Communications
in Computer and Information Science **990**

Commenced Publication in 2007
Founding and Former Series Editors:
Phoebe Chen, Alfredo Cuzzocrea, Xiaoyong Du, Orhun Kara, Ting Liu,
Dominik Ślęzak, and Xiaokang Yang

Editorial Board

More information about this series at http://www.springer.com/series/7899

Mohammad S. Obaidat · Enrique Cabello (Eds.)

E-Business
and Telecommunications

14th International Joint Conference, ICETE 2017
Madrid, Spain, July 24–26, 2017
Revised Selected Paper

 Springer

Editors
Mohammad S. Obaidat
University of Jordan
Amman, Jordan

Enrique Cabello
King Juan Carlos University
Madrid, Madrid, Spain

and

Nazarbayev University
Astana, Kazakhstan

ISSN 1865-0929   ISSN 1865-0937 (electronic)
Communications in Computer and Information Science
ISBN 978-3-030-11038-3   ISBN 978-3-030-11039-0 (eBook)
https://doi.org/10.1007/978-3-030-11039-0

Library of Congress Control Number: 2018966821

This Springer imprint is published by the registered company Springer Nature Switzerland AG
The registered company address is: Gewerbestrasse 11, 6330 Cham, Switzerland

Preface

The present book includes extended and revised versions of a set of selected best papers from the 14th International Joint Conference on e-Business and Telecommunications (ICETE 2017), held in Madrid, Spain, during July 24–26, 2017.

ICETE 2017 received 195 paper submissions from 48 countries, of which 7% are included in this book. The papers were selected by the event chairs and their selection is based on a number of criteria that includes the reviews and suggested comments provided by the Program Committee members, the session chairs' assessments and also the program chairs' global view of all papers included in the technical program. The authors of selected papers were then invited to submit a revised and extended version of their papers having at least 30% new material.

ICETE 2017 was a joint conference aimed at bringing together researchers, engineers, and practitioners interested in information and communication technologies, including data communication networking, e-business, optical communication systems, security and cryptography, signal processing and multimedia applications, and wireless networks and mobile systems. These are the main knowledge areas that define the six component conferences, namely: DCNET, ICE-B, OPTICS, SECRYPT, SIGMAP, and WINSYS, which together form the ICETE joint international conference.

The papers selected to be included in this book contribute to the understanding of relevant trends of current research in the areas of computer-based analysis of Tomatis Listening Test System audio data, Ka-band satellite applications for 5G systems, techniques to secure P2PSIP in MANETs, client-side localization of BGP hijack attacks, optical MIMO transmission systems, consumer awareness and interactions in online brand community, history-based throttling distributed denial-of-service attacks, resistance of the point randomization countermeasure, leak abuse attacks against symmetric searchable encryption, on the relation between SIM and IND-RoR security models, interoperable and IoT PKI, BoolTest as a fast randomness testing scheme, a representational requirements scheme, and optimizing link quality in wireless sensor networks.

We would like to thank all the authors for their contributions and also the reviewers who helped ensure the quality of this publication. We also thank the program chairs and Technical Program Committee, for their good work. Finally, we would like to thank the ICETE 2017 secretariat and the Institute for Systems and Technologies of Information, Control and Communication (INSTICC) leadership for their outstanding support.

July 2017

Mohammad Obaidat
Enrique Cabello

Organization

ICETE Conference Co-chairs

Mohammad Obaidat   University of Jordan,
       Jordan and Nazarbayev University, Kazakhstan

Enrique Cabello   Universidad Rey Juan Carlos, Spain

Program Co-chairs

DCNET

Christian Callegari   RaSS National Laboratory - CNIT, Italy

ICE-B

Marten van Sinderen   University of Twente, The Netherlands

OPTICS

Panagiotis Sarigiannidis   University of Western Macedonia, Greece

SECRYPT

Pierangela Samarati   Università degli Studi di Milano, Italy

SIGMAP

Sebastiano Battiato   University of Catania, Italy

WINSYS

Pascal Lorenz   University of Haute Alsace, France

DCNET Program Committee

Ishfaq Ahmad   University of Texas at Arlington, USA

Baber Aslam   National University of Sciences and Technology
               (NUST), Pakistan

Ilija Basicevic   University of Novi Sad, Serbia

Marco Beccuti   University of Turin, Italy

Pablo Belzarena   UdelaR, Uruguay

Giuseppe Bianchi   University of Rome Tor Vergata, Italy

Roberto Canonico   Università degli Studi di Napoli Federico II, Italy

Maurizio Casoni   University of Modena and Reggio Emilia, Italy

Fernando Cerdan   Polytechnic University of Cartagena, Spain

Paskorn Champrasert   Chiang Mai University, Thailand

Tatsuya Suda   University Netgroup Inc., USA
Vicente Traver   ITACA, Universidad Politécnica de Valencia, Spain
Kurt Tutschku   Blekinge Institute of Technology, Sweden
Adriano Valenzano   National Research Council of Italy, Italy
Bernd Wolfinger   University of Hamburg, Germany
Józef Wozniak   Gdansk University of Technology, Poland
Christos Xenakis   University of Piraeus, Greece
Jianbin Xiong   Guangdong University of Petrochemical Technology,
                            China
Cliff Zou   University of Central Florida, USA

DCNET Additional Reviewers

Habib Mostafaei   Università degli Studi Roma Tre, Italy
Benigno Rodríguez   Electrical Engineering Institute, UdelaR, Uruguay

ICE-B Program Committee

Andreas Ahrens   Hochschule Wismar,
                            University of Technology Business and Design,
                            Germany
Dimitris Apostolou   University of Piraeus, Greece
Ana Azevedo   CEOS.PP-ISCAP/IPP, Portugal
Elarbi Badidi   United Arab Emirates University, UAE
Ilia Bider   DSV, Stockholm University, Sweden
Efthimios Bothos   Institute of Communication and Computer Systems,
                            Greece
Christoph Bussler   Oracle Corporation, USA
Wojciech Cellary   Poznan University of Economics, Poland
Chun-Liang Chen   National Taiwan University of Arts, Taiwan
Dickson Chiu   The University of Hong Kong, SAR China
Michele Colajanni   University of Modena and Reggio Emilia, Italy
Rafael Corchuelo   University of Seville, Spain
Inma Hernández   University of Seville, Spain
Stephan Kassel   University of Applied Sciences Zwikau, Germany
Hurevren Kilic   Dogus University, Turkey
Abderrahmane Leshob   University of Quebec at Montreal, Canada
Yung-Ming Li   National Chiao Tung University, Taiwan
Rungtai Lin   National Taiwan University of Arts, Taiwan
Liping Liu   University of Akron, USA
Peter Loos   German Research Center for Artificial Intelligence,
                            Germany
Babis Magoutas   Information Management Unit,
                            National Technical University of Athens, Greece
Gianluca Carlo Misuraca   European Commission, Joint Research Centre, Spain
Wai Mok   The University of Alabama in Huntsville, USA

Maurice Mulvenna	Ulster University, UK
Paulo Novais	Universidade do Minho, Portugal
Krassie Petrova	Auckland University of Technology, New Zealand
Charmaine Plessis	University of South Africa, South Africa
Pak-Lok Poon	CQUniversity, Australia
Ela Pustulka-Hunt	FHNW Olten, Switzerland
Arkalgud Ramaprasad	University of Illinois at Chicago, USA
Manuel Resinas	University of Seville, Spain
Gustavo Rossi	Lifia, Argentina
Jarogniew Rykowski	The Poznan University of Economics (PUE), Poland
Ahm Shamsuzzoha	Sultan Qaboos University, Oman
Hassan Sleiman	Renault Group, France
Riccardo Spinelli	Università degli Studi di Genova, Italy
Athena Stassopoulou	University of Nicosia, Cyprus
Zhaohao Sun	PNG University of Technology;
	Federation University Australia, Papua New Guinea
James Thong	Hong Kong University of Science and Technology,
	SAR China
Ben van Lier	Centric, The Netherlands
Alfredo Vellido	Universitat Politècnica de Catalunya, Spain
Yiannis Verginadis	ICCS, National Technical University of Athens, Greece
Wlodek Zadrozny	University of North Carolina, Charlotte, USA
Edzus Zeiris	ZZ Dats Ltd., Latvia

ICE-B Additional Reviewer

Muller Cheung	Hong Kong University of Science and Technology,
	SAR China

OPTICS Program Committee

Hamada Al Shaer	University of Edinburgh,
	Li-Fi Research and Development Centre, UK
Tiago Alves	Instituto Superior Técnico/Instituto
	de Telecomunicações, Portugal
Nicola Andriolli	Scuola Superiore Sant'Anna, Italy
Hercules Avramopoulos	National Technical University of Athens, Greece
C. Chow	National Chiao Tung University, Taiwan
Giampiero Contestabile	Scuola Superiore Sant'Anna, Italy
Bernard Cousin	University of Rennes 1, France
Michael Crisp	University of Cambridge, UK
Brian Culshaw	University of Strathclyde, UK
Marija Furdek	KTH Royal Institute of Technology, Sweden
Habib Hamam	Université de Moncton, Canada
Sang-Kook Han	Yonsei University, Korea, Republic of
Nicholas Ioannides	London Metropolitan University, UK

Atsushi Kanno   National Institute of Information and Communications
                               Technology, Japan
Miroslaw Klinkowski   National Institute of Telecommunications, Poland
Tsuyoshi Konishi   Osaka University, Japan
Guifang Li   The University of Central Florida, USA
Qi Li   Columbia University, USA
Malamati Louta   University of Western Macedonia, Greece
Guo-Wei Lu   Tokai University, Japan
Paolo Martelli   Politecnico di Milano, Italy
Lenin Mehedy   IBM Research Australia, Australia
Maria Morant   Universitat Politècnica de València, Spain
Thas Nirmalathas   The University of Melbourne, Australia
Yasutake Ohishi   Research Center for Advanced Photon Technology,
                               Japan
Satoru Okamoto   Keio University, Japan
Albert Pagès   Universitat Politècnica de Catalunya, Spain
Anirban Pathak   Jaypee Institute of Information Technology, India
Jordi Perelló   Universitat Politècnica de Catalunya (UPC), Spain
Periklis Petropoulos   University of Southampton, UK
João Rebola   Instituto de Telecomunicações, ISCTE-IUL, Portugal
Enrique Rodriguez-Colina   Universidad Autónoma Metropolitana, Mexico
Nicola Sambo   Scuola Superiore Sant'Anna, Italy
Mehdi Shadaram   University of Texas at San Antonio, USA
Surinder Singh   Sant Longowal Instituite of Engineering
                               and Technology, Longowal, India
Georgios Siviloglou   University of Amsterdam, The Netherlands
Salvatore Spadaro   Universitat Politecnica de Catalunya, Spain
Michela Svaluto Moreolo   Centre Tecnologic de Telecomunicacions de Catalunya
                               (CTTC), Spain
Takuo Tanaka   RIKEN, Japan
Ashok Turuk   National Institute of Technology Rourkela, India
Bal Virdee   London Metropolitan University, UK
Peter Winzer   Nokia Bell Labs, USA
Kyriakos Zoiros   Democritus University of Thrace, Greece

OPTICS Additional Reviewer

Muhammad Imran   Scuola Superiore Sant'Anna, Italy

SECRYPT Program Committee

Luís Antunes   Universidade do Porto, Portugal
Alessandro Armando   FBK, Italy
Prithvi Bisht   Adobe, USA
Carlo Blundo   Università di Salerno, Italy
Francesco Buccafurri   University of Reggio Calabria, Italy

Silvio Ranise	Fondazione Bruno Kessler, Italy
Indrajit Ray	Colorado State University, USA
Indrakshi Ray	Colorado State University, USA
Nuno Santos	INESC, Portugal
Andreas Schaad	Huawei European Research Center, Germany
Cristina Serban	AT&T, USA
Daniele Sgandurra	Royal Holloway - University of London, UK
Juan Tapiador	Universidad Carlos III de Madrid, Spain
Vicenc Torra	University of Skövde, Sweden
Jaideep Vaidya	Rutgers Business School, USA
Corrado Visaggio	Università degli Studi del Sannio, Italy
Ivan Visconti	University of Salerno, Italy
Cong Wang	City University of Hong Kong, SAR China
Haining Wang	The College of William and Mary, USA
Lingyu Wang	Concordia University, Canada
Xinyuan Wang	George Mason University, USA
Edgar Weippl	SBA & FHSTP, Austria
Qiben Yan	University of Nebraska Lincoln, USA
Meng Yu	Virginia Commonwealth University, USA
Jiawei Yuan	Embry-Riddle Aeronautical University, USA
Lei Zhang	Thomson Reuters, USA
Yongjun Zhao	The Chinese University of Hong Kong, SAR China
Jianying Zhou	Institute for Infocomm Research, Singapore

SECRYPT Additional Reviewers

Tahir Ahmad	Foundazione Bruno Kessler, Italy
Monir Azraoui	EURECOM, France
Pedro Cabral	Faculdade de ciências/C3P, Portugal
Alejandro Calleja	Universidad Carlos III de Madrid, Spain
Maria Karyda	University of the Aegean, Greece
Frédéric Lafitte	Royal Military Academy, Belgium
Liran Lerman	Université Libre de Bruxelles, Belgium
Fudong Li	Plymouth University, UK
Christos Lyvas	University of Piraeus, Greece
Alessio Merlo	University of Genoa, Italy
Omid Mirzaei	Universidad Carlos III de Madrid, Spain
Melek Önen	EURECOM, France
Miguel Pardal	Instituto Superior Técnico, Universidade de Lisboa, Portugal
Nikos Pitropakis	Department of Digital Systems University of Piraeus, Greece
João Resende	University of Porto, Portugal
Andrea Saracino	Consiglio Nazionale delle Ricerche - Istituto di Informatica e Telematica, Italy
Vishal Saraswat	Indian Institute of Technology (IIT) Jammu, India

Giada Sciarretta	FBK, Italy
Stavros Shiaeles	Plymouth University, UK
Federico Sinigaglia	FBK, Italy
Patricia Sousa	FCUP, Portugal
Ingo Stengel	Germany
Cédric Van Rompay	EURECOM, France
Xiaomei Zhang	Penn State University, USA
Mingyi Zhao	Snap Inc., USA
Chen Zhong	Indiana University Kokomo, USA

SIGMAP Program Committee

Emmanuel Ifeachor	Plymouth University, UK
Harry Agius	Brunel University London, UK
Rajeev Agrawal	North Carolina Agricultural and Technical State University, USA
Gabriele Anderst-Kotsis	Johannes Kepler University Linz, Austria
Ramazan Aygun	University of Alabama in Huntsville, USA
Nicholas Bambos	Stanford University, USA
Arvind Bansal	Kent State University, USA
Chidansh Bhatt	FX Palo Alto Laboratory, Inc., USA
Adrian Bors	University of York, UK
Christian Breiteneder	Vienna University of Technology, Austria
Enrique Cabello	Universidad Rey Juan Carlos, Spain
Wai-Kuen Cham	The Chinese University of Hong Kong, SAR China
Amitava Chatterjee	Jadavpur University, India
Jianwen Chen	University of Electronic Science and Technology of China, China
Wei Cheng	Garena Online Pte. Ltd., Singapore
Cristina Conde	Universidad Rey Juan Carlos University, Spain
Carl Debono	University of Malta, Malta
Khaled El-Maleh	Qualcomm, USA
Giovanni Farinella	Università di Catania, Italy
Zongming Fei	University of Kentucky, USA
Jakub Galka	University of Science and Technology, Poland
Jerry Gibson	University of California Santa Barbara, USA
Seiichi Gohshi	Kogakuin University, Japan
Minglun Gong	Memorial University of Newfoundland, Canada
William Grosky	University of Michigan - Dearborn, USA
Malka Halgamuge	The University of Melbourne, Australia
Razib Iqbal	Missouri State University, USA
Li-Wei Kang	National Yunlin University of Science and Technology, Taiwan
Constantine Kotropoulos	Aristotle University of Thessaloniki, Greece
Adnane Latif	Cadi Ayyad University, Morocco
Choong-Soo Lee	St. Lawrence University, USA

Chengqing Li	Xiangtan University, China
Zhu Liu	AT&T, USA
Zitao Liu	University of Pittsburgh, USA
Martin Lopez-Nores	University of Vigo, Spain
Hong Man	Stevens Institute of Technology, USA
Manuel Marin-Jimenez	University of Cordoba, Spain
Daniela Moctezuma	Conacyt (CentroGEO), Mexico
Chamin Morikawa	Morpho, Inc., Japan
Alejandro Murua	University of Montreal, Canada
Noel O'Connor	Dublin City University, Ireland
Ioannis Paliokas	Centre for Research and Technology - Hellas, Greece
Ioannis Pratikakis	Democritus University of Thrace, Greece
Guoping Qiu	University of Nottingham, China
Peter Quax	Hasselt University, Belgium
Paula Queluz	Instituto Superior Técnico - Instituto de Telecomunicações, Portugal
Luis Rosales	CONACYT-Universidad Michoacana de San Nicolás de Hidalgo, Mexico
Simone Santini	Universidad Autónoma de Madrid, Spain
John Smith	IBM T. J. Watson Research Center, USA
Li Song	Institute of Image Communication and Network Engineering, Shanghai Jiao Tong University, China
Aristeidis Tsitiridis	University Rey Juan Carlos, Spain
Sudanthi Wijewickrama	University of Melbourne, Australia
Hongxun Yao	Harbin Institute of Technology, China
Kim-hui Yap	Nanyang Technological University, Singapore
Chang Yoo	KAIST, Korea, Republic of
Yongxin Zhang	Qualcomm R&D, USA
Bartosz Ziolko	AGH University of Science and Technology, Poland

SIGMAP Additional Reviewers

| Jeroen Put | EDM - Universiteit Hasselt, Belgium |
| Khomsun Singhirunnusorn | The University of Alabama in Huntsville, USA |

WINSYS Program Committee

Ali Abedi	University of Maine, USA
Taufik Abrão	Universidade Estadual de Londrina, Brazil
Ali Abu-El Humos	Jackson State University, USA
Fatemeh Afghah	Northern Arizona University, USA
Dharma Agrawal	University of Cincinnati, USA
Andreas Ahrens	Hochschule Wismar, University of Technology Business and Design, Germany
Aydin Akan	Istanbul University, Turkey

Vicente Alarcon-Aquino	Universidad de las Americas Puebla, Mexico
Hassan Artail	American University of Beirut, Lebanon
Nicholas Bambos	Stanford University, USA
Marko Beko	Universidade Lusófona de Humanidades e Tecnologias, Portugal
Luis Bernardo	Universidade Nova de Lisboa, Portugal
Dajana Cassioli	University of L'Aquila, Italy
Llorenç Cerdà-Alabern	Universitat Politècnica de Catalunya, Spain
Gerard Chalhoub	Clermont University, France
James Conrad	University of North Carolina at Charlotte, USA
Antonio Corradi	University of Bologna, Italy
Orhan Dagdeviren	Ege University, Turkey
Carl Debono	University of Malta, Malta
Bryan Dixon	California State University, USA
Christos Douligeris	University of Piraeus, Greece
Amit Dvir	BME-HIT, Hungary
Nancy El Rachkidy	LIMOS, France
Ozgur Ergul	Cankaya University, Turkey
Panagiotis Fouliras	University of Macedonia, Greece
Janusz Gozdecki	AGH University of Science and Technology, Poland
Fabrizio Granelli	Università degli Studi di Trento, Italy
Antonio Grilo	INESC/IST, Portugal
Dirk Grunwald	University of Colorado Boulder, USA
Alexander Guitton	University Blaise Pascal, France
Aissaoui-Mehrez Hassane	Mines-Telecom Institute/Telecom-ParisTech, France
Doan Hoang	University of Technology, Sydney, Australia
Cynthia Hood	Illinois Institute of Technology, USA
A. R. Hurson	Missouri S&T, USA
Hong Ji	Beijing University of Post and Telecommunications (BUPT), China
Josep Jornet	University at Buffalo, USA
Georgios Kambourakis	University of the Aegean, Greece
Ala' Khalifeh	German Jordanian University, Jordan
Abdelmajid Khelil	Landshut University of Applied Sciences, Germany
Gurhan Kucuk	Yeditepe University, Turkey
Wookwon Lee	Gannon University, USA
Wei Li	Univerity of Sydney, Australia
David Lin	National Chiao Tung University, Taiwan
Ju Liu	Shandong University, China
Elsa Macias López	University of Las Palmas de G.C., Spain
Reza Malekian	Malmö University, Sweden
Pietro Manzoni	Universidad Politecnica de Valencia, Spain
Luis Mendes	Escola Superior de Tecnologia e Gestão de Leiria, Portugal
Marek Natkaniec	AGH University of Science and Technology, Poland
Amiya Nayak	University of Ottawa, Canada

Cristiano Panazio	Escola Politécnica of São Paulo University, Brazil
Grammati Pantziou	Technological Educational Institution of Athens, Greece
Al-Sakib Pathan	IIUM, Malaysia and Islamic University in Madinah, KSA, Bangladesh
Jordi Pérez-Romero	Universitat Politècnica de Catalunya (UPC), Spain
Symon Podvalny	Voronezh State Technical University, Russian Federation
Jorge Portilla	Universidad Politécnica de Madrid, Spain
Julian Reichwald	Cooperative State University Mannheim, Germany
Heverson Ribeiro	University of Neuchâtel, Switzerland
Jörg Roth	University of Applied Sciences Nuremberg, Germany
Angelos Rouskas	University of Piraeus, Greece
Brian Sadler	Army Research Laboratory, USA
Farag Sallabi	United Arab Emirates University, UAE
Manuel García Sánchez	Universidade de Vigo, Spain
Altair Santin	Pontifical Catholic University of Paraná (pucpr), Brazil
Christian Schindelhauer	University of Freiburg, Germany
Kuei-Ping Shih	Tamkang University, Taiwan
Christopher Silva	The Aerospace Corporation, USA
Mujdat Soyturk	Marmara University, Turkey
Srinath Srinivasa	International Institute of Information Technology, India
Bala Srinivasan	Monash University, Australia
Alvaro Suárez-Sarmiento	University of Las Palmas de Gran Canaria, Spain
Cesar Vargas-Rosales	Tecnologico de Monterrey, Campus Monterrey, Mexico
Sheng-Shih Wang	Minghsin University of Science and Technology, Taiwan
Anne Wei	CNAM Paris, France
Shibing Zhang	Nantong University, China

WINSYS Additional Reviewers

Xi Li	Beijing University of Posts and Telecommunications, China
Marcelo Pellenz	Pontifical Catholic University of Parana, Brazil
Xin Tan	State University of New York at Buffalo, USA

ICETE Invited Speakers

Carlo Regazzoni	University of Genoa, Italy
Jan Camenisch	IBM Research Zurich, Switzerland
Jose Duato	UPV, Spain
Andreas Holzinger	Medical University Graz, Austria

Contents

Client Side Localization of BGP Hijack Attacks with a Quasi-realistic Internet Graph

Paulo Salvador[✉]

DETI, University of Aveiro, Instituto de Telecomunicações, Aveiro, Portugal
salvador@ua.pt
http://paulosalvador.net

Abstract. Internet routing relies completely on the Border Gateway Protocol (BGP) which is inherently insecure and allow the deployment of route hijacking attacks. The client side detection of such type of attacks can be achieved by detecting Round Trip Time (RTT) deviations from multiple points on the Internet to the target network. However, the localization of the autonomous systems where the attack originates can only be performed with an underlying realistic and precise model of the Internet interconnections. A usable and useful realistic Internet interconnections model does not exist. The existing interconnection models are to simplistic to be applicable in real scenarios and/or incorporate to much uncorrelated information that cannot be used due to its complexity.

This work presents a client side methodology to locate the source of BGP hijack attacks based on a quasi-realist graph that models the Internet as an all. The construction of such graph builds upon all known Internet exchange points (IX) and landing points of all known submarine cables. The lack of information about interconnections between Internet exchangers (IX) nodes and landing points is extrapolated from simple rules that take in consideration Earth geographic characteristics. This approach results in a graph that includes all major corner stones of the Internet while maintaining a simple structure. This underlying quasi-realist graph model of the Internet will allow the search for IX nodes where a false route could be injected to create a similar RTT anomaly observed during an attack.

With very simplistic assumptions as similar node, link loads and symmetric routing by the shortest path, and calibration using a relatively small set of world-scale measurements, the proof-of-concept results show that the model allows to locate the source of routing hijack attacks within a reasonable degree of efficiency.

Keywords: BGP · Route hijack · Routing attack · Attacker location
Internet graph model · Quasi-realistic · Real IX · Submarine cables

© Springer Nature Switzerland AG 2019
M. S. Obaidat and E. Cabello (Eds.): ICETE 2017, CCIS 990, pp. 1–15, 2019.
https://doi.org/10.1007/978-3-030-11039-0_1

1   Introduction

Since Pilosov and Kapela [1] proposed in 2008 an exploit of the BGP vulnerabilities to implement BGP route hijack attacks, it was reported several times evidences of active traffic redirection attacks [2–4]. BGP hijack attacks are performed by compromising and consequently configure an autonomous system BGP edge router to announce IP network prefixes (from the attack targets) with a manipulated path attribute. If the malicious announcement is more specific (shorter path) than the legitimate one, the traffic may be directed to the attacker router and subsequently subject to man-in-the-middle attacks. By announcing false network prefixes and route attributes, the compromised router may poison the Routing Information Base (RIB) of its peers and, after poisoning one peer, the malicious routing information could propagate to other peers, to other AS, and onto the broader Internet. After the fake route propagates, an Internet client contacting the attacked network may have its traffic illicitly redirect through the compromised router.

The detection of an active BGP hijack attack can only be performed: (i) at the ISP, by constantly monitoring the BGP updates and/or RIB changes [5,6], or (ii) at the client side, by constant motorization of round-trip time (RTT) to specific locations from multiple worldwide locations and looking for anomalous increments on the RTT [7,8]. However, at the client-side, upon the detection of the attack the localization of the source of the attack (the Autonomous System of the compromised router) is very difficult and must rely only on variation of the measured RTT values. In this work it is presented a methodology that achieves such goal by triangulating the source of the attack using multiple RTT measurements (and respective variations) to a specific site from multiple locations spread over the world. However, such methodology relies greatly on an effective Internet model to predict the transmissions times to and from any node on the Internet.

Internet complexity in terms of magnitude, unknown interconnectivity, and asymmetry restricts the construction of any useful and usable model. Internet quasi-realist models can be used to infer Internet communications performance at a world scale, specially when properties of nodes, links and addressing can be totally inferred while maintaining a close to real structure of relations. Therefore, to implement the proposed localization methodology it was necessary to develop a simple but realistic Internet graph model, based on real data, such as submarine cables landing points and IX locations, and constrained by Earth geographical characteristics [9]. The resulting graph has an open structure where nodes and links have properties (e.g., IX name, landing point name, and geographic distances) and is open to define other properties (e.g., node load, link load, link speed, etc. . .). The developed code for construction of the quasi-realistic Internet graph are publicly available at graph.netconfs.net.

2　Related Work

BGP hijack attack detection and source localization at the ISP level is complex because it requires constant monitoring of changes in the BGP updates and RIB [10,11]. However, from at the client side the detection of the attacks is possible [7,8], but the localization of the attack relies greatly on a precise model able to relate RTT to geographic locations and Internet distances.

Mapping RTT values to geographic distances have been analyzed and/or modeled in the past [12–14]. Landa et al. [14] presented a model for the analysis of Internet round trip time (RTT) and its relationship to geographic distance. The results show that it is possible to derive a relatively precise relation between the geographic locations and distances of two points and their logical distance (RTT). However, the results also show that the variability of RTT is high and that a relation between geographic and logical distances must include other variables to achieve higher precision.

Several works on mapping of the Internet have been presented, however, their are restricted to cataloging and visualization of Internet nodes and connections. Durairajan et al. [15,16] constructed a geographic database of the Internet based on real data, which result is publicly available (internetatlas.org) and allows data visualization and analysis. However, such compilation of data is easily usable in studies because it requires data aggregations in a valid model that incorporates all inter-connections and relations. Salvador proposed a first (non-calibrated) version of a quasi-realistic Internet model [9].

3　Quasi-realistic Internet Graph

3.1　Internet Elements and Interconnections

Nodes. The Internet graph nodes will be all known IX and landing points from submarine cables from data publicly available compiled by Tele-Geography. Submarine cable information is available on website TeleGeography Submarine Cable Map (www.submarinecablemap.com) and respective repository (github.com/telegeography/www.submarinecablemap.com). Internet exchanged information is available on website TeleGeography Internet Exchange Map (internetexchangemap.com) and respective repository (github.com/telegeography/www.internetexchangemap.com).

The available data in December 5th 2016, listed 1202 IX, however only 600 where considered. IX from the same provider at the same building or nearby buildings were merged and considered as a single IX node. At the same date, there were 368 listed submarine cables, with a total of 947 unique landing points (considering its identifier and geographical location). From the 947 unique landing points, two pairs of nodes had the same identifier but different however close geographic locations. Each of these pairs of points were merged into a single landing point. Therefore, only 945 landing points nodes were integrated into the graph.

Links. Internet link information is almost inexistent. The only real information must be extracted from the known submarine cables information, where is possible to assume that each cable landing point has a direct connection to all other landing points. However, the publicly available information does not define the order by which the landing points are connected, neither the geographic path that the cable follows. Therefore, all Internet oceanic links and respective path can be closely inferred from the available data by imposing constrains has geographic elevation (ocean depth) and geographic distances between points.

For Internet land links, available information is really limited by service providers and difficult to correlate with IX and landing points locations. Portals like Internet Atlas have information about some providers in restricted areas of the world, but is difficult to infer inter-connections between providers. In this work was choose a more heuristic approach in which land links were defined based on basic rules constrained by the maximum number of neighbor nodes within a geographical range.

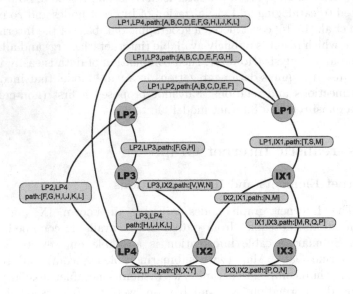

Fig. 1. Graph logical representation [9].

3.2   Graph Structure and Dynamics

It was assumed that Python is the nowadays language of election for fast and lightweight development. Therefore, the Internet graph was constructed using the Python package NetworkX (networkx.github.io/) which allows the creation, manipulation, and analysis of the structure and dynamics of complex networks. It was chosen a NetworkX Undirected Simple Graph for modeling the Internet nodes and inter-connections, because it is assumed that the link properties between two nodes is the same for both directions.

A NetworkX allows the addition of arbitrary attributes for graph nodes and links. Nodes will an identifier and two attributes `ntype` and `coord`, the first defines the type of node (IX or Landing Point - LP) and the second the geographic coordinate as a 2-tuple with latitude and longitude. Links (or edges under NetworkX nomenclature) are defined by the two end-point nodes and have three attributes `etype`, `dist` and `path`, the first defines the type of the link (Ocean, Land, Land to Ocean, etc...), the second attribute defines the geographical distance of the link and the final attribute defines the geographical path of the link as a list of geographical coordinates. The unidirectional nature of the graph implies that the attributes between node1 and node2, are the same as the ones between node2 and node1. Therefore, the geographical path may have to be inverted when starting from the node considered as the end of the path.

Figure 1 depicts a logical representation of the graph, where letters represent the geographic coordinates of the respective points.

3.3   Graph Construction

The graph construction algorithm, previously proposed by Salvador [9], can be divided in three main steps: (i) addition of nodes and links of the known submarine cables, (ii) addition of IX nodes, and links between IXs and between IXs and submarine cables landing points, finally (iii) guarantee the full interconnectivity of the graph, connecting all sub-graphs with additional links using land paths as attribute, or in case of impossibility direct links between nodes.

Steps 1 to 3 require an underlying ocean grid and land grid to determine/constrain the paths. This grids were defined also as unidirectional NetworkX graphs to allow the estimation of the best paths in ocean or land.

Both ocean and land grids were constructed based on elevation/depth information obtained from a geographic referenced tiff from the USA National Ocean and Atmospheric Administration (NOAA) depicted in Fig. 2. All geographic distances were calculated over the Earth Rhumb line between two locations [17].

Fig. 2. Earth elevation/depth map [9].

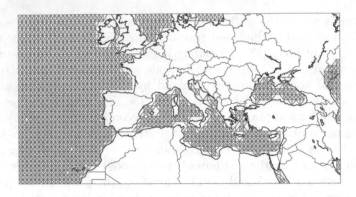

Fig. 3. Ocean grid [9].

The ocean grid construction started by defined a set of geographic underwater points from latitude $-51°$ to $78°$, and from longitude $-180°$ to $180°$ in one degree intervals. An Ocean Grid edge is included if both end-points are underwater and three equally spaced points between them are also underwater. A georeferenced point is considered underwater if its (average) elevation is zero or less. This rule may erroneously include land locations that are below sea level (e.g., Netherlands), and erroneously exclude locations, subject to high tides, that are not permanently covered by water. Moreover, the choice to consider zero elevation has threshold for allow the passage of a submarine cable was a conscious one; to compensate the low resolution (high distance between grid georeferenced points) that was excluding most of the water straits and channels of the world were submarine cables pass. Even with this relax elevation rule some important water straits and channels were not considered viable to pass a submarine cable and had to be manually added. Namely:

- Add connection over the Suez channel.
- Add connection over the Panama Chanel.
- Add connection over the English Chanel.
- Add connection near Isle of Man Channel (Irish Sea to Atlantic North).
- Add connection between the sea channel between Denmark and Sweden.
- Add connection from the White Sea to Barents Sea in Russia.
- Add connection from Mediterranean Sea to Istanbul and Black Sea, over Dardanelles strait and Sea of Marmara.
- Add connection over Malacca strait between Malaysia and Indonesia Sumatra Island.
- Add connection over the strait between Indonesian islands of Sumatra and Java.

Moreover some points of Ocean Grid located in Netherlands had to be removed because they were classified as underwater, because they are below the sea level however are dry land. The resulting ocean grid had only one unconnected subgraph (isolated ocean zone), namely the Caspian Sea with 80 nodes. The final ocean grid had 31434 nodes and 119229 edges. Figure 3 depicts a zoom area of the ocean grid that includes the Atlantic ocean, seas of the north of Europe, Mediterranean sea at the south and part of the Caspian sea. Note that, in the figure is visible some of the manual edge additions, namely the Panama Channel, around great Britain islands, between Denmark and Sweden and from Mediterranean Sea to Istanbul.

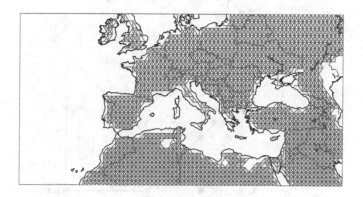

Fig. 4. Land grid [9].

The construction of the Land Grid followed a similar approach using as rule for a grid points and intermediary point an elevation higher then zero. It included geographic points above sea level points from latitude $-80°$ to $80°$, and from longitude $-180°$ to $180°$ in one degree intervals. Only two major faults on the grid had to be corrected, namely the addition of long bridges (e.g., between three of Japan main islands) that transport land data cables. Namely:

– One connection between Honshu and Kyushu islands in Japan.
– One connection between Honshu and Hokkaido islands in Japan.

The final land grid had 18312 nodes and 65690 edges. Figure 4 depicts a zoom area of the land grid that includes Europe and the north of Africa.

Figure 5 depicts a simple network example that can be used illustrate how the distance and (ocean or land) path between two nodes is determined. For any submarine cable landing point is determined the closest node of the ocean grid and the closest node of the land grid (e.g., nodes A and T for LP1 and nodes L and Y for LP4). For an IX is only determined the closest node of the land grid (e.g., node M for IX1 and node N for IX2). The path between two nodes is determined using the shortest path under water or in land. The path is simplified maintaining only the nodes were direction changes; e.g., ocean path between LP1 and LP3 is: A, B, C, D, E, G, H nodes of the ocean grid, and land path between IX2 and IX3 is: N, O, P nodes of the land grid. For each path is recorded the geographic coordinates of all used grid node and the overall geographic distance. The methods *pathByOcean(.)*, *distByOcean(.)*, *pathByOcean(.)*

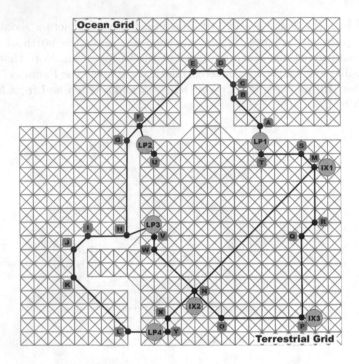

Fig. 5. Ocean and land grids usage example [9].

and *distByLand(.)* referenced in pseudo-code implement this algorithm for ocean and land grids, respectively.

The pseudo-code presented in Algorithm 1 details the algorithm for step 1; for each submarine cable it starts by determining the two landing points that are more distant using an ocean path [lines 2–8], one of the end-points is added as a graph node [lines 11–12], then starting from that end-point looks for the landing point with the shortest distance by ocean, add that landing point as a graph node, determines the ocean path between both nodes, and adds a link with that path and distance as attributes, restart using the new node until the other cable end-point its reached [lines 13–29]. At this moment, some of the cable landing points may not be in the graph yet, for each one of the unconnected landing points, adds it to the graph as node, searches for the closest node already connect, and adds a link for each new pair, then repeats until all submarine cable nodes are connected [lines 30–44].

The algorithm for step 2 is detailed in Algorithm 2; each IX is added as a graph node, and for each IX is determined the closest IXs with distances by land bellow a pre-determined threshold, links between the IXs are added to the graph [lines 1–7]. Then for all submarine cables landing points is determined the closest IXs with distances by land bellow a pre-determined threshold, links between each landing point and IXs are added to the graph [lines 8–13]. The pre-determined threshold values for this step were: (i) each IX connects to a maximum of 12 IX neighbors within a 2500 Km radius using land paths, (ii) each landing point connects to a maximum of 3 IX within a radius of 250 Km using a land path.

Finally in step 3 (see Algorithm 3); the unconnected nodes or sub-graphs were merged with the main graph with a land connection between the node closest to a main graph node and the respective closer node within 2000 Km [lines 1–12]. When no land connections were possible to merge the sub-graphs, direct connections (independent of ocean and land grids) were defined [lines 13–23].

In the last step, it was necessary to extend the maximum range of direct connections to 2000 Km, to include a connection in Sacalina Island, Russia to inter-connect the "Far East Submarine Cable System" to the remaining nodes.

The final Internet graph constructed as 1545 nodes (600 IX, and 945 Landing Points), and 10332 edges. Figure 6 depicts the Internet graph in a world map.

Fig. 6. Final quasi-realistic Internet graph [9].

3.4 Calibration

The model should be calibrated, i.e., determine the delay imposed by each node (adding it as a graph node attribute) and determine the data propagation speed for each link as a fraction of the speed of light (c). Within the scope of this work it is assumed that (i) the delays imposed by nodes and links data propagation speed are the same for all nodes and links, and (ii) routing is symmetric and uses the shortest path.

With that assumptions, the expected round-trip-time (RTT) between two nodes given by the graph is derived using the equation:

$$eRTT_{i,j} = 2\left(\frac{L_{i,j}}{\alpha c} + \beta N_{i,j}\right) \tag{1}$$

where c is the speed of light, α is the fraction of speed of light that defines a link data propagation speed, β is the delay imposed by each node, and $L_{i,j}$ and $N_{i,j}$ are, respectively, the geographic distance and the number of nodes between nodes i and j given by the Internet graph model.

Algorithm 1. Internet graph model construction step 1: submarine cables landing points.

```
 1: for cable in AllCables do
 2:     max_dist ← 0
 3:     for Lp1 in cable.LandingPoints do
 4:         for Lp2 in cable.LandingPoints do
 5:             dist ← distByOcean(Lp1,Lp2)
 6:             if dist > max_dist then
 7:                 max_dist ← dist
 8:                 cable.endPoints ← (Lp1,Lp2)
 9:     connectedLP ← emptyList
10:     unconnectedLP ← cable.LandingPoints
11:     cLp ← cable.endPoints[0]
12:     Graph ← Graph.AddNodeToGraph(best_uLp,type=LP)
13:     while cLp ≠ cable.endPoints[1] do
14:         add cLp to connectedLP
15:         remove cLp from unconnectedLP
16:         min_distance ← +∞
17:         for uLp in unconnectedLP do
18:             dist ← distByOcean(cLp,uLp)
19:             path ← pathByOcean(cLp,uLp)
20:             if dist < min_dist then
21:                 min_dist ← dist
22:                 best_uLp ← uLp
23:         add best_uLp to connectedLP
24:         remove best_uLp from unconnectedLP
25:         dist ← distByOcean(cLp,best_uLp)
26:         path ← pathByOcean(cLp,best_uLp)
27:         Graph ← Graph.AddNodeToGraph(best_uLp,type=LP)
28:         Graph ← Graph.AddLinkToGraph(cLp,best_uLp,attributes=[path,dist])
29:         cLp ← best_uLp
30:     for uLp in unconnectedLP do
31:         min_distance ← +∞
32:         for cLp in connectedLP do
33:             dist ← distByOcean(cLp,uLp)
34:             path ← pathByOcean(cLp,uLp)
35:             if dist < min_dist then
36:                 min_dist ← dist
37:                 best_cLp ← cLp
38:         add uLp to connectedLP
39:         remove uLp from unconnectedLP
40:         dist ← distByOcean(uLp,best_cLp)
41:         path ← pathByOcean(uLp,best_cLp)
42:         Graph ← Graph.AddNodeToGraph(uLp,type=LP)
43:         Graph ← Graph.AddLinkToGraph(uLp,best_cLp,attributes=[path,dist])
44:         cLp ← best_uLp
```

Algorithm 2. Internet graph model construction step 2: IX nodes and connections between them and submarine cables landing points.

```
 1: for ix1 in AllIX do
 2:     Graph ← Graph.AddNodeToGraph(ix,type=IX)
 3:     closerIX ← getCloserByLand(ix1,AllIX,Number1,maxDistance)
 4:     for ix1 in closerIX do
 5:         dist ← distByLand(ix1,ix2)
 6:         path ← pathByLand(ix1,ix2)
 7:         Graph ← Graph.AddLinkToGraph(ix1,ix2,attributes=[path,dist])
 8: for Lp in AllLandingPoints do
 9:     closerIX ← getCloserByLand(lp,AllIX,Number2,maxDistance)
10:     for ix in closerIX do
11:         dist ← distByLand(ix,Lp)
12:         path ← pathByLand(ix,Lp)
13:         Graph ← Graph.AddLinkToGraph(ix,Lp,attributes=[path,dist])
```

Algorithm 3. Internet graph model construction step 3: interconnection of subgraphs to create a single fully connected graph.

```
 1: mainGraph,subGraphs ← Graph.getSubGraphs()
 2: for sG in subGraphs do
 3:     max_dist ← MaxDistAllowed
 4:     for node1 in mainGraph do
 5:         for node2 in sG do
 6:             dist ← distByLand(node1,node2)
 7:             if dist < min_dist then
 8:                 min_dist ← dist
 9:                 best_pair ← (node1,node2)
10:     if best_pair not empty then
11:         path ← pathByLand(best_pair[0],best_pair[1])
12:         Graph ← Graph.AddLinkToGraph(best_pair[0],best_pair[1],attributes=[path,dist])
13: mainGraph,subGraphs ← Graph.getSubGraphs()
14: for sG in subGraphs do
15:     max_dist ← +∞
16:     for node1 in mainGraph do
17:         for node2 in sG do
18:             dist ← distDirect(node1,node2)
19:             if dist < min_dist then
20:                 min_dist ← dist
21:                 best_pair ← (node1,node2)
22:     path ← pathDirect(best_pair[0],best_pair[1])
23:     Graph ← Graph.AddLinkToGraph(best_pair[0],best_pair[1],attributes=[path,dist])
```

To infer the α and β parameters, multiple measurements were made using several servers spread all over the world (see Fig. 7). The RTT measurements were made over a period of one week (from March 10th to March 17th 2017) using `ping` and `traceroute`, respectively. Based on each server's approximated known location, each server was mapped to a specific IX node on the Internet graph model.

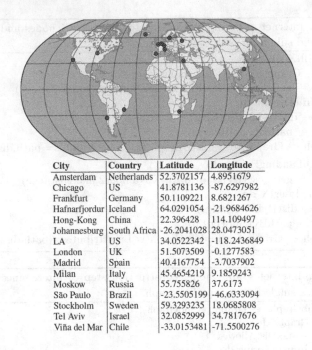

City	Country	Latitude	Longitude
Amsterdam	Netherlands	52.3702157	4.8951679
Chicago	US	41.8781136	-87.6297982
Frankfurt	Germany	50.1109221	8.6821267
Hafnarfjordur	Iceland	64.0291054	-21.9684626
Hong-Kong	China	22.396428	114.109497
Johannesburg	South Africa	-26.2041028	28.0473051
LA	US	34.0522342	-118.2436849
London	UK	51.5073509	-0.1277583
Madrid	Spain	40.4167754	-3.7037902
Milan	Italy	45.4654219	9.1859243
Moskow	Russia	55.755826	37.6173
São Paulo	Brazil	-23.5505199	-46.6333094
Stockholm	Sweden	59.3293235	18.0685808
Tel Aviv	Israel	32.0852999	34.7817676
Viña del Mar	Chile	-33.0153481	-71.5500276

Fig. 7. Model calibration and test server locations [9].

The following minimization process can be used to estimate α and β:

$$\min_{\alpha,\beta} \sum_i \sum_j \frac{|eRTT_{i,j} - mRTT_{i,j}|}{rRTT_{i,j}} \tag{2}$$

where $mRTT_{i,j}$ is the average RTT measured between servers i and j.

The calibration results inferred using the minimization process (2) were: $\alpha = 0.6853$ and $\beta = 2.6 \times 10^{-16}$ s. These values equate to an inferred data transmission speed of 68.53% of the speed of light and a close to zero delay imposed by nodes. The average absolute error of prediction was approximately 21.6% for the RTT and 36.1% for the number of nodes. To comparison, the average absolute predicting the RTT using the direct line geographic distance between any two points (and the same speed of data propagation) were 48.3%.

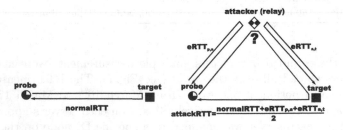

Fig. 8. Data path and RTT under normal circumstances (left) and under during a BGP hijack attack (right).

4 Attacks Source Localization

The attack localization methodology is based on the assumption that when traffic is sent from any point in the Internet (probe) to a specific network (target), the time data takes to go from probe to target and back in normal circumstances, is increased by a fraction of time when an attack is active, because data is now traveling from probe to the source of the BGP hijack attack (relay), to the target and back directly to the probe. Figure 8 illustrates this assumption, and relates the normal RTT (normalRTT) with the observed RTT during the attack (attackRTT), based on the expected RTT (eRTT) to the attacker from probe and target.

The algorithm to determine possible locations of the source of an attack (attacker) uses the underlying Internet graph model (see Algorithm 4). Using the model is possible to search IX nodes for which the triangular data path RTT during the attack can be similar to the anomalous RTT (attackRTT).

Algorithm 4. Attack localization algorithm.

1: **while** not under attack **do**
2:     $normalRTT_{p,t} \leftarrow mRTT_{p,t}$
3: $attackRTT_{p,t} \leftarrow mRTT_{p,t}$
4: possibleAttackerLocations $\leftarrow$ emptyList
5: **for** ix **in** Graph.AllIXNodes **do**
6:     $eAttackRTT_{p,a,t} = 0.5 * (normalRTT_{p,t} + eRTT_{p,a} + eRTT_{a,t})$
7:     **if** $|eAttackRTT_{p,a,t} - attackRTT_{p,t}| < \gamma$ **then**
8:         **add** ix **to** possibleAttackerLocations

To test the localization methodology a set of route hijack attacks were simulated using an overlay network between the test servers listed in Fig. 7. The overlay network and manipulated routing were deployed using IP GRE tunnels between the servers and `iptables` to force routing over the overlay network. The measurements of the RTT were performed using `ping` with TCP packets. The TCP port was used to control the data flow between the probes, attacker, and target serves. As target servers were chosen servers in Chicago (USA), Frankfurt (Germany), and London (UK). The simulated attackers were placed in Los Angels (USA), Madrid (Spain), Moscow (Russia), and São Paulo (Brazil). The remaining servers served as test probes. Assuming an error $\gamma = 20$ ms between observed RTT during the attack ($attackRTT_{p,t}$) and the expected RTT during the attack provided by the Internet graph model, the attack locations inferred are presented in Table 1.

The results show than any traffic deviation via Los Angels is almost perfectly located in the USA (West Cost IX), only one IX in Calcary (Canada) is wrongly identified as the source of the attack. When the simulated attacker were in Spain, the Internet model and algorithm is not able to identify the correct country and locates the attacker in neighbor European countries, mainly due to the high accepted RTT error of 20 ms and very small RTT values between

Table 1. Attacker location inference results. When multiple locations were found the probability of each one it is presented in parenthesis.

Target	Attacker location	Inferred attacker location(s)
Chicago (USA)	Los Angels (USA)	USA (95%), Canada (5%)
	Madrid (Spain)	UK (80%), France (20%)
	Moscow (Russia)	Netherlands (50%), UK (50%)
	São Paulo (Brazil)	Brazil
Frankfurt (Germany)	Los Angels (USA)	USA (95%), Canada (5%)
	Madrid (Spain)	Spain (25%), Germany (25%), Netherlands (25%), Italy (25%)
	Moscow (Russia)	Netherlands
	São Paulo (Brazil)	USA (80%), Brazil (20%)
London (UK)	Los Angels (USA)	USA
	Madrid (Spain)	Netherlands (25%), Germany (25%), Switzerland (25%), France (25%)
	Moscow (Russia)	Netherlands (40%), Sweden (40%), Denmark (20%)
	São Paulo (Brazil)	Brazil

Central and West Europe. For the attacker located in Moscow the algorithm fails in identifying the correct country but places the attacker closer to the Russia Internet entry point to Europe (Netherlands and Scandinavian countries). When considering the simulated attacker in São Paulo (Brazil), the algorithm performs perfectly for the UK and USA targets but fails for the German target by locating the attacker in the USA with a probability of 80%. The errors can be explained by the fact that some connections do not follow the assumptions made by the algorithm, namely, similar delays at nodes (0 ms). This is more clear on the Internet connections between Moscow and Europe, and in the connections from Brazil to the Internet using North American peers.

5   Conclusions

This work presented a methodology to detect the location of the source of BGP hijack attacks from the client side. The methodology relies on a quasi-realistic Internet graph that incorporates real infrastructure data. A proof-of-concept experiment, under simplistic assumptions on the Internet symmetry, with the Internet model graph and a localization algorithm proved the relatively efficiency of the proposed methodology.

Acknowledgements. This work was supported by the Fundação para Ciência e Tecnologia (FCT) through PTDC/EEI-TEL/5708/2014 and UID/EEA/50008/2013.

References

1. Pilosov, A., Kapela, T.: Stealing the internet - an internet-scale man in the middle attack. In: DEFCON 2016, August 2008
2. Cowie, J.: The New Threat: Targeted Internet Traffic Misdirection. Dyn Blog, November 2013. http://dyn.com/blog/mitm-internet-hijacking/
3. Madory, D.: On-going BGP Hijack Targets Palestinian ISP. Dyn Blog, January 2015. http://dyn.com/blog/going-bgp-attack-targets-palestinian-isp/
4. Madory, D.: UK traffic diverted through Ukraine. Dyn Blog, March 2015. http://dyn.com/blog/uk-traffic-diverted-ukraine/
5. Zhang, Z., Zhang, Y., Hu, Y.C., Mao, Z.M., Bush, R.: iSPY: detecting IP prefix hijacking on my own. IEEE/ACM Trans. Netw. 18(6), 1815–1828 (2010)
6. Liu, Y., Luo, X., Chang, R., Su, J.: Characterizing inter-domain rerouting by betweenness centrality after disruptive events. IEEE J. Sel. Areas Commun. 31(6), 1147–1157 (2013)
7. Salvador, P., Nogueira, A.: Customer-side detection of internet-scale traffic redirection. In: 16th International Telecommunications Network Strategy and Planning Symposium (NETWORKS 2014), September 2014
8. Silva, M., Nogueira, A., Salvador, P.: Modular platform for customer-side detection of BGP redirection attacks. In: Proceedings of the 4th International Conference on Information Systems Security and Privacy - Volume 1: ICISSP, pp. 199–206. INSTICC, SciTePress (2018)
9. Salvador, P.: A quasi-realistic internet graph. In: Proceedings of the 14th International Joint Conference on e-Business and Telecommunications (ICETE 2017), pp. 27–32 (2017)
10. Lad, M., Massey, D., Pei, D., Wu, Y., Zhang, B., Zhang, L.: PHAS: a prefix hijack alert system. In: Proceedings of the 15th Conference on USENIX Security Symposium - Volume 15. USENIX-SS 2006. USENIX Association, Berkeley (2006). http://dl.acm.org/citation.cfm?id=1267336.1267347
11. Schlamp, J., Holz, R., Jacquemart, Q., Carle, G., Biersack, E.W.: HEAP: reliable assessment of BGP hijacking attacks. IEEE J. Sel. Areas Commun. 34(6), 1849–1861 (2016)
12. Kasiviswanathan, S.P., Eidenbenz, S., Yan, G.: Geography-based analysis of the internet infrastructure. In: 2011 Proceedings IEEE INFOCOM, pp. 131–135, April 2011
13. Mátray, P., Hága, P., Laki, S., Csabai, I., Vattay, G.: On the network geography of the internet. In: 2011 Proceedings IEEE INFOCOM, pp. 126–130, April 2011
14. Landa, R., Araújo, J.T., Clegg, R.G., Mykoniati, E., Griffin, D., Rio, M.: The large-scale geography of internet round trip times. In: 2013 IFIP Networking Conference, pp. 1–9, May 2013
15. Durairajan, R., Ghosh, S., Tang, X., Barford, P., Eriksson, B.: Internet Atlas: a geographic database of the internet. In: Proceedings of the 5th ACM Workshop on HotPlanet, HotPlanet 2013, pp. 15–20. ACM, New York (2013). https://doi.org/10.1145/2491159.2491170
16. Durairajan, R., Barford, P., Sommers, J., Willinger, W.: Intertubes: a study of the us long-haul fiber-optic infrastructure. SIGCOMM Comput. Commun. Rev. 45(4), 565–578 (2015). https://doi.org/10.1145/2829988.2787499
17. Alexander, J.: Loxodromes: A rhumb way to go. Mathematics Magazine 77, December 2004

Ka-band High Throughput Satellites for 5G Based Applications: The Athena-Fidus Case Study

M. Luglio[1], C. Roseti[1], E. Russo[2], and F. Zampognaro[1(✉)]

[1] University of Rome "Tor Vergata", Via del Politecnico 1, 00133 Rome, Italy
zampognaro@ing.uniroma2.it
[2] Italian Space Agency (ASI), Rome, Italy
http://tlcsat.uniroma2.it
http://www.asi.it

Abstract. The 5G standardization activities are going to be finalized. The full set of specifications for the next generation telecommunication systems, which will be based on flexible network management and new services definition, is expected for mid 2018 (release 15) and for mid 2019 (release 16). At the same time, High Throughput Satellite (HTS) platforms faced a wide adoption for the provision of Internet access and are recently gaining a significant interest as complementary connectivity able to support 5G architectures, leading to significant investments for the development and deployment of future platforms. In the view of a synergy between terrestrial and satellite networks to provide 5G services, the satellite access can play a meaningful role to support/complement terrestrial networks for its peculiar characteristics of coverage, broadcasting/multicasting, synchronization, etc. To this aim, the system availability and bandwidths available must be carefully assessed when the hybrid network is tailored to specific 5G services. The Athena Fidus system has been realized to support civil and governmental services and is today operational. In this paper, the characteristics of Athena Fidus DVB-S2/DVB-RCS links are considered to identify the set of services that will be possible to offer, focusing on nominal IP-based bandwidth and availability. The objective is to draw the operational context to be considered for the potential utilization of Athena Fidus in the next communication systems.

Keywords: 5G · Athena Fidus · Link budget · Ka-band

1 Introduction

The forthcoming fifth generation of telecommunication networks is deemed to provide relevant advances and revolutions both for end-users and carriers. From the user point of view, the dramatic improvements on bandwidth and latency, together with the possibility of tailoring the network configuration and deploying

© Springer Nature Switzerland AG 2019
M. S. Obaidat and E. Cabello (Eds.): ICETE 2017, CCIS 990, pp. 16–37, 2019.
https://doi.org/10.1007/978-3-030-11039-0_2

application components at the network edge (mobile edge computing), pave the way to novel communication services including enhancing massive mobile broadband (eMBB), Ultra-Reliable and Low Latency Communications (URLLC) and mMTC (massive Machine Type Communications), with possible use cases ranging from 4K video, to Autonomous Driving to IoT/smart city related applications. From the operator point of view the introduced innovations are even more disruptive. The network functions will be softwarized and virtualised giving the capability to provide the "Network as a Service". The possibility to create slices leveraging network segments and function of different owners will open new business opportunities based on new business models. In other words, the envisioned 5G network aims at seamlessly supporting the widest range of services and applications ever witnessed in past wireless mobile networks. To realize such a vertical integrated vision of multiple end-to-end services deployed on the same mobile infrastructure, future 5G networks will embrace the vision of "customer-facing on-demand network slicing". As described in the 5GPP architecture white paper [1] a network slice is exactly "a composition of adequately configured network functions, network applications, and the underlying cloud infrastructure (physical, virtual or even emulated resources, RAN resources etc.), that are bundled together to meet the requirements of a specific use case, e.g., bandwidth, latency, processing, and resiliency, coupled with a business purpose".

High Throughput Satellites (HTS) platforms allow to achieve high rate (today up to 20 Mbit/s per user, with the goal of offering more than 100 Mbit/s in the next years) bi-directional links, through Very Small Aperture antenna satellite Terminals (VSATs) at the users premises. Such platforms are already available worldwide and represents currently an effective access link to the Internet. HTS typically use Ka-band, in a multi-spot beam configuration, and make use of geostationary satellites (such as Ka-Sat by Eutelsat). In addition, ongoing initiatives are designed to use LEO constellations, so that the experienced latency is greatly reduced, with the deployment of hundreds or thousand of satellites and the capability to offer very large data rate making this platforms suitable to 5G communications.

As introduced in [2], the feasibility of using HTS platforms to implement broadband service is already investigated, looking at well known problems in terms of propagation in Ka-band, opening the way to further 5G oriented integrations. In particular, the consensus and wider agreement on what satellite brings to achieving the 5G goals are:

Ubiquity. Satellite provides high speed capacity across the globe using the following enablers: capacity in-fill inside geographic gaps, overspill to satellite when terrestrial links are over capacity, general global wide coverage, backup/resilience for network fall-back and especially communication during emergency.

Mobility. Satellite is the only readily available technology capable of providing connectivity anywhere on the ground, sea or air for moving platforms, such as airplanes, ships and trains.

Broadcast (Simultaneity). Satellite can efficiently deliver rich multimedia and other content across multiple sites simultaneously using broadcast and multicast streams with information centric networking and content caching for local distribution.

All the three above features are due to satellite's ability to serve coverage areas much wider than those of other wireless communications technologies. Moreover, they can provide cost-effective coverage to many areas of the globe, which can go underserved by terrestrial infrastructures. In summary, satellite can offer complementary connectivity options, seamless user experience, and provide important benefits.

In this regard, over the last few years satellite networks have been envisioned as an important missing piece of 5G networks and several scenarios that could benefit from a mature satellite/terrestrial network integration have been identified [3]. Indeed, satellites are the only means to provide truly ubiquitous geographic coverage and mobility. This feature is important to the successful deployment and operation of 5G use cases, such as:

- Complementing connectivity to mobile nodes (aerial, maritime, vehicles and trains);
- Guarantee 5G connectivity in the areas not covered by terrestrial infrastructures;
- Ensuring 5G for rural connectivity (in both developed and underdeveloped countries);
- Providing emergency response/disaster relief recovery communications.
- Providing backhauling services to fixed and mobile stations
- Efficient content distribution to feed CDNs
- Remote automation and sensing
- Highly geographically distributed networks.

In this new very challenging scenario, the satellite can be fruitfully included in hybrid communication architectures, to contribute to ensure the full respect of all the requirements and capabilities associated to the 5G deployment, as preliminarily discussed in [4,5].

This paper investigates the potentiality of using IP-based bearer services offered by Athena Fidus, which is an operational HTS platform covering the Italian territory. The authors will describe in details its characteristics, configuration and, by means of simulations, link budget margins and achievable bitrates, suitable to support 5G applications, with a determined quality of service and availability.

The rest of the paper is organized as follows: Sect. 2 includes the description of the Athena Fidus platform; Sect. 3 describes the detailed radio-frequency channels specification in relation with system availability; in Sect. 4 a detailed analysis of Ka-band link attenuations is presented; in Sect. 5 simulation results including link-budgets and relative resulting bearer channel are shown. In Sect. 6 conclusions are drawn and possible future works are described.

2   Athena Fidus Characteristics and Architecture

The Athena Fidus (Access on THeaters for European allied forces Nations-French Italian Dual Use Satellite) system [6,7] is the result of a space program developed jointly by ASI (the Italian Space Agency) and CNES (Centre National d'Etudes Spatiales). The Athena Fidus satellite hosts Italian and a French payloads (which are completely independent in characteristics, operations and coverages), either for civil or military use; therefore, four separated and independent payloads are operative at the same time in a geostationary orbit, at a position of 37.8°E. Athena-Fidus has 14 antennas, 7 of which are steerable for dynamic spot-coverage (with a spot diameter of 1750 Km) to serve areas on demand at high bitrates; France owns 5 beams and Italy 2.

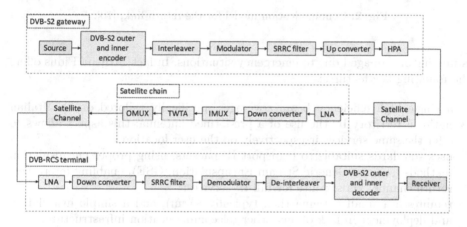

Fig. 1. Communication model for the forward link, [10].

The Athena Fidus goal is to support a telecommunication infrastructure able to replace or complement terrestrial networks for a large set of civil and governmental applications, both broadband and narrowband beams using different bands, namely Ka-band and EHF. While EHF is adopted for military operations, which are undocumented and outside the scope of this work, the civil allotment will be considered in the rest of the paper. More specifically, Italy is the geographical reference area considered, where a single beam in Ka-band is available, for broadband national services: the overall expected data rate is over 1 Gbit/s. In its current setup, Athena-Fidus ground segment makes us of DVB-RCS [8] for return link communications on a shared channel, and point to point links (for mesh communications) or DVB-S2 [9] broadcasting for forward links, to offer state of the art transmission efficiency and service availability.

Athena Fidus Italian civil payload can possibly enable new IP-based and 5G services in remote and underserved areas, or where the terrestrial infrastructure

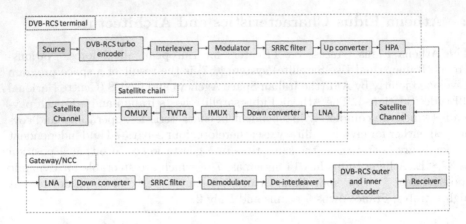

Fig. 2. Communication model for the return link, [10].

is missing or damaged due to emergency situations. In fact, Athena Fidus offers the following key features:

- a single high efficiency beam coverage, specifically tailored on the Italian national territory by the use of a pre-formed antenna: this aspect allows to offer the same services irrespectively on the user location;
- uses standards suitable to transport IP packets, using proper encapsulation methods (such as Generic Stream Encapsulation, GSE), enabling interactive return channel via satellite for full-IP services;
- requires a a small antenna (i.e., typically 85 cm), and a simple installation and deployment in lack of any other telecommunication infrastructure.

Nonetheless, the available capacity to the 5G/IP based service depends on the physical characteristics of the satellite channels which are defined to respect the transmission standards. In particular, the overall bandwidth allotment must be divided into sub-carriers with different layouts according to the type of service and the transmission direction. Furthermore, it is necessary to consider carefully other system parameters such as EIRP (Equivalent Isotropic Radiated Power) at transmission, G/T (Antenna gain-to-noise-temperature, the specific figure of merit of the antenna in use $= G_R/T$ in reception) and other losses (due to distortion, interferences, etc.).

To conclude the overview on Athena Fidus, a block diagram of the transmission and reception chain considered is provided for both DVB-S2 (used in forward link) and DVB-RCS links in [8] and [9] (used in return link) and shown in Figs. 1 and 2 respectively. All the functional blocks impact the overall performance and contribute to the determination of the Signal to Noise Ratio (SNR) thresholds for the link budget, and have been considered as well in the following analysis and simulations.

3   Service Overview and Channel Design

Link availability represents the percentage of time in which the link is suitable for transmission or, in other words, shows enough signal to noise margin to support the identified transmission mechanism. This value is calculated as a % over the year, and it is usually fixed to a target value agreed with users in the Service Level Agreement (SLA). While this value can be exactly calculated a-posteriori by continuous monitoring of the link status (i.e., to verify if the SLA was respected by the Satellite Operator), what is of interest is to consider this value as a statistical target and perform dimensioning and tuning of the system on that.

Therefore, the dimensioning of the system envisages first the determination of a reference link availability % and then the tuning of the best combination of other parameters (such as transmitter power, antenna gain, etc.), in accordance to statistical propagation models which take into account variable aspects such as rain attenuations, fading, etc. Once this activity, called link budget, is concluded, it is then finally possible to determining the modulation and coding to use and consequently the available bitrate at IP level.

Satellite commercial systems typically provide connectivity based services with 99.7% of availability. Of course, most critical services belonging to 5G specifications could require higher values so, in the analysis presented hereinafter, also values higher than 99.7% will be considered.

In order to perform an exhaustive analysis and determine the other system parameters, in this paper we considered a distribution of 2166 terminals across the Italian territory with the aim to cover different specific location characteristic (e.g., distance to the sea, altitude, rainy areas, etc.). The distribution of terminals adopted for the following simulations is represented in Fig. 3. The typical values for the current commercial Ka-band terminals which are used for the evaluation of link budget, which are: $G_R = 42$ dB and EIRP $= 48$ dBW [11].

Well assessed rain models are then applied using parameters which depend on the geographical location of the terminal. Each terminal location, expressed in terms of longitude, latitude and real altitude above sea level, will be used in all the calculations and simulations for the service evaluation.

On the basis of these simulations, and for each specific target Link availability (%), the nominal IP bandwidth that can be exploited by a Ka-band terminal by these characteristics can be evaluated taking into account the Carrier Symbol Rate (kbit/s) and the Modulation and Coding scheme (MODCOD) which can be used.

Table 1 summarizes the channel breakdown (bandwidth allotment) on the Athena Fidus transponder, as extracted from technical specifications available and considering the transmission and reception standards, equipment, antenna types and maximum amplifier power. For each channel the main parameters impacting the link budget computation are reported. In the present study, the star-based network architecture is considered as a baseline, where Athena Fidus makes use of a common broadband forward link, whereas a shared return link is used by many remote peers along the territory in time division.

Fig. 3. Identified terminal locations; Gateway is located at Fucino plateau.

Table 1. Athena Fidus channel repartition, [10].

Channel #	Connectivity	F_{UP} (MHz)	F_{DOWN} (MHz)	Carrier
15 + 17(1)	Star return (DVB-RCS)	29600	19520	10
15 + 17(2)	Star return (DVB-RCS)	29600	19520	144
15 + 17(3)	Star return (DVB-RCS)	29600	19520	116
16	Star forward (DVB-S2)	29427.5	19887.5	1
18	Star forward (DVB-S2)	29302.5	19762.5	1

The broadcast forward channels are number 16 and 18, with 75 and 125 MHz bandwidths respectively, making use of DVB-S2 standard. Then, Athena Fidus offers many carriers to be used in time division multiple access (TDMA defined in DVB-RCS standard) or as exclusive access. Such carriers are defined within the combination of channel 15 and 17, defining three different classes with different bandwidths (identified as (1), (2) and (3) leveraging the combined 15 + 17 channel). For each channel class, a different number of carriers is defined (last column) and, as reported in Table 2, a different respective bandwidth in MHz. Depending on the supported symbol rate/bandwidth per channel, this allows to create different narrowband links, with an overall bandwidth of about 200 MHz.

Table 2. Athena Fidus channel characteristics, [10].

Channel #	Symbol rate (MSym/s)	Roll-off	BW per carrier (MHz)	EIRP density (dBW/MHz)	G/T (dB/K)
15 + 17(1)	1.9	0.35	2.565	28	9
15 + 17(2)	0.64	0.35	0.864	28	9
15 + 17(3)	0.32	0.35	0.432	28	9
16	60	0.25	75	32.5	10
18	100	0.25	125	32.5	10

Definitively, the Athena Fidus terminals will be associated to only one of such carrier for the return link, and each single carrier can be associated to multiple terminals competing for the carrier bandwidth as defined by multiple access techniques required by DVB-RCS standard. Multiple access (TDMA) is normally enforced on channel $15 + 17(1)$, while the other 2 classes can be used also without contention (one carrier per terminal). On the other hand, for the forward link, all terminals will make use of the shared broadcast link (either channel 16 or 18).

4   Evaluation of Ka-band Attenuations

Once the channels are defined, the Ka-band propagation models [12–16] are applied to assess the attenuation margin as a function of the terminal coordinates/altitude above the sea level and of the target availability. This dynamic parameter, combined with the other system parameters discussed before, allows to evaluate accurate per-terminal link budgets. Taking as a reference the Athena Fidus coverage, the two frequencies $f_1 = 19.8$ GHz and $f_2 = 29.4$ GHz are considered as reference for downlink and uplinks, respectively, to show the attenuation margins. The other frequencies involved are considered in the correspondent simulations (e.g., 29.6 GHz for the return link uplink, and 19.52 MHz for the return link downlink), but attenuation results are not presented (presenting marginal differences with regard to the case discussed below).

Figure 4 shows the attenuation distribution due to propagation effects in the downlink (at $f_1 = 19.8$). It is obtained as a normalized histogram (so that the sum of all bins value equals to 1) of the values obtained from terminals, then representing an approximation of the Probability Density Function (PDF). This view allows to spot easily the attenuation trend, for different availability values of 99.9%, 99.5% and 99%, and the correspondent mean value. If the considered target application, which will make use of this kind of satellite segment, has an availability requirement of 99.9%, it can be satisfied designing the system to counteract an attenuation varying in the range 6–9.5 dB. The simulation results show that the higher attenuation values are encountered for sites located in North-East of Italy. With a lower availability requirement (i.e. 99.5%), the attenuation value to consider drops below 5 dB.

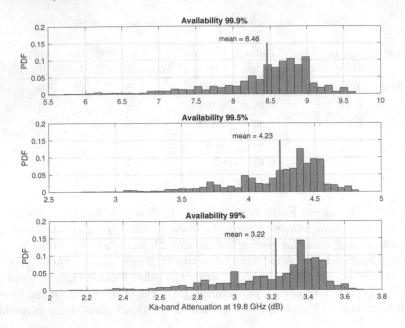

Fig. 4. Ka-band attenuation for $f_1 = 19.8$ GHz.

The same simulation output is reported for $f_2 = 29.4$ (related to the uplink) in Fig. 5. In comparison with the downlink, for an availability of 99.9%, the attenuation varies in the range 11–18 dB. This is due to the greater dependence on rain fading within this frequency range. It is clear that, for the overall link budget evaluation for a transparent HTS platform, such as the one considered in this paper, the uplink represents the most critical link with regard to the attenuation.

The same data have been post processed to provide another representation, where on the y-axis there is the attenuation value in ascending order and the x-axis represents the percentage of terminals considered in the simulation (from 0 to 100), positioned over the Italian territory as shown in Fig. 3. In this way, it is possible to assess the percentage of terminals of a given population which can be considered with attenuation below a target reference value. The results are shown in Fig. 6 for $f_1 = 19.8$ GHz, and in Fig. 7 for the uplink at $f_2 = 29.4$ GHz. This representation allows to focus on a specific percentage of terminals which will statistically suffer of that attenuation, allowing to support with more details the link budget evaluation for the system dimensioning, in case the position of the terminals to consider is not known in advance. It is possible for instance to identify the margin for the system dimensioning, only based on a subset of terminals. If considering 50% of terminals, it is possible to obtain the median of all attenuation values. For $f_1 = 19.8$ GHz and a required availability of 99.5% the median is 4.3 dB, while for $f_2 = 29.4$ GHz is 8 dB (so slightly different from the mean value showed before). As additional example, and reported with the

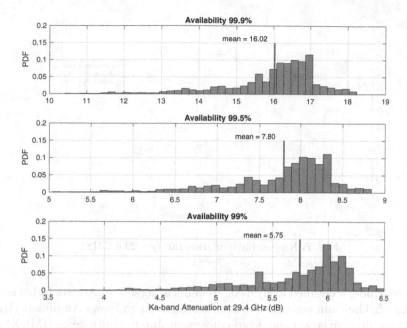

Fig. 5. Ka-band attenuation for $f_2 = 29.4$ GHz.

dotted lines in the plot, for an availability of 99.9% and considering the margin which allows to take into account 20% of terminals, the attenuation to consider is 8 dB for $f_1 = 19.8$ GHz and 14.7 for $f_2 = 29.4$ GHz, lower than both mean and median values. The presented results are referred to a distribution of terminals over the entire national territory but of course it would be possible to perform more limited analysis at regional level.

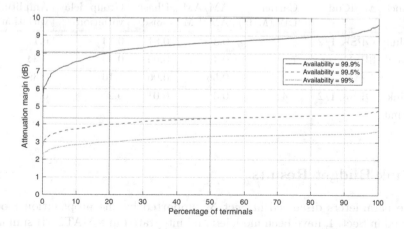

Fig. 6. Ka-band attenuation for $f_1 = 19.8$ GHz.

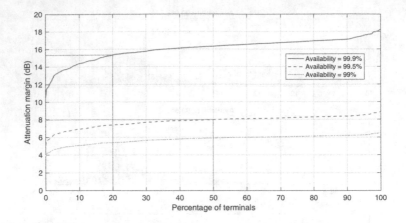

Fig. 7. Ka-band attenuation for $f_2 = 29.4$ GHz.

To conclude, a detailed analysis of "non-linear losses" in Athena Fidus is provided in [6]. The main loss contributions are due to High Power Amplifiers (HPA) distortions, up-conversion and down-conversion, Input-Multiplexed (IMUX) and Output-Multiplexer (OMUX) filters. An example of the main degradation contributions are summarized in Table 3, for some of the channels available and depending on the target modulation and coding scheme to use. For the simulations, they are combined as average in root sum square in order to consider adequately the overall attenuation value due to non-linear effects.

Table 3. Summary of Athena Fidus non-linear degradations.

Channel	ModCod	Carrier BW (MHz)	Average value of degradations (dB)			
			AM/AM AM/PM	Phase noise	Group delay variation	Amplitude variation
Fwd link	QPSK 1/2		0.3	0.01	0.34	0.1
Ka-band	8PSK 3/4	75	0.49	0.05	0.93	0.34
	16APSK 2/3		0.56	0.06	1.16	0.39
Ret link Ka-band	QPSK 1/2	5.4	0.3	0.01	0.2	0.1

5   Link Budget Results

All the parameters discussed in Sect. 3, supported by the propagation models described in Sect. 4, have been modeled and integrated in a MATLAB simulator aimed to compute link budget for both return and forward link of the target system, at all possible satellite links configurations. Relevant propagation models and ITU standards have been considered, specifically considering the attenuation margins achieved by previous simulations. The goal of the proposed analysis is to determine, given a certain degree of availability associated to a specific service, the useful channel capacity (in terms of available bit/s for TCP/IP traffic), which is indicated as C_{IP}.

Before computing link budget, the target signal-to-noise ratio (ideal SNR_0), to be used as lower-bound threshold for the link budget, were determined as a function of the eligible coding and modulation schemes and real channel choices. This in turns allows to determine the associated value of raw capacity available (C) in baseband, and consequently the capacity available at the IP level (C_{IP}) to support 5G services. In particular, the link budget requirements for a specific carrier are described in the next sections by means of:

- Mode – MODCOD reference for possible choice of *"Modulation scheme"* and *"coding rate"*;
- Target (ideal) E_b/N_0 – as obtained from standards and test results found in literature, i.e. [17];
- Spectral Efficiency (η) – transmitted bits per Hz, computed as ratio between radiofrequency bandwidth (IF) and channel bandwidth $C = SR \cdot R_c \cdot log_2(M)$, where SR = Symbol Rate, R_c = overall coding rate, M = number of modulation symbols);
- Target (ideal) SNR_0 – signal to noise ratio computed as $E_b/N_0 + \eta[dB] + SR[dB]$;

The simulations will allow to identify the MODCOD to use according to the required availability, for each of the channel identified, and then derive the associated baseband capacity C, using the spectral efficiency values reported in the tables. From this C value, it is then possible to derive C_{IP} (Mbit/s), which is the capacity effectively available at the IP layer using the relations, discussed in [18] for average sized IP packets, of $C_{IP} = C \cdot 0.95$ for the forward link and $C_{IP} - C \cdot 0.86$ for the return link. The required SNR_0 for decoding and attenuation are evaluated for each of the 2166 terminals for all possible channel configurations.

5.1   Return Link

The summary of the link budget requirements and MODCOD selection presented hereafter, are based on [19], where the values for E_b/N_0 are referred to the useful bit-rate, so taking into account the factor $10\ log_{10}188/204$ ($\approx 0,36$ dB) due to the Reed-Solomon outer code) and include the modem implementation margins.

Link Budget Requirements and Calculation of the Nominal Capacity. Considering the channel configuration characterized by a symbol rate of 320 kSym/s (carrier $15 + 17(3)$), the maximum throughput allowed at the IP level is below 400 kbit/s, as summarized in Table 4. This rate is sufficient to set up low

Table 4. DVB-RCS link budget requirements for 320 ksym/s channels, [10].

Mode	Ideal E_b/N_0 [dB]	Spectral efficiency (η)	Ideal SNR_0 [dB]	C_{IP} (kbit/s)
QPSK 1/2	4.5	0.57	**57.14**	**213**
QPSK 2/3	5	0.76	**58.89**	**284**
QPSK 3/4	5.5	0.86	**59.9**	**320**
QPSK 5/6	6	0.95	**60.86**	**356**
QPSK 7/8	6.4	1.0	**61.47**	**373**

data rate services such as messaging, Voice over IP (VoIP), small file transfer, small data M2M and sensor networks data exchange.

Table 5 summarizes requirements and associated maximum capacity available at the IP layer over channels with symbol rate equal to 640 ksym/s ($15 + 17(2)$). The allowed IP capacity ranges from 427 to 747 kbit/s depending on the selected MODCOD. Such values are compliant with application requirements of medium data rate such as real time video streaming, file transfer, web browsing, distributed monitoring [20]. In fact, the obtained data rates are comparable with the ones experienced in the common ADSL return link, allowing satellite either to offload traffic coming from congested terrestrial networks or to backup terrestrial links during failures or outages.

Table 5. DVB-RCS link budget requirements for 640 kSym/s channels, [10].

Mode	Ideal E_b/N_0 [dB]	Spectral efficiency (η)	Ideal SNR_0 [dB]	C_{IP} (kbit/s)
QPSK 1/2	4.5	0.57	**60.1**	**427**
QPSK 2/3	5	0.76	**61.9**	**569**
QPSK 3/4	5.5	0.86	**62.9**	**641**
QPSK 5/6	6	0.95	**63.8**	**712**
QPSK 7/8	6.4	1.0	**64.4**	**747**

Finally, Table 6 concerns requirements for connectivity over 1.9 MSym/s channels ($15-17(1)$). Of course, requirements in terms of C/N_0 are more severe, while the allowed IP capacity is much higher: from 1.2 Mbit/s up to more than 2 Mbit/s. With data rates in this range even wideband services such as HD TV can be provided. Also this configuration is considered for link budgets.

Link Budget Analysis. Figures 8, 9 and 10 show results of link budget calculations for the whole set of terminals in terms of SNR_0, obtained by setting the transmitting antenna gain at 42 dB. Note that the results for different gain

Table 6. DVB-RCS link budget requirements for 1.9 MSym/s Channels, [10].

Mode	Ideal E_b/N_0 [dB]	Spectral efficiency (η)	Ideal SNR_0 [dB]	C_{IP} (kbit/s)
QPSK 1/2	4.5	0.57	**64.87**	**1268**
QPSK 2/3	5	0.76	**66.62**	**1691**
QPSK 3/4	5.5	0.86	**67.63**	**1903**
QPSK 5/6	6	0.95	**68.59**	**2114**
QPSK 7/8	6.4	1.0	**69.2**	**2220**

values of the antenna (in dB) can be immediately obtained by linearly up or down shifting the curves. The link budget margin (SNR_0) is reported on the abscissa, sorted in ascending order, for different availability targets. On x-axis it is reported the % of terminals considered for the analysis, similarly to the previous figures related to the attenuation study. On each plot, the reference thresholds for the selection of a specific MODCOD are indicated, by means of dashed lines.

For the $15 + 17(3)$ channel, availability curves are shown in Fig. 8, ranging from 99.9% to 99.5%. In this configuration, about the 10% of the the terminals is able to exceed the QPSK 1/2 threshold for an availability of 99.9%. If considering a slightly lower availability target, all the terminals are able to

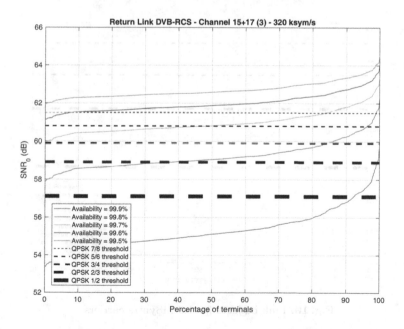

Fig. 8. Link budgets for 320 kSym/s carriers.

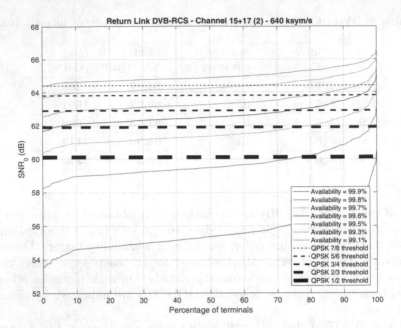

Fig. 9. Link budgets for 640 kSym/s carriers. (Color figure online)

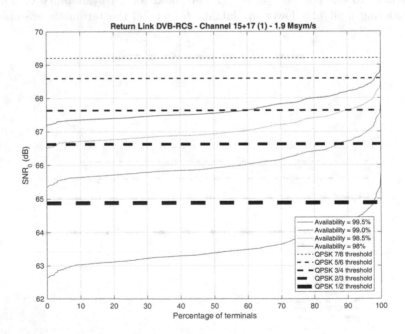

Fig. 10. Link budgets for 1.9 MSym/s carriers.

use the QPSK 1/2 and, in many cases, lower MODCODs. This type of channel, rather than offering multimedia and wide band communication, can become very important for narrow band ultra reliable services, part of the 5G applications portfolio. It is important to note that, narrow band channels can be achieved also if adopting bandwidth on demand (BoD) techniques, as described in DVB-RCS standard, or random access techniques [21], leveraging the broader channels (such as, $15 + 17(1)$). Nonetheless, this may require an higher SNR_0 as it will be shown in the following, although the channel can be shared among several terminals more efficiently rather than assigning a carrier in a dedicated way.

Figure 9 shows results for the $15 + 17(2)$ channel, offering a 640 ksym/s carrier, with the colored curves associated with different values of link availability selected for the link budget spanning from 99.1% (pink uppermost curve) up to 99.9% (blue curve). With an availability of 99.9% (blue curve), almost all the terminals are not able to comply with the link budget. A similar situation occurs with 99.8%, where only about 20% of terminals are above the QPSK 1/2 threshold. Setting availability to 99.7% (typical value exhibited for commercial services), all the terminals satisfy link budget requirements. About 20% of the terminals can even use more efficient MODCODs, thus working at rates up to 747 kbit/s. Finally, results improve even more when decreasing availability requirements. For instance, with 99.3% all terminals can work at a maximum rate higher than 700 kbit/s.

Figure 10 shows results when considering the highest capacity channels of 1.9 MSym/s. In order to guarantee that all the terminals satisfy link budget requirement, the target availability must go down to 99%. For higher values (i.e. 99.5%) only a small subset of terminals complies. On the other hand, while link budget respects the requirements, the amount of capacity available at the IP layer is much higher than the one allowed with the 640 ksym/s channel (in any configuration). In fact, with availability of 99% all the terminals can transmit at a maximum rate of at least 1.26 Mbit/s, while about 10% of the terminals can achieve up to 1.69 Mbit/s. As a general conclusion, these broad channels can be used for broadband applications that do not require commercial-like availability.

5.2   Forward Link

Communication on the forward link over channel #16, and Channel #18, characterized by parameters resumed in Tables 1 and 2, is specifically addressed. DVB-S2 standard is adopted, enabling a large number of combinations among modulation and coding schemes, as presented in [19]. For the evaluation of target E_b/N_0, and related ideal (nominal) SNR_0, Quasi Error Free conditions ($PER = 10^{-7}$) and white noise Gaussian channel are considered, with FEC Frame length set as normal (64800 bits). If considering short FEC Frame (16200 bits), an additional degradation of 0.2 dB to 0.3 dB has to be taken into account. Please note that the η efficiency parameter is the $(bit/s)/Hz$ ratio (considering the available baseband bitrate, or C), and not $(bit/s)/Sym$ as otherwise used.

Table 7. DVB-S2 link budget requirements for Channel #16, considering useful MOD-CODs.

Mode	Ideal E_b/N_0 [dB]	Spectral efficiency (η)	Ideal SNR_0 [dB]	C_{IP} (Mbit/s)
QPSK 1/4	−2.35	0.4	**75.43**	**28.53**
QPSK 1/3	−1.24	0.53	**76.54**	**38.04**
QPSK 2/5	−0.3	0.64	**77.48**	**45.64**
QPSK 1/2	1	0.8	**78.78**	**57.06**
QPSK 3/5	2.23	0.96	**80.01**	**68.47**
QPSK 2/3	3.1	1.06	**80.88**	**76.08**
QPSK 3/4	4.03	1.2	**81.81**	**85.59**
QPSK 4/5	4.68	1.28	**82.46**	**91.29**
8PSK 3/5	5.5	1.44	**83.28**	**102.7**
8PSK 2/3	6.62	1.6	**84.4**	**114.12**
8PSK 3/4	7.91	1.8	**85.69**	**128.38**
16APSK 2/3	8.97	2.13	**86.75**	**152.16**
16APSK 3/4	10.21	2.4	**87.99**	**171.18**
16APSK 4/5	11.03	2.56	**88.81**	**182.59**
16APSK 5/6	11.61	2.66	**89.39**	**190.2**
32APSK 3/4	12.73	3	**90.51**	**213.97**
32APSK 4/5	13.64	3.2	**91.42**	**228.24**
32APSK 5/6	14.28	3.33	**92.06**	**237.75**
32APSK 8/9	15.69	3.55	**93.47**	**253.6**
32APSK 9/10	16.05	3.6	**93.83**	**256.77**

Link Budget Requirements and Calculation of the Nominal Capacity. Some of several Modulation and Coding (MODCOD) configurations in the DVB-S2 forward link transmission are not of practical interest. Figure 11 shows the ideal SNR_0 as function of possible MODCODs for both Channel #16 and Channel #18, as inferred by the work by same authors in [10]. Some combinations of MODCODs at the same nominal SNR_0 offer a lower C_{IP} and can be discarded. For instance, if considering Channel #18 (100 MSym/s), and assuming a received SNR_0 in the range of 90–91 dB, either 8PSK 5/6, 8PSK 8/9, 8PSK 9/10 or 16APSK 3/4 offer a lower throughout at IP level compared to 16 APSK 3/4. Therefore, the possible channel configurations of interest for the forward link are presented for Channel #16 and Channel #18 respectively in Tables 7 and 8, where in particular η represents the spectral efficiency in terms of radio frequency bandwidth (MHz) and available bitrate (Mbit/s).

Link Budget Analysis. Target SNR_0 values are taken as thresholds to be compared to values achieved through link budget simulations related to all the

Table 8. DVB-S2 link budget requirements for Channel #18, considering useful MOD-CODs.

Mode	Ideal E_b/N_0 [dB]	Spectral efficiency (η)	Ideal SNR_0 [dB]	C_{IP} (Mbit/s)
QPSK 1/4	−2.35	0.4	**77.65**	**47.55**
QPSK 1/3	−1.24	0.53	**78.76**	**63.4**
QPSK 2/5	−0.3	0.64	**79.7**	**76.08**
QPSK 1/2	1	0.8	**81**	**95.1**
QPSK 3/5	2.23	0.96	**82.23**	**114.12**
QPSK 2/3	3.1	1.06	**83.1**	**126.8**
QPSK 3/4	4.03	1.2	**84.03**	**142.65**
QPSK 4/5	4.68	1.28	**84.68**	**152.16**
8PSK 3/5	5.5	1.44	**85.5**	**171.18**
8PSK 2/3	6.62	1.6	**86.62**	**190.2**
8PSK 3/4	7.91	2.8	**87.91**	**213.97**
16APSK 2/3	8.97	2.13	**88.97**	**253.6**
16APSK 3/4	10.21	2.4	**90.21**	**285.3**
16APSK 4/5	11.03	2.56	**91.03**	**304.32**
16APSK 5/6	11.61	2.66	**91.61**	**317**
32APSK 3/4	12.73	3	**92.73**	**356.62**
32APSK 4/5	13.64	3.2	**93.64**	**380.4**
32APSK 5/6	14.28	3.33	**94.28**	**396.25**
32APSK 8/9	15.69	3.55	**95.69**	**422.67**
32APSK 9/10	16.05	3.6	**96.05**	**427.95**

terminals. Results are shown in Fig. 12 for Channel #16. With a high availability of 99.9%, the totality of terminals show a link budget margin above the lower threshold (related to QPSK 1/4), so that connectivity requirement is always respected, giving at IP layer a capacity of at least 28 Mbit/s. In fact, most of the terminals are in conditions to work with QPSK 1/2, thus with a net IP capacity of 38 Mbit/s. Setting a slightly lower availability requirement (i.e. 99.5%), terminals can use a MODCOD much more efficient such as the QPSK 5/6 and then exploiting a capacity of about 95 Mbit/s.

Results for Channel #18, shown in Fig. 13, are very similar to those experienced in the previous forward link configuration, in terms of SNR_0. Of course, Channel #18 allows the achievement of much higher overall rates, once fixed the SNR leaving the same overall evaluation approach unchanged.

In conclusion, the forward link does not present any particular critical issue in the considered scenario, also for applications requiring high availability values.

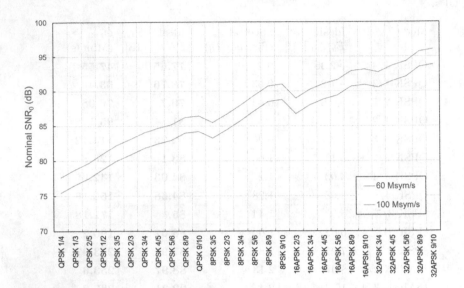

Fig. 11. Possible MODCODs in DVB-S2

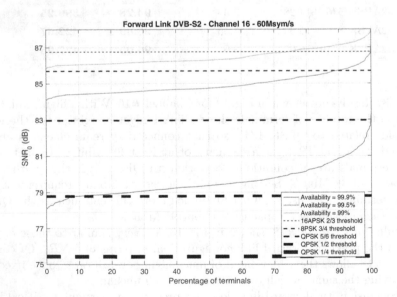

Fig. 12. Forward link ModCod configuration for Gateway - Channel #16.

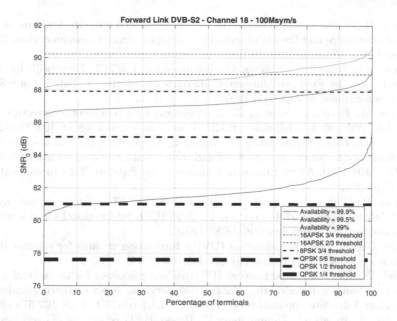

Fig. 13. Forward link ModCod configuration for Gateway - Channel #18.

6   Conclusion

In this paper we discuss in details the configuration and system specification of the Athena Fidus satellite platform, with a focus on its Italian Ka-band broadband interactive IP service. The Athena Fidus platform and its peculiar characteristics where presented and discussed in more details with regard to the previous work from the same authors [10]. Furthermore, this work represents an extension on previous works and available literature providing more details on system characteristics, and supporting with more details and additional simulations the possible system configuration for the Athena Fidus users and operators. From these outcomes, the identification of the most suitable configurations to support the provision of upcoming IP/5G services is possible. The authors are preparing an experimental campaign to compare the results presented in this paper with measures resulting by real installations. Once the analysis outcomes are confirmed, it will be important to test new transmission protocols and innovative approaches oriented to 5G communications on the real satellite links as in [22–24].

References

1. 5G-PPP: View on 5G Architecture. Version 1.0 edn. Architecture Working Group (2016)
2. Berretta, G., et al.: Improvement of ka-band satellite link availability for real-time IP-based video contribution. ICT Express **3**, 124–127 (2017)

3. Evans, B.G.: The role of satellites in 5G. In: Advanced Satellite Multimedia Systems Conference and the 13th Signal Processing for Space Communications Workshop. IEEE ASMS/SPSC (2014)
4. Luglio, M., Roseti, C., Savone, G., Zampognaro, F.: TCP Noordwijk for high-speed trains. In: First International Conference on Advances in Satellite and Space Communications, SPACOMM (2009)
5. Luglio, M., Roseti, C., Savone, G., Zampognaro, F.: Cross-layer architecture for a satellite-WiFi efficient handover. IEEE Trans. Veh. Technol. **58**(6), 102–106 (2009)
6. Iorio, E.D., Ruini, R., Nicola, V.D., Miglietta, A., Winkler, R.: End-to-end system performance evaluation in a forward and return satellite communications link. In: 2012 IEEE First AESS European Conference on Satellite Telecommunications, ESTEL (2012)
7. Sacco, P.: The italian assets for the CLOSEYE EU project: cosmo-skymed and Athena-Fidus satellite systems. In: 2016 IEEE International Geoscience and Remote Sensing Symposium, IGARSS (2016)
8. ETSI: Digital Video Broadcasting (DVB); Interaction channel for satellite distribution systems. V1.4.1 edn. ETSI EN 301 790 (2005)
9. ETSI: Digital Video Broadcasting (DVB): User guidelines for the second generation system for Broadcasting, Interactive Services, News Gathering and other broadband satellite applications (DVB-S2). V1.1.1 edn. ETSI EN 102 376 (2005)
10. Luglio, M., Roseti, C., Zampognaro, F., Russo, E.: Feasibility of 5G services over ka-band Athena-Fidus satellite - a study on ka-band frequency use for 5G based applications over satellite. In: 8th International Conference on Data Communication Networking, pp. 33–42 (2017)
11. EUTELSAT: "VSATs RF Performance", Type Approvals and Characterizations. Eutelsat Broadband Services (2016)
12. ITU-R: Attenuation by atmospheric gases, Recommendation P676–7. International Telecommunication Union (2007)
13. Rytir, M.: Radiowave Propagation at Ka-band (20/30 GHz) for Satellite Communication in High-Latitude Regions. Norwegian University of Science and Technology, NTNU (2009)
14. ITU-R: Propagation data and prediction methods required for the design of Earth-space telecommunication systems, Recommendation P618–9. International Telecommunication Union (2007)
15. ITU-R: Specific attenuation model for rain for use in prediction methods, Recommendation P838. International Telecommunication Union (2005)
16. ITU-R: Attenuation due to clouds and fog, Recommendation P840–3. International Telecommunication Union (1999)
17. ETSI: Digital Video Broadcasting (DVB); Interaction channel for Satellite Distribution Systems; Guidelines for the use of EN 301 790. V1.4.1 edn. ETSI TR 101 790 (2009)
18. Castro, M.A.V., Cardoso, A., Rinaldo, R.: Encapsulation and framing efficiency of dvb-s2 satellite systems. In: 2004 IEEE 59th Vehicular Technology Conference, VTC 2004-Spring, vol. 5, pp. 2896–2900 (2004)
19. ETSI: ETSI EN 301 210 Digital Video Broadcasting (DVB); Framing structure, channel coding and modulation for Digital Satellite News Gathering (DSNG) and other contribution applications by satellite. V1.1.1 edn. ETSI EN 301 210 (2000)

20. Carniato, L., Fongher, F., Luglio, M., Munarini, W., Roseti, C., Zampognaro, F.: Traffic analysis and network dimensioning through simulation and emulation for ka band high capacity satellite systems. In: The International Workshop on Computer-Aided Modeling Analysis and Design of Communication Links and Networks, CAMAD 2013, CAMAD (2013)
21. Bacco, M., Gotta, A., Roseti, C., Zampognaro, F.: A study on TCP error recovery interaction with random access satellite schemes. In: Advanced Satellite Multimedia Systems Conference and the 13th Signal Processing for Space Communications Workshop, ASMS SPSC (2014)
22. Cataldi, P., Gerla, M., Zampognaro, F.: Rateless codes for file transfer over DVB-S. In: 1st International Conference on Advances in Satellite and Space Communications, SPACOMM 2009 (2009)
23. Abdelsalam, A., Luglio, M., Roseti, C., Zampognaro, F.: A burst-approach for transmission of TCP traffic over DVB-RCS2 links. In: 2015 IEEE 20th International Workshop on Computer Aided Modelling and Design of Communication Links and Networks (2015)
24. Abdelsalam, A., Luglio, M., Roseti, C., Zampognaro, F.: TCP Wave: A new reliable transport approach for future internet. In: Computer Networks Volume 112, 15 January 2017, pp. 122–143 (2017)

Approaches to Securing P2PSIP
in MANETs

Alexandre Cormier[1], François Gagnon[2(✉)], Babak Esfandiari[1],
and Thomas Kunz[1]

[1] Department of Systems and Computer Engineering, Carleton University,
Ottawa, Canada
{alexandrecormier,babak,tkunz}@sce.carleton.ca
[2] Cybersecurity Research Lab, Cégep Sainte-Foy, Québec City, Québec, Canada
frgagnon@cegep-ste-foy.qc.ca

Abstract. This paper studies the security for Voice over IP in peer-to-peer (P2P) networks. Instead of taking a general approach to security in P2P, we focus on a specific use case, namely private (e.g. military) mobile ad hoc networks. This allows for security measures that are not necessarily applicable to general P2P networks, but elegantly solve the issues in the given context. We propose security measures for two different approaches to the P2P version of the Session Initiation Protocol in such networks, provide their implementations and present results from performing experimentations in a simulator.

Keywords: P2P · SIP · MANET · Security
Attacks and simulation experiments

1 Introduction

Telecommunication in areas without access to the Internet infrastructure can be enabled using mobile ad hoc networks (MANET). Securing such communication against hostile interference is a requirement in many domains, such as military or law enforcement. Voice over IP (VoIP) is a convenient means for such communication and, because VoIP connections are usually established using the Session Initiation Protocol (SIP), this paper focuses on securing peer-to-peer SIP (P2PSIP) in MANETs.

In [1], we presented our preliminary work toward securing a MANET used in such a scenario. This involved presenting a threat model for peer-to-peer SIP (P2PSIP) over MANETs, proposing a security solution for an approach to P2PSIP based on a distributed hash table (DHT) and providing experimental results for a partial implementation of this security solution, in $Omnet++^1$ using the P2P simulation framework $OverSim^2$. In this paper, we extend this work with:

---

[1] https://omnetpp.org/ [2].
[2] http://www.oversim.org [3].

© Springer Nature Switzerland AG 2019
M. S. Obaidat and E. Cabello (Eds.): ICETE 2017, CCIS 990, pp. 38–62, 2019.
https://doi.org/10.1007/978-3-030-11039-0_3

- Experimental results for full implementation of the DHT-based solution.
- A second security solution, built upon a flooding-based approach to P2PSIP.
- Experimental results for this new solution, also in *Omnet++*.

The remainder of this paper is organized as follows. Section 2 covers some background about MANETs, SIP and P2P. Section 3 then presents related work from literature before Sect. 4 describes in detail the two approaches to SIP over MANETs which our work is based on. Section 5 presents the threat model for our context, then Sects. 6 and 7 present our two security solutions, respectively built upon each of the two aforementioned approaches. Section 8 details experiments performed with these security mechanisms in a simulator and their results. Finally, Sect. 9 closes with a short summary of our findings and discussion of future work.

2   Background

The key concepts used throughout this paper consist of MANETs, SIP and P2P. They are covered in this section, where a short description of each is provided as background.

2.1   Mobile Ad Hoc Networks

MANETs [4] are infrastructure-less wireless networks in which every node acts as both an end device and a router. If a node needs to send a packet to another node that is not within communication range, a multi-hop path is created between those two nodes and the packet is routed to its destination wirelessly through intermediate nodes on this path.

MANETs thus do not require any kind of central administration and allow for dynamic topologies that can be changing constantly. Nodes are devices that can be carried by their users or even vehicles. These characteristics make MANETs ideal for scenarios where infrastructure may not be available or cannot be relied upon, such as emergency response and military networks. Even in the most hostile of environments, users can carry mobile devices and create a network in order to communicate with each other.

2.2   Session Initiation Protocol

SIP [5] is an IETF-standardized protocol used to initiate a session between two users' devices. The entire point of SIP is that this is not done using just IP addresses, but rather, users are identified by a human-readable identifier called a SIP URI. This is similar, both conceptually and in format, to an email address (e.g. sip:alice@example.com).

The heart of the protocol is thus mapping SIP URIs to a contact address, which is the current network location of the SIP client or, in other words, its IP address. This mapping of a SIP URI to a contact address is called an Address-of-Record (AOR). AORs are stored by registrars, whose role is to keep a registry of clients' location and perform the mapping from SIP URI to IP address at session initiation time. SIP being based on a client-server architecture, a number of SIP servers assume the role of registrars. Larger organizations or Internet service providers generally manage those.

Putting all the pieces together, this means that a client that needs to establish a connection with another one needs to first contact its own SIP server, which in turn needs to locate the destination client's SIP server. This is done using DNS, based on the domain part of the destination client's SIP URI. This SIP server has the destination client's AOR and can thus contact it to establish the session between the two clients.

2.3   P2P

As explained in Sect. 2.2, SIP is based on a client-server architecture, which means that it is not appropriate for MANETs. Centralized SIP servers, which serve as registrars, need to be replaced with a distributed solution. One way to do this is to build a P2P overlay network over the MANET, for example using a distributed hash table (DHT), to store and retrieve AORs. The RELOAD protocol [6], standardized by the IETF, is such an approach.

A P2P network [7] is a distributed network in which peers work together by sharing a part of their resources in order to provide a certain service or content. There's is no need for central intermediary entities for traffic to pass through, as participants can access each other directly. A *pure* P2P network is one in which peers can leave and rejoin without affecting the service being provided by the network as a whole, which means that it is completely decentralized. P2P is an ideal choice for MANETs because of those characteristics.

A DHT is one way to structure a P2P network. It stores $(key, value)$ pairs and provides peers with an easy and efficient way to retrieve the value associated with a given key as well as to store new pairs. To achieve this, nodes that form the DHT and keys need to share the same identifier space. A common way to assign node identifiers is to compute a hash of the node's IP address. The same hashing function can then be used to compute keys from meaningful names related to the values that need to be stored. The value is then stored on the node closest to the resulting key, for some definition of closeness.

3   Related Work

Implementing SIP over MANETs is not a new idea, and so a few solutions have been proposed. These can be grouped into distinct categories following the registration scheme used to replace SIP servers, as follows.

Local Storage. TacMAN [8] and a proposal by Banerjee et al. identified as "Loosely Coupled" [9] use local storage, meaning that each peer stores only its own information. A remote peer that needs to retrieve this information then broadcasts a request to locate it.

Network Subset Storage. AdSIP [10], another approach by Banerjee et al. identified as "Tightly Coupled" [11], MANETSip [12] and a solution by Aburumman et al. [13] instead stay closer to traditional SIP and select a subset of the network's peers to act as registrars. For the first two of those, in particular, the peers are chosen such that they form a dominating set of the network graph, meaning that all nodes have at least one neighbor in this subset and all lookups are at most one hop.

DHT Storage. Two unnamed proposals, by Wongsaardsakul et al. [14] and O'Driscoll et al. [15], implement a DHT over the MANET, in which AORs are stored in order to replace registrars. As mentioned in Sect. 2.3, this is also the approach used in the RELOAD protocol [6], standardized by the IETF.

For the most part, however, these solutions do not focus on security. RELOAD is the notable exception, with its three-level security model based on a central certificate authority (CA). TLS or an equivalent protocol is used for all communication between nodes, all messages are signed and stored objects are also signed by the node that creates them.

A few additional solutions also put the focus on securing a P2PSIP network: P2PNS [16] and two unnamed proposals, by Bryan et al. [17] and Seedorf [18]. The first two rely on public key cryptography to sign overlay messages. P2PNS additionally signs registration messages, while the solution by Bryan et al. involves signing the registrations themselves. Both rely on rate limiting mechanisms to make it hard for an attacker to get a valid key pair, rather than using a central CA. For the former, this mechanism is crypto-puzzles. Seedorf, on the other hand, proposes to use self-certifying SIP URIs to ensure the integrity of registrations. To achieve this, each node generates a key pair for itself. The user part of the SIP URI, instead of being a meaningful name like the user's first and last names, is then replaced with a hash of the node's public key. Finally, registrations are signed with the corresponding private key. A more thorough examination of security solutions for P2PSIP, with a focus on DHT security, is presented in [19].

To summarize, many proposals for SIP over MANETs simply do not consider security. Those that do, for the most part, make little assumptions about the context in which they will be used. This allows them to provide a general solution, suitable to many contexts. However, it means that these solutions are not tailored to any specific context, such as the context under focus for this paper (see Sect. 5). Consequently, it makes it more difficult or even impossible to provide the stricter security guarantees that more context awareness can provide.

4 Two Approaches to P2PSIP

We propose two approaches to building a secure MANET for P2PSIP. In this section, we focus on the details of the operation of the network for each approach. Both are based on general approaches seen in Sect. 3. The first one, described in Sect. 4.1, is a simple method in which network flooding is used to resolve SIP

URIs to IP addresses, while the other replaces SIP registrars with a DHT and is detailed in Sect. 4.2.

4.1 Flooding-Based P2PSIP

The first approach we propose is rather simplistic. It is based on a standard flooding protocol and is not expected to provide the best performance in terms of network utilization and latency, but Sects. 5 and 6 will show that it has some benefits, security-wise.

In this approach, rather than having SIP registrars keeping records of other nodes' AORs, each node is responsible for its own AOR. This means that the registration step of SIP is eliminated, as each node has knowledge of their own SIP URI and IP address.

When a node Q needs to reach another node R, it sends a resolve request to all of its neighbors, indicating R's SIP URI, as well as its own SIP URI and IP address. Any node S receiving such a request checks the SIP URI enclosed in the message and compares it to its own. If they do not match, meaning that $S \neq R$, S forwards the request to all of its neighbors. If the SIP URIs match, that is if $S = R$, R creates a response message by adding its IP address to the request and then broadcasts it to the network for it to be routed back to Q following the same mechanism. When Q receives this response, the connection is established and the two nodes can communicate using any IP-based MANET routing protocol. It is relevant to note, however, that if flooding is not used to carry this communication, it may be unsuccessful even after a successful resolve request. This is because flooding provides security advantages, as will be detailed in Sect. 6.

For this to work well, two last steps are required: preventing messages from remaining in the network and being perpetually forwarded between nodes, as well as collision avoidance. For the former, duplicate packet detection can be implemented, by adding a large random number to each message as an identifier and using it to detect and drop duplicate packets. Finally, to avoid collisions, a small random delay can be added before sending messages. This avoids a situation where all nodes forward or respond to a message at the same time, potentially interfering with each other.

4.2 DHT-Based P2PSIP

The second approach is more structured, as nodes in the network form a DHT that is used to replace SIP registrars.

Using this approach, all nodes need to register their SIP AOR with the DHT. A node R trying to do so uses a hash function to reduce its SIP URI to a value k in the key space of the DHT. It then sends a PUT request to that key with the value being its AOR. The node S responsible for this key k receives this PUT request and stores R's AOR.

When a node Q needs to reach R, it hashes R's SIP URI, which yields k. It then sends a GET request to the DHT for this key k. S receives this GET request, as it is responsible for this key, and responds with R's AOR. From the AOR, Q gets R's IP address and communication between Q and R can then be established.

Lastly, if IP addresses are not static, this scheme requires that nodes update their AOR that is stored in the DHT whenever their IP address changes.

5 Threat Model

Before we can discuss attacks to which the network is vulnerable, we need to detail the assumptions that we make with regard to the context in which it is used as well as the security properties that are important in this context. Our focus is on private networks, controlled and operated by a given entity (e.g. the army) that can assert who should and who should not be part of it. SIP URIs can thus be authorized by this central authority prior to the deployment of the network.

In this context, we are interested in protecting data integrity and service availability. The former means an attacker should not be able to fool a legitimate node with regard to the current location of another node, while the latter means an attacker should also not be able to prevent a legitimate node from locating another node.

A successful attack affecting these two properties also corresponds to the attacker's two objectives, with data integrity being the primary target and service availability the secondary. We consider that each malicious node is in full control of one legitimate device and that all malicious nodes can collude and communicate together via a dedicated channel.

We do not consider confidentiality nor anonymity, but they have been studied in P2P literature. For example, Tarzan [20], MorphMix [21] and Octopus [22] study confidentiality and [23] additionally considers anonymity. Our previous work in [1] also describes the entire context in greater depth.

Section 5.1 formally defines and extends the notation used in Sect. 4 and throughout this paper. Then, we present attacks on which the attacker can rely in Sects. 5.2 and 5.3, focusing on storage and retrieval attacks. Again, our previous work in [1], as well as [19], describe these in a more detailed fashion, along with impersonation attacks.

5.1 Notation

The notation used throughout this paper is that of [1], which is as follows:

- Q and R stand for legitimate nodes.
- x and y stand for legitimate users.
- Q and x denote an entity querying the SIP service.
- R and y denote an entity to communicate with.
- M stands for a malicious node.
- S stands for a generic node.

- A stands for a contact address.
- $P(x)$ denotes the node(s) responsible for storing x's AOR.

When describing attack scenarios, we assume the following context: node Q is querying the P2P network to get the current location of user y, which is node R's IP address. This query needs to be routed to $P(y)$. For flooding-based SIP resolution, $P(y)$ is simply R itself. Using the DHT-based approach, however, $P(y)$ could be any node, or even multiple nodes if redundant storage is used.

5.2   Attacks in a Flooding Context

There are two potential angles of attack for a malicious node in the flooding-based approach: attacking the resolve request messages and attacking the response messages. The simplest possible attack is a denial of service attack that can target both by simply dropping all messages. M can perform this attack on every single resolve request happening in the network, because all nodes receive all resolve requests and responses. We will call this the *Drop Messages Attack*.

To target data integrity, M can focus on request messages and respond to any of them, even if it is not the destination of the request. M's response can include invalid data to direct Q to the wrong node, for example M itself. We have implemented this attack and called it the *Resolve to Self Attack*. It causes Q to initiate a session with the malicious node M.

M could also focus on response messages by editing them with an invalid contact address, like its own, before forwarding it to its neighbors. We call this the *Edit Responses Attack*. This attack has the advantage of potentially preventing legitimate nodes from forwarding the valid response message if M's edited response makes it to their packet cache first. Vis-à-vis the *Resolve to Self Attack*, however, it has the disadvantage that M cannot respond to the request before R, thus making it less likely for its bogus response to make it to Q first.

5.3   Attacks in the DHT Context

When a DHT is used for P2PSIP, the attack surface gets larger. An attacker can target the DHT's routing mechanism, which is responsible of locating $P(y)$, the query mechanism or the insertion mechanism.

The simplest routing-based attack is for M to simply drop the message used to locate $P(y)$. To do this, M obviously needs to be on the path followed by this message. This attack is called a *Drop Find Node Attack* in *OverSim*. A more sophisticated routing attack consists in providing an incorrect response to the message. When M is asked for the next hop to reach $P(y)$, it sends Q on a false trail by answering with a random IP address or by saying that it is $P(y)$ itself, for example. *OverSim* calls these the *Invalid Nodes Attack* and *Is Sibling Attack*, respectively. The latter is illustrated in Fig. 1 and sets the table for a query-based attack, which would allow M to compromise data integrity rather than only availability.

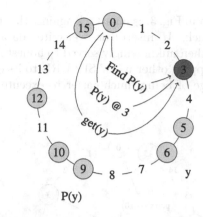

P(y)

Fig. 1. Is Sibling Attack.

A query-based attack is one that is performed by M when it happens to be $P(y)$ or when Q has been fooled into thinking M is $P(y)$. Again, the simplest case is a denial of service attack, by refusing to cooperate and not serving the data by not responding to the query. A more interesting case would be for M to answer the query with invalid data. *OverSim* implements this in its *Invalid Data Attack*, which causes malicious nodes to respond to DHT queries with random data. This data is not in the correct format for a P2PSIP response, so it is easily detected by Q without any security mechanism and thus only causes a denial of service. For M to target data integrity, we have implemented the *Resolve to Self Attack*. Akin to its flooding-based counterpart, it makes a malicious node M respond to Q's resolve request with its own contact address rather than R's. This is illustrated in Fig. 2.

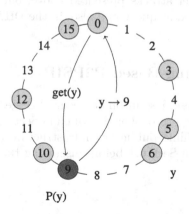

P(y)

Fig. 2. Resolve to Self Attack.

DHT poisoning, shown in Fig. 3, is an attack against the insertion mechanism of the DHT. In this attack, M inserts or overwrites data in the DHT with fabricated data, which is then unknowingly served to honest nodes. For example, M could insert AORs mapping other users' SIP URIs to its own IP address. For M, this has the advantage of being much easier to execute than a routing- or query-based attack.

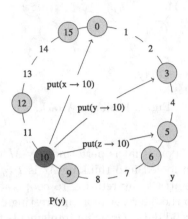

Fig. 3. DHT poisoning.

5.4   Replay Attack

A class of attack that is common to both the flooding and DHT scenarios is the replay attack. It consists in M intercepting a message from a legitimate node and reusing it at a later time when the information in the message is outdated. This is not as powerful as other attacks presented above, but it is more difficult to counter. It can be executed at query and also, in the DHT context, at insertion time.

6   Securing Flooding-Based P2PSIP

In this section, we propose a solution to secure SIP resolution in a MANET based on a simple flooding protocol as described in Sect. 4.1. At the heart of this security solution is an offline public key infrastructure (PKI). We first tackle the data integrity issue in Sect. 6.1 before discussing the system's resilience in Sect. 6.2.

6.1   Data Integrity

As a mirror of the attacker's main objective of compromising data integrity, our main goal for security is to protect this data integrity. This means that malicious nodes should not have the ability to fool a legitimate node Q into believing that user y is located at node S with address A if such is not the case. Q should have the ability to detect such an attempt from malicious nodes and stop trying to communicate with y before sending any meaningful data to S.

Because the flooding-based approach does not include the registration mechanism from SIP (each node stores its own AOR), the only attack vector is at query time. A malicious node will try to respond to Q's query with invalid data as discussed in Sect. 5.2.

When Q sends a query for y's current address, it may receive multiple responses: one from each of its physical neighbors. Because of the duplicate message detection, described in Sect. 4.1, only the first one is considered. If this first response is malicious, then Q is fooled. Waiting for all responses to arrive before trusting any of them would be an improvement, but that presents an issue: if more malicious responses are received than honest ones, then Q is still fooled as to y location.

To fix this issue, Q needs a way to differentiate malicious responses from legitimate ones. To achieve that, we propose using an offline PKI to authenticate responses.

Setup. An offline certificate authority (CA) creates a key pair for itself and the associated certificate. It also issues a certificate for every SIP URI in use in the system, signed by the CA's private key. Before the network is deployed, each node is given its own certificate (userCert) and the associated key pair, as well as the CA's certificate (rootCert), which contains the CA's public key. This is illustrated in Fig. 4 and, in the context in which we operate, described in Sect. 5, this is not a major overhead as a central authority figure owns and is in control of the network and all these nodes correspond to devices that will have to be prepared for missions before being deployed anyway.

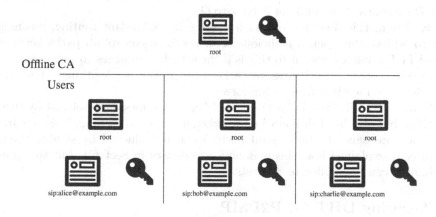

Fig. 4. PKI setup.

Details. With this setup in place, a node R, acting on behalf of user y, can now prove its real identity and authenticate its responses by using its private key to sign them and sending its certificate along with them. Other nodes can then validate these responses by verifying that:

- the SIP URI in the response corresponds to the one in the userCert,
- the message was indeed signed with the private key associated to the public key found in the userCert,
- the userCert was signed with the private key associated to the public key in rootCert.

If a node—Q or an intermediary node—cannot validate a response, it should drop it rather than adding it to the cache that is used for duplicate message detection. This way, a malicious node cannot forge a response, or it will simply be dropped.

One thing that still remains to be fixed, however, is replay attacks. A malicious node cannot forge responses, but it can still use previous responses from R with an outdated contact address in order to mislead Q. To fix this, we can require that the request message's identifier, which is random, be included in the response and signed. This acts as a nonce, meaning previously signed responses from R will not have the correct request identifier and will not be considered valid.

When Q receives a response that it can successfully validate, it can trust that it came from R and the session can be established.

6.2   Resilience

Once data integrity is fixed, an attacker may instead focus on denying service to legitimate nodes, preventing them from communicating together. To do so, this malicious entity needs to prevent the resolve request from Q from making it to R or R's response from making it back to Q.

By design, this flooding approach offers fully redundant routing, meaning that to achieve this goal, a malicious actor needs to control all paths between Q and R. The one exception to this is if the attacker manages to get an invalid message into other nodes' message cache, thus preventing legitimate messages with the same identifier from being forwarded.

A way to fix this issue is for nodes to differentiate messages not just by their identifier, but also by their source node, when it comes to caching. This requires that those messages be unforgeable, which can be achieved by signing them. We already explained how this is done for responses in Sect. 6.1, but the same mechanism can be applied to requests.

7   Securing DHT for P2PSIP

This section presents our multi-layer approach to securing the DHT-based SIP resolution mechanism described in Sect. 4.2. Just like our solution to the flooding-based approach, this one is centered around an offline PKI. First, we discuss how to address data integrity protection and, then, we focus on ensuring the system is resilient.

7.1 Data Integrity

Again, our main objective is to protect data integrity, which means a malicious actor should not be able to convince Q that y is currently located at address A if this is not the case. With the DHT-based approach, there are two vectors through which an attacker could attempt this. The attacker could act:

– at query time. When Q queries the DHT for y's AOR, a malicious node M could perform a query-based attack, as discussed in Sect. 5.3, possibly combined with a routing-based attack. This would allow M or an accomplice of M to respond to Q's query with false information.
– at insertion time. This means a malicious node M could insert invalid data into the DHT so that when Q requests y's AOR, $P(y)$ unknowingly responds to Q with tampered information. This corresponds to the DHT poisoning attack detailed in Sect. 5.3 and is particularly important because of its simplicity and efficiency compared to query time attacks.

In the context of P2PSIP, the simplest way for Q to ensure that the data retrieved by the DHT is valid is through a cryptographic challenge mechanism. At a high level, this works by having Q take the IP address from the AOR that it received and ask the node at this address to prove that it is indeed the intended destination user y. This counters attacks performed through both vectors above.

To achieve this, we make use of the same PKI setup described in Sect. 6.1. This gives R, acting on behalf of y, the technical means to sign Q's challenge. Some additional considerations need to be taken in order to make sure the answer to the challenge is not replayable nor transferable.

First, to avoid a malicious node M being able to intercept the challenge response from R and reuse it later to impersonate R and the associated user y, the challenge will include a random value, or nonce. R will sign the random value and send it back as its response along with its certificate. When Q receives the challenge response, it will validate that this nonce is the same as what it sent and that it is properly signed by R's private key. This way, if M attempts to reuse an old challenge response from R, the nonce will not match. M is obviously not capable of signing faking R's signature with the proper nonce.

Then, we need to ensure that if M managed to have y's SIP URI resolve to its own IP address, it cannot simply transfer the challenge to R before sending it back to Q. This means that the challenge response should be specific to y's location. The challenge response should thus include y's IP address as well as the nonce, all of which is signed. Q can then verify that the address received in the challenge response correspond to the one it sent the challenge to. If this is not the case, it means that the challenge was transfered from a malicious node to R.

Only when the challenge is successful should the session be initiated. If the challenge fails, it means that the node controlling the IP address to which Q's query resolved is malicious. In such a case, Q should halt its attempt to communicate with y.

7.2   Resilience

With the challenge mechanism described in Sect. 7.1, data integrity is protected. However, any attempt at compromising data integrity now results in a failed challenge and thus in denial of service. This means the system is not very resilient. To fix this, we will first tackle DHT poisoning and resource exhaustion attacks, followed by replay attacks and finally routing- and query-based attacks.

Preventing DHT Poisoning and Resource Exhaustion Attacks. With only the challenge mechanism in place, one way that malicious nodes can cause challenges to fail is by inserting invalid data into the DHT, either to overwrite valid entries or to use up all resources of a node and causing it to be unable to store valid entries. To prevent this, whenever a node is asked to store an AOR, it should be able to validate it first.

To achieve this, we also rely on the PKI and require that all AORs to be inserted into the DHT be signed by the node inserting it. The node responsible for storing this AOR then needs to validate that the SIP URI in the AOR corresponds to the SIP URI of the node that signed the entry, as indicated in the certificate sent along with the insertion request.

This signature validation ensures that a malicious node cannot insert invalid data into the DHT. This thus makes it impossible for it to perform a DHT poisoning or resource exhaustion attack, reducing the attack surface available to a malicious actor.

Limiting Replay Attacks. Now that a malicious node cannot insert arbitrary data into the DHT, an attacker may try a replay attack. For example, if y used to be located at an IP address A but has moved, a malicious node M may try reusing y's previous AOR that maps its SIP URI to A and inserting it into the DHT. If successful, this would cause a node Q trying to reach user y to be unable to do so.

To fix this, when receiving an insertion request, a node should be able to validate that this is a new AOR, rather than an outdated one. We propose doing this by adding a timestamp to AORs. Because the AOR needs to be signed, it is not possible for a malicious node to forge an invalid timestamp. Then, when a node receives a request to insert an AOR, it needs to validate the timestamp.

Say S receives a request to insert user y's AOR, located at node R and address A. If S already has an AOR for user y's SIP URI, it needs to validate that the timestamp in the new AOR is indeed more recent than the timestamp in the existing, already stored AOR. If this is not the case, it means that someone is trying to insert an older AOR into the DHT and S should reject it. If S does not already have an entry for y's AOR, it is unlikely that the insertion could be a replay attack because, in the vast majority of cases, this insertion request should be y's first, which means that there are no old requests to replay. However, it is possible that y's first insertion request did not make it to $P(y)$ but that M intercepted it. In this case, however, y is already unreachable, so the replay attack is harmless: when Q tries to contact R, the challenge will fail, resulting in the session initiation attempt being dropped, just like if $P(y)$ had no AOR for R.

Limiting the Effect of Retrieval Attacks. Attacks at insertion time are now taken care of, but there still remains routing- and query-based attacks. Those can be handled by adding redundancy to the storage and retrieval mechanism. The same AOR can be stored by multiple nodes and all of those nodes can be queried at session initiation time.

If the querier receives more than one response to their resolve request, it needs to be able to determine which one is the most trustworthy. This is simple: the correct AOR will be properly signed by the destination node's private key and it will be the latest AOR created by this node. The querier thus needs to trust the most recent properly signed AOR that it received, based on its timestamp.

To prevent the query from succeeding, a malicious node then needs to prevent all legitimate nodes from responding, be it by controlling all nodes responsible for the data or all paths to reach those nodes. Whether this malicious entity performs a typical DoS attack, for example a *Drop Find Nodes* attack, or a more elaborate attacking usually targetting data integrity like a query-based replay attack, the result will be the same. If this malicious actor manages to prevent all honest nodes from responding and itself sends outdated AOR entries for the destination node, the challenge will fail and service will be denied but data integrity will be preserved.

8   Experiments

In this section, we describe our experiments and results, starting with our methodology in Sect. 8.1, followed by the flooding-based solution in Sect. 8.2 and the DHT-based solution in Sect. 8.3. Then, in Sect. 8.4, we discuss the results of these experiments.

8.1   Methodology

As previously mentioned, we implemented simulations using *Omnet++*, along with the *OverSim* framework to implement the DHT. We simulated a network of 25 static nodes placed such that there exists at least one path between any to nodes, assuming all honest and cooperating nodes.

For simulations of attack scenarios, each node has a given probability of spawning as malicious, as indicated on each figure. In all experiments where the effect of changing the number of malicious nodes is evaluated, it ranges from no malicious node at all to each node having a 50% chance of being malicious.

Every node periodically tries, every 30 s, to resolve a SIP URI among those of all nodes. This process starts after 100 s, to let the network build itself and stabilize, which is important for the DHT approach. We simulated 600 seconds per simulation and each scenario was run 20 times in order to account for randomness and in order to get statistically significant results. Margins of error corresponding to 95% confidence intervals are also shown on all graphs.

Details specific to each of our two solutions will be included in their respective subsection.

8.2   Flooding-Based Solution

First, we cover experiments with the approach using network flooding. We go over our methodology and then present our results.

Methodology. The cache we used for duplicate message detection is a simple bounded queue with a capacity of 512 packets. The random delay used to prevent collisions varies from 0 to 10 ms and follows a uniform distribution.

The defense mechanism presented in Sect. 6 has been implemented, along with the *Drop Messages*, *Resolve to Self* and *Edit Responses* attacks discussed in Sect. 5.2.

Results. This sections shows the result of our simulations in which we evaluated the effect of different attacks on the resolve success rate as well as observed the total amount of traffic generated.

Drop Messages Attack. This attack is a denial of service attack for which our security solution itself is not expected to help, but the nature of the resolve mechanism, being based on flooding, is expected to provide great benefits: there needs to be a malicious node on all paths between the caller and the callee for the attack to have an effect.

Figure 5a shows the effect of the attack on the success rate of resolve calls. We notice that, evidently, the success rate goes down as the proportion of malicious nodes goes up. It drops faster than the increase in malicious nodes. This is because, given that a node is malicious with probability p, each resolve call fails, with probability p, due to the SIP URI being resolved belonging to a malicious node. In addition, it fails if malicious nodes cut all paths between the caller and the callee. Also, the two green lines overlap, confirming our expectation that the security mechanism does not play a role in this scenario.

Figure 5b shows the network utilization in this same scenario, calculated as the total amount of traffic by the MAC layer to the physical layer. It is indirectly proportional to the number of malicious nodes, as expected, because malicious nodes do not forward messages or respond to resolve requests. The amount of traffic when all nodes are honest is most interesting though, for comparison with the DHT-based solution results in similar circumstances, that follow in Sect. 8.3.

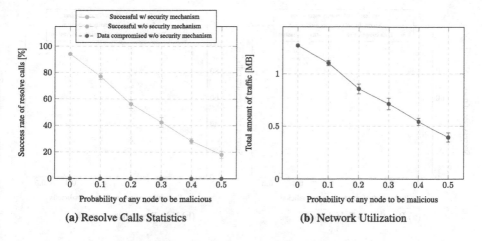

(a) Resolve Calls Statistics

(b) Network Utilization

Fig. 5. Drop Messages Attack statistics.

Resolve to Self Attack. This attack targets data integrity and is thus expected to be countered by the signature and verification mechanism of our security solution. Figure 6a shows that this is the case: there is only a slight decrease in the success rate of resolves as the number of malicious nodes increases. This decrease is due to situations where all paths between the calling and called nodes count at least one malicious node. In this case, the node attempting to resolve a SIP URI only receives invalid AORs, so the resolve fails, but no session is established because it detects that the AORs are invalid. Without the security mechanism and assuming the first resolve response received for a given request is always trusted, a few malicious nodes suffice to greatly affect the integrity of the network. This is shown with dashed lines in Fig. 6a, where the red one represents cases in which the session would be established with the wrong, malicious node.

Edit Responses Attack. With the security solution in place, this attack is expected to yield the same result as the *Resolve to Self Attack*, following the same reasoning. Figure 6b confirms that this is indeed the case. Without the security mechanism, this attack is less effective than the *Resolve to Self Attack*, however. This is due to the fact that, in a *Resolve to Self Attack*, malicious nodes respond to the request before the destination node does if they are closer to the querier, which is not the case with an *Edit Responses Attack*. Additionally, a response that has been edited keeps the same message identifier and thus may not be forwarded by all nodes because of the packet detection mechanism.

8.3   DHT-Based Solution

Now, we describe our experiments with the approach making use of a DHT before presenting our results.

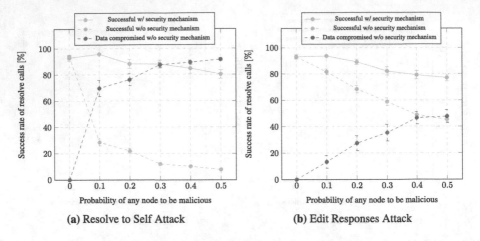

Fig. 6. Resolve calls statistics.

Methodology. These experiments were run using a Chord DHT [24] over an OLSR network [25]. After joining the DHT, nodes repeatedly try registering their AOR with the P2PSIP service by storing it in the DHT, until they succeed and nodes only try resolving SIP URIs that have been registered.

The full security solution presented in Sect. 7 has been implemented. Some of our experiments, however, focus on the data integrity aspect and used the PKI and cryptographic challenge mechanism in isolation. The *Resolve to Self Attack*, presented in Sect. 5.3, was also implemented.

Results. In this section, we show the results of our simulations with the DHT-based approach. These evaluate the effect of the different attacks on the ability of nodes to join the DHT, the success rate of resolve calls and the amount of network traffic generated. These statistics are evaluated for different proportions of malicious nodes, again ranging from none to half the total number of nodes, as well as the different levels of redundancy. Once more, the margin of error for 95% confidence intervals is displayed on all graphs.

Challenge Mechanism: Attacks in OverSim. We conducted some experiments with only part of our solution implemented: the challenge mechanism. We begin with results for attacks already present in *OverSim*, for which we do not expect to observe benefits from the challenges. This is because these attacks are either DoS attacks or are detectable, in the context of P2PSIP, without any security mechanism.

Graphs for resolve calls statistics show four relevant statistics. The solid green line shows the success rate of resolve calls, meaning that a response was received, the challenge succeeded and communication could be established. The orange line indicates the percentage of resolve requests that yielded a properly formatted response, but for which the challenge failed because the data had been tampered with. The dashed green line is a combination of these last two statistics and represents the percentage of resolve requests that would be considered successful without the challenge mechanism. In some cases, it overlaps with the solid green line. Finally, the red line shows the percentage of resolve requests that failed because no response was received or the response was incorrectly formatted, meaning it did not contain an IP address.

Drop Find Node and Invalid Nodes Attacks. These two attacks are very similar. They both target the mechanism responsible for locating a node in the DHT. The first one does so by simply dropping the message while the second one responds with an invalid node that, in most cases, will not exist. They thus present very similar results, as shown in Figs. 7 and 8. In both cases, the attack affects the capacity of nodes to join the DHT, as it goes down when more malicious nodes are present. We also notice that the success rate of resolve requests goes down in the same circumstances. The challenge mechanism has no effect, as expected, because these are DoS attacks.

Invalid Data Attack. This attack, in the general DHT case, targets data integrity. However, in a P2PSIP context, the data returned by a malicious node is not in the correct format for the expected response. This means that the attack is detected and the resolve request fails even without a security mechanism in place, turning it into a DoS attack for which the challenge mechanism is not expected to help. This is exactly what Fig. 9a shows. Resolve failures increase as the number of malicious nodes increases.

Is Sibling Attack. This attack, by itself, is a DoS attack. This means that the challenge mechanism is not expected to provide benefits and that the success rate is expected to go down with more malicious nodes. Figure 9b confirms that.

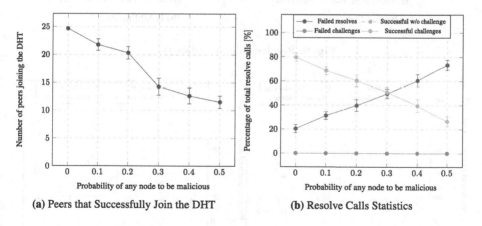

(a) Peers that Successfully Join the DHT

(b) Resolve Calls Statistics

Fig. 7. Drop Find Node Attack statistics [1].

Attacks Demonstrating the Effectiveness of the Challenge Mechanism. To demonstrate the effectiveness of the challenge mechanism, we conducted some

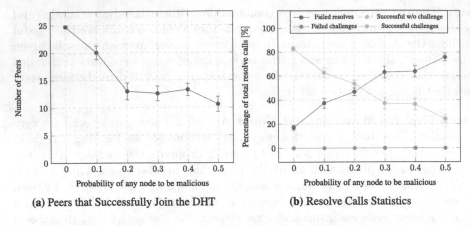

(a) Peers that Successfully Join the DHT   (b) Resolve Calls Statistics

Fig. 8. Invalid Nodes Attack statistics [1].

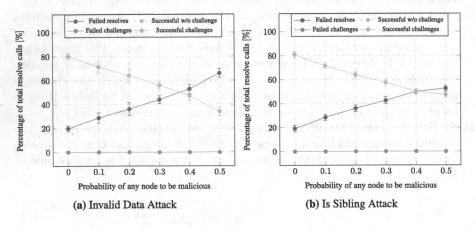

(a) Invalid Data Attack   (b) Is Sibling Attack

Fig. 9. Resolve calls statistics [1].

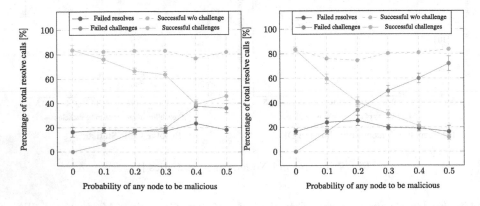

Fig. 10. Resolve to Self Attack alone (left) and with the Is Sibling Attack (right) [1].

experiments with only this part of the security solution enabled. Only the *Resolve to Self Attack* is expected to have an effect because it is the only one that targets data integrity and is undetectable without a security solution in place. This attack can be amplified by combining it with the *Is Sibling Attack*, so we go over both scenarios (Fig. 10).

Resolve to Self Attack. Because the data sent by malicious nodes is in a valid format, this attack cannot be detected without implementing a security solution. Figure 9 shows this in the number of failed challenges and the difference between the amount of successful resolves with and without the challenge mechanism.

Resolve to Self Attack and Is Sibling Attack. Figure 9 shows that this combination of attacks has the same effect as the *Resolve to Self Attack* by itself, but it is amplified. This is because, when trying to locate the node responsible for a given AOR, the first malicious node reached will resolve the query to its own IP address.

Full Security Solution. To evaluate our complete security solution for the DHT-based approach, including AOR signatures and redundancy in addition to the challenge mechanism, we simulated a combination of the *Resolve to Self* and *Is Sibling Attacks* with different levels of redundancy and for different probabilities of a given node being malicious.

Figure 11 shows the result. The green line shows the success rate of resolve requests while the red one is the amount of failures due to network issues or otherwise not receiving a response. Both orange lines capture resolve failures resulting from the attack but where data integrity was preserved thanks to the defense mechanism. The dashed orange line represents cases where none of the responses received were properly signed and the solid line represents failed challenges. As explained in Sect. 7.2, only one properly signed response is required and that, if multiple such responses are received, the most recent one according to the included timestamp will be trusted. The challenge is then sent to the contact address found in this trusted response to validate its identity and establish the connection. It is also interesting to note that, if malicious nodes performed a query-based replay attack instead of the *Resolve to Self Attack*, the two orange lines would be switched. This is because the *Resolve to Self Attack* creates improperly signed messages, causing a signature validation failure before the challenge is even sent, while a replay attack would use properly signed messages pointing to the wrong node.

The amount of network failures shown in Fig. 11, even in Fig. 11a, seems to go up quickly as more redundancy is added. This is counter-intuitive, but can be explained by the fact that only 100 seconds are reserved for the DHT to build itself before starting resolve requests and data collection. The more redundancy is used, the longer it takes for the DHT to reach a stable state.

The most important statistic to note is the rate at which resolves fail because no properly signed response was received—the dashed orange line. We note a great improvement in this regard from no redundancy to 5 replicas, but the rate of improvement slows down as more replicas are added.

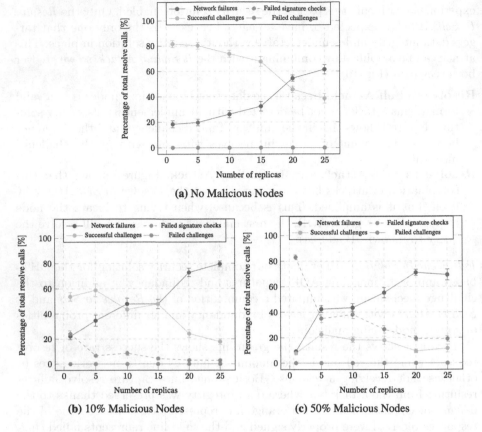

(a) No Malicious Nodes

(b) 10% Malicious Nodes

(c) 50% Malicious Nodes

Fig. 11. Statistics for resolve to self and Is Sibling Attacks with different probabilities of each node being malicious and the full security solution in place.

Figure 12 shows the amount of traffic sent over the network during the entire simulation and per 50 successful resolve requests, for different levels of redundancy. It shows that the more redundant the network is, the more traffic is generated, including all DHT and OLSR control messages. Even without redundancy, the amount of traffic generated by the DHT-based approach is an order of magnitude higher than that of the flooding-based approach. This traffic includes DHT maintenance messages, register messages, resolve requests and responses as well as challenges and the associated response.

8.4 Discussion

As expected, we have demonstrated that both of our security solutions are effective. For both solutions, we have shown that the PKI, with the signature and cryptographic challenge schemes, protect the integrity of the network and ensure that a malicious node cannot fool a legitimate one into establishing a connection

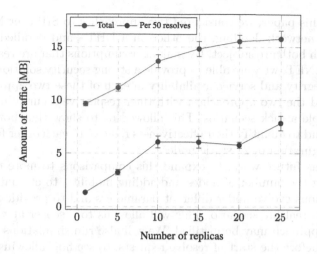

Fig. 12. No attack—network utilization.

with an unintended node. We have also shown that the same PKI, combined with storage and routing redundancy, helps to maintain the resilience of the network when it is subject to an attack.

For the DHT-based approach, we found that adding redundancy makes it harder for the DHT to stabilize, causing resolve request failures while the DHT has not finished building itself. The return of redundancy in terms of mitigating attacks is also great for a small number of replicas but diminishes as more are added. This means that a good balance would need to be found between DHT stability and effectiveness of the security solution in order to determine an appropriate level of redundancy for a given scenario.

We have also shown that for our configuration of 25 static nodes, maintaining a DHT brings a lot of overhead compared to flooding-based approach. Maintaining the distributed data structure, in itself, is complex and the attack surface is also higher with the DHT, making the security solution more complex also. The amount of traffic generated was also an order of magnitude higher with the DHT and the success rate was lower because of the lower stability of the network. We can conclude that, for such a small network, implementing a solution based on a DHT is not worth it compared to the much simpler approach using flooding. This may not be true for bigger networks though, as DHTs are designed to scale, with lookups in a logarithmic number of logical hops with regard to the total number of nodes, while flooding does not scale as well.

9 Conclusion

The implementation of SIP over MANETs and the security of P2P networks have both been the subject of research. Few have combined both to study the security of P2PSIP over MANETs and those who have made little assumptions about the context in which the network is used in order to provide very general solutions. In this paper, we considered two approaches to SIP over MANETs—one based on network flooding, the other on a DHT—and detailed the threat model to which both are subject. By making assumptions that are reasonable for a military MANET, we were able to provide a strong security solution to protect both data integrity and service availability in each of these two approaches. We then simulated the two approaches, with their respective security mechanisms, against multiple attack scenarios. This allowed us to show that both solutions are effective and to quantify their effectiveness relative to each other for a specific network configuration of 25 static nodes.

We plan, as future work, to expand this comparisons to more diverse networks, varying the number of nodes and adding mobility, to evaluate how both security solutions evolve under different parameters and to provide results that are closer to a real life scenario. This will allow us to discover at what scale a DHT-based approach may be justified. We will also run simulations with longer time periods before the start of resolve requests, to see how allowing more time for the DHT to build and stabilize itself improves its effectiveness. We will also implement more attack scenarios, for example the DHT poisoning attack and replay attacks, and evaluate their effect against our security solutions. Finally, we intend on comparing both of our solutions to existing ones to examine their differences and how it effects the network. A comparison with RELOAD, in particular, will be interesting due to its similarity to our DHT-based solution.

Acknowledgment. The research was sponsored by the Army Research Laboratory/US Army RDECOM-Americas and was accomplished under Cooperative Agreement Number W911NF-16-1-0345. The views and conclusions contained in this document are those of the authors and should not be interpreted as representing the official policies, either expressed or implied, of the Army Research Laboratory/US Army RDECOM-Americas or the U.S. Government. The U.S. Government is authorized to reproduce and distribute reprints for Government purposes notwithstanding any copyright notation herein.

References

1. Cormier, A., Gagnon, F., Esfandiari, B., Kunz, T.: Toward testing security attacks and defense mechanisms for P2PSIP in MANETs with a simulator. In: Proceedings of the 14th International Joint Conference on e-Business and Telecommunications - Volume 3: DCNET, (ICETE 2017), INSTICC, pp. 43–54. SciTePress (2017)
2. Varga, A., Hornig, R.: An overview of the OMNeT++ simulation environment. In: Proceedings of the 1st International Conference on Simulation Tools and Techniques for Communications, Networks and Systems & Workshops, ICST (Institute for Computer Sciences, Social-Informatics and Telecommunications Engineering), p. 60 (2008)
3. Baumgart, I., Heep, B., Krause, S.: OverSim: a flexible overlay network simulation framework. In: Proceedings of 10th IEEE Global Internet Symposium (GI 2007) in Conjunction with IEEE INFOCOM 2007, Anchorage, AK, USA, pp. 79–84 (2007)
4. Giordano, S., et al.: Mobile ad hoc networks. In: Handbook of Wireless Networks and Mobile Computing, pp. 325–346 (2002)

5. Rosenberg, J., et al.: SIP: Session Initiation Protocol. RFC 3261 (2002)
6. Jennings, C., Lowekamp, B., Rescorla, E., Baset, S., Schulzrinne, H.: REsource LOcation and Discovery (RELOAD) Base Protocol. RFC 6940 (2014)
7. Schollmeier, R.: A definition of peer-to-peer networking for the classification of peer-to-peer architectures and applications. In: First International Conference on Peer-to-Peer Computing, Proceedings, pp. 101–102. IEEE (2001)
8. Li, L., Lamont, L.: Support real-time interactive session applications over a tactical mobile ad hoc network. In: Military Communications Conference, MILCOM 2005, pp. 2910–2916. IEEE (2005)
9. Banerjee, N., Acharya, A., Das, S.K.: Peer-to-peer SIP-based services over wireless ad hoc networks. In: BROADWIM: Broadband Wireless Multimedia Workshop (2004)
10. Yahiaoui, S., Belhoul, Y., Nouali-Taboudjemat, N., Kheddouci, H.: AdSIP: decentralized SIP for mobile ad hoc networks. In: 2012 26th International Conference on Advanced Information Networking and Applications Workshops (WAINA), pp. 490–495 (2012)
11. Banerjee, N., Acharya, A., Das, S.K.: Enabling SIP-based session setup in ad hoc networks. In: Proceedings of INFOCOM (2005)
12. Fudickar, S., Rebensburg, K., Schnor, B.: MANETSip - a dependable SIP overlay network for MANET including presentity service. In: Fifth International Conference on Networking and Services, ICNS 2009, pp. 314 319 (2009)
13. Aburumman, A., Seo, W.J., Esposito, C., Castiglione, A., Islam, R., et al.: A secure and resilient cross-domain SIP solution for MANETs using dynamic clustering and joint spatial and temporal redundancy. In: Practice and Experience, Concurrency and Computation (2016)
14. Wongsaardsakul, T.: P2P SIP over mobile ad hoc networks. Ph.D. thesis, Evry, Institut national des télécommunications (2010)
15. O'Driscoll, A., Rea, S., Pesch, D.: Hierarchical clustering as an approach for supporting P2P SIP sessions in ubiquitous environments. In: 9th IFIP International Conference on Mobile Wireless Communications Networks, MWCN 2007, Cork, Ireland, 19–21 September 2007, pp. 76–80. IEEE (2007)
16. Baumgart, I.: P2PNS: a secure distributed name service for P2PSIP. In: Sixth Annual IEEE International Conference on Pervasive Computing and Communications, PerCom 2008, pp. 480–485. IEEE (2008)
17. Bryan, D.A., Lowekamp, B.B., Zangrilli, M.: The design of a versatile, secure P2PSIP communications architecture for the public internet. In: IEEE International Symposium on Parallel and Distributed Processing, IPDPS 2008, pp. 1–8. IEEE (2008)
18. Seedorf, J.: Using cryptographically generated SIP-URIs to protect the integrity of content in P2P-SIP. In: Third Annual VoIP Security Workshop (2006)
19. Davoust, A., Gagnon, F., Esfandiari, B., Kunz, T., Cormier, A.: Towards securing peer-to-peer sip in the manet context: existing work and perspectives. In: 2017 IEEE International Conference on Internet of Things (iThings) and IEEE Green Computing and Communications (GreenCom) and IEEE Cyber, Physical and Social Computing (CPSCom) and IEEE Smart Data (SmartData), pp. 223–229. IEEE (2017)
20. Freedman, M.J., Morris, R.: Tarzan: a peer-to-peer anonymizing network layer. In: Proceedings of the 9th ACM Conference on Computer and Communications Security, CCS 2002, Washington, DC, USA, 18–22 November 2002, pp. 193–206 (2002)

21. Rennhard, M., Plattner, B.: Introducing MorphMix: peer-to-peer based anonymous internet usage with collusion detection. In: Proceedings of the 2002 ACM Workshop on Privacy in the Electronic Society, WPES 2002, Washington, DC, USA, 21 November 2002, pp. 91–102 (2002)
22. Wang, Q., Borisov, N.: Octopus: a secure and anonymous DHT lookup. In: 2012 IEEE 32nd International Conference on Distributed Computing Systems (ICDCS), pp. 325–334. IEEE (2012)
23. Fonville, M.: Confidential peer-to-peer file-sharing using social-network sites. In: 13th Twente Student Conference on IT, June, vol. 21, p. 10 (2010)
24. Stoica, I., Morris, R., Karger, D., Kaashoek, M.F., Balakrishnan, H.: Chord: a scalable peer-to-peer lookup service for internet applications. ACM SIGCOMM Comput. Commun. Rev. **31**, 149–160 (2001)
25. Clausen, T., Jacquet, P.: Optimized Link State Routing Protocol (OLSR). RFC 3626 (2003)

How Marketers Can Induce Consumer Awareness and Interactions in Facebook Brand Pages? - Drivers and Outcomes

Mathupayas Thongmak[✉]

Thammasat Business School, Thammasat University, Bangkok 10200, Thailand
mathupayas@tbs.tu.ac.th

Abstract. Marketer-generated content influence the fans' responses to social media. Provide the right content to the right target audiences at the right time could increase online engagement. Brands existing in online social media could attain brand awareness and engagement. Therefore, this paper aims to analyze the factors determining consumer awareness and interactions with the brand-posted content and consequences of this awareness and interactions, by collecting the objective measures from the secondary sources. Data such as posts per day, engagement rate, PTAT are collected from almost 300 famous national and international brand fan pages from 9 industries in Thailand. An empirical analysis using simple and multiple linear regression is conducted to test the proposed hypotheses. The results show the insights of social media strategies among 9 brand categories. Pictures and videos are popularly used as the content strategies. However, the percentage of the picture and video posts do not directly affect the engagement rate. Total fans significantly determine the consumer awareness and interactions (PTAT), which later drive more of the new likes. This study contributes to the existing literature in terms of using objective measures and widely exploring brands in various categories, filling the research gaps with interesting results and guiding what should be added for brands in each category.

Keywords: Facebook fan pages · Social interactions · PTAT
Online engagement · Marketer-generated content

1 Introduction

Social media, particularly social networking sites, provide firms opportunities to communicate with prospect consumers and enable the consumers to online engage with brands [1]. They are also alternative channels offering cost advantages with personal and social nature over traditional media channels [2, 3]. If applied them correctly, positive economic effects could be happened to brands and companies [4]. Facebook is a leading social networking site, which had 1.09 billion daily active users on average for March 2016. More than eighty percent of active users were outside the US and Canada [5].

Social interactions on a social networking site reflect insights for each brand [6]. Successful online brand communities such as a Facebook fan page needs fans' engagement and interactions [7, 8]. In addition, online brand community participation

M. S. Obaidat and E. Cabello (Eds.): ICETE 2017, CCIS 990, pp. 63–80, 2019.
https://doi.org/10.1007/978-3-030-11039-0_4

affects community consequences of participation, which later impacts brand consequences of participation [9]. However, in Facebook brand pages, consumers generally act in lurking behaviour than posting behaviour [1, 10]. Therefore, social media management such as monitoring social interactions (user posts and corresponding likes, comments, or shares) is required to enable suitable reaction strategies for negative social interactions [6]. The strategies regarding number of posts, relevant and popular content, high information quality, advantageous campaigns, etc. should completely engage, integrate, and immerse fans into the vivid and interactive brand community [8, 11–15].

Some studies explore the engagement and interactions of consumer in social media. Coursaris, Van Osch and Balogh [2] conduct a longitudinal study on brand posts of big three firms in Fortune 110 companies, to offer a set of topology regarding Facebook page marketing messages. The proposed topology consists of seven post categories: brand awareness, corporate social responsibility, customer service, engagement, product awareness, and promotional, seasonal, and 23 sub-categories. Rohm, Kaltcheva and Milne [16] examine the role of social media among digital natives. Results indicate that brand engagement are driven by five consumer motivations: entertainment, connection to the brand, timeliness of information and service responses, product information, promotions and incentives. Saji, Chauhan and Pillai [17] examine the impact of content strategy consisting of content types, posting agility, posting day, and the context of content on customer engagement regarding the number of likes and comments. The content type and content agility have significant influence on engaging customers in brand communities created on social media. Hutter, Hautz, Dennhardt and Füller [4] analyse how activities in a car manufacturer's Facebook page and fan interactions affects consumers' brand awareness, word of mouth (WOM) actions, and purchase decision.

Kim, Sung and Kang [18] investigate the effect of consumers' relationships with brands on consumers' engagement in retweeting Twitter messages about brands. Habibi, Laroche and Richard [19] explore how consumers' relationship elements such as brand, product, company, and other consumers affect brand trust. Findings sum that three of four factors positively drive brand trust. Chan, Zheng, Cheung, Lee and Lee [20] test the influence of system support, community value, freedom of expression, and rewards and recognition on customer engagement and the effect of customer engagement on repurchase intention and word-of-mouth intention. Angela Hausman, Kabadayi and Price [21] study factors influencing likes and comments on Facebook brand pages and the mediating effect of modes of interaction on the relationship between personal traits and consumers' liking and commenting behavior. Sabate, Berbegal-Mirabent, Cañabate and Lebherz [13] empirically test a conceptual model regarding the impact of content richness and timeframe on the number of likes and comments. Stavros, Meng, Westberg and Farrelly [22] reveal four motivations underpinning fans' desires to engage Facebook sites of National Basketball Association teams, which are passion, hope, esteem, and camaraderie.

Kim and Hettche [23] conduct a content analysis of posts on corporate Facebook pages to examine the social media marketing practices of those global brands in terms of their media types, content orientation, and the number and type of users responding to the content. Chua and Banerjee [24] investigate the association of brand posts' incentives, vividness and interactivity and users' attention (likes, comments, and shares of brand posts). Touchette, Schanski and Lee [25] explore the social media strategy of apparel brands' Facebook pages. Photos and advertisements are applied to promote products and sales without utilizing a specific play theme such as play as frivolity. Hsu, Wang, Chih and Lin [26] analyse a proposed model integrating the use and gratification theory with the dual mediation hypothesis. Findings reveal that both perceived news' entertainment and informativeness positively affect the interests of attitude toward the news, which later influence the hedonic and utilitarian dimensions of attitude toward Facebook fan pages.

Schultz [6] explores consumer social interactions on social networking sites of six apparel retail brands, by analysing the fan number, brand posts, and response behaviour, and consumer activities such as liking and sharing. Zoha, Hasmah, Kumaran, Sedigheh and Mohd Hairul Nizam [27] explore the impact of the most frequently posted contents of 14 international brands of electronics firms on the brand fan pages' People Talking About This (PTAT) metric. De Veirman, Cauberghe and Hudders [1] investigate consumers' motivations differing the level of activeness and public visibility on Facebook brand pages. Results show that both lurking and posting behaviours are driven by social interaction desires. Lurking behaviour is also impacted by entertainment motives and posting behaviour is affected by empowerment motives. Schultz [28] explains brand post interactions by post vividness, interactivity, and content. Vividness and content types positively and negatively affect the brand post interactions. Interactive characteristics have a positive influence on users' social interactions.

Even though the existing literature investigates social interactions in brand communities, social marketing and social media engagement strategies are still at the early stage and are quite limited such as the unknown about how social media channels are being used, what their potentials are, and how consumers interact [1, 16, 21, 29, 30]. The literature also generally focuses on a specific brand category or message category [2]. Factors driving consumers to contribute in online social pages are yet to be thoroughly explored [10]. Also, only few researches explore the effects of brand activities (marketer-generated content) on consumers' social awareness and interactions. The goals of this paper are thus (1) to evaluate the effect of marketers' activities in the Facebook brand pages together with the fan bases on consumer awareness and interactions represented by the PTAT metric, (2) to examine the consequence of the PTAT, (3) to understand the effects of different content formats on the engagement rate (PTAT/total likes) and (4) to compare different strategies applied by nine brand categories in terms of the post frequency, the popularity of posts, media types, hashtags, and average response time.

2 Related Literature

2.1 Facebook Brand Pages

Brand communities are another form of consumer communities representing social networks of consumer knowledge and companionship. Social networking sites and brand communities have the same basic property in terms of their members interacting with each other [31]. Social media-based brand communities encompass five unique dimensions: social context (members can obtain a great deal of information about other members), structure (no explicit or implicit structure), scale (brand communities can reach millions of members), storytelling (more interactive from using video and photos accompanied by texts), and numerous affiliated brand communities (the cost of creating a brand community is close to zero) [19]. Brand communities can influence consumers to feel favorable toward brands. Some studies confirm that brand communities affect consumers' satisfactions that eventually enhance brand loyalty. Good relationship in a brand community also has a positive impact on purchase intentions, increasing sales. Consumers' relationships with brands, products, or companies positively affect brand trust. Those relationships are stronger for highly-engaged customers more than lower engaged customers [8, 19, 26, 29]. Social media-based brand communities also enable brand owners the ability to increase value, brand trust, and brand loyalty [32].

Facebook, the dominant social networking site, provides five tools for firms to use the platform for marketing purposes, including Facebook ads, Facebook brand pages, social plugins, Facebook applications and sponsored stories [3, 29]. Facebook fan page, emerged in 2007, is an open platform that can help enterprises to initiate a brand community for direct interaction with consumers such as customer service, sharing news, or offering product information to their consumers [29, 32–34]. Fan pages can be used for presenting business advertisements, commercial marketing, or professional knowledge [33]. Companies use Facebook fan pages because of increasing trustworthiness and goodwill, lead generation, ability to engage with consumers, accessing to customer's feedback, and cheaper form of advertising [10]. A company can generate interactions with consumers by writing on a company's wall or creating posts. Companies are flexible to choose media types such as status, link, photos, or app in order to spread information in their ways [27, 35]. The news feed linked to a brand page is sent to members connecting to the page and their online friends through a ticker, enhancing word-of-mouth effects and enabling push-based customer relationship management [33, 36–38]. Nowadays, almost every major brands have Facebook fan pages [12].

Ongoing interactions are crucial for social networks, whereas social relationships are important for brand communities [31]. The Facebook fan pages or brand pages are prominent due to their rapid membership growth [33]. Facebook fan pages could be used as an explicit brand communication and interaction channel, to be first of all a connection between consumers and the brand [8]. Fans can engage or interact with a company, improving their brand experience, by posting content on the wall, commenting on existing posts, giving likes, sharing posts on their profile, and so on. These actions represent a form of word-of-mouth communication, which significantly increases brand commitment, purchase decision making, and sales [21, 27, 29, 35, 39].

2.2 Posted Content and Customer Engagement

Customer engagement starts from initializing a relationship with fans to generating brand activities (posts or user posts) and supporting consumer activities (likes, comments, and shares) [6]. Customer engagement in online brand community is positively related to repurchase intention and WOM intention. It is the strategy for establishing and retaining competitive advantages [20]. However, generally only 1 percent of fans contributing a lot by posting messages, responding to other members' questions, joining brand contests, and share their experiences about the brand with other members [9].

Although Facebook users tend to follow many brand pages, not all brand posts are popular, attracting significant likes, comments, or shares [11]. Valuable content, both hedonic and functional, are thus crucial for attracting consumers to brand fan pages. In addition, delivering interesting, entertaining, and innovative content to fan page users are important [8]. Online-passing behaviour occurs in social networking sites when consumers pass along content such as information about products or brands by liking, commenting, or sharing the posted content [18]. Popularity of brand posts is shown by receiving the number of likes, comments, and shares [11]. Facebook brand pages implement the algorithm containing factors such as post popularity (likes and comments), content types (photos, videos, status updates) to select the relevant content among a lot of content to push to the fans' news feeds [37]. Facebook posts also have a positive effect on sales because customers immediately react to posts by visiting the brand store [3]. Therefore, good and persuasive content could create the ripple effect on Facebook brand pages.

3 Research Framework and Hypotheses

3.1 Marketer-Generated Content: Posts per Day, Post Timing, Average Length of Posts, Curiosity, Hashtags, and Enabling Fan Posts

Good content strategy increases consumers' interactions [17, 29, 35, 40, 41]. Consumer-brand relationships and post content are crucial factors motivating fans to participate and contribute to online brand communities [7]. If companies provide entertainment, brand-related information, and remuneration, engagement motivations of fans will be met, increasing the number of likes and comments and gaining more interaction duration [29]. Informational supports also positively impact brand community commitment [42]. Generating more brand-related information drives the number of likes, comments, and interaction duration on brand fan pages [29, 35]. De Vries, Gensler and Leeflang [35] proposes that posting informational and entertain content may increase the brand post popularity in terms of the volume of likes and comments.

Online engagement depends on the various content of posts [38]. Posting and response behaviour is shown by the average posts per day and the average response rate per day orderly [6]. Posting daily challenges could enhance the learning experience of fan members [31]. Brand post vividness, interactivity, and content type are expected to have a significant impact on post interactions [28]. Different types of posts have different impact on PTAT, especially image posts with details and feature videos [27]. Content types, media types, and posting times tend to relate to online engagement [28, 29].

Schultz [28] proposes that the publication day of post would significantly impact post interactions. Posts created on weekdays and during business hours may receive higher post popularity [13]. Posting day of the week is a relevant factor for choosing the appropriate time for posts [43]. It is possible that users would visit brand fan pages during the weekends than on weekdays, resulting in higher post popularity [35]. Posting content on weekdays is important for the user engagement in terms of likes and comments because people are possibly willing to spend this time on the workdays [29].

Schultz [28] proposes that the longer a brand post placed at the top of page generates the higher post interactions. Lengths of messages may impact click-through rates of advertisements [35]. Posts with a proper amount of texts are may gained higher popularity than posts with no or a lot of texts [37]. If posting content is favourable, brand owners should listen to their fans and response to their questions and suggestions. Brand pages may be applied as crowdsourcing channels, by asking consumers' opinions [1]. Brand post topics such as questions have a significant influence on the number of likes and comments [28]. The marketing strategy of a well-known company such as Starbucks is using the hashtag to advise customers to create, order, and modify their own drinks, for instance, #protip [44]. Social media enable customers to be the active content creators online [45]. Creating a positive word of mouth from those customers makes brands gain brand awareness [46].

Hence, hypotheses are proposed as follows:

H1: Posts per day on an online brand community have an impact on consumer awareness and interactions (PTAT).

H2: Post timing on an online brand community have an impact on consumer awareness and interactions (PTAT).

H3: Average length of posts on an online brand community has an impact on consumer awareness and interactions (PTAT).

H4: Curiosity (amount of posting questions) on an online brand community have an impact on consumer awareness and interactions (PTAT).

H5: Hashtags on an online brand community have an impact on consumer awareness and interactions (PTAT).

H6: Enabling posts from fans (everyone can post) have an impact on consumer awareness and interactions (PTAT).

3.2   Number of Fans (Total Likes)

A Facebook fan page's popularity is important since the fan page should have as many users as possible to view the brand's posts [37]. The engagement rating relates to the number of fans [47]. Total fans show the market developments, for instance, expansion strategies. Decrease of fan numbers reflect some problems in the consumer-brand relationship [6]. The like button on a fan page is a straightforward tool to engage fans into brand communications and co-creations [48]. Total likes are the multiplier of possible reach. So, they affect a brand's social media strategy. The number of fans shows the ability to influence users' friends and the potential to provide insights about sales or brand value [6]. Facebook points that people who liked Facebook fan pages are more engaged, active, and connected than others. Total likes are also the measure of the return on investment in social media [48]. Likes on Facebook fan pages enable firms to increase their brand awareness and engagement, which later contributes to companies' return on investment [21].

There is a positive relationship of the number of followers over customer engagement regarding the number of likes and comments [13]. The total fans on the publication date of the brand post negatively affect the post popularity in terms of shares [28]. In a virtual community, users' normative influence and informative influence have positive effects on the eWOM review's credibility and adoption [33]. The number of pages that users followed or liked could drive overall consumer engagement and consuming level [38]. The intensity of a brand fan page usage significantly increases the fan-page engagement and brand loyalty [8].

Hence, a hypothesis is proposed as follows:

H7: The number of fans on an online brand community have an impact on consumer awareness and interactions (PTAT).

3.3 People Talking About This

PTAT metric reflects a Facebook fan page's awareness and interaction over time [49]. It integrates stories, for instance, liking/commenting/sharing posts, answering questions, responding to events, or claiming offers [50]. Likes, comments, and shares provide a method to measure consumer-brand interactions [23]. Liking posts are in turn spreading content for their personal networks [41]. A single like can refer a post to hundreds of friends and to other friends' networks who liked the post, generating social contagion effects [40]. More likes a post received, the probability that the post is sent to more fans' news feed [37]. Higher social interaction and brand interaction significantly bring more fan engagement [8]. Higher levels of brand awareness also significantly lead to higher WOM activities and purchase intentions [4]. Social interaction is a common motivation for engaging activities in online brand communities such as Facebook fan page [1]. Strong consumer participation can drive a brand forward, creating reaches for each post [49].

A Facebook fan page's popularity is important since the fan page should have as many users as possible to view the brand's posts [37]. The engagement rating relates to the number of fans [47]. Total fans show the market developments, for instance, expansion strategies. Decrease of fan numbers reflect some problems in the consumer-brand relationship [6]. The like button on a fan page is a straightforward tool to engage fans into brand communications and co-creations [48]. Total likes are the multiplier of possible reach. Therefore, they affect a brand's social media strategy. The number of fans shows the ability to influence users' friends and the potential to provide insights about sales or brand value [6]. Facebook points that people who liked Facebook fan pages are more engaged, active, and connected than others. Total likes are also the measure of the return on investment in social media [48]. Likes on Facebook fan pages enable firms to increase their brand awareness and engagement, which later contributes to companies' return on investment [21].

Hence, hypotheses are proposed as follows:

H8a: Consumer awareness and interactions (PTAT) positively affect fan growth by day.

H8b: Consumer awareness and interactions (PTAT) positively affect fan growth by week.

H8c: Consumer awareness and interactions (PTAT) positively affect fan growth by month.

3.4 Content Types: Images and Videos

Consumers are engaged in brand-related activities differently. For example, some consumers consume brand-related media such as pictures or movies. Some consumers comment on posts or like content, turning them from being observers to media contributors. Sometimes they also upload pictures or videos on Facebook, being the creators of brand-related content [51]. Consumer engagement and contributing of consumers are sharing companies' posts on their social networking systems such as videos, audios, pictures, or texts, or uploading product-related videos, audios, images, and so on [52].

Image and video post formats are statistically relevant factors driving more likes. Post formats are the significant factors defining comments, particularly for posts with plain texts or images. They significantly increase the number of shares [53]. The richness of content including images and videos have an influence on the number of likes. Posting images in the proper-time publication significantly increases the number of comments. Posts using images also significantly generate more likes and shares [13]. Many scholars support that pictures are the most effective content type [44]. Pictures create more likes than posts with plain texts [53]. Funny images with animals are popular for the drugstore chain's Facebook pages, gained a high level of engagement from fans such as likes or shares the posts [54]. In terms of information sharing, many respondents like to post updates and share images on social media [55].

Posts using videos are significantly received higher levels of brand post popularity in terms of likes [13]. Games or videos generated by brands positively drive consumers to interact with brands on social media [56]. Entertainment such as watching videos is the reason why respondents use social media platforms [55]. Content in a video format is shared more frequently than a link or a plain text [53]. The number of comments received on a YouTube video in the first 15 days has a statistically positive influence on total views on that video after 60 days passed [57].

Hence, hypotheses are proposed as follows:

H9a: The percentage of picture posts have an influence on the engagement rate of a brand page.
H9b: The percentage of video posts have an influence on the engagement rate of a brand page.

4 Methodology: Data Sample and Data Collection

To choose the best players on social networking platforms, top one-hundred Facebook fan pages, ranked based on the number of fans, listed on Socialbakers.com [58] were applied to identify brand pages and to select studied samples. Other brand pages in the same categories were collected more with the same proportion as top one-hundred Facebook pages (to make sure about the active pages with high engagement rates) to complete the samples, under criteria that brands had concrete products or services and they were top brands in each category. The list consisted of various brand categories including Fast-Moving Consumer Goods (FMCG), e-commerce, retail foods, telecommunications, electronics, fashion, finance, jewellery & watches, and retail.

The unit of analysis was per brand page. The Facebook fan pages of 328 brands were analysed from the page themselves, free statistics from Socialbakers.com, and free statistics from Likealyzer.com, using one-month period. Free statistics from various sources because of their objective measures. Focusing on marketer-generated content on each brand page, collected information for this study comprised of fans growth (by day/by week/by month) from Socialbakers.com, likes, PTAT, engagement rate, posts per day, likes, comments and shares per post, posts per type (picture/video/message/ Pinterest), timing, length of posts, curiosity, enabling post by fans, hashtags, response time, and response rate from Likealyzer.com. Engagement rate is calculated from the total PTAT divided by the total likes. Curiosity is how frequent is a brand page poses questions to its fans. Way off, slightly off, and perfect of timing were turned to 1 to 3 respectively. Way off means "You publish many posts between 00–03 (GMT). But posts published between 15–18 (GMT) engage more users". Slightly off means "So close! You publish many posts between 15–18 (GMT). But posts published between 18–21 (GMT) engage more users.". Perfect means "You publish the majority of your posts between 15–18 (GMT). At this time, your followers seem to be most active." [59]. Length of posts were converted "less than 100 characters" to 1, "100–500 characters" to 2, "more than 500 characters" to 3, and "more than 500 words" to 4. Curiosity, enabling post by fans, and hashtags were coded as dummy variables. There are missing data of some variables (posts by fans, response rate, and response times) since the Likealyzer.com cannot fetch the data from some Facebook pages, leading to the total percentage less than 100 in Table 3.

After data collection by the research assistant was completed, 31 brands were excluded from data analysis due to too much lack of data about brand pages. Final dataset encompassed 297 fan pages in Thailand (both local and international brands) from 9 brand categories.

5 Results

5.1 Descriptive Statistics

Of 297 brand fan pages, there are 82 pages from Fast-Moving Consumer Goods (FMCG), 44 pages from e-commerce, 33 pages from retail foods, 8 pages from telecommunications, 30 pages from electronics, 41 pages from fashion, 34 pages from finance, 4 pages from jewellery & watches, and 21 pages from retails. According to the statistics from the public Facebook pages, 160 pages, 116 pages, 19 pages, 1 page and 1 page have fans in the age groups 18 to 24 years old, 25 to 34 years old, 18 to 34 years old, 13 to 17 years old, and 13 to 24 years old, accounting for 53.87%, 39.06%, 6.40%, 0.3%, and 0.3% of all pages, respectively.

From highest to lowest average fans per page, the brand categories are as follows: (1) electronics, (2) FMCG, (3) fashion, (4) retail foods, (5) jewellery & watches, (6) telecommunications, (7) finance, (8) e-commerce, and (9) retail, as shown in Table 1. Posts from FMCG, telecommunications, and electronics receive a high engagement in terms of average likes, comments, and shares per post. However, telecommunication brands are the most outstanding brands in terms of average fans growth by day, average fans growth by week, average fans growth by month, and average engagement rate. They are also the fastest brands replying to the users' posts on their pages, showing by the lowest average response time. Although fashion and jewellery & watches brands have a number of fans, they are the lowest two brands that have low fan growth rates and low engagement rates, as shown in Table 1.

Table 1. Information about fan pages, classified by brand categories [61].

Brand category	Avg. fans	Avg. fan growth by day	Avg. fan growth by week	Avg. fan growth by month	Avg. likes, comments & shares per post	Avg. engagement rate (%)	Avg. response time (mins)
FMCG	2,121,549	332	2,310	11,525	2,317	5.2	3,681
E-commerce	596,581	648	5,193	22,410	649	4.3	1,915
Retail Foods	1,767,610	311	2,178	9,228	796	4.4	1,168
Telecommunications	863,106	1,589	6,571	29,427	1,215	7.9	86
Electronics	2,375,338	897	6,415	31,145	1,143	5.8	1,166
Fashion	1,774,408	188	1,352	5,786	446	3.0	1,836
Finance	926,074	457	3,087	11,644	648	3.9	1,059
Jewellery & watches	1,049,355	87	654	3,232	699	3.6	696
Retail	389,973	340	2,494	12,755	481	7.0	993

Table 2. Information about the frequency of posting and posted content.

Brand category	Avg. posts/day	Avg. picture posts (%)	Avg. video posts (%)	Avg. message posts (%)	Avg. Pinterest posts (%)
FMCG	3.3	91.95	4.11	1.66	2.29
E-commerce	10.8	76.85	2.60	5.66	14.90
Retail Foods	1.9	93.29	1.77	1.89	3.05
Telecommunications	6.0	79.16	6.78	5.73	8.33
Electronics	2.6	84.22	5.70	1.81	8.61
Fashion	3.2	91.19	3.81	2.03	2.98
Finance	2.9	82.86	3.59	6.06	7.50
Jewellery & watches	3.2	96.85	0.00	1.05	2.10
Retail	17.2	94.84	2.58	1.39	1.20

Retail and e-commerce brands are quite active in daily communicating messages as shown in Table 2. Considering posted content, fan pages in every brand category heavily pay attention to picture posting, especially FMCG, retail foods, fashion, jewellery & watches, and retail brands. Comparing to others, telecommunications, electronics brand pages utilize videos more than brands in other categories. Posts including images and videos are significantly popular than posts without them [37]. Image posts significantly receive more likes and comments [27]. Photos, videos, and status updates also are top three post types that receive a high volume of likes and comments [60]. Therefore, the post strategy of those brands may move in the right direction. E-commerce, telecommunications, and finance pages sometimes apply texts to convey marketing messages to consumers. E-commerce brands show the remarkable use of Pinterest posts.

Table 3. Other details about fan pages, classified by brand categories.

Topic	G1	G2	G3	G4	G5	G6	G7	G8	G9
Posted timing									
(1) Way off	35	17	15	4	14	14	18	2	9
	(42.7%)	(38.6%)	(45.5%)	(50%)	(46.7%)	(34.1%)	(52.9%)	(50%)	(42.9%)
(2) Slightly off	24	16	10	1	9	16	11	1	6
	(29.3%)	(36.4%)	(30.3%)	(12.5%)	(30.0%)	(39.0%)	(32.4%)	(25%)	(28.6%)
(3) Perfect	23	11	8	3	7	11	5	1	6
	(28%)	(25%)	(24.2%)	(37.5%)	(23.3%)	(26.8%)	(14.7%)	(25%)	(28.6%)
Length of posts									
(1) <100 characters	29	10	15	4	10	11	9	0	4
	(35.4%)	(22.7%)	(45.5%)	(50%)	(33.3%)	(26.8%)	(26.5%)	(0.0%)	(19%)
(2) 100–500 characters	51	33	18	4	19	26	22	3	15
	(62.2%)	(75%)	(54.5%)	(50%)	(63.3%)	(63.4%)	(64.7%)	(75%)	(71%)
(3) >500 characters	0	0	0	0	0	4	3	0	0
	(0.0%)	(0.0%)	(0.0%)	(0.0%)	(0.0%)	(9.8%)	(8.8%)	(0.0%)	(0.0%)
(4) >500 words	2	1	0	0	1	0	0	1	2
	(2.4%)	(2.3%)	(0.0%)	(0.0%)	(3.3%)	(0.0%)	(0.0%)	(25%)	(9.5%)
Curiosity (posted questions)									
(1) You should ask more questions	81	43	30	8	30	39	33	4	20
	(98.8%)	(97.7%)	(90.9%)	(100%)	(100%)	(95.1%)	(97.1%)	(100%)	(95.2%)
(2) A good amount of questions	1	1	3	0	0	2	1	0	1
	(1.2%)	(2.3%)	(9.1%)	(0.0%)	(0.0%)	(4.9%)	(2.9%)	(0.0%)	(4.8%)
Hashtags									
(1) Not using	32	18	17	5	7	22	23	3	10
	(39.0%)	(40.9%)	(51.5%)	(62.5%)	(23.3%)	(53.7%)	(67.6%)	(75%)	(47.6%)
(2) Using	50	26	16	3	23	19	11	1	11
	(61.0%)	(59.1%)	(48.5%)	(37.5%)	(76.7%)	(46.3%)	(32.4%)	(25%)	(52.4%)
Everyone Can Post									
(1) No	9	6	6	0	4	1	6	0	5
	(11.0%)	(13.6%)	(18.2%)	(0.0%)	(13.3%)	(2.4%)	(17.6%)	(0.0%)	(23.8%)
(2) Yes	73	38	27	8	26	40	28	4	16
	(89.0%)	(86.4%)	(81.8%)	(100%)	(86.7%)	(97.6%)	(82.4%)	(100%)	(76.2%)
Posts by fans									
(1) Very rarely	4	4	4	0	2	1	2	1	1
	(4.9%)	(9.1%)	(12.1%)	(0.0%)	(6.7%)	(2.4%)	(5.9%)	(25.0%)	(4.8%)
(2) Once or twice a week	12	7	4	1	6	12	8	0	2
	(14.6%)	(15.9%)	(12.1%)	(12.5%)	(20.0%)	(29.3%)	(23.5%)	(0.0%)	(9.5%)
(3) Happens on a daily basis	45	18	18	3	14	15	14	2	12
	(54.9%)	(40.9%)	(54.5%)	(37.5%)	(46.7%)	(36.6%)	(41.2%)	(50.0%)	(57.1%)
Response rate									
(1) Catastrophic	17	9	11	0	5	9	8	0	0
	(20.7%)	(20.5%)	(33.3%)	(0.0%)	(16.7%)	(22.0%)	(23.5%)	(0.0%)	(0.0%)
(2) Bad	13	5	2	1	4	5	4	1	2
	(15.9%)	(11.4%)	(6.1%)	(12.5%)	(13.3%)	(12.2%)	(11.8%)	(25.0%)	(9.5%)
(3) Poor	17	12	6	1	9	8	10	0	3
	(20.7%)	(27.3%)	(18.2%)	(12.5%)	(30.0%)	(19.5%)	(29.4%)	(0.0%)	(14.3%)
(4) Good	10	7	4	2	6	5	4	1	5
	(12.2%)	(15.9%)	(12.1%)	(25.0%)	(20.0%)	(12.2%)	(11.8%)	(25.0%)	(23.8%)
(5) Perfect	2	1	0	0	0	0	0	1	1
	(2.4%)	(2.3%)	(0.0%)	(0.0%)	(0.0%)	(0.0%)	(0.0%)	(25.0%)	(4.8%)

Note: G1 = FMCG, G2 = E-Commerce, G3 = Retail Foods, G4 = Telecommunications, G5 = Electronics, G6 = Fashion, G7 = Finance, G8 = Jewellery & Watches, and G9 = Retail

Table 3 summarizes the additional aspects of brands in each category from Likealyzer.com. Proper timing of posts significantly affects the number of comments [13], but post timing of all brand categories is generally way off the suitable time. In terms of the length of posts, most of brands normally generate a post with 100–500 characters. Almost all brands rarely ask questions. FMCG, e-commerce, electronics, and retail brands commonly use hashtags, whereas retail foods, telecommunications, fashion, finance, and jewellery & watches brands do not use hashtags. Brands in all categories are open to posts from fans on their brand fan pages, which happen on a daily basis. Only the response rate of the brands in telecommunications, jewellery & watches, and retail are good.

5.2 Data Analysis

Multiple regression and simple linear regression are applied to verify the proposed framework. As shown in Table 4, only the number of fans significantly has a positive impact on consumer awareness and interactions. Therefore, $H1$–$H6$ are rejected, whereas $H7$ are confirmed. It was found that PTAT level explains a significant amount of the variance in the value of fans growth by day ($F(1, 295) = 58.416$, $p < .01$, $R^2 = .165$, $R^2_{Adjusted} = .162$). The analysis shows that PTAT level significantly predict fans growth by day ($Beta = .407$, $t(295) = 7.643$, $p = .000$). When fans growth by week was predicted, it was found that PTAT level ($Beta = .405$, $p < .01$) was a significant predictor. The overall model fit was $R^2 = .164$. The result of the simple linear regression also indicated that PTAT explained 20.8% of the variance ($R^2 = .208$, F $(1,295) = 77.355$, $p < .01$). The PTAT positively increase fans growth by week ($Beta = .456$, $p < .01$). Therefore, $H8a$–$H8c$ are accepted.

Table 4. Summary of multiple regression analysis of variables on PTAT (N = 297).

Variable	B	SE B	Beta
Posts per day	282.644	245.231	.054
Timing	2276.174	4170.967	.025
Length of posts	−5571.702	5546.984	−.046
No. of fans (Likes)	.010	.001	.627**
Curiosity	−8494.000	19698.333	−.020
Hashtags	−1782.525	6795.443	−.012
Posts by fans	−2635.633	10558.226	−.012
R^2		.411	
F for change in R^2		28.774***	

$*p < .05$. $**p < .01$.

Multiple regression analysis is also applied to examine the relationship between different post types and the engagement rate. The engagement rate is total PTAT divided by total likes. Both the ratio of image and video posts has no significant impact on the engagement rate, as shown in Table 5. Thus, H9a and H9b are rejected. The rejection of hypotheses is explained by the unclear difference between the effects of content types such as videos and other content types on comments or shares [53].

Table 5. Summary of multiple regression analysis of content types on the engagement rate (N = 297).

Variable	B	SE B	Beta
The percentage of picture posts	−.009	.026	−.021
The percentage of video posts	−.002	.074	−.002
R^2		.000	
F for change in R^2		.063	

$*p < .05. **p < .01.$

6 Discussion and Implications

Testing hypotheses support literature research. For instance, fans' impressions drive fan pages' engagement [60]. The effects of day and time on likes per post are not supported [13]. A post published on weekdays or weekends has no impact on social interactions. Longer posts decrease the number of likes, comments, and shares [28]. Posts with a moderate amount of texts are more accepted than posts with too few or too many texts [37]. Posts created in the peak hours have no influence on the engagement level [29]. Electronic WOM is transmitted in an exponentially growing nature through social media [62].

However, this study yields some different results from the past studies. For example, in sport context, 72% of posts from the health coach received social interactions at least once, showing the importance of average posts per day [63]. Saji, Chauhan and Pillai [17] confirms that content agility significant affects the number of likes and comments. Content agility is the timing of the day during which the post is made. They divided total hours of a day into 6 slots, 4 h each. Total fans have a negative influence on sharing behaviour [28]. A report from Socialbakers.com points that in general more fans decrease engagement rates. However, a study of Laurens [47] indicates that the number of fans has no significant influence on the engagement rates, but the friends among fans have a positive effect on the engagement rate of brand pages [47]. There is no significant effect of like rations on interaction duration. Posted days significantly affect the comments [43].

In sum, this study support that the number of fans affects consumer awareness and interactions, but in the positive way. The consumer awareness and interactions in terms of PTAT later significantly increase more fans daily, weekly, and monthly. Giving different results from the literature research, marketer-generated content in terms of average posts per day, post timing, average length of posts, and average posted questions insignificantly affect social interactions.

This study extends the framework in the literature studies by adding the aspect of strategies applied by marketers in terms of posts per day, post timing, average length of posts, and curiosity. To my best knowledge, there are few studies analysing the effects of marketer-generated content on consumer interactions, using objective measures. For practical implications, this study confirms the importance of fan bases on consumer awareness and interactions, which finally affect future fans. The quantity of marketer-generated content is not much important as the quality or the variety of posting content. There are still more rooms for brands in various brand categories to promote their brand pages to increase the number of fans. Although the pictures and videos do not directly attract more consumers to engage with the posts, various content types should be added as the experiment for the appropriate content types to increase PTAT of each brand. Brands in all categories can also ask questions more to drive consumers' participation and PTAT. PTAT is important to involve more non-fans to become fans and to participate in quality posts of brands in the future, creating a ripple effect. In addition, brands should not neglect to quickly respond to their fans because brands in many categories still have poor response rates and bad response times.

7 Conclusion, Limitations and Future Works

This paper collects the secondary data of objective measures from leading Facebook brand fan pages in Thailand, from 9 brand industries, to understand how the owners of fan pages communicate with their fans and how content generated by brands affect the consumer awareness and interactions. Marketer-generated content are collected in various aspects that are posts per day, post timing, average length of posts, curiosity, hashtag, and enabling fan posts. These data together with the fan growth by day, the fan growth by week, and the fan growth by month are compared across all brand categories. The effectiveness of post types (images and videos) on the engagement rate is also examined. The results indicate the importance of content quality rather than the content quantity. In addition, findings point the significance of fan bases on fans' awareness and interactions, that subsequently affect future fan bases. Images are a dominant content type used by all brand categories. However, all brands should conduct some experiments with various combinations of content types to select the proper content type for their brands since the percentage of image and video posts does not directly influence the engagement rate. Content strategy from the successful brand industry that are telecommunications, FMCG, and electronics such as faster response times could be applied to brands in other industries. Post timing, response rate, and response time of brands in many brand categories should be adjusted.

Limitations of this study are relying on a social networking system, Facebook brand pages, and collecting inequality numbers of fan pages in each category because of the widespread acceptance of some page categories. Nevertheless, this study significantly contributes to the literature since most studies are conducted in the Western environments and Thailand is topmost three countries with the highest Facebook users [64]. To my knowledge, the results from Facebook fan pages in 9 brand categories are presented for the very first time. Further studies should replicate this research to other social media. More pages in some categories should be collected to compare the same proportion of fan pages from different industries. Other factors such as specific content types or formats affecting the awareness and interaction of pages should be explored by brand categories. The comparative study among the Southeast Asian countries should be conducted.

References

1. De Veirman, M., Cauberghe, V., Hudders, L.: Why are people interacting with brands on Facebook: unraveling consumers' motivations for lurking and posting on Facebook brand pages. In: European Marketing Academy Conference (EMAC) (2016)
2. Coursaris, C.K., Van Osch, W., Balogh, B.A.: A social media marketing typology: classifying brand Facebook page messages for strategic consumer engagement. In: The 21st European Conference on Information Systems (ECIS), pp. 1–12 (2013)
3. Augar, N., Zeleznikow, J.: 'I just saw this on Facebook, I need it now': exploring small business use of Facebook. In: 24th Australasian Conference on Information Systems (ACIS), pp. 1–11. RMIT University (2013)
4. Hutter, K., Hautz, J., Dennhardt, S., Füller, J.: The impact of user interactions in social media on brand awareness and purchase intention: the case of MINI on Facebook. J. Prod. Brand. Manag. **22**, 342–351 (2013)
5. http://newsroom.fb.com/company-info/
6. Schultz, C.D.: Insights from consumer interactions on a social networking site: findings from six apparel retail brands. Electron. Mark. **26**, 203–217 (2016)
7. Huang, F.-H.: Motivations of Facebook users for responding to posts on a community page. In: Ozok, A.A., Zaphiris, P. (eds.) OCSC 2013. LNCS, vol. 8029, pp. 33–39. Springer, Heidelberg (2013). https://doi.org/10.1007/978-3-642-39371-6_4
8. Jahn, B., Kunz, W.: How to transform consumers into fans of your brand. J. Serv. Manag. **23**, 344–361 (2012)
9. Madupu, V., Cooley, D.O.: Antecedents and consequences of online brand community participation: a conceptual framework. J. Internet Commer. **9**, 127–147 (2010)
10. Leach, H.S., Komo, L.W., Ngugi, I.K.: Engaging consumers through company social media websites. Comput. Inf. Syst. **16**, 5–20 (2012)
11. Chua, A.Y., Banerjee, S.: Marketing via social networking sites: a study of brand-post popularity for brands in Singapore. In: Proceedings of the International MultiConference of Engineers and Computer Scientists (2015)
12. Jayasingh, S., Venkatesh, R.: Customer engagement factors in Facebook brand pages. Asian Soc. Sci. **11**, 19 (2015)
13. Sabate, F., Berbegal-Mirabent, J., Cañabate, A., Lebherz, P.R.: Factors influencing popularity of branded content in Facebook fan pages. Eur. Manag. J. **32**, 1001–1011 (2014)
14. Erdoğmuş, İ.E., Cicek, M.: The impact of social media marketing on brand loyalty. Procedia Soc. Behav. Sci. **58**, 1353–1360 (2012)
15. Chow, W.S., Shi, S.: Investigating customers' satisfaction with brand pages in social networking sites. J. Comput. Inf. Syst. **55**, 48–58 (2015)
16. Rohm, A., Kaltcheva, D.V., Milne, G.R.: A mixed-method approach to examining brand-consumer interactions driven by social media. J. Res. Interact. Mark. **7**, 295–311 (2013)
17. Saji, K., Chauhan, K., Pillai, A.: Role of content strategy in social media brand communities: a case of higher education institutes in India. J. Prod. Brand. Manag. **22**, 40–51 (2013)
18. Kim, E., Sung, Y., Kang, H.: Brand followers' retweeting behavior on Twitter: how brand relationships influence brand electronic word-of-mouth. Comput. Hum. Behav. **37**, 18–25 (2014)
19. Habibi, M.R., Laroche, M., Richard, M.-O.: The roles of brand community and community engagement in building brand trust on social media. Comput. Hum. Behav. **37**, 152–161 (2014)

20. Chan, T.K., Zheng, X., Cheung, C.M., Lee, M.K., Lee, Z.W.: Antecedents and consequences of customer engagement in online brand communities. J. Mark. Anal. **2**, 81–97 (2014)
21. Angela Hausman, D., Kabadayi, S., Price, K.: Consumer–brand engagement on Facebook: liking and commenting behaviors. J. Res. Interact. Mark. **8**, 203–223 (2014)
22. Stavros, C., Meng, M.D., Westberg, K., Farrelly, F.: Understanding fan motivation for interacting on social media. Sport. Manag. Rev. **17**, 455–469 (2014)
23. Kim, D.-H., Lisa, S., Hettche, M.: Analyzing media types and content orientations in Facebook for global brands. J. Res. Interact. Mark. **9**, 4–30 (2015)
24. Chua, A.Y., Banerjee, S.: How businesses draw attention on Facebook through incentives, vividness and interactivity. IAENG Int. J. Comput. Sci. **42**, 275–281 (2015)
25. Touchette, B., Schanski, M., Lee, S.-E.: Apparel brands' use of Facebook: an exploratory content analysis of branded entertainment. J. Fash. Mark. Manag. **19**, 107–119 (2015)
26. Hsu, L.-C., Wang, K.-Y., Chih, W.-H., Lin, K.-Y.: Investigating the ripple effect in virtual communities: an example of Facebook fan pages. Comput. Hum. Behav. **51**, 483–494 (2015)
27. Zoha, R., Hasmah, Z., Kumaran, S., Sedigheh, M., Mohd Hairul Nizam, M.: Determining the relationship between fanpage contents and PTA metrics (2016)
28. Schultz, C.D.: Driving likes, comments, and shares on social networking sites: how post characteristics affect brand interactions in apparel retailing. In: Proceedings of the 18th Annual International Conference on Electronic Commerce: e-Commerce in Smart connected World, p. 9. ACM (2016)
29. Cvijikj, I.P., Michahelles, F.: Online engagement factors on Facebook brand pages. Soc. Netw. Anal. Min. **3**, 843–861 (2013)
30. Cervellon, M.-C., Galipienzo, D.: Facebook pages content, does it really matter? Consumers' responses to luxury hotel posts with emotional and informational content. J. Travel. Tour. Mark. **32**, 428–437 (2015)
31. Zaglia, M.E.: Brand communities embedded in social networks. J. Bus. Res. **66**, 216–223 (2013)
32. Chen, H., Papazafeiropoulou, A., Duan, Y., Chen, T.-K.: The antecedents and outcomes of brand experience on the social networking site. In: European Conference on Information Systems, p. 10 (2013)
33. Hsu, L.-C., Chih, W.-H., Liou, D.-K.: Investigating community members' eWOM effects in Facebook fan page. Ind. Manag. Data Syst. **116**, 978–1004 (2016)
34. Beukeboom, C.J., Kerkhof, P., de Vries, M.: Does a virtual like cause actual liking? how following a brand's Facebook Updates enhances brand evaluations and purchase intention. J. Interact. Mark. **32**, 26–36 (2015)
35. De Vries, L., Gensler, S., Leeflang, P.S.: Popularity of brand posts on brand fan pages: an investigation of the effects of social media marketing. J. Interact. Mark. **26**, 83–91 (2012)
36. Podobnik, V.: An analysis of Facebook social media marketing key performance indicators: the case of premier league brands. In: 12th International Conference on Telecommunications (ConTEL), pp. 131–138. IEEE (2013)
37. Trefzger, T.F., Baccarella, C.V., Kai-Ingo, V.: Antecedents of brand post popularity in Facebook: the influence of images, videos, and text. In: The 15th International Marketing Trends Conference, pp. 1–8 (2016)
38. Luarn, P., Lin, Y.-F., Chiu, Y.-P.: Influence of Facebook brand-page posts on online engagement. Online Inf. Rev. **39**, 505–519 (2015)
39. Shen, B., Bissell, K.: Social media, social me: a content analysis of beauty companies' use of Facebook in marketing and branding. J. Promot. Manag. **19**, 629–651 (2013)

40. Swani, K., Milne, G., Brown, B.P.: Spreading the word through likes on Facebook: evaluating the message strategy effectiveness of Fortune 500 companies. J. Res. Interact. Mark. **7**, 269–294 (2013)
41. Malhotra, A., Malhotra, C.K., See, A.: How to create brand engagement on Facebook. MIT Sloan Manag. Rev. **54**, 18–20 (2013)
42. Chen, J., Shen, X.-L.: Consumers' decisions in social commerce context: an empirical investigation. Decis. Support Syst. **79**, 55–64 (2015)
43. Pletikosa Cvijikj, I., Michahelles, F.: A case study of the effects of moderator posts within a Facebook brand page. In: Datta, A., Shulman, S., Zheng, B., Lin, S.-D., Sun, A., Lim, E.-P. (eds.) SocInfo 2011. LNCS, vol. 6984, pp. 161–170. Springer, Heidelberg (2011). https://doi.org/10.1007/978-3-642-24704-0_21
44. Taecharungroj, V.: Starbucks' marketing communications strategy on Twitter. J. Mark. Commun. **23**, 552–571 (2016)
45. Hajli, N.: Social commerce constructs and consumer's intention to buy. Int. J. Inf. Manag. **35**, 183–191 (2015)
46. Tsimonis, G., Dimitriadis, S.: Brand strategies in social media. Mark. Intell. Plan. **32**, 328–344 (2014)
47. Laurens, A.: Who Likes to Engage? An Investigation of the Influences of Facebook Fan Page Characteristics on the Engagement Rate. Faculteit economie en bedrijfswetenschappen, vol. master in de toegepaste economische wetenschappen (2013)
48. Wallace, E., Buil, I., de Chernatony, L., Hogan, M.: Who "likes" you… and why? a typology of Facebook fans. J. Advert. Res. **54**, 92–109 (2014)
49. http://www.socialbakers.com/resources/studies/a-marketers-guide-to-facebook-metrics
50. Othman, I., Bidin, A., Hussain, H.: Facebook marketing strategy for small business in Malaysia. In: 2013 International Conference on Informatics and Creative Multimedia (ICICM), pp. 236–241. IEEE (2013)
51. Schivinski, B., Christodoulides, G., Dabrowski, D.: Measuring consumers' engagement with brand-related social-media content. J. Advert. Res. **56**, 64–80 (2016)
52. Tsai, W.-H.S., Men, L.R.: Consumer engagement with brands on social network sites: a cross-cultural comparison of China and the USA. J. Mark. Commun. **23**, 1–20 (2014)
53. Valerio, G., Herrera-Murillo, D.J., Villanueva-Puente, F., Herrera-Murillo, N., del Carmen Rodríguez-Martínez, M.: The relationship between post formats and digital engagement: a study of the Facebook pages of Mexican universities. Revista de Universidad y Sociedad del Conocimiento **12**, 50–63 (2015)
54. He, W., Tian, X., Chen, Y., Chong, D.: Actionable social media competitive analytics for understanding customer experiences. J. Comput. Inf. Syst. **56**, 145–155 (2016)
55. Whiting, A., Williams, D.: Why people use social media: a uses and gratifications approach. Qual. Mark. Res. Int. J. **16**, 362–369 (2013)
56. Enginkaya, E., Yılmaz, H.: What drives consumers to interact with brands through social media? a motivation scale development study. Procedia Soc. Behav. Sci. **148**, 219–226 (2014)
57. Susarla, A., Oh, J.-H., Tan, Y.: Influentials, imitables, or susceptibles? virality and word-of-mouth conversations in online social networks. J. Manag. Inf. Syst. **33**, 139–170 (2016)
58. http://www.socialbakers.com/blog/1515-february-2013-social-media-report-facebook-pages-in-thailand
59. http://likealyzer.com/
60. Lee, D., Hosanagar, K., Nair, H.: The effect of social media marketing content on consumer engagement: Evidence from Facebook. Available at SSRN 2290802 (2014)

61. Thongmak, M.: Consumer awareness and interactions in online brand community-antecedents and consequences. In: The International Conference on e-Business, pp. 28–37 (2017)
62. Kaplan, A.M., Haenlein, M.: Two hearts in three-quarter time: how to waltz the social media/viral marketing dance. Bus. Horiz. **54**, 253–263 (2011)
63. Merchant, G., et al.: Click "like" to change your behavior: a mixed methods study of college students' exposure to and engagement with Facebook content designed for weight loss. J. Med. Internet Res. **16**, e158 (2014)
64. https://www.statista.com/statistics/193056/facebook-user-numbers-in-asian-countries/

How to Manage and Model Unstructured Business Processes: A Proposed List of Representational Requirements

Zaharah Allah Bukhsh[1](✉), Marten van Sinderen[2], Klaas Sikkel[2], and Dick Quartel[3]

[1] Department of Construction Management and Engineering, University of Twente, Drienerlolaan 5, 7522 NB Enschede, The Netherlands
z.allahbukhsh@utwente.nl
[2] Department of Computer Science, University of Twente, Drienerlolaan 5, 7522 NB Enschede, The Netherlands
{m.j.vansinderen,k.sikkel}@utwente.nl
[3] BiZZdesign BV, Capitool 15, 7521 PL Enschede, The Netherlands
d.quartel@bizzdesign.com

Abstract. Recent advancements in technology have enabled businesses to automate their structured business processes, thus requiring minimum intervention from end-users. This has shifted attention towards less structured processes, which are ad-hoc, often undocumented and demand frequent human decision-making. These processes are referred to as Unstructured Business Processes (UBP). Currently available tools and technologies are mainly focused on structured processes and therefore not optimally suited for management of UBP. With a representative example, we performed an experiment to compare and assess the ability of existing process support paradigms, i.e. Business Process Management and Case Management, to manage UBP. Moreover, we also investigated the limitations of Business Process Model and Notation (BPMN) and Case Management Model and Notation (CMMN) for modeling UBP. Based on our findings, a set of requirements are derived that are needed for optimally managing and modeling UBP. These requirements allow to express end-to-end business processes while providing flexibility for run-time changes. The requirements are also demonstrated with a possible extension of BPMN.

Keywords: Business Process Management · Case Management
Business Process Model and Notation
Case Management Model and Notation · BPMN · CMMN
Unstructured Business Process · Flexibility

1 Introduction

Business Process Management (BPM) has popularized the concept of business process automation, optimization and monitoring. The purpose of BPM is to innovate, maintain and optimize the business process by defining, modeling and

© Springer Nature Switzerland AG 2019
M. S. Obaidat and E. Cabello (Eds.): ICETE 2017, CCIS 990, pp. 81–103, 2019.
https://doi.org/10.1007/978-3-030-11039-0_5

automating it at design time. The design-time defined process is executed any number of times with various process instances. In BPM, it is assumed that each process instance has the same characteristics and will follow the process exactly in a manner that is defined at design time. However, not all the business processes can be planned and executed as defined at design time. According to a report by AIIM [19], for 51% of the companies polled, more than half of their business processes are unstructured and unpredictable in nature. Various studies [2,15,18] have defined the classification of business processes based on their level of structuredness. A business process having an ordered set of planned activities which are defined at design time, is said to be a *Structured Business Process (SBP)*. While a business process which depends on real-time events, available data and knowledge of knowledge workers is referred as an *Unstructured Business Process (UBP)*.

Companies adopt various methodologies (e.g., in-house collaborative systems, process management suites, etc.) to deal with the shift in focus from structured to unstructured business processes. Traditionally, UBP are dealt with a structured way [10]. For example, a business process is modeled at design time using Business Process Model and Notation (BPMN) while Business Process Management Suite (BPMS) implements the designed business process. Such process automation provides efficiency, however, it limits the process engineer to predefined activities and conditional flows.

Considering these limitations, some new and/or modified process management paradigms and modeling languages have been suggested that are specifically targeted to provide the flexibility for management of UBP. van der Aalst et al. [3] proposed case handling/management as a new paradigm to deal with UBP. To support the dynamic nature of business processes, a number of new modeling constructs were added in the BPMN v2.0 release [21]. Moreover, OMG proposed a new modeling language called Case Management Model and Notation (CMMN) for modeling processes where the process activities depend on real-time evolving circumstances [22]. The availability of a number of process modeling paradigms, with their advertised vendor solutions, pushes companies to rethink their tools that are used for process management. On one hand, BPMN is usually preferred since it is widely adopted and understood as an industry standard. On the other hand, the new proposed modeling language (i.e. CMMN) is attractive since it promises an increased level of expressibility for modeling of evolving business processes. The current scientific literature on process modeling languages lacks a comparison and capability assessment of BPMN and CMMN for UBP. However, a number of online discussions[1,2] and a recently published study by Hinkelmann [14] suggests the integration of BPMN and CMMN for improved process modeling benefits.

This study intends to fill the gap in the scientific literature by assessing the modeling capabilities of BPMN and CMMN with respect to UBP. Similarly, a comparison of the existing process support paradigms, i.e. BPM and Case

---

[1] https://www.linkedin.com/groups/1175137/1175137-5868060474150502404.
[2] http://brsilver.com/bpmn-cmmn-compared/.

Management (CM) is also performed in order to assess their support for UBP. The result of this study can assist companies, and specifically their process engineers and process consultants, in making a careful selection of the most suitable modeling and management paradigm for the process at hand by considering its requirements. Therefore, a number of representational and management requirements has been derived from literature. We believe, a process modeling language that is able to fulfill these representational requirements can model the SBP and UBP, while keeping their run-time flexibility. The work presented in this chapter is an extension of a previous study [5].

The rest of this chapter is structured as follows: characteristics of UBP are provided in Sect. 2. The details of an experiment that assess the capabilities of process support paradigms for UBP is provided in Sect. 3. To assess the capabilities of modeling languages proposed by OMG, a sample business process is modeled with BPMN and CMMN in Sect. 4. Based on the results of the capability assessment, a number of representational requirements for UBP are derived in Sect. 5. The representational requirements are demonstrated by means of an application scenario in Sect. 6. The validation of representational requirements with three business process modeling experts is presented in Sect. 7. Finally, Sect. 8 provides our conclusion.

2 Properties of UBP

Many literature studies have discussed the characteristic of UBP under the title of case management [9,16,20,31]. Following are some of the aspects of UBP which make them different from SBP.

Data Dependent: In UBP, process and data are strictly integrated which makes them data dependent [8]. The modification, addition or deletion of process data defines the future activities of the process. However, the unavailability of particular data may halt the processing of the whole process.

Goal Oriented: UBP are goal oriented, which means a process evolves through a series of sub-goals and milestones [9]. The achievement of each goal depends on a number of factors, e.g. availability of required data, execution of activities, decisions of knowledge workers, and responses from customers. Every sub-goal of a process is well-integrated with one final goal. An achieved sub-goal can be modified or proven wrong as more data and knowledge emerges as the process progresses [20].

Business Rule Driven: Conformance to business rules and standards is one the most convincing arguments to automate a business process. However, due to the uncertain and emergent nature of UBP, knowledge workers are required to maintain the business rules and standards during process execution. All the process activities are influenced by particular rules and policies of business [9].

Coordination and Collaboration: Execution of UBP highly relies on the coordination and collaboration among the knowledge workers [20]. Usually, a single process involves many knowledge workers [9]. As the process progresses, new knowledge workers may get involved or existing knowledge workers may leave their roles.

To sum up, it is argued that in SBP the predefined routing rules drive the process while in UBP the characteristic of the particular process instance drive the process [1]. UBP requires tacit knowledge, collaboration and decision making skills from knowledge workers. The knowledge work of an organization cannot be straight-jacketed into an automated process and electronic forms due to its unstructured and evolving nature [3]. Eshuis et al. [11], suggested an approach to convert the UBP to SBP to be able to model them with imperative modeling languages.

3   Process Support Paradigm for UBP

For effective resource utilization, business organizations employ various methods, techniques and methodologies to optimize their business operations. Due to various types of process, process support and process improvement paradigms, an organization has to make a decision on which process support paradigm is more useful in dealing with a particular type of business processes. In this section, two process support paradigms are compared to better understand their strengths and weaknesses in managing UBP. For comparison purposes, an experiment is conducted. The experiment will provide us insight about which process support paradigm is more efficient and easy to use for implementing and maintaining an UBP.

3.1   Experiment Setup

Business Process Management (BPM) and Case Management (CM) are process support paradigms with difference in focus. An experiment is planned to assess and compare the capabilities of BPM and CM to manage UBP. The approach of the experiment is adopted from [30]. This section details the experiment setup, factors and factor level and threats to validity.

1. Subject: The purpose of this experiment is to understand the BPM and CM methodological differences while dealing with an UBP. Considering the purpose of this experiment, the subject of this experiment is only one researcher who is also responsible for experiment setup as well as for experiment execution.

2. Object of Study: The object of study is the admission of a student to a university, which is, to some extent, a UBP. The detailed process description is provided in Sect. 4.1.

3. Factors and Factor Levels: The factor or independent variable of this experiment is process support paradigm with two factor levels which are BPM and CM. Bizagi modeller and Bizagi Studio [6] are selected as BPMS to analyse the BPM capabilities. According to the Gartner magic quadrant [26], Bizagi is one of the visionary vendors of BPMS. As a CM, the Cognoscenti software tool is used. Cognoscenti [27] is one of the few CM tools that is available free of cost for research purposes [29].

4. Response Variable: The response or dependent variable of this experiment is 'effort of implementing an unstructured process'. The usage effort will be measured by implementing an admission process with Bizagi (BPM) and with Cognoscenti (CM).

5. Analysis Procedure: The analysis procedure provides the design of experiment. It is difficult to quantitatively gauge the effort of implementing UBP as well as to assess the differences between the BPM and the CM process management methodology. Hence, certain aspects of process management are proposed for analysis purposes. These aspects include (a) process/case modeling, (b) data management (c) business rules specification (d) user roles specification (e) process/case progress view (f) process/case control (g) activities execution and (h) process/case setup effort.

6. Threats to Validity: We identified the following threats to validity for this experiment:

1. It is planned to assess the difference in methodology of BPM and CM based on their software suites. However, the platform-specific features provided by these suites can influence the results of this experiment.
2. The experiment has very limited subjects, i.e. only one researcher.
3. The object of this study, i.e. the admission process, can have possible biases for one process support paradigm over the other.

To mitigate the effect of these threats, some additional steps are performed. For example, Bizagi provides the functionality of process modeling while Cognoscenti lack this feature. To bring balance of functionality between both platforms, a Microsoft Visio stencil was created and used for modeling the case using CMMN. The second threat of validity is mitigated by presenting the results of the experiment to two experienced BPM practitioners as well as to three experienced researchers. The third and final threat of validity is difficult to mitigate. As depending on the particular process instance and the choices made by designer/modeler, the admission process can be more structured or unstructured.

3.2 Experiment Execution

The implementation procedure of the admission process can be broadly divided into design-time planning and run-time execution. In design-time planning of the process, the process is defined and modeled. While, in run-time a process instance is created as a result of process initiation. In the following paragraphs, the implementation of the admission process is discussed with the software suites of Bizagi (BPM) and Cognoscenti (CM).

Admission Process with Bizagi (BPM). For the implementation of the admission process in Bizagi, process modeling is the first and most pivotal part of the process management life cycle. Based on the process model, the data model, business rules, user roles and electronic forms are designed. After deployment of the designed process, the process can be accessed on the work portal of Bizagi. On the work portal, a process instance can be initiated. The process of implementing the admission process with Bizagi is depicted in Fig. 1.

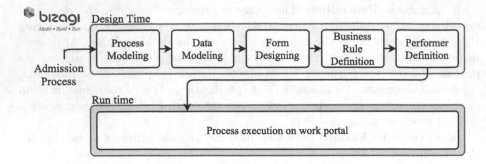

Fig. 1. Implementation step of admission process in Bizagi [4].

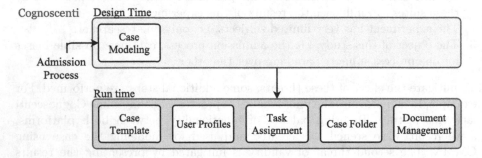

Fig. 2. Implementation step of admission process in Cognoscenti [4].

Admission Process with Cognoscenti (CM). Cognoscenti, an open source software, is available for research purposes. According to Swenson [28], Cognoscenti is not a complete product, but a testbed to show the capabilities of case management. Due to this reason, Cognoscenti has limited features.

As compared to Bizagi, the process implementation steps in Cognoscenti are directed. Cognoscenti does not automate the business process but facilitates in its management. Figure 2 provides the steps that assist in process management in a flexible manner. It is important to notice that the execution steps of the admission process are performed at the runtime with no directed links.

3.3   Results of the Experiment

As mentioned earlier, the procedure of implementing the business process is dependent on the functionalities provided by software suites. Each software suite has different capabilities, which can either make the process management more or less difficult. Execution of this experiment is assessed based on the process management aspects defined in the above-mentioned analysis procedure. Table 1 provides a summary of the experiment execution process.

Considering the result of this experiment, it can be said that BPM and CM are significantly different in managing an UBP. However, both paradigms have its strengths and weaknesses. From the UBP perspective, BPM straitjackets the

Table 1. Difference between BPM and CM process paradigms [4].

Business Process Management (Bizagi)	Case Management (Cognoscenti)
Process/Case modeling	
The process model is the first and most important activity in the process specification as all other process activities (e.g. data modeling, electronic forms design) are dependent on it. The process model is used as a road map which is followed by each process instance on run-time	Case modeling is a useful activity in which activities and goals of a case are defined. The case model provides guidance for case processing. It is not necessarily followed by case instances at run-time
Data management	
In BPM, visibility of data is very limited to users. End-users can provide and obtain data only through the electronic forms	The focus of CM is on data. A case folder maintains all the relevant records of the particular case. Based on available data, the further goals of the case are defined and assigned to knowledge workers
Business rules specification	
Business rules can be defined at design time. These rules specify the flow and execution of activities of the process	Cognoscenti, as a tool, does not provide the functionality to define the business rules. However, in CM, the specification of business rules is an important task
Users role specification	
In the BPM process model, the lanes are used to define the user roles. The activities assigned to users are defined on the process model. User roles and assigned activities cannot be modified at run-time	User roles are assigned as soon as the case is created. New users can be added at run-time as well as existing users can be deleted. Each uploaded document can be assigned with different access level permissions
Process/Case progress view	
A limited view of the overall process progress is visible to end-user. The process view is only accessible by electronic forms, where process model is not visible during process execution	With the milestone concept of CMMN, the process view is visible to process engineers on the process/case model
Process/Case control	
A BPM system is able to conform to the business level standards. Sequential and conditional flow of the process, predefined input of data and inherited business rules provide control to the business. But on the downside, it limits the process on the predefined flow of activities which might not depict real-world situations	The CM system is an open-ended platform where conformance to standards is a difficult task. It does not provide the conditional flows or predefined forms for data input. But on the positive side, it can represent the real-world situation by performing the needed activities
Activities execution	
The focus is on activities and control. Activities defined in the process model are executed with certain sequential flow and control. All the activities that are defined in the process model need to be performed except if omitted by if-else conditions	New activities can be initiated during run-time, while, the defined activities can be skipped, executed or deleted. Activities are defined and executed at run-time based on the data
Setup effort	
A BPM process requires intensive setup steps at design time. The setup includes process modeling, data modeling, forms design, business rules specification, users' profiles specification and finally deployment of the process. The setup efforts also require some prior knowledge of data modeling and form designing	A case does not require intensive setup steps before the execution. The setup step includes only case modeling and the creation of the particular case project. The case project can be considered as a case folder which contains all the information about the case and its processing

process into predefined activities and flow, but at the same time conformance to business rules and business standards are assured. On the other hand, CM provides an open-ended platform that provides run-time activity specification, task assignment and collaboration among knowledge workers, thus providing the required flexibility to unstructured business processes. However, without the predefined users and activities, the case/process can take longer in its processing than expected. For example, the run-time task assignment to users can cause resource dependency or even deadlocks in certain situations.

By analysing the strengths and weaknesses of both paradigms, it can be concluded that a software suite that contains the features of BPMS and CMS will facilitate management of an UBP in the most effective way. For example, most of the processes of a business are combination of structured and unstructured activities.

4   Evaluating BPMN and CMMN for Modeling UBP

Two process modeling languages i.e. BPMN and CMMN have been introduced and evaluated, respectively, to assess their ability to model UBP. We use an application scenario of an admission process to investigate and compare the capabilities of these notations to model an UBP.

4.1   Application Scenario

The admission process is a knowledge intensive unstructured process which demands collaboration and communication among number of departments to perform the smooth intake of students. Following is the detailed description of the admission process.

> With the announcement of admission, the students can send their documents to the university through an online form. Students are required to submit their personal information with their academic certificates, motivation letter and language certificate. Once the admission application is *submitted* by the student, the **admission office** is *notified*. Based on documents received, each admission file might go through at number of assessments before the final decision can be made. Initially, the **admission administrator** *checks* the application for its correctness and completeness. The admission file is then forwarded to the corresponding department of university for *assessment*. The **admission coordinator** will *review* the admission file to check the attached academic certificates. The final *decision* can be made by the admission coordinator only or it can require the *discussion* and *decision* from the **admission panel**. During the decision process, the provided details can be *verified* and new documents can be requested from the student. At the end, a student can be admitted, rejected or conditionally admitted. The involved knowledge workers and the decision highly depend on the particular admission file. Finally, the student is *informed* about the decision based on his admission file.

In this scenario description, verbs in italic letters show the activities of the admission process while nouns in bold letters represent the involved knowledge workers.

4.2   Modeling UBP with BPMN

BPMN is one of the widely adopted process modeling notations due to its ease of use and expressibility. A BPMN process model provides a layout of the business process by modeling the set of ordered activities, events, and process flow logic [10]. BPMN is often regarded as the modeling notation of choice for SBP [24]. Figure 3 shows the admission process modeled using BPMN modeling constructs.

Following are some problems of modeling an UBP with procedural modeling language like BPMN [25].

Task Ordering: BPMN, as a procedural modeling languages, poses the ordering and task dependency in process executions. For example, in Fig. 3, the task ordering implies that the activity *'Send certificate for authentication'* will be only performed after the task *'Review admission form'* has been completed. While, in reality, the verification of certificates and review of admission form can be performed in parallel.

Unavailable Optional Tasks: In BPMN, the execution of tasks can be skipped only by employing conditions on an exclusive gateway. However, tasks that are defined with a sequential flow on the process model without any conditions cannot be skipped. Even if the tasks are not required by the particular process instance, the tasks are needed to be executed to continue the process flow. For example, the activity *'Send certificates for authentication'*, in Fig. 3, should be regarded as an optional activity if the authentication is not needed.

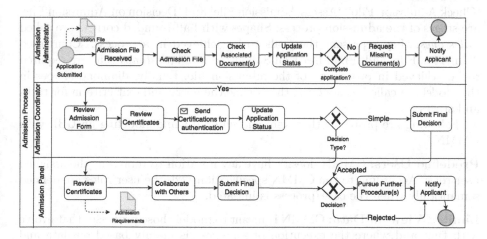

Fig. 3. Process model of admission process using BPMN [5].

Limited View on Data: BPMN provides a very limited view on data. Business processes like the admission process are data-intensive in nature; the provided data can define the flow of activities. With BPMN, the data input and output flow can be depicted, but the changing state of data can not be defined.

Some of the problems that are highlighted with BPMN can be mitigated by using the extended BPMN elements [21, p. 30]. The concept of ad-hoc subprocess has been found to be most useful for modeling an UBP. An ad-hoc sub-process does not specify the ordering among activities. The activities in an ad-hoc sub-process can be executed any number of times without any pre-defined ordering. Based on process instance requirements, the activities of ad-hoc sub-processes can be done, redone or even skipped. However, according to the BPMN version 2.0 standard specification [21], many process engines don't provide support for ad-hoc sub-process execution. Moreover, use of extended BPMN elements results in a very complex process model. The activities defined inside the ad-hoc sub-process cannot be labeled to indicate whether activities are optional, required or re-executable. The use of various events and sub-processes can negatively influence the understandability and readability of the process model.

4.3   Modeling UBP with CMMN

CMMN is for modeling the case/process where the activities are not strictly defined, but dependent on evolving circumstances and decisions of knowledge workers [22]. As compared to BPMN, CMMN is a relatively new process modeling language with unique constructs. Modeling construct of CMMN, which are exploited in Fig. 4 for admission process model, are the following:

A rectangle shape with the title of 'Admission Process' is called *case folder*, while the title depicts the name of the case/process. A *case folder* is a container that consists of all CMMN elements to model the process. A rectangular shape with angled corners shows the episodes of a process which are called *stages*. 'Check Admission File', 'Assess Admission File' and 'Decision on Admission File' are stages of the admission process. Shapes with half-rounded corners are called *milestones*; they represent the goals to be achieved in a process. 'Completed Admission File' and 'Final Decision Submitted' are *milestones* that are required to be achieved in processing of the admission file. Finally, diamond shapes in the model are called as *sentries*; they define the entry and exit criteria for tasks and stages.

Following are problems that were encountered while modeling an UBP with CMMN.

Predefine Users: CMMN doesn't have any notation to represent the assigned user roles. According to the CMMN specification [22], the user roles are defined semantically when the case/process is initiated.

Limited View on Data: CMMN is meant to model those processes that evolve with time and where the execution of a process is mainly based on data and knowledge workers' decisions. CMMN has a concept of case file along with file

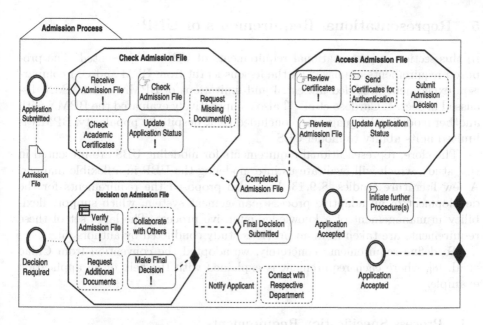

Fig. 4. Case model of admission process using CMMN [5].

versioning. However, the versioning of a case file is defined semantically. From a visualization perspective, CMMN provides a very limited view on data.

Task Dependency: Connectors and sentries represent the concept of task dependency in CMMN. The tasks will be executed only if the entry/exit condition, associated with it, is fulfilled. However, as compared to BPMN, the combination of connector and sentries provides poor readability. For example, in Fig. 4, the stage of *Assess Admission File* will only be executed if the milestone *Application Check Completed* has been achieved.

Unlike BPMN, CMMN is a declarative language. It is used to specify what should be done in the process instead of how it should be done. The purpose of a CMMN model is to provide a guidance map which instructs the process engineers on what can be done for successful process execution. Instead of design-time defined conditional flows, the evolving data and knowledge of knowledge workers drive the process execution. Consequently, BPMN is more expressive in its process flows as compared to CMMN. On the other hand, the discretionary tasks and stages of CMMN provide a better understanding of which tasks can be skipped during process execution as compared to ad-hoc sub-processes of BPMN. A detailed comparison of BPMN and CMMN notations is provided in [4, Sect. 4.4].

5   Representational Requirements of UBP

In this section, representational requirements of UBP are presented. The proposed requirements are based on the lessons learnt from BPM and CM comparison experiment provided in Sect. 3 and limitations of BPMN and CMMN discussed in Sect. 4. Cardoso et al. [7] also comparatively evaluated the BPMN with another modeling language and concluded that, despite its popularity, BPMN is limited in its ability to model UBS.

Therefore, representational requirements for modeling UBS are presented in this study, which will facilitate us into modeling the UBP in a flexible manner. A few literature studies [8,9,13] have also proposed the requirements for the development of an adaptive process management system, which support flexibility in management of a knowledge-intensive process. The large set of these requirements are taken from an previous study conducted by authors [5].

To define requirements concretely, we adopted the convention from Chiao et al. [8], where each requirement is explained with the help of an application example.

5.1   Process Specification Requirements

Each process has some general requirements that need to be fulfilled to represent the real-world scenarios.

Support to Capture Real-Time Events: It should be possible for UBP to capture and respond to real-time events. These real-time events can be related to process start or end, arrival of data, modification of existing data, or they can be triggered by user activity.

> When an applicant submits his admission application, the admission office is notified. The *notify event* can be a start event to initiate the admission process.

Support to Quantify and/or Qualify the Conditions: On certain steps in processing of an UBP, the decision to execute next process activities is taken. It should be possible to represent the conditional flow on process model.

> A complete check in admission process is an example of quantifying condition.

5.2   Activities Specification Requirements

Activities define the work that is expected to be performed for successful execution of a process. The requirements of activities specification from the perspective of an UBP are discussed below.

Support for Ordered and Unordered Activities: A business process consists of structured and unstructured parts of the process. It should be possible to define and follow the control flow among the activities as well as skip the activities' execution, if needed.

Ordered Activities: The steps like *submission* of admission file by student and *notifying* it to admission office are ordered set of activities. These process activities are required to be executed one after another.

Unordered Activities: An *assessment* activity which consist of check on academic certificates, analysis of their authenticity and review of other related documents are example of unordered process activities.

Support for Required and Optional Activities: Due to nondeterministic and emergent nature of UBP, it should be possible to define the process activities as optional or required.

Required Activities: Irrespective of type of admission file, it is required to inform the student about the status of his application.

Optional Activities: During the *assessment* activity, the activity of certificates authentication can be treated as an optional activity based on admission application.

Support for Re-execution and Undo Activities: An UBP mainly relies on decisions made by knowledge workers. Such decisions may lead to undo or re-execute the previously performed activities.

Re-execution of Activities: An admission application from the recognized national university might require single review while the international admission application might go through a number of reviews.

Undo Activities: For example, a request to defer the admission for a specific time can lead to undo certain activities that had marked the student as an upcoming admitted student.

Support for Collaboration Among Activities: In addition to parallel execution of activities, it should be possible to define and depict the collaboration among the individual process activities. BPMN depicts the collaboration between the external and internal process through message passing but not within a process.

The activities of *discussion* and *decision* require collaboration and can further leads to *verification* of the admission application. Therefore, the collaboration activities should be explicit.

Support for Varying Levels of Granularity: A process model with low level of granularity provides the flexibility for knowledge workers in process execution while a process with high level of granularity limits the knowledge workers' freedom.

Assessment and *verification* are examples of those activities that be modeled with varying level of granularity.

Support for Process and Data Alignment: Unlike traditional business process, where data are limited to defining control flows, UBP have an abundance of data with changing states. With process and data alignment, it should be possible to trace back data through a process and vice versa.

Almost each activity of admission process have associated data e.g. admission documents, remarks, decisions, etc.

Support for Process/Activity Call: It should be possible to model the already available process or activity. The callable aspect will reduce the burden of re-modeling/re-doing the same activity.

In case the applicant, who had applied for admission, also submitted his application for a scholarship. With activity/process call, the results of the authentication activities can be reused from admission process.

5.3   Data Specification Requirements

UBP are fundamentally data-centric, which means that the process and data are strictly bounded [3,17]. The execution of process highly relies on available and evolving process data.

Support for Data Representation: UBP produce and consume data during execution. It should be possible to clearly define the inflow and outflow of data files for a particular process activity.

In the *assessment* activity, the admission application can be represented as an input data file while remarks as an output data file.

Support for Data Authorization: With the involvement of number of knowledge workers in UBP, it is should be possible to define the access level of data.

The admission application should not be accessible to the admission coordinator and admission panel before it is verified by admission administrator.

Support for Version Control of Data: Due to evolving nature of data, the version control of data is important. The concept of versioning for UBP is introduced by OMG in CMMN version 1.0 [22]. Data versioning can be modelled as data states on a process model.

The remarks and the decision on the admission file have evolving nature which can be revised, added or deleted.

5.4   Business Rules Specification Requirements

To conform to standards and business policies, business rules need to be employed during process execution. These rules provide information on how certain business processes should be performed and how the resources can be used [23]. The alignment of process with business rules will answer the questions about 'how and why certain activities were performed and specific decisions were made'.

The admission deadline defined by an institute is one example of business rule, which is related to admission process.

5.5   Process Goals Specification Requirements

Goal-orientedness is one of the most distinguishing characteristics of UBP. Based on the main goal, a process evolves into a number of sub-goals and milestones as process progresses. To provide an overview of process, it should be possible to model goals and sub-goals.

The main goal of admission process is final verdict of acceptance or rejection of admission application, while the other goals can be 'application received', 'application reviewed', and 'application verified'.

5.6   Knowledge Workers' Specification Requirements

Knowledge workers play a critical role in managing and solving UBP. Knowledge workers' primary job is to create, distribute and apply their tacit and explicit knowledge to comprehend the process, analyze related information and make decisions [12].

Support for Knowledge Workers' Roles Assignment: Due to involvement of many knowledge workers in process management, it should be possible to define the roles of each knowledge worker along with their assigned tasks.

> Admission administrator, admission coordinator, and admission decision panel are knowledge workers of the admission process with their assigned set of tasks.

Support to Capture Knowledge Workers' Decisions: One of the most important tasks of knowledge workers is to utilize their tacit knowledge, available data and process context to take the certain decisions. The decisions made by knowledge workers affect the process running time, its control flow, final outcome and many other process related aspects. It should be possible to capture every decision of knowledge workers.

> The admission administrator needs to make a decision about the completeness of the admission application before forwarding it to admission coordinator.

Table 2. Extended Modeling Constructs of BPMN (Demonstration) [5].

No	Name	Notations	Semantics
1	Collaborative Subprocess		Collaborative subprocess represents collaboration among different activities of the process
2	Decision Activity		Decision activity shows a decision taken during the course of process execution
3	Optional Activity		Optional activity defines an activity that can be skipped during the process execution considering the process context
4	Required Activity		Required activity defines a process activity that must be executed
5	Undo Activity		Undo activity represents an activity that can be undone considering the particular process context
6	Goal		Goal represents the purpose of the process
7	User Role		User role represents a person or a class of people who are assigned to perform the process execution
8	Business Rule		Business rule represents a related business rule on the process model

6   Illustration of Representational Requirements

To demonstrate the proposed representational requirements, a few extended modeling constructs based on BPMN are suggested in Table 2. The reason to demonstrate representational requirements with BPMN is twofold: First, as compared to CMMN, BPMN is widely known and adopted by process engineers. Second, many available modeling constructs provided by BPMN are able to fulfill a number of representational requirements.

Using BPMN and the extended modeling construct, an admission process is modeled in Fig. 5. The description of each construct is provided as added comments in Fig. 5 and with Table 1. All the activities without incoming and outgoing sequential flow are unordered, while the sequential flow defines the order between activities. Moreover, a subprocess can be attached to the conditional flow to reach to the goal. For instance, the goal *Application verified* can only be reached if the condition *verification completed* is met. Data objects with their changing states are also represented in the process model. The position of data objects in the process model shows the data access levels for the involved performers. For example, the data object applicant file with created and verifying state is only accessible by the admission administrator while the applicant file with verified state can be accessed by all the involved performers.

To improve the readability, comments have been added in Fig. 5. The whole process is placed within a single lane container, which is associated with a process name and a main goal. Each process has a number of other goals that are achieved during process execution. The admission process consists of three main sub-processes, namely *Application Intake, Application Assessment* and *Application Decision*. Each of these sub-processes has one associated 'goal' and one assigned 'user role'. The start of the admission application process is depicted with the timer catch event. *Receive application* is the required activity which will create an applicant's admission file. The data object file represents the name of the file as well as the state of data in file. The next step of *Verify Application* is demonstrated as sub-process which can be repeated any number of times as marked with re-executable marker. For example, *verify certificates* and *verify personal data* are marked as 'optional activities' which can be executed or skipped considering the provided data from applicant file. While the activities like *Check application completeness* and *Create Verification report* have a sequential flow that defines ordering of these activities. Moreover, an activity with the incoming sequential flow is always required. The conditional flow on the boundary of the sub-process *Application Intake* represents that the goal *Application Verified* will only be reached once the verification of the application is completed. The sub-process *Application Assessment* will start only if the 'goal' *Application Verified* has been achieved. In the review application step, the applicant file is reviewed considering the admission requirement. The admission requirement that is set by the institute is represented as 'business rule' data item. Once the application is reviewed, the activities that belong to *Application Decision* are performed. *Discussion for Decision* is a 'collaborative sub-process' which shows the interaction among user activities. All the activities inside the

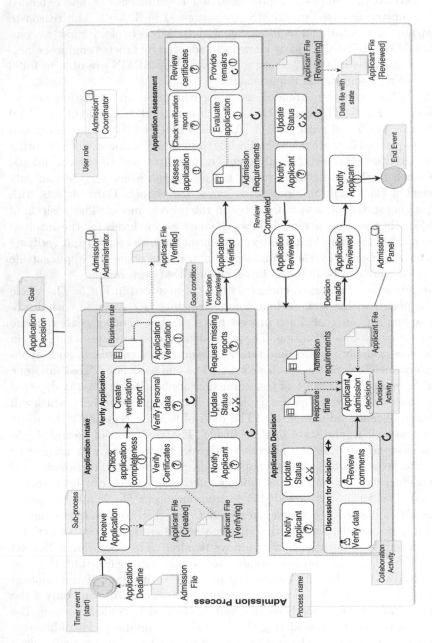

Fig. 5. Process model of admission process [5].

collaborative sub-process are dependent on each other. The final 'decision activity' takes the input from the applicant file, collaborative sub-process, business rules and finally provides the final decision. Once the decision has been made, the application decision goal and main goal of the process has been achieved and the applicant is notified.

As compared to the admission process model presented in Figs. 3 and 4, the admission model that fulfills the representational requirements offers a number of advantages.

Expressive Process Model: As compared to CMMN, the process model provided in Fig. 5 has a well-defined process start and end event. Moreover, the modeling constructs to show the required, optional, decision and collaborative tasks makes the process model easy to read and communicate.

Ability to Model (un)Structured Process: The process model shown in Fig. 5 represents the structured and unstructured process parts. Sequential flow represents the task ordering and task dependency between tasks which is a must requirement to model structured process. CMMN doesn't have the concept of sequential flow while in BPMN the use of the sequential flow inside the ad-hoc subprocess yields a semantically incorrect process model.

Ability to Model User Roles: With the user role notation, a person or group or department can be set as responsible to perform certain activities. CMMN and BPMN don't have any notation to define the user roles on the process model. However, in BPMN lanes are used for this purpose.

Ability to Model Data Access Level: The data access level is defined based on data object position on the process model. A data object that is defined inside the subprocess belongs to the assigned user only, while, the data object outside any subprocess is accessible by all the involved users of a process.

Ability to Model Related Business Rules: With BPMN and CMMN, it is feasible to represent business rule related activities either by a business rule task or planning table. However, in order to show the effect of business rules on process control flow, an extended modeling construct is used in Fig. 5.

Ability to Model Collaborative Activities: The process model provided in Fig. 5 shows the collaboration among the activities. The collaboration among activities presents that the activities are dependent on each other for their execution.

7 Validation

The validation of proposed representational requirements and their demonstration with extended BPMN constructs were performed with three experienced business process modeling practitioners. Each of these practitioners has considerable working experience with the BPMN process modeling language. Semi-structured qualitative interviews were conducted with each participant in separate sessions that lasted from 60 to 90 min.

The suggested representational requirements and their demonstration with BPMN extended constructs were mainly validated for their usefulness, ease of understanding and correctness. The result of validations is provided as follows:

Usefulness: The concepts of required, optional, collaborative sub-process, goal and decision activity are regarded as very useful for modeling unstructured business processes. However, the concept business rule is termed as unnecessary because business rules are often extensive and are difficult to be included in process model. Apart from business rules, the respondents found the concepts of data specification very powerful. According to one of the respondents, the demonstration of data specification in Fig. 5 is very intuitive as compared to technical specification of BPMN.

Ease of Understanding: The suggested representational requirements are easy to understand and yield flexibility for modeling UBS. However, the demonstration of representational requirements in Fig. 5 is indicated as difficult to read when compared to BPMN process model (see Fig. 3) and easy to read when compared to CMMN process model (Fig. 4).

Correctness: Some of the comments regarding similarities of BPMN with suggested concepts as requirements were highlighted. According to one of the respondents, the concept of optional task can be achieved by employing the BPMN gateway. But he also acknowledges the involved complexity of modeling an optional task with gateway (requiring three constructs) as compared to using a simple optional task. Moreover, the concept of undo and compensation event of BPMN is found to be similar. Another respondent suggested to keep one concept for required and optional as if some task is not required then it would be optional. However, other respondents find the separate concepts of required and optional very useful as it will bring clarity to the process model.

Overall it is found that representational requirements and a set of extended BPMN constructs are able to model USB without incorporating unnecessary details and complexity while representing the needed run-time flexibility.

8   Conclusion

Unlike structured business process, UBP are goal-oriented, data dependent, emergent, and demand run-time flexibility. Business Process Management (BPM) and Case Management (CM) as a process support paradigm are compared in order to assess their support for UBP. The results of the comparison suggest that BPM provide no flexibility for UBPm however, it assures the conformance to business rules and standards. CM, in contrast, enables the activities specification and task collaboration at run-time, however, it does not explicitly define the users. From the modeling perspective, taking the unique nature of UBP into consideration, a number of modeling limitations of BPMN and CMMN are identified. For instance, BPMN introduces task dependency in process execution whereas CMMN is unable to model user roles/task assignments in process modeling. Although BPMN provides a number of useful constructs (e.g. ad-hoc sub-processes, re-execute task) for modeling UBP. But use of various modeling constructs results into a very complex process model, which is difficult to communicate to business people along with its semantic content. On the other hand, the expressibility of CMMN modeling constructs is found to be insufficient for process modeling.

The main contribution of this paper is to derive explicit requirements for management and modeling that must be supported by a process support paradigm and a modeling language to optimally manage UBP. The modeling requirements of UBP are demonstrated by defining an extension to BPMN. We do not claim that this extension is the only or the best notations possible, but it does show that more adequate modeling notations for UBP are feasible.

Since a structured business process often consists of unstructured activities and vice versa, the future work of this study aims to seek or develop a comprehensive modeling language along with a support paradigm that is able to fulfill the requirements of structured and unstructured business processes without introducing unnecessary complexity and hindering the process run-time flexibility.

References

1. van der Aalst, W.M., Berens, P.: Beyond workflow management: product-driven case handling. In: Proceedings of the 2001 International ACM SIGGROUP Conference on Supporting Group Work, pp. 42–51. ACM (2001)
2. van der Aalst, W., Van Hee, K.M.: Workflow Management: Models, Methods, and Systems. The MIT Press, Cambridge (2004)
3. van der Aalst, W., Weske, M., Dolf, G.: Case handling: a new paradigm for business process support. Data Knowl. Eng. **53**(2), 129–162 (2005)
4. Allah Bukhsh, Z.: BPMN Plus: a modelling language for unstructured business processes, master thesis, University of Twente (2015). http://essay.utwente.nl/67945/
5. Allah Bukhsh, Z., van Sinderen, M., Sikkel, K., Quartel, D.: Understanding modeling requirements of unstructured business processes. In: Proceedings of the 14th International Joint Conference on e-Business and Telecommunications - Volume 4: ICE-B (ICETE 2017), pp. 17–27. INSTICC, SciTePress (2017)
6. Bizagi: Bizagi studio (2015). Software. http://www.bizagi.com/en/bpm-suite/bpm-products/studio
7. Cardoso, E., Labunets, K., Dalpiaz, F., Mylopoulos, J., Giorgini, P.: Modeling structured and unstructured processes: an empirical evaluation. In: Comyn-Wattiau, I., Tanaka, K., Song, I.-Y., Yamamoto, S., Saeki, M. (eds.) ER 2016. LNCS, vol. 9974, pp. 347–361. Springer, Cham (2016). https://doi.org/10.1007/978-3-319-46397-1_27
8. Chiao, C.M., Künzle, V., Reichert, M.: Enhancing the case handling paradigm to support object-aware processes. In: Proceedings of the 3rd International Symposium on Data-Driven Process Discovery and Analysis (SIMPDA 2013). CEUR Workshop Proceedings, CEUR-WS.org (2013)
9. Di Ciccio, C., Marrella, A., Russo, A.: Knowledge-intensive processes: characteristics, requirements, and analysis of contemporary approaches. J. Data Semant. **4**(1), 29–57 (2015)

10. Dumas, M., García-Bañuelos, L., Polyvyanyy, A.: Unraveling unstructured process models. In: Mendling, J., Weidlich, M., Weske, M. (eds.) BPMN 2010. LNBIP, vol. 67, pp. 1–7. Springer, Heidelberg (2010). https://doi.org/10.1007/978-3-642-16298-5_1
11. Eshuis, R., Kumar, A.: Converting unstructured into semi-structured process models. Data Knowl. Eng. **101**, 43–61 (2016)
12. Grudzińska-Kuna, A.: Supporting knowledge workers: case manangement model and notation (CMMN). Inf. Syst. Manag. **2**(1), 3–11 (2013)
13. Hauder, M., Munch, D., Michel, F., Utz, A., Matthes, F.: Examining adaptive case management to support processes for enterprise architecture management. In: IEEE 18th International Enterprise Distributed Object Computing Conference Workshops and Demonstrations (EDOCW), pp. 23–32. IEEE (2014)
14. Hinkelmann, K.: Business process flexibility and decision-aware modeling—the knowledge work designer. In: Karagiannis, D., Mayr, H., Mylopoulos, J. (eds.) Domain-Specific Conceptual Modeling, pp. 397–414. Springer, Cham (2016). https://doi.org/10.1007/978-3-319-39417-6_18
15. Kemsley, S.: The changing nature of work: from structured to unstructured, from controlled to social. In: Rinderle-Ma, S., Toumani, F., Wolf, K. (eds.) BPM 2011. LNCS, vol. 6896, p. 2. Springer, Heidelberg (2011). https://doi.org/10.1007/978-3-642-23059-2_2
16. Kitson, N., Ravisanskar, R., Soudamini, R.N.: Case management - managing chaos: unstructured processes and dynamic BPM (2012). Capgemini Whitepaper. www.capgemini.com/bpm-trends
17. Marin, M., Hull, R., Vaculín, R.: Data centric BPM and the emerging case management standard: a short survey. In: La Rosa, M., Soffer, P. (eds.) BPM 2012. LNBIP, vol. 132, pp. 24–30. Springer, Heidelberg (2013). https://doi.org/10.1007/978-3-642-36285-9_4
18. Mccready, S.: There is more Than One Kind of Workflow Software. Computerworld - COWO (1992)
19. Miles, D.: Case management and smart process applications. Technical report, Association for Information and Image Management (AIIM) (2014)
20. Mundbrod, N., Kolb, J., Reichert, M.: Towards a system support of collaborative knowledge work. In: La Rosa, M., Soffer, P. (eds.) BPM 2012. LNBIP, vol. 132, pp. 31–42. Springer, Heidelberg (2013). https://doi.org/10.1007/978-3-642-36285-9_5
21. OMG^{TM}: Business process and model notation (2011). http://www.omg.org/spec/BPMN/2.0
22. OMG^{TM}: Case management model and notation (CMMN) (2014). www.omg.org/spec/CMMN/
23. Penker, M., Eriksson, H.E.: Business Modeling with UML: Business Patterns at Work. John Wiluv & Sum 220 M. Godowski and D. Czyrnek/Requirement Management in Practice (2000)
24. Rosenfeld, A.: BPM: structured vs. unstructured. BPTrends, September 2011. http://bit.ly/1I6Ev3W
25. Rychkova, I., Nurcan, S.: The old therapy for the new problem: declarative configurable process specifications for the adaptive case management support. In: zur Muehlen, M., Su, J. (eds.) BPM 2010. LNBIP, vol. 66, pp. 420–432. Springer, Heidelberg (2011). https://doi.org/10.1007/978-3-642-20511-8_39
26. Sinur, J., Hill, J.B.: Magic quadrant for business process management suites. Gartner RAS Core research note, pp. 1–24 (2010)
27. Swenson, K.D.: Cognoscenti (2014). Open Source Software. https://code.google.com/p/cognoscenti/

28. Swenson, K.D.: Cognoscenti open source software for experimentation on adaptive case management approaches. In: IEEE 18th International Enterprise Distributed Object Computing Conference Workshops and Demonstrations (EDOCW), pp. 402–405. IEEE (2014)
29. Swenson, K.D., Palmer, N., Silver, B.: Taming the Unpredictable: Real World Adaptive Case Management: Case Studies and Practical Guidance. Future Strategies Inc., New York (2011)
30. Weber, B., Mutschler, B., Reichert, M.: Investigating the effort of using business process management technology: results from a controlled experiment. Sci. Comput. Program. **75**(5), 292–310 (2010)
31. White, M.: Case management: Combining knowledge with process. BPTrends, July 2009

Optical MIMO Transmission Focusing on Photonic Lanterns and Optical Couplers

Andreas Ahrens[(✉)], André Sandmann, and Steffen Lochmann

Department of Electrical Engineering and Computer Science,
Communications Signal Processing Group, Hochschule Wismar,
University of Applied Sciences: Technology, Business and Design,
Philipp-Müller-Straße 14, 23966 Wismar, Germany
{andreas.ahrens,andre.sandmann,steffen.lochmann}@hs-wismar.de
http://www.hs-wismar.de

Abstract. The exploitation of the spatial domain with the concept of multiple-input multiple-output (MIMO) is a promising approach to further improve the cost efficiency in fiber-optic communications. Historically, the first optical MIMO systems utilized multi-mode couplers for the purpose of mode multiplexing (MUX) and demultiplexing (DEMUX). However, their high insertion losses and asymmetries demand for alternative components. Nowadays, next to optical couplers, photonic lanterns have become considerably more attractive offering low insertion losses and being able to excite individual modes. Therefore, they are in the focus of this contribution. A setup of 6-port photonic lanterns is evaluated by measurements and compared with other multiplexing components. The measurement results and the simulated bit-error rate performances highlight that photonic lanterns are well-suited for optical MIMO communications.

Keywords: Optical MIMO · Photonic lantern
Space division multiplexing

1 Introduction

The growing demand of bandwidth particularly driven by the developing Internet has been satisfied so far by optical fiber technologies such as dense wavelength division multiplexing, polarization division multiplexing and multi-level modulation. These technologies have now reached a state of maturity [1]. The only way to further increase the available data rate is now be seen in the area of spatial multiplexing [2], which is well-established in wireless communications [3]. Nowadays several novel techniques such as mode group division multiplexing or multiple-input multiple-output (MIMO) are in the focus of interest [4]. Among these techniques, the concept of MIMO transmission over multi-mode fibers has

© Springer Nature Switzerland AG 2019
M. S. Obaidat and E. Cabello (Eds.): ICETE 2017, CCIS 990, pp. 104–122, 2019.
https://doi.org/10.1007/978-3-030-11039-0_6

attracted increasing interest in the optical fiber transmission community, targeting at increased fiber capacity [4–6]. The fiber capacity of an multi-mode fiber is limited by the modal dispersion compared to single-mode transmission, where no modal dispersion except for polarization exists. In theory, the optical MIMO concept is well-described [4]. However, the practical realization of the optical MIMO channel requires substantial further research regarding mode combining, mode maintenance and mode splitting [7,8]. Hence, photonic lanterns (PLs) have attracted a lot of attention in the research community [9,10]. Compared to other passive devices used for mode combining and mode splitting such as optical couplers, PLs offer the benefit of a low loss transition from the input fibers to the modes supported by the waveguide at its output which makes such devices very attractive for optical MIMO communication.

Against this background, the contribution of this paper is that based on measurements the suitability of PLs for mode combining and splitting is studied by computer simulations. The measurement results and the simulated bit-error rate performances highlight that photonic lanterns are well-suited for optical MIMO communications. In addition, other multiplexing components are studied and compared to the photonic lantern approach. Furthermore, a proof of concept is made by an end-to-end (2×2) MIMO transmission through 0.5 km of multi-mode fiber (MMF), using fusion couplers for multiplexing and demultiplexing with a gross rate of 5 Gbps.

The remaining parts of this paper are structured as follows: Sect. 2 introduces the studied optical MIMO system based on PLs and shows measured characteristics of a 6-port PL. Based on these characteristics in Sect. 3 a corresponding electrical MIMO channel model is derived. The block-oriented and SVD-based broadband MIMO system is described in Sect. 4. The associated performance results are presented and interpreted in Sect. 5. Section 6 shows an end-to end (2×2) MIMO transmission over 0.5 km multi-mode fiber. Finally, Sect. 7 provides the concluding remarks.

2 Physical Characteristics of an Optical MIMO Transmission

One approach to form an optical MIMO system is to transmit multiple data signals on different spatial modes through a few-mode fiber (FMF) or MMF. In this work, photonic lanterns are studied in order to transfer the binary information carried on the LP_{01} mode in n_T single-mode fibers (SMFs) to discrete modes in a FMF and vice versa. The physical transmission model is depicted in Fig. 1. The FMF carries n_M modes depending on the geometric as well as the physical structure of the fiber and the operating wavelength. Subsequent to the transmission through a FMF of length ℓ, the modes are demultiplexed to n_R SMFs with an inversely arranged PL.

In theory, for transitioning the incident modes of the SMF to the respective modes carried in the few mode fiber with low loss the condition $n_T = n_M = n_R$ needs to be respected [11]. However, measurements of the transfer characteristic

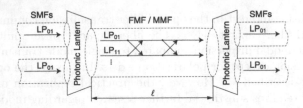

Fig. 1. Multi-mode MIMO transmission model using photonic lanterns for mode combining and splitting (Source [9]).

of the fusion type PL with 6-ports shows quite a noticeable insertion loss and slight asymmetries between the different SMF inputs, see Table 1. Still, these asymmetries are relatively small when comparing to the insertion loss differences of an optical MIMO system based on offset SMF to MMF splices and fusion couplers as shown in the same table [12]. Contrary to expectations, the photonic integrated circuit (PIC) type 6-port PL shows the best results with respect to the insertion loss. Extending a fusion coupler based system to 6-ports requires the concatenation of multiple 2-port systems which is accompanied by a significant insertion loss increase.

Table 1. Insertion loss measurements when launching from different SMF inputs through a fusion type and photonic integrated circuit (PIC) type 6-port photonic lantern compared to a 2-port fusion coupler based system (Source [9]).

SMF input number	1	2	3	4	5	6
Fusion type PL insert. loss [dB]	6.7	6.7	4.2	4.1	7.0	4.1
PIC type PL insert. loss [dB]	1.7	2.2	1.5	2.2	2.0	1.7
Fusion coupler insert. loss [dB]	0.1	8.1	–	–	–	–

Considering the modal behavior, under ideal conditions the PL transfers the signals from each SMF to a discrete mode in the FMF, see Fig. 2. In contrast, three spatial intensity patterns measured at the output of the 6-port PL, compare Fig. 3, show that a real PL excites a combination of modes which are superimposed in the FMF, e.g. the LP_{01} and LP_{11} modes. This can be interpreted as cross-talk. In addition to the cross-talk introduced by the PLs, mode mixing during the transmission through the FMF occurs due to micro bends etc. The idea is to apply MIMO signal processing in order to remove the cross-talk. For this purpose, the transmission relations are described in an electrical system model.

In addition to the above discussed photonic lanterns and fusion couplers, other components can be utilized for optical MIMO as well. An overview of different components, their use for optical MIMO and their advantages and disadvantages are summarized in Table 2.

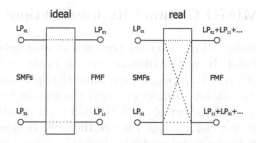

Fig. 2. Comparing the spatial mode transformation characteristic of a real PL with an ideal PL (Source [9]).

Fig. 3. Example of measured spatial intensity patterns at the output of a fusion type PL using different input SMFs at an operating wavelength of $\lambda = 1550$ nm; the dotted line represents the 30 µm fiber core diameter (Source [9]).

Table 2. Component overview for realizing different tasks in an optical MIMO transmission.

Component	Task(s)	Pros and Cons
Digital Light Processor (DLP)	Mode transformation and Mode MUX/ DEMUX	+ Freely configurable + Mode transformation and Mode MUX in a single step − Difficult mechanical alignment − Complexity − Attenuation due to the free-space transmission and masking by the micro mirror patterns
SMF to MMF splice with offset	Mode transformation	+ Simple realization + Low insertion loss + Passive component − Individual modes cannot be excited − Additional component for mode MUX required (e.g. fusion coupler)
Specific MMF fusion coupler	Mode MUX/DEMUX	+ Simple realization + Passive component − High insertion loss specifically for high order MIMO systems − Low mode selectivity for high order modes
Fixed mask/spatial filter	Mode transformation	+ Passive component − Not reconfigurable − Attenuation due to masking
Photonic lantern (PL)	Mode transformation and Mode MUX/DEMUX	+ Excitation of individual modes is possible + Low insertion loss + Mode transformation and Mode MUX in a single step + Passive component − Specific input phase required to excite individual modes − Complex manufacturing

3   Electrical MIMO Channel Representation

The electrical baseband MIMO channel representation employing PLs and a FMF is shown in Fig. 4. Here, the transmitter-side photonic lantern is fed by the signals $a_\mu(t)$, with $\mu = 1, \ldots, n_T$, representing the optical signals carried on the LP_{01} mode in the SMFs. Correspondingly, the signals $b_\beta(t)$ represent the guided spatial modes at the input of the FMF and $c_\kappa(t)$ are the resulting FMF output signals, where $\beta, \kappa = 1, \ldots, n_M$. Finally, the receiver-side PL transfers the modes of the FMF to fundamental modes in the SMFs, represented by the signals $d_\nu(t)$, with $\nu = 1, \ldots, n_R$. For simplification purposes and in order to create the prerequisites for a near lossless transmission the number of input SMFs n_T, the number of guided modes in the FMF n_M and the number of output SMFs n_R are assumed to be identically. In this work, these numbers are chosen to be $n_T = n_M = n_R = 2$ and therefore only the LP_{01} and LP_{11} modes can propagate implying a V-number in range $2.405 < V < 3.832$ when transmitting through a step-index profiled FMF. The degenerate modes of LP_{11}, i.e. LP_{11a} and LP_{11b}, are summarized.

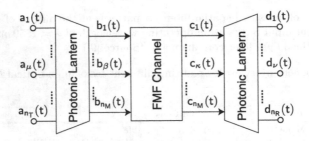

Fig. 4. Electrical MIMO channel model (Source [9]).

3.1   FMF Channel

The transmission properties of the FMF are represented by the model depicted in Fig. 5. In time-domain, the system characteristics of the FMF channel are given as follows [9]

$$
\begin{aligned}
c_1(t) &= k_{11}^{(CH)}\, b_1(t) & + k_{12}^{(CH)}\, b_2(t - \Delta\tau/2) \\
c_2(t) &= k_{21}^{(CH)}\, b_1(t - \Delta\tau/2) + k_{22}^{(CH)}\, b_2(t - \Delta\tau),
\end{aligned}
\tag{1}
$$

describing the mode-coupling of the underlying channel. Herein, the parameter $\Delta\tau$ describes the differential mode delay between the fundamental mode LP_{01} and the mode LP_{11}, which is identified to be $\Delta\tau = 200$ ps for the considered fiber length of $\ell = 2$ km. The effect of the chromatic dispersion is not analyzed in this contribution since a zero chromatic dispersion wavelength is assumed

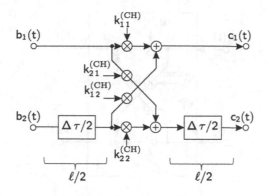

Fig. 5. Underlying FMF channel model of length ℓ designed for two mode propagation ($n_M = 2$) (Source [9]).

which is in the region of 1300 nm. However, for different wavelengths chromatic dispersion can be taken into account by a simple convolution with a Gaussian function. The optical field coupling coefficients $k_{\kappa\beta}^{(CH)}$ describe the coupling from the mode LP_{01} to the mode LP_{11}, from the mode LP_{11} to the mode LP_{01} and so forth. Since a lossless transmission through the FMF is assumed, the coupling coefficients have to fulfill the following condition [9]

$$\sum_{\kappa=1}^{n_M} \left| k_{\kappa\beta}^{(CH)} \right|^2 = 1 \quad \forall \quad \beta. \tag{2}$$

3.2 Photonic Lanterns

Hereinafter, the mode combining and mode splitting process conducted by the photonic lanterns is studied. Considering a (2×2) PL the corresponding electrical representation for the transmitter-side PL is shown in Fig. 6. At the transmitter-side the mapping of the incident LP_{01} modes, represented by the signals $a_\mu(t)$, by the PL can be described with the corresponding coupling matrix [9]

$$\mathbf{K}^{(TX)} = \begin{bmatrix} k_{11}^{(PL,\,TX)} & \cdots & k_{1\,n_T}^{(PL,\,TX)} \\ \vdots & \ddots & \vdots \\ k_{n_M\,1}^{(PL,\,TX)} & \cdots & k_{n_M\,n_T}^{(PL,\,TX)} \end{bmatrix}, \tag{3}$$

with $k_{\beta\mu}^{(PL,\,TX)}$ denoting the transmitter-side coupling coefficients. Having an ideal PL, compare Fig. 2, the coupling matrix is given by an identity matrix considering $n_M = n_T$. Since the receiver-side PL is inversely arranged and is assumed to have identical properties to the transmitter-side PL, the corresponding coupling matrix is the transpose denoted by $(\cdot)^T$ of the transmitter-side coupling matrix, i.e. $\mathbf{K}^{(RX)} = \left(\mathbf{K}^{(TX)} \right)^T$. Here, it is worth noting that under

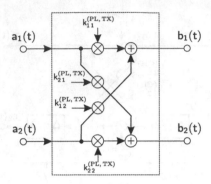

Fig. 6. Electrical system model of the transmitter-side PL ($n_T = n_M = 2$) (Source [9]).

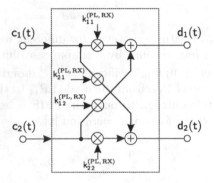

Fig. 7. Electrical system model of the receiver-side PL ($n_M = n_R = 2$) (Source [9]).

practical assumptions the output LP_{01} modes of the receiver-side PL appear as superpositions of the LP_{01} and LP_{11} modes of the FMF as highlighted in Fig. 2. Having a non-ideal PL, the corresponding electrical system model is shown in Fig. 7 for the receiver-side PL. Here, $k_{\nu\kappa}^{(\text{PL, RX})}$ denotes the receiver-side coupling coefficients, being summarized in the coupling matrix $\mathbf{K}^{(\text{RX})}$. Based on the short fiber length, the PL is assumed to be flat in the considered frequency band. Since no power-loss is assumed, the transmitter-side PL coupling coefficients are required to comply to [9]

$$\sum_{\beta=1}^{n_M} \left| k_{\beta\mu}^{(\text{PL, TX})} \right|^2 = 1 \quad \text{for} \quad \mu = 1, \ldots, n_T \tag{4}$$

and the receiver-side PL coupling coefficients need to fulfill the following condition [9]

$$\sum_{\nu=1}^{n_R} \left| k_{\nu\kappa}^{(\text{PL, RX})} \right|^2 = 1 \quad \text{for} \quad \kappa = 1, \ldots, n_M. \tag{5}$$

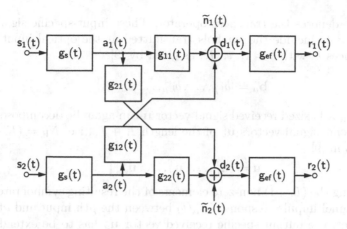

Fig. 8. Electrical (2×2) MIMO transmission model.

Considering the overall MIMO channel model, compare Fig. 4, as a black box with two in- and outputs the transfer characteristic can be described by the corresponding MIMO impulse responses $g_{\nu\mu}(t)$. Including pulse shaping and receive filtering functionality the overall (2×2) MIMO transmission model is depicted in Fig. 8. Rectangular pulses of frequency $f_T = 1/T_s$ are used for pulse shaping and receive filtering, i. e. $g_s(t)$ and $g_{ef}(t)$ and hence the overall impulse responses $h_{\nu\mu}(t)$ are formed as follows [9]

$$h_{\nu\mu}(t) = g_s(t) * g_{\nu\mu}(t) * g_{ef}(t), \qquad (6)$$

where $*$ denotes the convolution operator. An additional component to be considered is the additive white Gaussian noise (AWGN) denoted by the term $\tilde{n}_\nu(t)$. The sampled overall impulse responses are used for the broadband MIMO system model, being described in the next section.

4   Broadband MIMO System Description

Considering a frequency-selective MIMO link, composed of n_T optical inputs and n_R optical outputs, the resulting electrical discrete-time block-oriented system is modeled referring to [9,13,14] as follows

$$\mathbf{u} = \mathbf{H} \cdot \mathbf{b} + \mathbf{n}. \qquad (7)$$

Vector $\mathbf{b}$ of size $(N_T \times 1)$ contains the input symbols transmitted over n_T optical inputs in K consecutive time slots, i. e. $N_T = K\,n_T$. This vector can be decomposed into n_T input-specific signal vectors $\mathbf{b}_\mu$ according to [9]

$$\mathbf{b} = \left[\mathbf{b}_1^T, \ldots, \mathbf{b}_\mu^T, \ldots, \mathbf{b}_{n_T}^T\right]^T, \qquad (8)$$

where $(\cdot)^\mathrm{T}$ denotes the transpose operator. These input-specific signal vectors of size $(K \times 1)$ include the symbols transmitted at the optical input μ for all time instances k, with $k = 1, \ldots, K$, as given by [9]

$$\mathbf{b}_\mu = [b_{1\,\mu}, \ldots, b_{k\,\mu}, \ldots, b_{K\,\mu}]^\mathrm{T}. \tag{9}$$

The $(N_\mathrm{R} \times 1)$ sized received signal vector $\mathbf{u}$ can again be decomposed into n_R output-specific signal vectors $\mathbf{u}_\nu$ of the length $K + L_\mathrm{c}$, i.e. $N_\mathrm{R} = (K + L_\mathrm{c})\,n_\mathrm{R}$, and results in [9]

$$\mathbf{u} = [\mathbf{u}_1^\mathrm{T}, \ldots, \mathbf{u}_\nu^\mathrm{T}, \ldots, \mathbf{u}_{n_\mathrm{R}}^\mathrm{T}]^\mathrm{T}. \tag{10}$$

By taking the $(L_\mathrm{c}+1)$ non-zero elements of the resulting symbol rate sampled overall channel impulse response $h_{\nu\,\mu}(t)$ between the μth input and νth output into account, the output-specific received vector $\mathbf{u}_\nu$ has to be extended by L_c elements, compared to the transmitted input-specific signal vector $\mathbf{b}_\mu$ defined in (9). The $((K + L_\mathrm{c}) \times 1)$ signal vector $\mathbf{u}_\nu$ received by the optical output ν can be constructed, including the extension through the multi-path propagation, as follows [9]

$$\mathbf{u}_\nu = [u_{1\,\nu}, u_{2\,\nu}, \ldots, u_{(K+L_\mathrm{c})\,\nu}]^\mathrm{T}. \tag{11}$$

Correspondingly, the $(N_\mathrm{R} \times 1)$ sized vector $\mathbf{n}$ denotes the AWGN after receive filtering with $g_{\mathrm{ef}}(t)$ and sampling. Finally, the $(N_\mathrm{R} \times N_\mathrm{T})$ sized system matrix $\mathbf{H}$ of the block-oriented system model describes the symbol rate sampled overall MIMO channel $h_{\nu\,\mu}(t)$ consisting of the frequency-flat transmitter- and receiver-side PL models as well as the frequency-selective FMF model, the transmit and receive filter. The channel matrix $\mathbf{H}$ is composed as follows [9]

$$\mathbf{H} = \mathbf{H}^{(\mathrm{RX})} \cdot \mathbf{H}^{(\mathrm{CH})} \cdot \mathbf{H}^{(\mathrm{TX})}. \tag{12}$$

Herein, the $(n_\mathrm{M}\,(K + L_\mathrm{c}) \times n_\mathrm{M}\,K)$ sized matrix $\mathbf{H}^{(\mathrm{CH})}$ describes the frequency-selective representation of the FMF channel, compare Fig. 5, being structured as follows [9]

$$\mathbf{H}^{(\mathrm{CH})} = \begin{bmatrix} \mathbf{H}^{(\mathrm{CH})}_{1\,1} & \cdots & \mathbf{H}^{(\mathrm{CH})}_{1\,n_\mathrm{M}} \\ \vdots & \ddots & \vdots \\ \mathbf{H}^{(\mathrm{CH})}_{n_\mathrm{M}\,1} & \cdots & \mathbf{H}^{(\mathrm{CH})}_{n_\mathrm{M}\,n_\mathrm{M}} \end{bmatrix} \tag{13}$$

and consists of $n_\mathrm{M}\,n_\mathrm{M}$ single-input single-output (SISO) channel matrices $\mathbf{H}^{(\mathrm{CH})}_{\kappa\,\beta}$. Every of these matrices $\mathbf{H}^{(\mathrm{CH})}_{\kappa\,\beta}$ of the size $((K + L_\mathrm{c}) \times K)$ describes the $L_\mathrm{c} + 1$

non-zero elements of resulting symbol rate sampled impulse response of the FMF channel representation including transmit and receive filtering, resulting in [9]:

$$
\mathbf{H}_{\kappa\beta}^{(\mathrm{CH})} =
\begin{bmatrix}
h_{\kappa\beta}[0] & 0 & \cdots & 0 \\
h_{\kappa\beta}[1] & h_{\kappa\beta}[0] & \cdots & 0 \\
h_{\kappa\beta}[2] & h_{\kappa\beta}[1] & \cdots & 0 \\
\vdots & \vdots & \ddots & \vdots \\
h_{\kappa\beta}[L_{\mathrm{c}}] & h_{\kappa\beta}[L_{\mathrm{c}}-1] & \cdots & \\
0 & h_{\kappa\beta}[L_{\mathrm{c}}] & \cdots & \\
\vdots & \vdots & \ddots & \vdots \\
0 & 0 & \cdots & h_{\kappa\beta}[L_{\mathrm{c}}]
\end{bmatrix}.
\tag{14}
$$

Since the transmitter-side PL is assumed to be frequency-flat it can be described by a $((n_{\mathrm{M}}\,K) \times (n_{\mathrm{T}}\,K))$ pre-processing matrix [9]

$$
\mathbf{H}^{(\mathrm{TX})} = \mathbf{K}^{(\mathrm{TX})} \otimes \mathbf{I}_K,
\tag{15}
$$

where $\otimes$ denotes the Kronecker product, $\mathbf{K}^{(\mathrm{TX})}$ is the transmitter-side PL coupling matrix and $\mathbf{I}_K$ defines a $(K \times K)$ identity matrix. Matrix $\mathbf{H}^{(\mathrm{TX})}$ is composed of concatenated $(K \times K)$ sized diagonal matrices weighted by the corresponding coupling factors $k_{\beta\mu}^{(\mathrm{PL,\,TX})}$. Correspondingly the receiver-side PL can be described by a $(n_{\mathrm{R}}\,(K + L_{\mathrm{c}}) \times n_{\mathrm{M}}\,(K + L_{\mathrm{c}}))$ post-processing matrix [9]

$$
\mathbf{H}^{(\mathrm{RX})} = \mathbf{K}^{(\mathrm{RX})} \otimes \mathbf{I}_{K+L_{\mathrm{c}}},
\tag{16}
$$

with $\mathbf{K}^{(\mathrm{RX})}$ denoting the receiver-side PL coupling matrix. The interference, which is introduced by the off-diagonal elements of the channel matrix $\mathbf{H}$, requires appropriate signal processing strategies.

The MIMO block diagram of the transmission model is shown in Fig. 9. A popular technique is based on the singular-value decomposition (SVD) of the system matrix $\mathbf{H}$, which can be written as $\mathbf{H} = \mathbf{S} \cdot \mathbf{V} \cdot \mathbf{D}^{\mathrm{H}}$, where $\mathbf{S}$ and $\mathbf{D}^{\mathrm{H}}$ are unitary matrices and $\mathbf{V}$ is a real-valued diagonal matrix of the positive square roots of the eigenvalues of the matrix $\mathbf{H}^{\mathrm{H}}\,\mathbf{H}$ sorted in descending order. In order to remove the interferences pre-processed symbols $\mathbf{b} = \mathbf{D} \cdot \mathbf{c}$ are transmitted, with vector $\mathbf{c}$ denoting the unprocessed transmit symbols. In turn, the receiver multiplies the received vector $\mathbf{u}$ by the matrix $\mathbf{S}^{\mathrm{H}}$. Thereby, neither the transmit power nor the noise power is enhanced. The overall transmission relationship is defined as [9]

$$
\mathbf{y} = \mathbf{S}^{\mathrm{H}}\,(\mathbf{H} \cdot \mathbf{D} \cdot \mathbf{c} + \mathbf{n}) = \mathbf{V} \cdot \mathbf{c} + \mathbf{w}.
\tag{17}
$$

As a consequence of the processing in (17), the channel matrix $\mathbf{H}$ is transformed into independent, non-interfering layers having unequal gains [13, 14]. In MIMO communication, singular-value decomposition (SVD) has been established as an efficient concept to compensate the interferences between the different data streams transmitted over a dispersive channel: SVD is able to transfer the whole system into independent, non-interfering layers exhibiting unequal gains per layer as highlighted in Fig. 10, where as a result weighted AWGN channels appear.

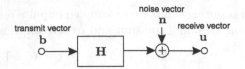

Fig. 9. Transmission system model (Source [9]).

Analyzing the considered (2×2) MIMO system, the data symbols at the time k, i.e. c_{1k} and c_{2k} are weighted by the positive square roots of the eigenvalues of the matrix $\mathbf{H}^H \mathbf{H}$, i.e. $\sqrt{\xi_{1k}}$ and $\sqrt{\xi_{2k}}$. The terms w_{1k} and w_{2k} denote the noise subsequent to the SVD post-processing. It is worth noting that the number of readily separable layers is limited by $\min(n_T, n_R)$. Therefore, in this work the maximum number of layers is given by $L = 2$. Based on this non-interfering layer-specific transmission model the bit-error rate performance can be calculated [15].

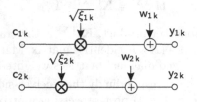

Fig. 10. SVD-based layer-specific transmission model (Source [9]).

5   Performance Results

In this section the bit-error rate (BER) performance of the beforehand introduced photonic lantern model is evaluated. Additionally, an optical MIMO system, using multi-mode fusion couplers as spatial MUX devices, is assessed.

5.1   Photonic Lantern

In this section the BER quality, transmitting through the (2×2) MIMO channel employing PLs for mode combining and splitting, is studied using fixed transmission modes with a spectral efficiency of 4 bit/s/Hz. The analyzed quadrature amplitude modulation (QAM) constellations are listed in Table 3. This bit allocation approach is combined with a power allocation method that equalizes the signal-to-noise ratios on all layers and time instances k in a data block for optimizing the BER performance [16].

In order to compare the performance of ideal PLs to real PLs different cross-talk parameters have been considered relating to the above described electrical MIMO channel model. Since both PLs are assumed to have identical properties in both directions and are also assumed to be symmetric the PL cross-talk parameter is defined as follows [9]

Table 3. Transmission modes (Source [9]).

Spectral efficiency	Layer 1	Layer 2
4 bit/s/Hz	16	0
4 bit/s/Hz	4	4

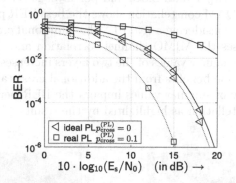

Fig. 11. BER performance when transmitting with the (16,0) QAM constellation (dotted lines) and the (4,4) QAM constellation (solid lines) assuming 10% FMF cross-talk, i.e. $p_{\mathrm{cross}}^{(\mathrm{CH})} = 0.1$, at a symbol frequency of $f_{\mathrm{T}} = 1\,\mathrm{GHz}$ (Source [9]).

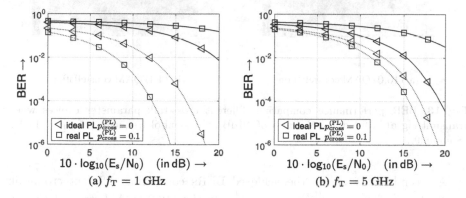

(a) $f_{\mathrm{T}} = 1\,\mathrm{GHz}$ (b) $f_{\mathrm{T}} = 5\,\mathrm{GHz}$

Fig. 12. BER performance comparing different symbol rates f_{T} when transmitting with the (16,0) QAM constellation (dotted lines) and the (4,4) QAM constellation (solid lines) assuming 30% FMF cross-talk, i.e. $p_{\mathrm{cross}}^{(\mathrm{CH})} = 0.3$ (Source [9]).

$$
\begin{aligned}
p_{\mathrm{cross}}^{(\mathrm{PL})} &= \left| k_{1\,2}^{(\mathrm{PL,TX})} \right|^2 = \left| k_{2\,1}^{(\mathrm{PL,TX})} \right|^2 \\
&= \left| k_{1\,2}^{(\mathrm{PL,RX})} \right|^2 = \left| k_{2\,1}^{(\mathrm{PL,RX})} \right|^2 ,
\end{aligned}
\tag{18}
$$

describing the electrical power transfer. The few-mode fiber channel cross-talk is assumed to be symmetric as well as defined by [9]

$$p_{\text{cross}}^{(\text{CH})} = \left| k_{12}^{(\text{CH})} \right|^2 = \left| k_{21}^{(\text{CH})} \right|^2. \tag{19}$$

The calculated BER results as a function of the signal energy to noise power spectral density E_s/N_0 are depicted in Figs. 11 and 12 for different FMF cross-talk parameter choices, i.e. $p_{\text{cross}}^{(\text{CH})}$, and symbol frequencies f_T. In all simulations the number of symbols per data block and per layer is selected to be $K = 15$. Choosing the (16,0) QAM constellation shows the best BER performance results for all configurations considering a real PL. The additional cross-talk introduced by a real PL increases the MIMO channel correlation and thus the amplitude ratio comparing the singular values of the two layers increases as well. Therefore, the (16,0) QAM scheme benefits from the additional cross-talk. In contrast, the increased asymmetry of singular values impairs the BER performance choosing the (4,4) QAM constellation as highlighted by the results.

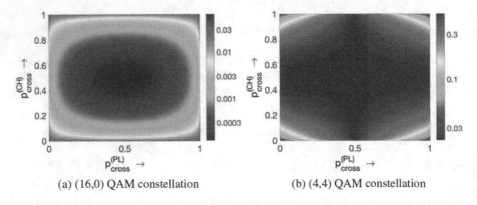

(a) (16,0) QAM constellation   (b) (4,4) QAM constellation

Fig. 13. BER performance comparing different cross-talk parameter choices when transmitting at a fixed E_s/N_0 ratio of 10 dB at a symbol frequency of $f_T = 1$ GHz (Source [9]).

A second study shows the achieved BERs comparing different cross-talk parameter choices, i.e. $p_{\text{cross}}^{(\text{CH})}$ and $p_{\text{cross}}^{(\text{PL})}$, for the (16,0) QAM constellation in Fig. 13(a) and for the (4,4) QAM scheme in Fig. 13(b) at a fixed E_s/N_0 ratio of 10 dB. This study confirms that the (16,0) QAM constellation benefits from high cross-talk values whereas the (4,4) QAM constellation shows a contrary behavior. It should be noted that 0.5 for $p_{\text{cross}}^{(\text{CH})}$ as well as for $p_{\text{cross}}^{(\text{PL})}$ is the value where the most cross-talk is introduced into the system. All in all, the best BER results are achieved with the (16,0) QAM constellation in combination with high cross-talk values when considering the studied simulation environment.

5.2   Multi-mode Fusion Coupler

In addition to the photonic lantern, an optical MIMO setup employing multi-mode fusion couplers is studied for comparison. The system properties of this setup are measured in form of their specific impulse responses with the setup depicted in the Fig. 14. Here, a picosecond laser unit is chosen for generating the input pulse, exhibiting a full width at half maximum of approximately 25 ps. This input pulse is used to measure separately the different SISO channels within the MIMO system. Since the used picosecond laser unit does not guarantee a fully flat frequency spectrum in the region of interest, the captured signals have to be deconvolved [16]. The estimated impulse responses $g_{\nu\,\mu}(t)$ with the input index $\mu = 1, \ldots, n_{\mathrm{T}}$ and the output index $\nu = 1, \ldots, n_{\mathrm{R}}$ are depicted in Fig. 15 measured at 1326 nm as well as at 1576 nm operating wavelength. It should be noted that the measured impulse responses are real valued since the testbed has currently the limitation that the phase information cannot be extracted. The measured impulse responses at 1576 nm clearly show the effect of chromatic dispersion indicated by the pulse broadening, being a typical characteristic at this operating wavelength in a standard fiber. On the other hand at 1326 nm the modal structure, characterized by the short pulses at different time instances which represent the different delays of each mode group, is clearly visible. Since the chromatic dispersion is nearly zero a pulse broadening is almost non-existent at this wavelength.

Rectangular transmit and receive filtering with the symbol frequency of $f_{\mathrm{T}} = 620\,\mathrm{MHz}$ is applied to the measured impulse responses at 1576 nm and subsequently they are sampled at the same rate. At this symbol rate the discrete channel impulse responses with coefficients $h_{\nu\,\mu}[k]$ are composed of three non-zero real valued channel taps each. Higher rates would produce more inter-symbol interferences, resulting in a higher number of non-zero channel taps.

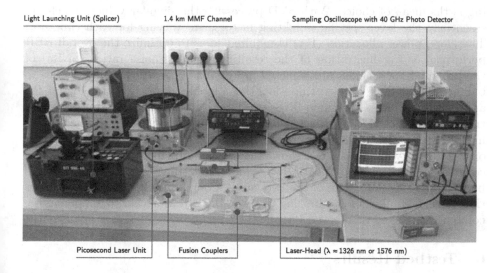

Light Launching Unit (Splicer)   1.4 km MMF Channel   Sampling Oscilloscope with 40 GHz Photo Detector

Picosecond Laser Unit   Fusion Couplers   Laser-Head ($\lambda \approx$ 1326 nm or 1576 nm)

Fig. 14. Measurement setup for determining the MIMO specific impulse responses.

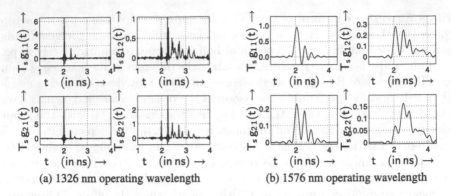

(a) 1326 nm operating wavelength   (b) 1576 nm operating wavelength

Fig. 15. Measured electrical MIMO impulse responses with respect to the pulse frequency $f_T = 1/T_s = 620\,\text{MHz}$.

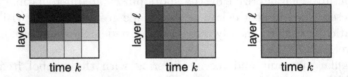

Fig. 16. Illustration of the remaining SNRs in SVD systems without applying PA (left), with layer-based PA (center) and with combined layer and time PA (right). The color black refers to high and white to low SNR values.

In order to remove the occurring interferences, again SVD based processing is the mean of choice. With SVD processing the singular values, which are essentially the layer specific weighting factors, are varying for each time-slot. Therefore, power allocation (PA) is required so as to optimize the overall BER performance. An illustration of the resulting signal-to-noise ratios (SNRs) of the proposed PA schemes are depicted in Fig. 16. The layer-specific PA tries to balance the SNR at a given time-slot, the combined layer and time-based PA approach guarantees the same SNR on all activated layers and time-slots per transmitted block [17]. The corresponding SVD-based BER results when transmitting with a spectral efficiency of 8 bit/s/Hz are depicted in Fig. 17. Activating only one layer with a 256 QAM shows the best performance as a result of a high correlation between the optical MIMO channels, leading to extreme differences between the singular values of the two layers. Comparing the PA schemes shows that PA is helpful when minimizing the overall BER. Moreover, by applying the combined layer and time-based PA, the BER performance increases significantly.

6   Testbed Results

Finally, after studying the photonic lantern model and evaluating the BER performance of a fusion coupler setup based on measured impulse responses, a real (2×2) MIMO end-to-end transmission is demonstrated over 500 m MMF with

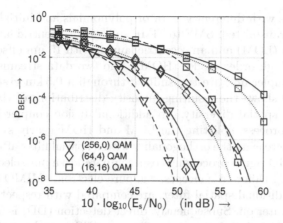

Fig. 17. BER applying SVD-based equalization with layer and time-based PA (dashed line), with layer-specific PA (dotted line) and without PA (solid line) when transmitting over the optical (2×2) MIMO channel

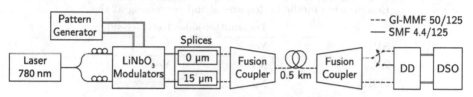

Fig. 18. MIMO testbed configuration.

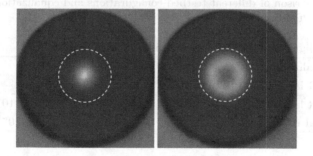

Fig. 19. Intensity distributions at the end of an MMF when launching centric $\delta = 0\,\mu m$ (left) and with an eccentricity of $\delta = 15\,\mu m$ (right); the dashed line represents the $50\,\mu m$ core size.

a gross data rate of 5 Gbit/s. The corresponding setup is depicted in Fig. 18. At the transmitter two independent intensity modulated data streams with on-off keying are generated with lithium niobate modulators and are transmitted at an operating wavelength of 780 nm. Despite the different operating wavelengths used in measurements throughout this paper, the frequency-selective characteristic of the MIMO channel still remains. Two independent $2^{15} - 1$ pseudo-random binary sequences with different generator polynomials and initialization vectors are repeatedly transmitted. SMF to MMF splices with centric launch excite the low order modes (LOM) and an eccentric launch with 15 μm offset transfers the data stream to high order modes (HOM). The two data streams are combined with a fusion coupler and are transmitted through a 0.5 km graded-index (GI) MMF. Figure 19 shows the resulting intensity distributions of the two streams, highlighting the spatial diversity. An additional fusion coupler is used for the demultiplexing process, splitting the LOM and HOM nearly symmetrically to both outputs. Increasing the orthogonality with a spatial filter after the DEMUX reduces the MIMO signal processing costs compared to a pure electronic interference removal [18]. Different concepts, e.g. pure electronic MIMO equalization or the use of an additional spatial filter, are compared with respect to their transmission quality later on. Subsequently, direct detection (DD) is applied and the data is saved at the digital storage oscilloscope (DSO) and processed offline.

Table 4. Requirements for the implementation of different equalization strategies.

Equalization method	Requires signal processing at the	
	Transmitter-side	Receiver-side
SVD	Yes	Yes
ZF	No	Yes
OSIC	No	Yes

Table 5. Comparison of different testbed configurations and equalization approaches analyzing a selected frame.

Configuration	Without spatial filter		With spatial filter	
Equalization	ZF	OSIC	ZF	OSIC
BER layer 1	$4 \cdot 10^{-3}$	$4 \cdot 10^{-3}$	0	0
BER layer 2	$73.2 \cdot 10^{-3}$	$4.3 \cdot 10^{-3}$	$6.98 \cdot 10^{-5}$	$10.46 \cdot 10^{-5}$
Total BER	$38.6 \cdot 10^{-3}$	$4.15 \cdot 10^{-3}$	$\mathbf{3.49 \cdot 10^{-5}}$	$5.23 \cdot 10^{-5}$

In the offline signal processing, a least squares channel estimation is used to obtain the current channel state information. Since our testbed does not allow signal processing at the transmitter-side, zero forcing (ZF) equalization and ordered successive interference cancellation (OSIC) is applied to counter the occurring inter-symbol and inter-channel interferences [19]. A qualitative comparison of these equalization strategies in terms of the required signal processing at the transmitter- and receiver-side is shown in Table 4.

The bit-error rate (BER) results of a selected frame for the two testbed configurations and equalizer concepts are compared in Table 5. They show that using a spatial filter in the testbed configuration greatly improves the BER performance. Furthermore, ordered SIC can significantly improve the BER over ZF equalization in the setup without spatial filter.

In Fig. 20 the BERs dependency on different transmission frames is illustrated as empirical complementary cumulative distribution functions (CCDF). This way of illustration allows a worst case assessment when considering multiple transmission frames. Both equalization approaches with spatial filter achieve BER results below the 10^{-3} forward error correction (FEC) threshold.

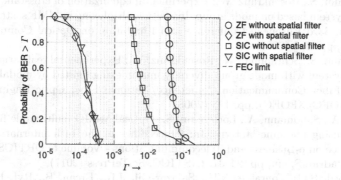

Fig. 20. Empirical CCDFs showing the BER dependency on the analyzed 38 frames.

7 Conclusions

In this work the performance of different spatial multiplexing and demultiplexing devices for fiber-optic communications have been analyzed, focusing on photonic lanterns and optical couplers. Therefore, a time-domain MIMO simulation model for a system based on photonic lanterns has been developed. It has been used for studying the effect of different cross-talk parameter settings on the overall system performance in form of the total bit-error rate. The results show that cross-talk does not necessarily impair the performance. As highlighted by the results, photonic lanterns seem to be well-suited for optical MIMO systems. As an alternative to the photonic lanterns, fusion couplers as spatial multiplex devices have been evaluated by the BER based on measured impulse responses. Finally, an end-to-end optical MIMO transmission at 780 nm with a gross data rate of 5 Gbit/s through a 0.5 km MMF channel has been demonstrated.

References

1. Winzer, P.J.: Optical networking beyond WDM. IEEE Photonics J. **4**, 647–651 (2012)
2. Richardson, D.J., Fini, J.M., Nelson, L.E.: Space division multiplexing in optical fibres. Nat. Photonics **7**, 354–362 (2013)
3. Tse, D., Viswanath, P.: Fundamentals of Wireless Communication. Cambridge University Press, New York (2005)

4. Singer, A.C., Shanbhag, N.R., Bae, H.M.: Electronic dispersion compensation - an overview of optical communications systems. IEEE Signal Process. Mag. **25**, 110–130 (2008)
5. Foschini, G.J.: Layered space-time architecture for wireless communication in a fading environment when using multi-element antennas. Bell Labs Tech. J. **1**, 41–59 (1996)
6. Winzer, P.J., Foschini, G.J.: Optical MIMO-SDM system capacities. In: Optical Fiber Communications Conference and Exhibition (OFC), pp. 1–3 (2014)
7. Schöllmann, S., Rosenkranz, W.: Experimental equalization of crosstalk in a 2×2 MIMO system based on mode group diversity multiplexing in MMF systems @ 10.7 Gb/s. In: 33rd European Conference and Ehxibition on Optical Communication (ECOC), pp. 1–2 (2007)
8. Schöllmann, S., Schrammar, N., Rosenkranz, W.: Experimental realisation of 3×3 MIMO system with mode group diversity multiplexing limited by modal noise. In: Optical Fiber Communication Conference/National Fiber Optic Engineers Conference (OFC/NFOEC), pp. 1–3 (2008)
9. Ahrens, A., Sandmann, A., Lochmann, S.: Optical MIMO multi-mode fiber transmission using photonic lanterns. In: Proceedings of the 14th International Joint Conference on e-Business and Telecommunications - Volume 5: OPTICS, (ICETE 2017), Madrid, Spain, pp. 24–31. INSTICC, SciTePress (2017)
10. Leon-Saval, S.G., Fontaine, N.K., Salazar-Gil, J.R., Ercan, B., Ryf, R., Bland-Hawthorn, J.: Mode-selective photonic lanterns for space-division multiplexing. Opt. Express **22**, 1036–1044 (2014)
11. Leon-Saval, S.G., Argyros, A., Bland-Hawthorn, J.: Photonic lanterns. Nanophotonics **2**, 429–440 (2013)
12. Sandmann, A., Götten, M., Ahrens, A., Lochmann, S.: MIMO signal processing in optical multi-mode fiber transmission using photonic lanterns. In: 11th International Conference on Mathematics in Signal Processing, Birmingham, United Kingdom (2016)
13. Raleigh, G.G., Cioffi, J.M.: Spatio-temporal coding for wireless communication. IEEE Trans. Commun. **46**, 357–366 (1998)
14. Pankow, J., Aust, S., Lochmann, S., Ahrens, A.: Modulation-mode assignment in SVD-assisted optical MIMO multimode fiber links. In: 15th International Conference on Optical Network Design and Modeling (ONDM), Bologna, Italy (2011)
15. Proakis, J.G.: Digital Communications. McGraw-Hill, Boston (2000)
16. Sandmann, A., Ahrens, A., Lochmann, S.: Zero-forcing equalisation of measured optical multimode MIMO channels. In: Obaidat, M.S., Holzinger, A., Filipe, J. (eds.) ICETE 2014. CCIS, vol. 554, pp. 115–130. Springer, Cham (2015). https://doi.org/10.1007/978-3-319-25915-4_7
17. Sandmann, A., Ahrens, A., Lochmann, S.: Evaluation of polynomial matrix SVD-based broadband MIMO equalization in an optical multi-mode testbed. In: Advances in Wireless and Optical Communications (RTUWO), Riga, Latvia, pp. 1–11 (2017)
18. Sandmann, A., Ahrens, A., Lochmann, S.: Successive interference cancellation in spatially multiplexed fiber-optic transmission. In: Advances in Wireless and Optical Communications (RTUWO), Riga, Latvia, pp. 91–95 (2017)
19. Wolniansky, P.W., Foschini, G.J., Golden, G.D., Valenzuela, R.A.: V-BLAST: an architecture for realizing very high data rates over the rich-scattering wireless channel. In: International Symposium on Signals, Systems and Electronics (ISSSE), Pisa, pp. 295–300 (1998)

BoolTest: The Fast Randomness Testing Strategy Based on Boolean Functions with Application to DES, 3-DES, MD5, MD6 and SHA-256

Marek Sýs, Dušan Klinec, Karel Kubíček, and Petr Švenda[✉]

Masaryk University, Brno, Czech Republic
{syso,ph4r05,karel.kubicek}@mail.muni.cz, svenda@fi.muni.cz

Abstract. The output of modern cryptographic primitives like pseudo-random generators and block or stream ciphers is frequently required to be indistinguishable from a truly random data. The existence of any distinguisher provides a hint about the insufficient confusion and diffusion property of an analyzed function. In addition to targeted cryptoanalysis, statistical tests included in batteries such as NIST STS, Dieharder or TestU01 are frequently used to assess the indistinguishability property. However, the tests included in these batteries are either too simple to spot the common biases (like the Monobit test) or overly complex (like the Fourier Transform test) requiring an extensive amount of data. We propose a simple, yet surprisingly powerful method called *BoolTest* for the construction of distinguishers based on an exhaustive search for boolean function(s). The *BoolTest* typically constructs distinguisher with fewer input data required and directly identifies the function's biased output bits. We analyze the performance on four input generation strategies: counter-based, low hamming weight, plaintext-ciphertext block combination and bit-flips to test strict avalanche criterion. The *BoolTest* detects bias and thus constructs distinguisher in a significantly higher number of rounds in the round-reduced versions of DES, 3-DES, MD5, MD6 and SHA-256 functions than the state-of-the-art batteries. Finally, we provide a precise interpretation of *BoolTest* verdict (provided in the form of *Z-score*) about the confidence of a distinguisher found. The *BoolTest* clear interpretation is a significant advantage over standard batteries consisting of multiple tests, where not only a statistical significance of a single test but also aggregated decision over multiple, potentially correlated tests, needs to be correctly performed.

Keywords: Statistical randomness testing · Hypothesis testing
Boolean function

The *BoolTest* implementation and paper supplementary material can be found at https://crocs.fi.muni.cz/papers/booltest2018.

M. S. Obaidat and E. Cabello (Eds.): ICETE 2017, CCIS 990, pp. 123–149, 2019.
https://doi.org/10.1007/978-3-030-11039-0_7

1   Introduction

Both newly designed as well as widely used cryptographic primitives (block cipher, stream cipher, hash function, pseudo-random generators, etc.)[1] are subjected to various analysis techniques like linear, differential and algebraic cryptanalysis which looks for flaws or information leakage in the primitive design. The standard techniques try to find any significant correlations between the tested primitive input (plaintext), output (ciphertext) and key bits (if used). The existence of correlated bits indicates a weakness of the function, which might be exploitable to predict bits of a secret key or next output bits of the pseudorandom generator. Although these techniques can be partially automated, the aid of the skilled cryptanalyst is still needed.

Fully automated but weaker statistical test suites (e.g., NIST STS, Dieharder, Test-U01) are often used as a quick and cheap tool before the deeper cryptanalysis is performed [2]. Commonly, well-designed crypto-primitives should produce output with the same characteristics as truly random data. Test suites examine the correlation of function output bits through randomness analysis of data it produces. Each test suite (often called battery) usually consists of tens of empirical tests of randomness. Each test looks for a predefined pattern of bits (or block of bits) in data, and thus it examines randomness property from its specific point of view. Each test computes a histogram of a specific feature of bits (or block of bits). The histogram is statistically compared with the expected histogram (for random data). The result (p-$value$) of the test is probabilistic measure how well both histograms match. Data are considered to be non-random if histograms differ significantly. Although there is an unlimited number of tests in principle, batteries opt for implementation of only several selected ones for the practical reasons. The randomness in such a context is a probabilistic property, and we can commit two types of errors – Type I (truly random data rejected) and Type II (non-random data not rejected).

The batteries implement many tests of various complexity – from the very simple Monobit computing statistic of bits (frequency of ones and zeros) to the very complex statistics computed from large blocks (e.g., computation of linear profile). The complexity of tests usually determines the amount of data necessary to compute the histograms for comparison. In order to decrease the Type I and II errors, sufficiently many data sequences (up to several GBs of data) are required in practice.

We can identify the following generic limitations of standard batteries with respect to the analysis of cryptographic functions:

1. **An Insufficient Strength to Detect Bias in Unweakened Functions**
   – The tests included in a battery are usually too weak to detect biases in an output of a modern cryptographic function with a full number of rounds and other standard security parameters.

---

[1] This is extended version of the paper 'The Efficient Randomness Testing using Boolean Functions' [1, SeCrypt].

2. **An Insufficient Detection Sensitivity if Only a Small Amount of Data is Available** – The tests might be too insensitive to detect biases when an only limited amount of data is available for the testing. The tests usually require from 10 MB up to several GBs of data which may not be available in particular test scenario.
3. **The Difficulty of Test Results Interpretation** – The interpretation of test results is often only generic in the form of "something is wrong with the provided data". Only a few tests are able to identify concrete dependent bits and provide this crucial information to a cryptanalyst.

Our goal is to resolve the last two aforementioned problems and to construct the set of statistical tests that will be stronger in detecting the bias when given a limited amount of data yet directly identifying the biased output bits. In fact, we are looking for the strongest distinguisher possible (of cryptographic function from the truly random data) within the given amount of tested data and complexity of a distinguishing function. A distinguisher is iteratively constructed in the form of simple function starting from the simplest possible and proceeding towards the more and more complex boolean functions. Surprisingly, such a test is missing from all three commonly used test suites. Our approach is a generalization of the simple Monobit test and was practically tested on the wide range of cryptographic functions of various types – block and stream ciphers, hash functions and pseudo-random number generators (PRNGs). We have found practical strong distinguishers which can also be used as the bit predictors (although usually weak) for the corresponding functions.
In short, we make the following contributions:

- **Simple, Yet Strong Test:** We designed the principally simple, yet surprisingly strong test called *BoolTest* based on the boolean functions with an easy interpretation whether a robust distinguisher for tested data and function was found (or not). The standard batteries are notoriously difficult to interpret as both the results of a single test as well as multiple, potentially cross-correlated tests needs to be properly reasoned about.
- **Interpretable Test for Small Data:** We have shown that *BoolTest* not only requires significantly less data and runs faster (seconds) but also allows for the direct interpretation of a distinguisher found – which particular bits in tested function output are biased together and how.
- **Large Number of Function Analyzed:** The *BoolTest* sensitivity was tested on common and widely used cryptographic functions like AES or SHA-3 (with over 20 functions tested total), all with a gradually reduced complexity via the decreased number of internal rounds. The sensitivity of *BoolTest* is mostly equal to the state-of-the-art batteries like TestU01 when tested on 100 MB data streams with some notable differences. The counter-based input generation strategy results in more internal rounds still distinguishable by *BoolTest* for DES, 3-DES, Keccak, MD5, MD6, SHA-1, SHA-256, and TEA functions when no bias is detected anymore by the standard batteries. Conversely, the TestU01 battery is able to distinguish a higher number of rounds

in DES, MD5, MD6, and SHA-1 functions when the strict-avalanche testing input generation strategy is used.

- **A Different Strategies for Input Data Generation Examined:** A tested cryptographic function is first repeatedly executed to produce a sufficiently long output data stream, which is then supplied for the testing. However, the properties of the inputs supplied to the tested function during the output generation are crucial and significantly influence the randomness properties of generated output. The four different input data generation strategies were tested: (1) counter-based, where input block is in the form of incremental counter, (2) very low hamming weight block, (3) random input block with a corresponding pair formed by single bit flip (focused on the analysis of strict avalanche criterion) and (4) random input block, but also inserted into the output data stream to test for input/output correlation.
- **Practical Distinguisher for *C/Java rand*:** Among others, we found previously unknown biases in the output of *C rand()* and *Java Random* pseudo-random generators forming surprising strong practical distinguishers regardless of the initial seed used. A deeper analysis of these distinguishers is provided.
- **Open-source Implementation:** We release the code of *BoolTest* [3] as an open-source to facilitate further research in this area and complement the standard test batteries.

The paper is organized as follows: Sect. 2 describes principles of the commonly used batteries and provides the motivation for more efficient tests. Section 3 provides background and detailed description of our strategy for distinguisher construction based on boolean functions with relevant implementation details which significantly speed up the computations. The comparison of results with common statistical batteries on more than 20 functions are provided in Sect. 4 together with the detailed discussion of practical distinguishers found for the Java and C pseudo-random generators and other functions. Section 5 is devoted to the statistical interpretation of results reported by *BoolTest*. Section 6 surveys the previous work and is followed by the conclusions given in Sect. 7.

2 Motivation for Better Tests

Tests in batteries can be roughly divided into three main categories w.r.t. their complexity. (1) The very simple tests compute statistic of bits (e.g., a histogram of ones and zeros) within an entire tested sequence or within smaller parts of the whole sequence. (2) The slightly more complex and usually slower tests compute statistic of a small block of bits (e.g., an entropy of 8-bit blocks) within a sequence. (3) The complicated and slow tests compute a complex statistic (e.g., the histogram of rank for matrices, linear complexity) within the large parts of the sequence.

How well the common batteries perform in the analysis of crypto primitives? Let's take the 100 MB data produced by truly random number generator (which should pass all tests), divide it into 128-bit blocks and introduce minor modification to original random stream – the last bit (b_{127}) of every block is changed so that *xor* with the very first bit (b_0) of that block gives always 0 as the result ($b_0 \oplus b_{127} = 0$) instead of in only half of the cases as expected. Even such a strong bias is detected only by a handful of tests, most significantly by the block frequency test. If the resulting 0 is produced 1 % more frequently than 1 (instead of always as previously), only one test of the TestU01 battery detects the bias. Moreover, for 0.1 % none of the standard tests (batteries NIST STS, Dieharder and TestU01) detect this – still significant – bias. The problem lays in a structure of patterns the tests are searching for in tested data.

Dieharder and NIST STS batteries analyze randomness according to consecutive m bits for small m (typically $m < 20$). The tests included in TestU01 take a different approach as data are transformed into series of real values with first r bits (of every real value) discarded and only next s bits used for the analysis. TestU01 analyzes data usually as point in k dimensions and thus t consecutive blocks of s bits represent point in t dimensions. Values of r, s are typically in range $[0, 32]$ and t is usually small value < 10.

Very simple and bit-oriented tests like Monobit test are usually also the fastest. Besides the speed, the additional advantage of simple tests is usually the small amount of data necessary to compute correct results (statistic distribution is approximated well). The more complex tests need significantly more data for the sufficient approximation and thus also for detection of bias (if present). Another drawback of standard tests is a lack of possibility to retrospective identify the exact biased or correlated bits even when a test is able to detect some bias. The observed statistic computed by a test is given by frequencies (histogram) of some feature. For more than two bins we are usually unable to identify which bin has unexpectedly high or low value (w.r.t. reference values). Hence we cannot identify the concrete input bits responsible for the production of the extreme value of the observed statistic. On the other hand, if histogram contains only two bins, the value in one bin automatically determines the value of the second bin.

According to the previous reasoning, the histogram (of frequencies) should preferably consist of two bins. To identify the biased or correlated bits, the searched relation should be bit-oriented as well. One statistical test of randomness can be used to examine only one relation of specific bits (within a block). In order to find correlated bits, we need to repeat the process many times with many different relations and bits selected. The time required to evaluate the tests should be reasonably small, and therefore the inspected relation represented as a simple boolean function is a natural choice. Such representation is fast to compute as only bitwise operations are used to compute the required histogram. Moreover, the exact (and not only approximated) reference distribution expected for the truly random data can be computed analytically. Finally, one can easily order two candidates (boolean functions) based on their complexity (degree and number of components) and find the simplest function which exhibits unexpected bias thus providing a more sensible guide for cryptanalyst. The following section provides more details for the constructions of such distinguishers.

3 The Randomness Distinguisher Based on the Boolean Functions

Our approach is inspired by the Monobit test which examines the proportion of ones and zeros within the provided sequence. The frequencies of ones and zeros computed in Monobit test represent results of a boolean function $f(x_1) = x_1$ when applied to all bits of the sequence. This can be generalized to an arbitrary boolean function $f(x_1, x_2, \cdots, x_m)$ of m variables applied to non-overlapping blocks of m bits.

In our approach, we construct set of boolean functions (potentially distinguishers) defining different tests of randomness. All tests (functions) are applied the same way (see Sect. 3.2) to given sequence resulting in a set of test statistics. The results of our approach are the maximal observed test statistic and the corresponding boolean function.

The maximal observed test statistic and the boolean function can be used to evaluate the randomness of analyzed sequence or a new sequence:

- Maximal observed test statistic can be directly used to assess the randomness of the analyzed sequence. The interpretation of maximal test statistic is based on the distribution of maximal test statistic obtained for reference random data (see Sect. 5).
- Found boolean function can also be used to assess the randomness of a new sequence from the same source as described in Sect. 3.2.

The distinguisher (boolean function) is constructed iteratively from simpler and weaker distinguishers (simpler boolean functions). Besides the fact that simpler distinguishers are found first, this also allows to speed up the entire process since many intermediate computational results (for simpler functions) can be reused.

3.1 Test of Randomness

The majority of empirical randomness tests are based on the statistical hypothesis testing. Tests are formulated to evaluate the null hypothesis – "data being tested are random". Each test computes a specific statistic of bits or block of bits which is a function of tested data. Firstly, a histogram of patterns for the given dataset is computed by the test. Then the histogram is transformed into a single value – observed test statistic which represents randomness quality of a sequence according to an analyzed feature. The distribution (null distribution) of the test statistic under the null hypothesis (data are random) is used to evaluate the test. Exact null distribution of a test statistic is usually complex function hence its close approximation is used instead. The most of the tests have χ^2 or *normal distribution* as their null distribution. A test checks where the observed test statistic appears within the null distribution. The hypothesis is rejected if value happens to be in extreme parts of the null distribution (tail). In such a case, the tested data are considered to be non-random. An observed test statistic is usually transformed to a *p-value* (using the null distribution). The *p-value* represents the probability that a perfect random number generator would have produced a sequence "less random" (more extreme according to analyzed feature) than the tested sequence [4]. The *p-value* is compared with the significance level α typically set to smaller values $0.01, 0.005$ or 0.001 for the randomness testing. If the *p-value* is smaller/bigger than α hypothesis is rejected/accepted and data are considered to be non-random/random. The following example illustrates how *p-value* is computed for the Monobit test.

Example 1. The Monobit test examines whether number of ones ($\#1$) and zeros ($\#0$) in a sequence of n bits are close to each other as would be expected for random data. The test statistic is computed as $s_{obs} = \frac{|\#0 - \#1|}{\sqrt{n}}$. The reference distribution of the test statistic is half normal as stated in [4] but this is just approximation. The *p-value* is computed in the Monobit test as:

$$p\text{-}value = \text{erfc}\left(\frac{s_{obs}}{\sqrt{2}}\right) = \text{erfc}\left(\frac{|\#0 - \#1|}{\sqrt{2n}}\right)$$

using the well-known complementary error function (erfc) [5]. Same *p-value* can be computed for statistic $s_{obs} = \#1$. The exact distribution of $\#1$ is binomial distribution $B(n, 0.5)$ for a sequence of n bits. Figure 1a illustrates the exact reference binomial distribution for $s_{obs} = \#1$ and sequences of $n = 100$ random bits (bins). The figure also shows that the discrete binomial distribution can be approximated well by the continuous normal distribution for sufficiently large n (documentation of NIST STS recommends $n \geq 100$). The *p-value* represents the probability that RNG would generate data with more extreme test statistic

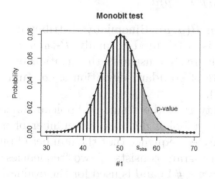
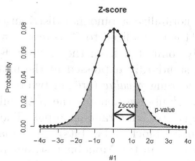

(a) Discrete binomial distribution $B(100, 0.5)$ and its approximation by continuous normal distribution $\mathcal{N}(50, 25)$. Area in the right tail represents *p-value* for the test statistic defined by $s_{obs} = \#1$ for a sequence with $n = 100$ bits [1].

(b) The relation of *Z-score* and *p-value*. *Z-score* is expressed in the units of the standard deviation [1].

Fig. 1. Monomial bit test and Z-score.

than s_{obs}. A *p-value* can be computed as an area below the normal distribution in the tail bounded by the observed test statistic s_{obs}. Figure 1a illustrates the value of *p-value* for $n = 100$ and $s_{obs} = 56$.

3.2   Distinguisher Evaluation

In order to evaluate the strength of the distinguisher (test), we use common principles from randomness testing. We adapt and generalize the Monobit test. The distinguisher (boolean function) defines the test of randomness, and the computed test statistic is used directly as the measure of the strength of distinguishers. A more extreme value of observed statistic means stronger distinguisher and conversely. To generalize the Monobit test, let us characterize steps of a test of randomness.

An empirical test of randomness consists (in general) of the following steps:

1. Compute the histogram H of some features (within data).
2. Compute (transform the histogram to) the observed test statistic s_{obs}.
3. Compute the null distribution (exact or its close approximation) $D(x)$ of the test statistic under the null hypothesis (random data).[2]
4. Compute the *p-value* from s_{obs} using the distribution $D(x)$.

In our approach, the histogram of results of the boolean function $f(x_1, \cdots, x_m)$ of m variables applied to non-overlapping m-bit blocks of the sequence is computed. Our test statistic is *Z-score* [6] defined as:

$$Z\text{-}score = \frac{\#1 - pn}{\sqrt{p(1-p)n}}, \tag{1}$$

which normalize a binomial distribution $B(n, p)$. Binomially distributed variable $\#1$ is normalized to *Z-score* which is distributed normally. *P-value* can be directly computed from the *Z-score*. Figure 1b illustrates the relation of a *Z-score* (standardly expressed in the units of standard deviation $x \cdot \sigma$) and the corresponding *p-value* (area of two tails).

The symbol p denotes the probability that the result of boolean function f is equal to 1 for random input. The symbol n denotes the number of non-overlapping blocks (of m bits) in the analyzed sequence (not the number of bits). Similarly, as in the Monobit test, our histogram consists of two frequencies $\#1$ and $\#0$, but only $\#1$ is computed ($\#0 = n - \#1$) and is used for the evaluation. The only difference is that the expected probability p is not $p = 0.5$. In general, p is arbitrary value from the interval [0,1] which depends on the given boolean function f. The *Z-score* and relevant statistical theory is discussed in Sect. 5 in more details.

Figure 2 illustrates our approach with the boolean function $f(x_1, \cdots, x_m) = x_2 + x_{89} + x_{94}$. Firstly, data to be analyzed are divided into multiple non-overlapping blocks. Then the number of results equal to one ($\#1$) is computed

---

[2] In most cases distribution $D(x)$ is given.

(blocks serve as the inputs for the function f). The final result – *Z-score* is computed as the statistical distance between observed and expected number of ones (#1).

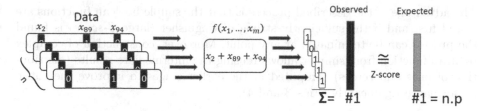

Fig. 2. Our approach and the computation of *Z-score* using boolean function $f(x_1, \cdots, x_m) = x_2 + x_{89} + x_{94}$. *Z-score* is computed as the statistical distance of observed #1 for tested data and #1 $= p.n$ expected for truly random data [1].

To perform the test, we have to compute only #1 and the expected probability p (as the p changes with the function f). The algorithm for the computation of p is described in Sect. 3.5. We may omit the computation of the *p-value* since the strength of distinguishers can be compared directly using their *Z-scores*. The bigger *Z-score* is, the stronger distinguisher is obtained and vice versa.

3.3 Distinguisher Construction

Our approach assumes that stronger and more complex distinguishers can be obtained as a combination of the weaker and simpler ones. This assumption is natural in a sense that if this would not be true, we have to find more complex distinguishers by brute force anyway. As we start with a test of the simpler candidate distinguishers first, we naturally obtain the simplest possible yet strong enough distinguisher. The potentially stronger, but more complex distinguishers are evaluated later. We work with the boolean functions of m variables for some fixed m. The construction is iterative. We first start with the simplest boolean functions $f(x_1, \cdots, x_m) = x_i$ for $i \in \{1, 2, \cdots, m\}$ and construct more and more complex (more monomials, higher degree) functions. Since we want to find the weakness (biased bits) in the output of a tested cryptographic function, the number of variables m of a boolean function should correspond with the size of function's output. Therefore, the typical value of m is set to $m = 128$ or to its small multiple 256, 384, 512 to match frequent block sizes used in common cryptographic functions. For such small values of m, we can check all such simple boolean functions by brute force. The construction is divided into two phases:

1. Firstly, the set S of k strongest and simple distinguishers is found: We search through the set of monomials $(x_i, x_i.x_j, x_i.x_j.x_k)$ of small degree $\leq deg$ since a total number of functions raise exponentially with the degree. We assess the strength of all monomials and set S of strongest (biggest *Z-score*) t distinguishers ($|S| = t$) is sent to the next phase.

2. In the second phase, we construct more complex distinguishers: The simple distinguishers (elements of S from the first step) are combined using the addition (XOR) operator. We construct all possible functions in the form of $f(x_1, \cdots, x_m) = b_1 + b_2 + \cdots + b_k$ such that $b_i \in S$ and k is fixed.

The advantage of the described process is that the simple boolean functions are tested first and if the sufficiently strong distinguisher (large Z-score) is found the process can be terminated at any point. Moreover, construction of complex boolean function from simpler allows reusing the intermediate results (distribution of ones and zeroes) computed in the earlier stages to improve the entire performance significantly (Figs. 3 and 4).

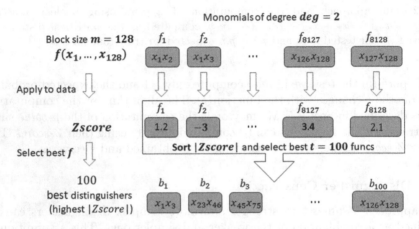

Fig. 3. Illustration of the first phase of distinguisher construction. The phase is parametrized by parameters m, deg, t. Input to this phase is data (fixed) to be analyzed. All Boolean functions in the first (and also in the second) phase are defined over m variables ($m = 128$ here). Each monomial (out of $\binom{m}{deg}$ monomials) of degree deg ($deg = 2$ here) is applied to data and corresponding Z-score is computed. Then absolute values of Z-scores are computed and sorted. The result of the first phase is set of t ($t = 100$) strongest distinguishers – Boolean functions b_i (monomials) with highest absolute values of Z-score.

3.4   Implementation Details

A result of the boolean function $f(x_1, \cdots, x_m)$ can be computed efficiently using fast bitwise operators AND and XOR. Moreover, these operators allow us to compute 32, 64 or 128 results at once (based on the CPU architecture and the instruction set). The principle follows the way how the distinguisher is constructed. We firstly compute "basis" of results for the simple boolean functions when applied to all input blocks (of m-bits) of a given sequence. Then the basis vectors are used to compute results for the arbitrary complex boolean function applied to the same inputs.

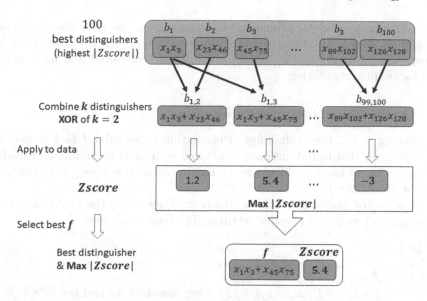

Fig. 4. Distinguisher construction – second phase. Second phase is parametrized by parameters m, k. The inputs to this phase are: the same data (as in previous phase) to be analyzed, and the set t of best distinguishers b_i found in the first phase. In this phase new Boolean functions are constructed as sum (XOR) of k Boolean functions b_i. All constructed B.f. are applied to data corresponding Z-score is computed. The result of this phase and of entire approach is the function f – distinguisher, and the value – Z-score. The $Z-score$ can be used to assess the randomness of analyzed data.

- Firstly, a "basis" of results is constructed. For each variable $x_i, i \in \{1, \cdots, m\}$ we fill the basis vector X_i (bit vector) by results of boolean function $f_i(x_1, \cdots, x_m) = x_i$ when applied to all input m-bit blocks of the tested data.
- The vector of all results X_f of the function f can be computed using our vector basis X_i in the same way as result of f is computed using x_i. In fact, to compute the vector of all results, it suffices to perform same operations with vectors X_i instead of x_i where AND and XOR are operators of boolean vectors now. The basis vectors are packed into words for more efficient computation.

The principle can be illustrated on the following example. Let assume that we want to compute 64 results of the boolean function $f(x_1, x_2, x_3, x_4) = x_1 x_2 + x_3$ for 64 blocks B_i each having 4-bits. We firstly compute basis bit-vector X_i that represents results (64 bits) of boolean function $f_i(x_1, x_2, x_3, x_4) = x_i$ applied to all blocks B_i. Vector of results X_f for the function f (applied to B_i) can be computed as

$$X_f = (X_1 \text{ AND } X_2) \text{ XOR } X_3$$

for operators AND, XOR working with bit-vectors. The vector of results X_f can be computed using just two bitwise operations working with 64-bits words. The longer sequences should be divided into words of 64 bits.

In our approach, boolean functions of a small degree and with the small number of monomials (t) are constructed. Therefore vectors X_i, $X_{i,j} = X_i$ AND X_j corresponding to functions x_i, $x_i \cdot x_j$ are fully pre-computed and used as the basis for result computation.

3.5   On the Computation of Expected p

Determining p, i.e., the probability of evaluating polynomial f to 1 under the null hypothesis that tested data are random, is equivalent to finding all variable settings under which f evaluates to 1. This problem is exponentially complex with the size of the f.

Let p_i be the probability of x_i evaluating to one, $P(f)$ the probability of f evaluating to 1 under all possible settings. The basic cases are:

1. $P(x_i) = 0.5$
2. $P(x_i x_{i+1} \cdots x_{i+k-1}) = p_i p_{i+1} \cdots p_{i+k-1} = 2^{-k}$
3. $P(x_i + x_j) = p_i(1 - p_j) + (1 - p_i)p_j$
4. $P(x_i + x_j + x_k) = P((x_i + x_j) + x_k)$ using associativity and the rule 3.

By using these rules, it is easy to determine $P(f)$ for a general polynomial in algebraic normal form (ANF) in linear time w.r.t. a number of variables (under the assumption of disjoint terms). However, the evaluation is more time-consuming if the terms are dependent, as the relations above do not hold. The solution for the problem with dependent terms requires to evaluate a polynomial for all possible variable settings, then count the number of cases where $f(x) = 1$ and finally compute resulting $P(f)$. This time complexity of the algorithm is exponential with respect to the number of variables.

Table 1. Experimental execution time of *BoolTest* running on Python 3.6.4, Intel Xeon CPU E5-2630 v3 2.40. *BoolTest* configuration is: block bit size - degree - term combination degree.

Data \ conf	256-2-3	256-3-3	512-2-3	512-3-3
10 MB	23 s	1 m 12 s	21.1 s	3 m 29 s
100 MB	2 m 40 s	9 m 53 s	1 m 42 s	31 m 30 s

We use few tricks to reduce the computation time. Let denote $f = b_1 + b_2 + \cdots b_k$, where $b_i = \prod_{j=1}^{deg} x_j$ is a term of degree deg. If $deg(f) = 1$ the rule 2 is used. In case of dependent terms we fall-back to naïve algorithm – evaluate f in all settings.

As example, lets examine the polynomial $f_1 = x_1 x_2 x_3 + x_1 x_5 x_6 + x_7 x_8 x_9$. Using naïve approach the f_1 is evaluated 2^8 times. With the closer look it can be evaluated as: $P((b_1 + b_2) + b_3)$, as b_3 is independent of other terms so whole evaluation is done only in 2^5 steps and one rule 3 application. To generalize this trick we just need to compute dependency components between terms b_i.

The terms b_i, b_j are dependent if $b_i \cap b_j \neq \emptyset$, i.e., they share at least one variable. The trick is to apply the naïve algorithm to all dependent components of the polynomial, then merge the components using rules 3, 4 as they are pairwise independent. Component finding is implemented with *Union-Find* algorithm with complexity $O(\alpha(n))$ which yields the resulting complexity $O(n\,\alpha(n))$.

To further optimize the evaluation, we can convert the input polynomial to a canonical form by renumbering the variables and sorting the terms. E.g. $x_{60}x_{120}x_{48} \rightarrow x_1x_2x_3$. Then by caching previous computations (e.g., LRU), we can avoid some expensive computations in a dependent component evaluation.

Another optimization is to use pruning and recursive application of the rules above when evaluating dependent components. Consider $b = x_1x_2x_3 + x_1x_5x_6$. In branch $x_1 = 0$ we directly have $b = 0$ thus all evaluation sub-branches are pruned. In branch $x_1 = 1$ we have $b' = x_2x_3 + x_5x_6$. By applying the algorithm recursively, we see x_2x_3, x_5x_6 are independent and no naïve algorithm is used, only rules 2, 3, 4.

In practice, we use polynomials and terms of a relatively small degree, so we do not use optimization with pruning and LRU caching as evaluating terms by the naïve algorithm is faster with this sizes. The overall benefit is the fast dependent component detection, and in practice, the vast majority of polynomials have independent terms which yield very fast $P(f)$ computation, in $O(n\,\alpha(n))$. Practical running times of the overall BoolTest are stated in Table 1.

4   Testing Methodology and Results

To demonstrate the practical usability of the proposed approach, we tested the approach on a variety of cryptographic primitives – hash functions, block and stream ciphers and truly- and pseudo- random number generators (TRNG, PRNG). The results are compared with the existing automated approaches utilized by the randomness statistical test batteries NIST STS, Dieharder and TestU01. The data used for analysis are generated using four different strategies.

4.1   Preparation of Data for Testing

Several different data generation strategies were used to analyze target function output confusion and diffusion properties, namely *CTR*, *LHW*, *SAC* and *RPC* as shown in Fig. 5 and explained below. With the given strategy, the 100 MB of output data are generated and used as an input for the randomness testing battery.

The *CTR* strategy generates blocks of particular size each containing the current block index. Intuitively the high bits are set to zero while the low bits are iterating until the 100 MBs of data is generated.

The *LHW* stands for low Hamming weight as it generates function's input blocks with the fixed and low Hamming weight. The weight is derived from the block size as it is required to avoid cycling of the generator, i.e., depleting of all options on the block size. If tested function f has input block size of 128 bits, the

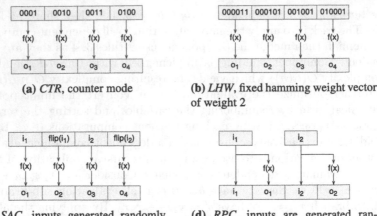

(a) *CTR*, counter mode

(b) *LHW*, fixed hamming weight vector of weight 2

(c) *SAC*, inputs generated randomly, $flip()$ flips one bit at random position.

(d) *RPC*, inputs are generated randomly

Fig. 5. Data generation modes and formation of output stream for testing.

Hamming weight is set to 4, because $16\binom{128}{4} \approx 170\,\text{MB}$. For 64-bit input block, the minimal required Hamming weight is 6, as $8\binom{64}{6} \approx 600\,\text{MB}$. The idea behind the *LHW* strategy is to cover the whole input block with small changes only, keeping the total Hamming weight low thus feeding the minimal possible entropy to a function. Both *CTR* and *LHW* serve as low-entropy input generators.

The *SAC* strategy aims to test the Strict Avalanche Criterion. It generates pairs of blocks where the first block in the pair is randomly generated and the second one is almost the same except for single bit flip at a randomly selected position. Both blocks are then used as an input to tested function f.

The *RPC* strategy stands for random-plaintext-ciphertext and generates random input block p_i, which is an input to a tested function f. The resulting data block used for statistical analysis is then $p_i \| f(p_i)$, the concatenation of plaintext and ciphertext. This particular testing method adds additional entropy to the tested function making the detection more difficult, e.g., it is expected that number of function's internal rounds with still detectable bias would be lower when compared to low-entropy inputs such as *CTR* and *LHW*. On the other hand, we can directly analyze function's input-output correlation.

4.2 Parameters of Boolean Functions

Our approach is parameterized by the parameters deg, m, t and k. We search for the distinguisher with m variables and of k monomials each with degree of deg. The parameter t represents the number of best monomials used to construct distinguisher in the second phase (as described in Sect. 3.3). For instance, parameters $deg = 2$, $m = 4$, $t = 128$, $k = 3$ means that we searched for 128 strongest distinguishers (boolean functions) of the form $f(x_1, x_2, x_3, x_4) = x_i x_j$ for different $x_i, x_j \in \{x_1, x_2, x_3, x_4\}$ in the first phase. In the second phase we combine every k-tuple of them to find the strongest distinguisher of the form $f(x_1, x_2, x_3, x_4) = x_i x_j + x_k x_l + x_r x_s$ among the all possible combinations. We tested data produced by various crypto functions with various settings. We used the combination deg, m, t, k where $deg \in \{1, 2, 3\}$, $m \in \{128, 256, 384, 512\}$, $t = 128$, and $k \in \{1, 2, 3\}$.

4.3 Common Cryptographic Functions with CTR Strategy

In order to compare our results with the standard batteries, we tested the data generated with *CTR* strategy both with *BoolTest* and NIST STS, Dieharder and TestU01 test suites (Alphabit, BlockAlphabit, Rabbit, Small Crush). Table 2 summarizes the results and strength of tools according to a number of rounds for which deviation from distribution expected for random data (null hypothesis) is detected by the respective tool for 100 MB of data. We consider tested data to be rejected by a battery if at least one test from the battery fails with the conservative significance level set to $\alpha = 1\%$.

Table 2. The number of rounds (of selected primitives and PRNGs) in which non-randomness was detected for 100 MB data for NIST STS (NI), Dieharder (Di) and TestU01 (U01). Our approach is presented for two well performing settings Bool1($deg = 2$, $k = 1$, $m = 384$) and Bool2($deg = 2$, $k = 2$, $m = 512$). Character '*' means that more rounds were distinguished by boolean function found with other parameters than two presented. Adapted from [1].

function	NI	Di	U01	Bool1	Bool2
AES	3	3	3	3	3
ARIRANG	3	3	4	3	3
AURORA	2	2	4	2	2
BLAKE	1	1	1	1	1
Cheetah	4	4	6	4	4
CubeHash	0	0	1	0	0
DCH	2	2	2	1	1
Decim	6	6	6	5	5
Echo	1	1	1	1	1
Grain	3	2	2	2	2
Grøstl	2	2	2	2	2
Hamsi	0	0	0	0	0

function	NI	Di	U01	Bool1	Bool2
JH	6	6	6	6	6
Keccak	2	2	2	3	3
Lex	3	3	3	3	3
Lesamta	2	3	3	2	2
Luffa	7	7	7	7	7
MD6	8	8	8	9	8
Simd	0	0	0	0	0
Salsa20	6	4	6	4*	4*
TEA	4	4	4	4*	4*
TSC-4	13	12	13	13*	13*
Twister	6	6	7	6	6

Table 2 shows the best results of our tool obtained for two particular *BoolTest* settings: *Bool1*($deg = 2$, $k = 1$, $m = 384$) and *Bool2*($deg = 2$, $k = 2$, $m = 512$). In 15 out of 24 functions tested, *BoolTest* was able to detect non-randomness in stream produced by the same number of rounds in round-reduced cryptographic functions when compared to NIST STS. The more and fewer rounds were distinguished for Keccak, MD6, and DCH, Decim, Grain, Salsa20 functions respectively.

It should be noted that *BoolTest* was able to find boolean functions with other parameters than *Bool1* and *Bool2* capable of detecting non-randomness of Salsa20 with 4 rounds, TEA reduced to 5 rounds, and TSC-4 reduced to 14 rounds, but performing same or worse on the remaining configurations.

The second practically important property of any test is the least amount of data necessary to spot the bias (if present). We tested and compared the performance of *BoolTest* with statistical batteries using 10 MB, 100 MB, and 1 GB of input data. The results are summarized in Table 3. For test suites, the number of passed tests are shown. The computed *Z-scores* are shown for the *BoolTest* and two best settings according to given a set of analyzed functions. The results of *BoolTest* and test suites which can be interpreted as detected non-randomness (null hypothesis rejected) are highlighted in gray. Based on the results, we can conclude that test based on boolean functions usually requires an order of magnitude fewer data to detect bias than common batteries.

Table 3. Results of NIST STS (NI), Dieharder (Di), TestU01 (U01) and our approach with two settings Bool3($deg = 1$, $k = 2$, $m = 384$, $t = 128$) and Bool4($deg = 1$, $k = 2$, $m = 512$, $t = 128$) obtained for 10 MB, 100 MB and 1 GB of data produced with primitives with limited number of rounds [1].

size	func	NI	Di	U01	Bool3	Bool4
	AES (3)	∀	18	15	8.6	6.7
	TEA (4)	∀	20	∀	20.6	11.5
	Keccak (3)	∀	∀	15	3.7	5.3
10 MB	MD6 (9)	∀	∀	∀	3.9	13.3
	SHA-256 (3)	0	0	6	88.7	242
	AES (3)	∀	16	15	8.9	15.0
	TEA (4)	14	21	∀	73.6	5.2
	Keccak (3)	14	22	15	3.8	9.2
100 MB	MD6 (9)	∀	∀	∀	3.7	26.4
	SHA-256 (3)	0	0	4	50.7	828
	AES (3)	9	18	14	12.8	41.2
	TEA (4)	13	24	∀	127	4.3
	Keccak (3)	∀	26	15	3.5	32.0
1 GB	MD6 (9)	13	25	15	4.1	26.4
	SHA-256 (3)	0	1	3	78.0	3043

4.4 Comparison of Data Generation Strategies on Selected Functions

The four different data generation strategies described in Sect. 4.1 and their impact on the randomness properties of tested function output is shown in Table 4. The notable results are as follows:

- MD5 hash function reduced to 18 rounds and with *LWH* data generation mode as tested by TestU01. The test smarsa_BirthdaySpacings from

Table 4. The number of rounds (of selected primitives) in which non-randomness was detected for 100 MB data for NIST STS (NI), Dieharder (Di) and TestU01 (U01) compared to our approach *BoolTest* (BT). The input generation is described in Subsect. 4.1. Gray highlight the best result for given function on every data generation strategy.

Scenario	CTR				LHW				SAC				RPC			
Fun.\Tests	NI	Di	U01	BT	NI	Di	U01	BT	NI	Di	U01	BT	NI	Di	U01	BT
AES	3	3	3	3	2	3	3	3	2	2	2	2	-	1	1	1
Blowfish	2	2	2	2	2	3	3	3	2	2	3	3	-	1	1	1
DES	4	4	4	5	4	4	4	5	4	4	5	4	1	1	2	4
3-DES	2	2	2	3	2	2	3	3	2	2	2	2	1	1	1	2
Grøstl	2	2	2	2	2	2	2	2	-	-	-	-	-	-	-	-
JH	6	6	6	6	6	6	6	6	6	6	6	5	2	2	2	3
Keccak	2	2	2	3	2	2	2	3	2	2	2	2	1	-	1	1
MD5	9	10	9	11	12	13	20	13	9	11	14	12	3	3	4	6
MD6	8	8	8	8	8	8	8	9	7	7	8	7	5	5	7	5
SHA-1	12	12	13	14	16	16	16	16	11	15	16	14	4	4	5	7
SHA-256	6	6	6	7	12	12	12	13	11	11	12	13	3	4	4	4
TEA	4	4	4	5	3	3	3	4	3	4	3	3	-	2	1	1

TestU01 Small Crush consistently evaluates the input as non-random. The test's *p-value* increases with increasing number of rounds up to 18, but it is always significant ($\leq 10^{-9}$). The test snpair_ClosePairsBitMatch from TestU01 Rabbit fails with even more extreme *p-values*. This test fails even for MD6 reduced to 20 out of total 64 rounds (*p-values* $\leq 10^{-19}$).

- Among the input generation strategies, *RPC* is consistently the scenario which is the most difficult to distinguish from the truly random stream. The *SAC* is more difficult than *CTR* and *LHW*, which are roughly comparable. However, for SHA-256 the *CTR* scenario is more difficult than both *LHW* and *SAC*. We hypothesize that *CTR* difficulty is caused by more chaotic bit-flips within two consecutive blocks compared to other scenarios.
- *BoolTest* is among the most successful tests for *CTR*, *LHW* and *RPC* inputs for tested data with 100 MB length. For *SAC* generation strategy, TestU01 is the most sensitive battery, while *BoolTest* performs similarly to Dieharder battery.

Note, that the interpretation of *BoolTest* result (if the tested sequence is random or non-random) is more straightforward than for the standard batteries. While *BoolTest* consists of only a single test and resulting single *Z-score*, standard batteries consist of multiple statistical tests, each with own *p-value* interpretation and also potentially correlated to other tests. This property was also confirmed while comparing the results shown in the Table 4.

4.5 Pseudo-random Number Generators

The proposed approach was tested on several commonly used non-cryptographic pseudo-random number generators (PRNGs): Mersenne Twister 19937, Multiply-with-Carry C++ generator, Ranlux24, T800, TT800 from TestU01 and *C stdlib rand()* and *Java java.util.Random*. The practical distinguishers were found for the last two generators (as discussed below) and no distinguisher was found for any tested parameters and data sizes up to 1 GB for the remaining ones.

Using *BoolTest*, we were able to find universal distinguishers i.e., which work for large groups of PRNG seeds, for *C stdlib rand()* and *Java java.util.Random* (*C rand, Java rand* in short). We tested *BoolTest* on 1000 different bit streams generated by the C *rand* respectively, each bit stream generated by using a different random seed from the interval $[0, 2^{32} - 1]$.

Let define an input bit stream as τ_i and the best distinguisher and its corresponding *Z-score* value for τ_i returned by *BoolTest* as (ξ_i, δ_i). Figures 6, 7 and 8 depict the set of the best distinguishers $\xi_i \in \{f_1, f_2, f_3, f_4, f_5, f_6\}$ and their *Z-scores*[3] found by *BoolTest* on input bit streams $\tau_1, \ldots, \tau_{1000}$. In order to emphasize the *Z-score* deviation polarity each distinguisher has, the *Z-score* results are split into two box plots, for positive and negative *Z-scores* values. The number of occurrences of the distinguisher f_1^+ is $|f_1^+| = |\{i; \xi_i = f_1 \wedge \delta_i \geq 0\}|$. E.g., the f_1^- column represents all the *Z-score* values $\delta_i < 0$ where $\xi_i = f_1$ and the f_1^+ column represents $\delta_i \geq 0$ where $\xi_i = f_1$.

Note for the *C rand* the deviation is only positive while for *Java Random* it is usually symmetric.

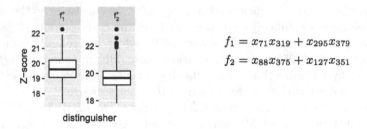

$$f_1 = x_{71}x_{319} + x_{295}x_{379}$$
$$f_2 = x_{88}x_{375} + x_{127}x_{351}$$

Fig. 6. The best distinguishers, *C rand()*, $1000 \times 1\,\text{MB}$ data samples, 384-bit block, random 32-bit seed, Ubuntu 16.04. The best distinguisher occurrences in 1000 tests: $|f_1^+| = 520$, $|f_2^+| = 480$ [1].

The distinguishers from Fig. 7 were discovered with the parameters ($deg = 3$, $k = 3$, $m = 512$). In this setting the *BoolTest* examined input bit stream of increasing sizes: $\{19200, \ldots, x_j, 2x_j, \ldots, 300 \cdot 1024^2\}$ bytes and found $\{f_3, f_4, f_5, f_6\}$ distinguishers after examining 37.5 MB bit stream. In the previous iterations with smaller input bit stream only weak distinguishers were found.

---

[3] $f_1, f_2, f_3, f_4, f_5, f_6$ are particular boolean functions.

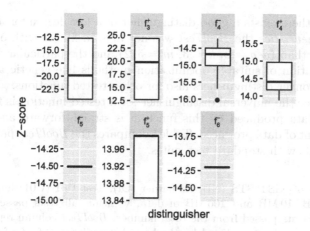

$$|f_3^-| = 352, |f_3^+| = 374, |f_4^-| = 48, |f_4^+| = 86$$
$$|f_5^-| = 45, \quad |f_5^+| = 63, \quad |f_6^-| = 32, |f_6^+| = 0$$

$$f_3 = x_{38}x_{326} + x_{39}x_{327} + x_{326}x_{486}$$
$$f_4 = x_{38}x_{326} + x_{205}x_{327} + x_{326}x_{486}$$
$$f_5 = x_{38}x_{326} + x_{326}x_{486} + x_{327}x_{359}$$
$$f_6 = x_{38}x_{326} + x_{167}x_{327} + x_{326}x_{486}$$

Fig. 7. The best distinguishers, *Java Random*, $1000 \times 1\,\text{MB}$ data samples, 512-bit block, random 32-bit seed. Java OpenJDK 1.8.0_121, Oracle Java 1.7.0_6, 1.8.0_65, [1].

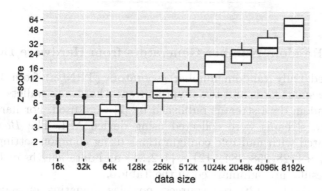

Fig. 8. The size of the input bit stream vs. $|Z\text{-}score|$ using distinguishers $\{f_3, f_4, f_5, f_6\}$ for *Java Random*, 1000 random seed samples per data size category. Dashed line represents ref. $Z\text{-}score$ value for the test, [1].

When using different settings $(deg, m, k) \in \{\{1, 2, 3\} \times \{128, 258, 384, 512\} \times \{1, 2, 3\}\}$ we were able to find only weaker distinguishers which required significantly more data to achieve the same $Z\text{-}score$. Interestingly, $\{f_3, f_4, f_5, f_6\}$ we discovered after examining 37.5 MB bit stream work very well also for smaller data sizes, as depicted in Fig. 5.

It is evident there exists a good distinguisher of a low degree for *Java Rand* but due to *top-heuristics* the *BoolTest* was not able to find it with other combinations rather than $(deg = 3, k = 3, m = 512)$ and the particular size of the data. The utilization of suitable optimization methods like genetic algorithms could lead to stronger distinguishers also for other tested functions.

Note that once the universal distinguisher for a tested function is found, the application on data produced by this function is straightforward and requires only small amount of data produced. Table 5 compares the *BoolTest* performance for tested PRNGs with standard test suites.

Table 5. Results of NIST STS (NI), Dieharder (Di), Test U01 (U01) and *BoolTest* obtained for 1 MB, 10 MB and 100 MB of data. $\forall$ means all tests passed, fraction means number of tests passed from the total number. *BoolTest* column represents an average of $|Z\text{-}score|$ values produced by the best distinguishers $\{f_1, f_2, f_3, f_4, f_5, f_6\}$ on 1000 randomly seeded input bit streams [1].

size	func	NI	Di	U01	*BoolTest*
1 MB	c	-	$\forall$	$\forall$	19.67
	java	-	$\forall$	$\forall$	17.78
10 MB	c	$\forall$	$\forall$	$\forall$	60.92
	java	$\forall$	$\forall$	$\forall$	55.98
100 MB	c	$\forall$	22/23	$\forall$	191.37
	java	$\forall$	$\forall$	15/16	176.62

4.6 Truly Random Number Generators from Hardware Devices

We also tested truly random number generators (TRNGs) from 13 different cryptographic smartcards and two cryptocurrency hardware wallets. For smartcards, the random data streams published by [7] were used. For hardware wallets, new data streams were collected using device API. The *BoolTest* testing was executed with multiple configurations using common settings $(deg, m, k) \in \{\{1, 2, 3\} \times \{128, 258, 384, 512\} \times \{1, 2, 3\}\}$ and data lengths of 1, 5, 10 and 95MB. The results are summarized in the Table 6.

For the majority of tested sources, no bias deviating enough from the expected reference values of Z-score was found – tested streams are therefore

Table 6. TRNG testing results of smart cards and hardware wallets.

Source	Min data	Z-SCORE	deg, m	Polynomial
Infineon CJTOP 80K	5 MB	4.78	1, 2	$x_{107} + x_{115}$
Oberthur Cosmo Dual 72K	1 MB	142.42	3, 3	$x_2 x_{67} x_{118} + x_3 x_{14} x_{54} + x_{25} x_{35} x_{86}$
Smartcards and hardware wallets with no detection				
Feitian JavaCOS A22, G_D SmartCafe {3.2, 4.x, 6.0}, JavaCOS A40, NXP {CJ3A080, CJ3A081, J2A080 80K, J2D081, J2E145G, JCOP41 v221}, Oberthur Cosmo 64				
Ledger Nano S, Trezor Model T				

indistinguishable (by *BoolTest*) from the truly random data. Only two smart-cards exhibited a larger Z-score than expected, signalizing the significantly biased output – a fact already known from the previous research [7]. *BoolTest* was able to spot bias already in the one megabyte of data tested. The Infineon CJTOP 80K is known to produce output stream which will never have two consecutive bytes with the same value. To detect this behavior, the resulting best distinguisher found by *BoolTest* is looking at an XOR of the bits at position 107 and 115 – precisely 8 bits apart – as one would expect. We performed a specific experiment for Infineon card and a block with 16 bits only (the smallest size previously tested was 128 bits, which is unnecessarily long for such a specific bias), which produced even larger Z-score, further confirming the presence of this specific bias. The exact structure of the bias in case of Oberthur Cosmo Dual 72K card is unknown, and best-performing distinguisher found by *BoolTest* for this card is also more complex with a polynomial of degree three and consisting of three monomials. The analysis of distinguisher found is left for the future work.

We can conclude that *BoolTest* was able to find for tested TRNGs precisely the biases already detected by the standard randomness testing batteries (and no more) with only small amount of data required.

5   The Statistical Interpretation

The result of *BoolTest* is the maximal *Z-score* computed within a set of boolean functions. The interpretation of *Z-score* for a single boolean function is simple and straightforward. *Z-score* is normally distributed random variable and *p-value* can be computed directly from it. However, the computation of *p-value* from the maximal *Z-score* (denoted as *Z-SCORE*) computed by our tool is more complicated. In this Section, we describe the *Z-score*, the *p-value* and the statistical theory related to our approach. Afterward, we discuss interpretations of the result of *BoolTest* based on reference results computed for truly random data (Table 7).

5.1   *P-value* and *Z-score*

The *p-value* represents the probability that more extreme results are obtained (for the true hypothesis) than we observed (s_{obs}). In our case, *p-value* represents the probability that a perfect random number generator would produce less random sequences than the sequence being tested. The *p-value* is computed from the observed test statistic s_{obs} and the reference distribution D or its close approximation. The null distribution of many tests is binomial distribution $B(n, p)$. It is approximated well (for $n > 10p$ and $n \cdot (1 - p) > 10$) by normal distribution $\mathcal{N}(\mu, \sigma^2)$ [8]. Normal distribution is symmetric around mean μ and therefore *p-value* is computed as an area under bell curve in both tails (see Fig. 1b). Sometimes *Z-score* is computed instead of *p-value* since they are related

$$p\text{-}value = \text{erfc}\left(\frac{Z\text{-}score}{\sqrt{2}}\right)$$

[9] and computation of $Z\text{-}score$ is simpler and faster. The $Z\text{-}score$ represents the distance from the mean μ in units of σ. The binomial distribution $B(n, p)$ is approximated by $\mathcal{N}(\mu, \sigma^2)$, with the parameters $\mu = np$ and $\sigma^2 = np(1 - p)$ [6] i.e. $Z\text{-}score$ of binomially $(B(n, p))$ distributed #1 is computed as

$$Z\text{-}score = \frac{\#1 - pn}{\sqrt{p(1 - p)n}} = \frac{\#1 - \mu}{\sigma}.$$

Table 7. The mean (μ) and the standard deviation (σ) of maximal $Z\text{-}SCORE$ computed by *BoolTest* for various settings k, $deg \in \{1, 2, 3\}$, $m \in \{128, 256, 384, 512\}$ and $t = 128$. Improved results w.r.t. [1].

deg	1			2			3		
m \ k	1	2	3	1	2	3	1	2	3
The mean (μ)									
128	2.80	3.96	4.81	3.87	5.35	5.80	4.71	6.56	7.61
256	3.05	4.00	4.81	4.23	5.66	6.01	5.13	7.10	8.24
384	3.14	4.01	4.77	4.39	5.86	6.19	5.32	7.41	8.55
512	3.24	3.92	4.79	4.55	6.02	6.28	5.54	7.64	8.86
The standard deviation (σ)									
128	0.39	0.25	0.25	0.33	0.30	0.32	0.27	0.23	0.27
256	0.42	0.30	0.24	0.36	0.31	0.26	0.28	0.23	0.26
384	0.37	0.31	0.25	0.26	0.27	0.26	0.25	0.22	0.23
512	0.37	0.30	0.23	0.31	0.30	0.27	0.28	0.20	0.31

5.2   Maximal Z-Score

In order to interpret result ($Z\text{-}SCORE$) of our tool we have to find expected distribution f_{max} of $Z\text{-}SCORE$ for the null hypothesis i.e. random data. The value of $Z\text{-}SCORE$ is determined by the boolean functions constructed in two phases using setting deg, m, k, t. The value $Z\text{-}SCORE$ is computed as a maximal $Z\text{-}score$ for a set of $Z\text{-}scores$ corresponding to constructed boolean functions. The theoretical assessment of the distribution f_{max} should follow the process of the construction of the best distinguisher with maximal $Z\text{-}score$ (in absolute value). It is hard to theoretically derive probability density function (pdf) f_{max} for settings with $k > 1$. But for the settings with $k = 1$ the pdf f_{max} can be derived much easier.

– For $k = 1$ the resulted $Z\text{-}SCORE$ is equal to a maximal $Z\text{-}score$ computed for boolean functions constructed in the first phase, since in the second phase no functions are constructed. While $Z\text{-}scores$ corresponding to boolean functions (monomials x_i for $i \in 1, \cdots, m$) of degree $deg = 1$ are independent normally distributed random variables, the $Z\text{-}scores$ of functions of higher degrees are dependent since these functions share variables e.g. $x_1.x_2$ and $x_1.x_3$. The correlation is not significant and variables can be modeled as independent with small bias when compared to empirically obtained f_{max}.

- In the case of $k > 1$ the situation is quite different. First of all, Z-scores for the best t distinguishers selected in the first phase are normally distributed but with different means and standard deviations. It is clear that the pdf of a maximum of t normal variables is different to pdf of the second largest normal variable. The reason is obvious: the probability $P(\max(X_i) = V)$ that maximum (l-th order statistic) of normal variables $X_1, \cdots, X_l$ is equal to very large value is strictly smaller than probability that second maximal value (within V_i) is equal to V. Second of all dependency of boolean functions constructed in the second phase is bigger, more complex since these functions are constructed as a sum of several (two or three) partially dependent functions. Therefore to derive theoretical expected pdf f_{max} for $k > 1$ is hard task in general.

In the case $k = 1$, the theoretical pdf f_{max} can be derived using the fact that pdf f_{max} of largest X (l-th order statistic) for independent and identically random variables $X_1, \cdots, X_l$ with pdf f is given by

$$f_{max}(x) = l \cdot f(x) \cdot F(x)^{l-1},$$

for the cumulative distribution function F of variables X_i. We are looking for f_{max} for maximum of absolute values of Z-scores hence $f(x) = 2 \cdot \varphi(x)$ and $F(x) = 2 \cdot (\Phi(x) - 0.5)$ for standard normal distribution $\varphi(x)$ and corresponding cdf $\Phi(x)$. The pdf f_{max} of Z-SCORE for $k = 1$ can expressed as:

$$f_{max}(x) = l \cdot \varphi(x) \cdot (2 \cdot \Phi(x) - 1)^{l-1}$$

for $l = \binom{m}{deg}$ representing number of boolean functions constructed in the first phase. We computed functions $f_{max}(x)$ for settings k, $deg \in \{1, 2, 3\}$, $m \in \{128, 256, 384, 512\}$ and realized that function f_{max} represent normal distribution with mean μ very close to average Z-score obtained empirically. Table 8 shows theoretical μ computed in statistical software R.

Table 8. The mean (μ) of maximal Z-SCORE computed by BoolTest and reference theoretical computation in statistical software R (R-soft) for various settings $k = 1$, $deg \in \{1, 2, 3\}$, $m \in \{128, 256, 384, 512\}$.

deg	1		2		3	
m	BoolTest	R-soft	BoolTest	R-soft	BoolTest	R-soft
128	2.80	2.70	3.87	3.85	4.71	4.68
256	3.05	2.92	4.23	4.18	5.13	5.09
384	3.14	3.03	4.39	4.36	5.32	5.32
512	3.24	3.12	4.55	4.48	5.54	5.48

6   Related Work

NIST STS [4], Dieharder [10] (an extended version of the Diehard [11]) and TestU01 [12] are the most commonly used batteries for statistical randomness testing. The NIST STS is the basic battery required by NIST to test RNGs of cryptographic devices by the FIPS 140-2 certification process [13] with four out of total 15 of NIST STS tests required as power-up tests executed on-device. The Dieharder battery is an extension of original Diehard battery [11] with some (but not all) NIST STS tests also included. Overall, Dieharder consists of 76 test variants. Dieharder is generally more powerful than NIST STS with the ability to detect smaller biases as it may analyze longer data stream.

TestU01 can be viewed as the current state-of-the-art of randomness testing. TestU01 is a library that implements more than 100 different tests of randomness. These tests are grouped into six sub-batteries called Small Crush, Crush, Big Crush, Rabbit, Alphabit, BlockAlphabit. The first three sub-batteries are proposed to test floating point random numbers from the interval [0,1]. The fastest is Small Crush (10 tests), significantly slower is Crush (96 tests) and very slow but powerful is Big Crush battery (all 106 tests). The amount of data used for analysis increases with the number of tests and their complexity. The Small Crush/Crush/Big Crush need at least 206 MB/2.6 GB/51.3 GB data to run all tests of the battery. Other three batteries are proposed for testing the binary sequences specifically. The Rabbit (26 tests), Alphabit (9 tests) and BlockAlphabit (54 tests) batteries are not limited in fact (Rabbit is restricted to 500 bits) in the size of data they need for the analysis. Other statistical testing tools we are aware of are: Donald Knuth's tests [14], Crypt-X suite [15], PractRand [16], RaBiGeTe [17], CryptoStat [18], YAARX [19], ENT [20], SPRNG [21], gjrand [22] and BSI's test suite [23].

Batteries analyze data with an assumption that data were generated by a black box function. It is clear that more information we have about the generator the better randomness analysis we can perform. There are three basic approaches (linear, differential and algebraic cryptanalysis) for randomness analysis of data produced by a primitive which are based on its internal structure. Nice tutorial on linear and differential cryptanalysis can be found in [24]. Various methods of algebraic cryptanalysis are described in the book [25]. There are several automated tools that implement aforementioned approaches. These tools look for dependency between inputs and outputs of the primitive (and key, IV bits). List of current such cryptanalytical methods and tools implemented in recent years can be found at [26].

In [27] a new and strong method of statistical testing of hash functions and symmetric ciphers was proposed. In this approach, each output bit is described as a boolean function in the algebraic normal form (ANF). The test statistic is based on a number of monomials in ANF. Since the number of monomials is exponential in the number of variables, the randomness is evaluated based on the number of monomials of degree exactly d which has χ^2 distribution for random boolean functions. Another automated cryptanalytic tool [28] is based on the strong d-monomial test. In [28] monomial test was generalized to perform chosen

IV statistical attacks on stream ciphers. In [29], a greedy method was proposed to find distinguishers from randomness for stream and block ciphers. The method is based on maximum degree monomial test similar to d-monomial test. Previous methods are based on ANF of analyzed function which is statistically compared with ANF of random boolean function expected for the truly random data. This is completely different to our approach, where the boolean function itself defines the statistic of a test of randomness.

The automated testing tool for cryptographic primitives named Crypto-Stat [30] is focused on testing block ciphers and message authentication codes. CryptoStat consists of several tests each computing the probability that block of bits of the ciphertext equals to bits taken from plaintext and key. Bits are selected either randomly, or block of consecutive bits are taken. The tests of CryptoStat are reducible to Bernoulli trials, and they are evaluated using Bayesian conditional probability.

Hernández and Isasi proposed an automated construction of distinguisher for TEA block cipher [31]. They searched for a distinguisher in the form of input bitmask of the 192-bit block (64-bit plaintext and 128-bit key). As the search space of all possible bitmasks is too large, a heuristic based on genetic algorithm was used to construct a distinguisher for TEA limited up to 4 rounds. In the [32], authors optimized the Hernández's approach with a quantum-inspired genetic algorithm and found distinguisher for TEA limited to 5 rounds. *BoolTest* is performing same as shown in Table 4, yet the scenarios are not directly comparable.

The similar but more general approach is used in EACirc framework [33] which constructs distinguisher (test of randomness) for crypto primitive without knowledge about primitive design (black-box). In the EACirc test of randomness is constructed for the predefined representation as circuit-like software over the set AND, XOR, NOR, NOT of boolean operations. The ciphers with a limited number of rounds were tested with results comparable to NIST STS battery. Although the Dieharder battery still provides overall better randomness analysis EACirc was able to detect some non-randomness for Hermes and Fubuki [34] where both batteries failed to detect any deviances.

7 Conclusion

This paper provides deeper analysis of newly proposed statistical testing tool called *BoolTest* [1, SeCrypt]. In the former work, authors focused on randomness testing of an output of cryptographic functions and random generators. In this work, we present three new strategies focusing on the correlation of input and output bits of cryptoprimitives. To compare the new strategies to the former one, we analyzed the same functions, and we extended the testbed with six new cryptoprimitives (Blowfish, DES, 3-DES, MD5, SHA-1, and SHA-256).

The new results show that *BoolTest* is filling the gap among most common statistical batteries like NIST STS, Dieharder, and TestU01. For *CTR* and *RPC* strategies, *BoolTest* is on average capable of detecting bias in one additional round. It performs comparable for *LHW* strategy and slightly worse in *SAC* strategy.

Additionally, the bias spotted is directly interpretable as a relation between several fixed output bits of the analyzed function. The *BoolTest* can be used as a fast alternative to existing batteries and to complement its results. The direct interpretability of a boolean function based distinguisher adds benefit for human cryptologist interested in the more detailed analysis of weakness present in an inspected cryptographic function.

The future work will address speeding up the brute-force part of the computation by utilizing the FPGA and smarter selection of terms using a heuristic.

Acknowledgements. We acknowledge the support of the Czech Science Foundation, project GA16-08565S. Computational resources were provided by the CESNET LM2015042 and the CERIT Scientific Cloud LM2015085, provided under the programme "Projects of Large Research, Development, and Innovations Infrastructures".

References

1. Sýs, M., Klinec, D., Švenda, P.: The efficient randomness testing using boolean functions. In: 14th International Conference on Security and Cryptography (Secrypt 2017). SCITEPRESS, pp. 92–103 (2017)
2. Simion, E.: The relevance of statistical tests in cryptography. IEEE Secur. Priv. **13**, 66–70 (2015)
3. Sýs, M., Klinec, D.: Booltest - a tool for fast randomness testing (2017). http://crocs.fi.muni.cz/papers/secrypt2017
4. Rukhin, A.: A statistical test suite for the validation of random number generators and pseudo random number generators for cryptographic applications, version STS-2.1, NIST (2010)
5. Press, W.H., Teukolsky, S.A., Vetterling, W.T., Flannery, B.P.: Numerical Recipes 3rd Edition: The Art of Scientific Computing. Cambridge University Press, New York (2007)
6. Sheskin, D.J.: Handbook of Parametric and Nonparametric Statistical Procedures. CRC Press, Boca Raton (2003)
7. Svenda, P., et al.: The million-key question - investigating the origins of RSA public keys. In: The 25th USENIX Security Symposium (UsenixSec 2016), USENIX, pp. 893–910 (2016)
8. Wackerly, D.D., Mendenhall III, W., Scheaffer, R.L.: Mathematical statistics with applications, Duxbury Advanced Series (2002)
9. Chevillard, S.: The functions ERF and ERFC computed with arbitrary precision and explicit error bounds. In: Academic Press Inc, Information and Computation, vol. 216. Academic Press, Inc., pp. 72–95 (2012)
10. Brown, R.G., Eddelbuettel, D., Bauer, D.: Dieharder: a random number test suite 3.31.1 (2013). http://www.phy.duke.edu/~rgb/General/dieharder.php
11. Marsaglia, G.: Diehard: a battery of tests of randomness (1995). https://web.archive.org/web/20040810115625/http://stat.fsu.edu/~geo/diehard.html
12. L'Ecuyer, P., Simard, R.: TestU01: a C library for empirical testing of random number generators. ACM Trans. Math. Softw. **33**, 22 (2007)
13. NIST: FIPS 140–2 security requirements for cryptographic modules, NIST (2001)
14. Knuth, D.E.: The Art of Computer Programming, vol. 2, 1st edn. Addison-Wesley Longman Publishing Co., Inc., Boston (1969)

15. Caelli, W., et al.: Crypt-X suite (1998). https://web.archive.org/web/19990224063612/http://www.isrc.qut.edu.au/cryptx/index.html
16. Doty-Humphrey, C.: Practically random: Specific tests in practrand (2014). http://pracrand.sourceforge.net/
17. Piras, C.: RaBiGeTe documentation (2004). http://cristianopi.altervista.org/RaBiGeTe_MT/
18. Kaminsky, A., Sorrell, J.: Cryptostat: A Bayesian Statistical Testing Framework for Block Ciphers and Macs. Rochester Institute of Technology, Rochester (2013)
19. Biryukov, A., Velichkov, V.: Automatic search for differential trails in ARX ciphers. In: Benaloh, J. (ed.) CT-RSA 2014. LNCS, vol. 8366, pp. 227–250. Springer, Cham (2014). https://doi.org/10.1007/978-3-319-04852-9_12
20. Walker, J.: ENT: a pseudorandom number sequence test program (2008). https://www.fourmilab.ch/random/
21. Mascagni, M., Srinivasan, A.: Algorithm 806: Sprng: a scalable library for pseudorandom number generation. ACM Trans. Math. Softw. (TOMS) 26, 436–461 (2000)
22. Jones, G.: gjrand random numbers (2007). http://gjrand.sourceforge.net/
23. Schindler, W., Killmann, W.: Evaluation criteria for true (Physical) random number generators used in cryptographic applications. In: Kaliski, B.S., Koç, K., Paar, C. (eds.) CHES 2002. LNCS, vol. 2523, pp. 431–449. Springer, Heidelberg (2003). https://doi.org/10.1007/3-540-36400-5_31
24. Heys, H.M.: A tutorial on linear and differential cryptanalysis. Cryptologia 26, 189–221 (2002). Bristol, PA, USA, Taylor & Francis, Inc
25. Bard, G.V.: Algebraic Cryptanalysis. Springer Publishing Company, Boston (2009). https://doi.org/10.1007/978-0-387-88757-9. ISBN 978-0-387-88756-2
26. Mouha, N.: Ecrypt II: tools for cryptography (2010). http://www.ecrypt.eu.org/tools/overview
27. Filiol, E.: A new statistical testing for symmetric ciphers and hash functions. In: Deng, R., Bao, F., Zhou, J., Qing, S. (eds.) ICICS 2002. LNCS, vol. 2513, pp. 342–353. Springer, Heidelberg (2002). https://doi.org/10.1007/3-540-36159-6_29
28. Englund, H., Johansson, T., Sönmez Turan, M.: A framework for chosen IV statistical analysis of stream ciphers. In: Srinathan, K., Rangan, C.P., Yung, M. (eds.) INDOCRYPT 2007. LNCS, vol. 4859, pp. 268–281. Springer, Heidelberg (2007). https://doi.org/10.1007/978-3-540-77026-8_20
29. Stankovski, P.: Greedy distinguishers and nonrandomness detectors. In: Gong, G., Gupta, K.C. (eds.) INDOCRYPT 2010. LNCS, vol. 6498, pp. 210–226. Springer, Heidelberg (2010). https://doi.org/10.1007/978-3-642-17401-8_16
30. Kaminsky, A., Sorrell, J.: Cryptostat, a bayesian statistical testing framework for block ciphers and MACS (2014). http://www.cs.rit.edu/~ark/students/jls6190/report.pdf
31. Hernández, J., Isasi, P.: Finding efficient distinguishers for cryptographic mappings, with an application to the block cipher TEA. In: Computational Intelligence, vol. 20, pp. 517–525, Blackwell (2004)
32. Garrett, A., Hamilton, J., Dozier, G.: A comparison of genetic algorithm techniques for the cryptanalysis of TEA. Int. J. Intell. Control Syst. 12, 325–330 (2007). Springer
33. EACirc: EACirc project (2017). https://github.com/CRoCS_MUNI/EACirc
34. Sýs, M., Švenda, P., Ukrop, M., Matyáš, V.: Constructing empirical tests of randomness. In: SECRYPT 2014, ICETE (2014)

Resistance of the Point Randomisation Countermeasure for Pairings Against Side-Channel Attack

Damien Jauvart[1]([⊠]), Nadia El Mrabet[2], Jacques J. A. Fournier[3], and Louis Goubin[4]

[1] Aix-Marseille Université, 163 Avenue de Luminy, 13009 Marseille, France
damien.jauvart@univ-amu.fr
[2] Mines Saint-Étienne, 880, route de Mimet, 13541 Gardanne Cedex, France
nadia.el-mrabet@emse.fr
[3] CEA LETI, 17 rue des Martyrs, 38054 Grenoble Cedex 9, France
jacques.fournier@cea.fr
[4] Laboratoire de Mathématiques de Versailles, UVSQ, CNRS,
Université Paris-Saclay, 78035 Versailles, France
louis.goubin@uvsq.fr

Abstract. Pairing-based cryptography (PBC) has been significantly studied over the last decade, both in the areas of computational performance and in establishing security and privacy protocols. PBC implementations on embedded devices are exposed to physical attacks such as side channel attacks. Such attacks which are able to recover the secret input used in some PBC-based schemes are our main focus in this paper. Various countermeasures have consequently been proposed in the literature. The present paper provides an updated review of the state of the art countermeasures against side channel attacks against PBC implementations. We especially focus on a technique based on point blinding using randomization. Furthermore, we propose a collision based side-channel attack against an implementation embedding the point randomization countermeasure. This raises questions about the validation of countermeasures for complex cryptographic schemes such as PBC. We also discuss about ways of defeat our attack. This article is in part an extension of the paper [20] published at Secrypt 2017.

Keywords: Pairing-based cryptography · Miller's algorithm
Side-channel attack · Collision side-channel attack · Countermeasures

1 Introduction

Bilinear pairings are used in cryptography for various innovative protocols. In 2001, Boneh and Franklin published the Identity-Based Encryption (IBE) scheme based on Pairings [10]. The one-round tripartite key exchange [22] based on Pairings is another interesting practical use of such cryptographic primitives.

© Springer Nature Switzerland AG 2019
M. S. Obaidat and E. Cabello (Eds.): ICETE 2017, CCIS 990, pp. 150–172, 2019.
https://doi.org/10.1007/978-3-030-11039-0_8

Both protocols have been rewarded by the 2013 Gödel price for their advance in the cryptographic area.

Several studies have investigated about the vulnerability of PBC to side-channel attacks. The first papers to consider the security of pairings regarding side-channel attacks were mainly concerned with elliptic curves defined over small fields of characteristics 2 and 3 is Page *et al.* [36]. Although Joux [23] and Barbulescu [3] recently suggested that such fields should be avoided, some of those techniques intended for small characteristic fields can nevertheless be applied over large prime fields. At high level a pairing is a bilinear and not degenerate map denoted $e : \mathbb{G}_1 \times \mathbb{G}_2 \rightarrow \mathbb{G}_3$ where $\mathbb{G}_1$, $\mathbb{G}_2$ and $\mathbb{G}_3$ are abelian groups of the same order l. In an IBE [10] scheme that uses pairings, a cipher is decrypted by the computation of a pairing between a **secret** point and another point that is part of the **input** cipher. In a nutshell, in the IBE [10] scheme the decryption step consists in deciphering the ciphertext constituted by the pair $\{U, V\}$ with $U \in \mathbb{G}_1$ and $V \in \{0, 1\}^n$ using the private key D. The entity needs to compute $e(D, U)$. Side-channel attacks against such a scenario aim at exploiting the interaction between the **known ciphertext point** and the **secret point** (which is part of the private secret key). A pairing calculation has a *double-and-add* structure, as is the case in Elliptic Curve Cryptography (ECC). However, with PBC the problem regarding side-channel attacks is different: the number of iterations and the scalar are known; and the secret is one of the arguments of the pairing. Consequently, side-channel attacks on PBC implementations are more likely to rely on Correlation Power Analysis-like (CPA) techniques to target the secret point (compared to using Simple Power Analysis-like (SPA) approaches to target the scalar in the double-and-add structure).

In this paper, we review various side-channel attacks used against PBC implementations and the associated countermeasures. We then focus on one of those countermeasures in order to explain and illustrate how to defeat it with an attack that has never been developed against PBC. The paper is organized as follows. The Sect. 2 recalls the bases on the pairings necessary for their comprehension for this article. We review related work concerning side-channel around PBC in the Sect. 3. The Sect. 4 provides an analysis of a countermeasures under our investigation and explains how this protection can be defeated. Then the Sect. 5 describes the practical experiments and results obtained when implementing this attack against a software pairing calculation running on a 32-bit platform. A conclusion is then proposed in the Sect. 6.

2 Pairings as a Cryptographic Application

In this section, we provide the concepts and notations that will be used throughout this paper. For a detailed explanation of pairings we refer the reader to [40].

2.1 Pairing Description

Let q be a large prime number and E be an elliptic curve defined over $\mathbb{F}_q$. E can be written as in the Eq. 1, this is the well known Weierstrass form.

$$E = \{(x,y) \in \mathbb{F}_q \times \mathbb{F}_q | y^2 + a_1 xy + a_3 y = x^3 + a_2 x^2 + a_4 x + a_6\} \cup \{\mathcal{O}\}, \quad (1)$$

where $\mathcal{O}$ denotes the point at infinity: it is the identity element for the addition group law. The set of l-*torsion points of* E is $E[l] := \ker[l]$ (the set of points P in E such that $[l]P = \mathcal{O}$), the *rational torsion points* are given by $E(\mathbb{F}_q)[l] := E(\mathbb{F}_q) \cap E[l]$. The smallest positive integer k such that l divides $q^k - 1$ is called the embedding degree of $E(\mathbb{F}_q)$ with respect to l. As soon as $k > 1$, the group $E(\mathbb{F}_q)[l]$ is included into $E(\mathbb{F}_{q^k})$. Let $\mathbb{G}_1 = E(\mathbb{F}_q)[l] \cup E(\mathbb{F}_q)$, $\mathbb{G}_2 = E(\mathbb{F}_{q^k}) \cup E(\mathbb{F}_q)[l]$ and $\mathbb{G}_3$ be the group of l-roots of unity in $\mathbb{F}_{q^k}$.

1. Non-degeneracy: $\forall P \in \mathbb{G}_1 \setminus \{\mathcal{O}\} \quad \exists Q \in \mathbb{G}_2$ such that $e(P,Q) \neq 1$,
2. Bilinearity:

$$e([a]P_1 + [b]P_2, Q) = e(P_1, Q)^a e(P_2, Q)^b, \text{for } a,b \in \mathbb{F}_l$$
$$e(P, [a]Q_1 + [b]Q_2) = e(P, Q_1)^a e(P, Q_2)^b.$$

The above properties can be verified by using groups of points on elliptic curves for both abelian groups.

The Tate Pairing. The widely used Tate pairing [6,13,16,39] takes as inputs two points P and Q such that $P \in E(\mathbb{F}_q)[l]$ and $Q \in E(\mathbb{F}_q)$ as provided in Eq. 2 where μ_l is the group of the l-th roots of unity such that $\mu_l = \{\xi \in \mathbb{F}_{q^k}^\star | \xi^l = 1\}$. A final exponentiation $\frac{q^k-1}{l}$ is applied to the output $f_P(Q)$ in order to obtain a unique value of order l.

$$\tau_l : E(\mathbb{F}_q)[l] \cup E(\mathbb{F}_q) \times E(\mathbb{F}_{q^k}) \setminus E(\mathbb{F}_q)[l] \rightarrow \mathbb{F}_{q^k}^\star/(\mathbb{F}_{q^k}^\star)^l \rightarrow \mu_l \subset \mathbb{F}_{q^k}^\star$$
$$P, Q \qquad\qquad\qquad \mapsto f_{l,P}(Q) \quad \mapsto f_P(Q)^{\frac{q^k-1}{l}} \qquad (2)$$

where $f_{l,P}$ represents the Miller's function.

The Barreto–Naehrig Curves [5]. This family of curves is widely used to get efficient implementations of pairings. The pairing-friendly ordinary elliptic curves over a prime field $\mathbb{F}_q$ are defined by $E : y^2 = x^3 + b$ where $b \neq 0$. Their embedding degree is $k = 12$. The order of E is l, a prime number. The BN curves are parametrized with p and l as follows:

$$p(t) = 36t^4 + 36t^3 + 24t^2 + 6t + 1,$$
$$l(t) = 36t^4 + 36t^3 + 18t^2 + 6t + 1, \qquad (3)$$

where $t \in \mathbb{Z}$ is chosen in order to get $p(t)$ coprime to $l(t)$ and large enough to guarantee an adequate security level. We use the same notation as in the original paper [20], Eq. 3. According to recent development on the resolution of discrete logarithm, the BN curves could be no longer the most accurate choice for an efficient pairing implementation. We demonstrate our work using BN curves as we had an existing efficient implementation. However, our approach is independent from the family.

The Miller's Function. The Miller's function $f_{l,P}$ is a rational function defined by its divisor: $Div(f_{l,P}) = l(P) - ([l-1]P) - (\mathcal{O})$. The computation of such a map is a well known problem [6] and an efficient way of computing such pairings was proposed as a recursive scheme by Miller [32]. Miller's algorithm, which works as the main calculation to compute a pairing, uses an iterative relation to construct the rational function $f_{l,P}$. The Miller's loop is given in Algorithm 1.

Algorithm 1. Miller's algorithm.

> **Data:** $l = (l_{n-1} \ldots l_0)_2$, $P \in \mathbb{G}_1$ and $Q \in \mathbb{G}_2$
> **Result:** $f_{l,P}(Q) \in \mathbb{G}_3$
>
> 1 $T \leftarrow P$;
> 2 $f \leftarrow 1$;
> 3   **for** $i = n - 1$ **downto** 0 **do**
> 4 $f \leftarrow f^2(l_{T,T}(Q))$;
> 5 $T \leftarrow [2]T$;
> 6   **if** $l_i == 1$ **then**
> 7 $f \leftarrow f(l_{T,P}(Q))$;
> 8 $T \leftarrow T + P$;
> 9   **end**
> 10 **end**
> 11 **return** f;

In Algorithm 1:

1. $l_{T,T}(Q)$ is the equation of the tangent at T evaluated at point Q.
2. $l_{T,P}(Q)$ is the equation of the line through T and P evaluated at point Q.

These equations are optimized by using mixed system coordinates for the points' representations as suggested in [1, 2, 8, 27, 35]:

1. P and Q are in affine coordinates.
2. T is in Jacobian coordinates, i.e. if $T = (x_T, y_T) = \left(\frac{X_T}{Z_T^2}, \frac{Y_T}{Z_T^3}\right)$ in affine coordinates then $T = (X_T : Y_T : Z_T)$ in Jacobian.

With this representation the tangent and line equation are shown in Eq. 4. With the same notation as in [20], Eq. 4.

$$
\begin{aligned}
l_{T,T}(Q) &= 2y_Q Y_T Z_T^3 - 2Y_T^2 - (3X_T^2 + aZ_T^4)(x_Q Z_T^2 - X_T) \\
l_{T,P}(Q) &= (y_Q - y_P) Z_T (X_T - Z_T^2 x_P) - (Y_T - Z_T^3 y_P)(x_Q - x_P)
\end{aligned}
\tag{4}
$$

In the following, our implementation is a Tate pairing over Barreto and Naehrig curves [5].

2.2 Application to Identity-Based Encryption

An IBE scheme can be used to simplify a widely known issue in public key cryptography: the key exchange [24]. A Public-Key Infrastructure (PKI) based on IBE is less complex and more scalable compared to classical schemes (with certifications).

In an IBE, the public key of a character **is** its identity. The associated private key can't be computed by this character, but generated by the Private Key Generator (PKG). Of course, the decryption should be possible only with the private key.

A simplified version of the scheme of Boneh-Franklin [10] work in four steps:

1. *Setup.* The PKG have to generate some public parameters for the pairings. Let $\mathbb{G}_1$ and $\mathbb{G}_2$ be two groups of order l such that $e : \mathbb{G}_1 \times \mathbb{G}_1 \to \mathbb{G}_2$ is a bilinear pairing. Let $P \in \mathbb{G}_1$ be a generator of $\mathbb{G}_1$. Let $H_1 : \{0,1\}^* \to \mathbb{G}_1^*$ and $H_2 : \mathbb{G}_2 \to \{0,1\}^n$ be two cryptographic hash functions. Let $s \in \mathbb{Z}_r$ be random, s is their private key (a master key of the system). Let $P_{PUB} = [s]P$ be the global public key. The set of public parameters is

$$\{r, n, \mathbb{G}_1, \mathbb{G}_2, e, P, P_{PUB}, H_1, H_2\}.$$

2. *Extraction.* The extraction algorithm supplies the private key of a user. Let $ID =$ "Bob" $\in \{0,1\}^*$ be the identity of a user Bob. The PKG hashes this string into $\mathbb{G}_1$ in order to obtain $Q_B = H_1(ID)$. Bob's private key is $d_B = [s]Q_B$ (computed and transmitted to Bob by the PKG).

3. *Encryption.* Alice wants to send a message $M \in \{0,1\}^n$ to Bob, she proceeds as follows:
   1. She computes $Q_B = H_1$ ("Bob").
   2. She randomly picks k.
   3. She computes $g_B = e(Q_B, P_{PUB}) \in \mathbb{G}_2^*$.
   4. Then, she computes the ciphertext $C = \{[k]P, M \oplus H_2(g_B^k)\}$ and sends it to Bob.

4. *Decryption.* Bob wants to decrypt the ciphertext $C = \{U, V\}$ where $U \in \mathbb{G}_1, V \in \{0,1\}^n$, he proceeds as follows:
   1. He computes $e(d_B, U)$ which is equal to $e([s]Q_B, [k]P) = e(Q_B, P)^{sk} = e(Q_B, [s]P)^k = e(Q_B, P_{PUB})^k = g_B^k$.
   2. He gets the message $M = V \oplus H_2(g_B^k)$.

3   Related Work and Contributions

Differential Power Analysis (DPA) attacks have been first introduced by Kocher *et al.* in [29]. Since then, DPA-like techniques have been successfully used to attack implementations of most cryptographic algorithms.

3.1   Related Work in Side-Channel Attacks Against Pairings

The first paper to investigate about the physical security of pairing algorithms was published in 2004. In this paper, Page and Vercauteren [36] simulated an attack on the Duursma–Lee Algorithm [12] which is used to compute Tate pairings using elliptic curves over finite fields of characteristic 3. The authors exposed the vulnerability of such pairings with respect to active (fault injections) and passive (side-channel observations) attacks. The authors also proposed two countermeasures to thwart side channel attacks.

The first countermeasure is based on the bilinearity of the pairing where, if a and b are two random values, then we have the equality: $e(P,Q) = e([a]P,[b]Q)^{1/ab}$. The second countermeasure, proposed in [36], works for cases where P is secret and a mask is added to the point Q as follows: select a random point $R \in \mathbb{G}_2$ and compute $e(P,Q+R)e(P,R)^{-1}$ instead of $e(P,Q)$, with different random values of R at every call to e.

The main inconvenience of these countermeasures is the computation overhead where two pairings are calculated instead of one.

Pan and Marnane [37] simulated a side-channel attack where they proposed a CPA based on a Hamming distance model to target a pairing over a base field of characteristic 2 over super-singular curves. The practical results obtained by Pan and Marnane can be used to assess the feasibility of using CPA to target pairings on an FPGA platform.

Kim et al. [25] also examined the security of pairings over binary fields. They addressed timing, SPA, and DPA attacks targeting arithmetic operations. In order to propose a more efficient countermeasure to protect Eta pairings, Kim et al. [25] implemented the third countermeasure proposed by Coron [11], which uses random projective coordinates. The randomization countermeasure proposed by Kim et al. adds just one step at the beginning. For greater efficiency, when P is secret, they randomized only the known input point Q. Its effect is "removed" during the final exponentiation.

This approach can be adapted to other pairing algorithms that are based on either small or large characteristic prime fields. This method is similar to the countermeasure suggested by Scott [39]. It consists in randomizing the Miller variable in Algorithm 1 by multiplying the operations 4 and 7 by a random $\lambda \in \mathbb{F}_q^*$. The result is correct because the random element is eliminated through the final exponentiation.

In the end, these countermeasures only add few modular multiplications, which means a small overhead.

Whelan and Scott [43] studied pairings with different base field characteristics. They analyzed the arithmetic operations and concluded that the secret can be recovered by using a CPA. But the authors specified the need to have the point Q (second entry) as secret for the attack to work. The latter conclusion was refuted by El Mrabet in [14], which, to our best knowledge, is the first paper to present a concrete attack on Miller's algorithm with P (first input) as secret.

Another attack, this time on an FPGA platform, is proposed by Ghosh et al. [17]. They performed a bitwise DPA attack on an FPGA platform by measuring the power consumption leakages during the modular subtraction operations. To counteract this attack, the authors proposed a "low-cost" protection based on a rearrangement principle whose aim is to prevent interaction between a known value and a secret input as it happens in the calculations involved in the tangent or line evaluations. To achieve this, the authors proposed to rewrite the line equation to prevent the addition and/or subtraction operations between the known and secret data. They used the distributivity properties, i.e. if an instruction is $(k - y_1)y_2$ with k being the secret and y_1, y_2 being known integers, then the target operation is $(k - y_1)$. To avoid this, the authors proposed to rewrite it as $ky_2 - y_1y_2$. Indeed, this trick avoids the critical subtraction. However, this time this trick does not protect the modular multiplication and fails to protect against classical attack schemes as presented in [9,14,43].

Moreover, Blömer et al. [9] studied DPA attacks by targeting modular addition and multiplication operations of finite field elements with large prime characteristics. Their paper describes an improved DPA for cases in which modular addition is targeted by combining information derived from manipulations of the least and most significant bits. In addition, the study provided simulation results to prove the feasibility of the attack. Furthermore, they propose a new countermeasure. In the reduced Tate pairing, the set of the second argument input is the equivalence class $E(\mathbb{F}_{q^k})/lE(\mathbb{F}_{q^k})$. If the random point T is chosen initially from $E(\mathbb{F}_{q^k})$ of order r, coprime to l, then $T + Q \sim Q$. Hence, $e(P, Q + T) = e(P, Q)$. This trick makes it possible to obtain a countermeasure as powerful as that of [36] with no overhead.

The importance of implementing countermeasures is supported by the recent results of Unterluggauer and Wenger [41] and Jauvart et al. [21], where attacks are presented in the real world environment. Indeed, Ate pairings implemented on Virtex-II FPGA, ARM Cortex-M0 and ARM Cortex-M3 have been broken efficiently with CPA attacks.

Despite all this existing literature on side-channel countermeasures for Pairings, to our best knowledge, none have actually tested or validated the efficiency of those countermeasures when considering analysis attack. In this paper we investigate about the level of protection provided by the randomization of coordinates which seems to be a classy and efficient countermeasure. To our best knowledge, except for fault attacks, no particular problem has been reported in the literature regarding this countermeasure applied to Pairings. But our analysis shows that this countermeasure can be defeated by a collision-based attack.

3.2 Collision Based Side Channel Attacks

The use of "collisions" as a means of exploiting side channel attacks is not something new in the literature. In this section we provide a quick review of the existing background in this very precise field before describing our approach and the differences with the existing state-of-the-art.

Collision attacks were first introduced in [38]. The main idea is to use the side-channel leakages to detect collisions in the encryption function, such collisions may appear internal to the function, in their attack it is not mandatory to observe collisions only at the output. Collisions inside the Data Encryption Standard (DES) can be detected using side-channels and exploited in order to retrieve the secret key used by the algorithm. This new class of attack was later used to circumvent countermeasures used in "secure" implementations of the Advanced Encryption Standard (AES) in [34].

The use of collisions against implementations of public key cryptographic algorithms have also been described. To achieve this, Fouque and Valette [15] use the following assumption: if two operations involve a common operand then the use of this common operand, can be detected using side-channels for attacking, in their example, the RSA exponent. More precisely, even if an adversary is not able to tell which computation is done by the device, he can at least detect when the device does the same operation twice. For example, if the device computes $2.A$ and $2.B$, the attacker is not able to guess the value of A nor B but he is able to check if $A = B$.

Similar work has been suggested by Bauer et al. in [7]. This time the target is a scalar multiplication over an elliptic curve. The assumption is still the same: the adversary can detect when two field multiplications have at least one operand in common. In a double-and-add algorithm the doubling step and the addition have a slight difference. One of them (depending on the curve representation) performs two modular multiplications with the same operand. Collision detection allows to distinguish between the doubling and the addition operations, from which the secret scalar can be deduced.

In [42], the authors target a protected Elliptic Curve Digital Signature Algorithm (ECDSA) implementation. One of the weak points of this protocol is the calculation of a modular multiplication between a known variable and the secret key. Thus a DPA is able to recover the key [18]. To counteract this attack, a trick consists in distributing a calculus to remove such critical operations. As an example, whenever the operation $mask(plaintext + public\_key \times secret\_key)$ must be computed, they propose to do $mask \times plaintext + (mask \times secret\_key)public\_key$ instead. The drawback revealed by Varchola et al. is that the additional calculation is between the known message and the temporary mask (which changes from one execution to another) while another calculation is made between this same mask and the secret. Thus, with the same assumption that in the previous cases [7, 15], the collision detection will make it possible to discover whether the known (and controllable) message is equal to the secret key.

Our contribution adapts the principle of collision detection – based on the detecting when the same operand is used twice – to circumvent the randomization of Jacobian coordinates countermeasure used to protect pairing.

4   Security Analysis of the Countermeasure Based on Randomized Jacobian Coordinates

The previously described countermeasures have been proposed without any theoretical security proofs, and to the best of our knowledge, no practical evidence has been provided neither. In this section, we first introduce the classical CPA against an unprotected pairing implementation. This will allow us to show how the countermeasure analysed in this paper plays an important role. Next, we will be able to compare the effectiveness of an attack on an unprotected and a counter-measured pairing to note the effectiveness of the countermeasure. The analysed countermesure is the Miller's algorithm with randomized Jacobian coordinates. We show how collisions can be used to make this countermeasure fail. We introduce a first "straight-forward" scheme to detect collisions and we show that this approach has its limits in practice. Then we adapt a refined method proposed in [42] for detecting collisions by implementing it on our target device and we show how practical results of how this collision-detection scheme defeats the point randomization countermeasure.

4.1 Classical Side-Channel Attack Against Unprotected Pairing Implementation

For performance reasons, the use of mixed affine-Jacobian coordinates has been often proposed in the literature [1,2,8,27,35]. In this case, at the beginning of the Miller's algorithm, the point P is assigned to T, with T expressed in Jacobian coordinates. This operation comprises the following steps:

1. $X_T \leftarrow x_P$; $Y_T \leftarrow y_P$; $Z_T \leftarrow 1$,
2. $T \leftarrow (X_T : Y_T : Z_T)$.

We are looking for an operation that takes as operands: known data and secret data. Such operation appear during the first iteration of the Miller loop. More precisely, in the calculation of the tangent line, the evaluation of the tangent line is as follow:

$$2Y_T Z_T^3 y_Q - 2Y_T^2 - (3X_T^2 + aZ_T^4)(x_Q Z_T^2 - X_T), \tag{5}$$

where a is a parameter for the BN curves. The attacked coordinates are x_Q and y_Q, they are respectively involved in the multiplications $x_Q(Z_T^2)$ and $(2Y_T Z_T^3)y_Q$. The secret coordinates are attacked with a CPA against the modular multiplication. The coordinates of the point $T = (X_T : Y_T : Z_T)$ are known since they are initialized to those of the known point P.

Attack Against the Modular Multiplication. The context is the following: the targeted modular multiplication $a \times b \mod p$ is a Montgomery's CIOS Multiprecision Multiplication Algorithm 2. It is a common choice for cryptographic applications due to its low cost, this choice does not affect the attack anyway. For more details about Montgomery multiplication implementation, we recommend to read [28].

The operation which involves known and unknown data is the following (line 5):

$$(uv) \leftarrow \underbrace{c_j}_{\text{carry}} + \underbrace{a_j b_i}_{\text{word integers}} + \underbrace{u}_{\text{register}}. \tag{6}$$

Algorithm 2. CIOS Modular Montgomery Multiplication

Data: The modulus $p = (p_{\mathfrak{N}-1} \ldots p_0)_{\overline{\mathfrak{W}}}$ coprime with $\overline{\mathfrak{W}}$, $\mathfrak{R} = \overline{\mathfrak{W}}^{\mathfrak{N}}$, p' such that
$\mathfrak{R}\mathfrak{R}^{-1} - pp' = 1$ and two integers $a = (a_{\mathfrak{N}-1} \ldots a_0)_{\overline{\mathfrak{W}}}$ and
$b = (b_{\mathfrak{N}-1} \ldots b_0)_{\overline{\mathfrak{W}}}$.

Result: The unique integer $c = (c_{\mathfrak{N}-1} \ldots c_0)_{\overline{\mathfrak{W}}}$ such that
$c = \text{REDC}(ab) = (ab\mathfrak{R}^{-1}) \mod p$.

```
 1  c ← 0 ;
 2  for i = 0 to 𝔑 − 1 do
 3      u ← 0 ;
 4      for j = 0 to 𝔑 − 1 do
 5          (uv) ← c_j + a_j b_i + u ;
 6          c_j ← v ;
 7      end
 8      (uv) ← c_𝔑 + u ;
 9      c_𝔑 ← v ;
10      c_{𝔑+1} ← u ;
11      m ← c_0 p'_0 mod 𝔚̄ ;
12      (uv) ← c_0 + m p_0 ;
13      for j = 1 to 𝔑 − 1 do
14          (uv) ← c_j + m p_j + u ;
15          c_{j−1} ← v ;
16      end
17      (uv) ← c_𝔑 + u ;
18      c_{𝔑−1} ← v ;
19      c_𝔑 ← c_{𝔑+1} + u ;
20  end
21  if (c_{𝔑−1} … c_0)_𝔚̄ < p then
22      c ← (c_{𝔑−1} … c_0)_𝔚̄ ;
23  else
24      c ← (c_{𝔑−1} … c_0)_𝔚̄ − p ;
25  end
26  return c ;
```

The 64-bit registers (uv) are affected into the new variable. In this new variable appear the product $a_j b_i$, two interesting machine words. One of them (a_j) is a word of the secret integer, i.e. derived from the point Q. While b_i is a word from the known integer P inputs in the Miller algorithm. The 32-bit of the secrete word are recover byte by byte. Thus, the known word is over 32 bits several leakage models are possible, the paper of Jauvart et al. [21] show some difference and select one of them. Figure 1 summarizes the choice of the 16-bit model.

The aim of correlation power analysis is to compare, by a correlation calculus, the side-channel leakages and the hypothetical intermediate state during the multiplication procedure. The side-channel leakages are the measurement traces. The intermediate state is computed between the known input (b_i) and all of

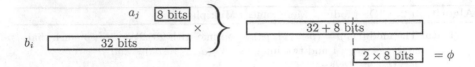

Fig. 1. Word machine leakage model.

the $2^8 = 256$ key hypothesis for the least significant byte. This intermediate calculus is mapped in intermediate state by the well know Hamming weight leakage model. The key whose calculation of correlation between the derived intermediate state and the side-channel traces which maximizes the correlation is retained as the candidate key.

Afterward, the others 3 bytes are Attacked in the Same Way.

4.2 The Miller's Algorithm with Randomized Jacobian Coordinates

Such protection is convenient to be applied in the Miller's algorithm using the mixed affine-Jacobian coordinates and relies on the homogeneity of Jacobian coordinates. The above steps in Sect. 4.1 are replaced by the proposed countermeasure, for which the input point P is **known**, and Q is the **secret** point:

1. $\lambda \in \mathbb{F}_q^*$ is randomly generated,
2. $X_T \leftarrow x_P \lambda^2; \quad Y_T \leftarrow y_P \lambda^3; \quad Z_T \leftarrow \lambda,$
3. $T \leftarrow (X_T : Y_T : Z_T).$

The full Miller algorithm that integrates this countermeasure is given in Algorithm 3.

Algorithm 3. Miller's algorithm with randomization of Jacobian coordinates.

Data: $l = (l_{n-1} \ldots l_0)$ radix 2 representation, $P \in \mathbb{G}_1$ and $Q \in \mathbb{G}_2$
Result: $f_P(D_Q) \in \mathbb{G}_3$

1 $\lambda \in \mathbb{F}_q^*$ is randomly generated ;
2 $X_T \leftarrow x_P \lambda^2;$
3 $Y_T \leftarrow y_P \lambda^3$;
4 $Z_T \leftarrow \lambda;$
5 $f \leftarrow 1;$
6 **for** $i = n - 1$ **downto** 0 **do**
7 $\quad\quad f \leftarrow f^2(l_{T,T}(Q));$
8 $\quad\quad T \leftarrow [2]T;$
9 $\quad\quad$ **if** $l_i == 1$ **then**
10 $\quad\quad\quad\quad f \leftarrow f(l_{T,P}(Q));$
11 $\quad\quad\quad\quad T \leftarrow T + P;$
12 $\quad\quad$ **end**
13 **end**
14 **return** $f;$

All attacks against pairings proposed so far are DPA/CPA-like approaches that target arithmetic operations such as modular additions or multiplications between a known (public) value and a secret (key) one. Our attack scheme is different as it exploits collisions which may appear during the same execution of a pairing.

Of course, since the recent results of Joux [23] and Barbulescu [3], pairings in small characteristic based field are no longer recommended. Nevertheless, the proposed countermeasures in such fields can also be used in other fields with a very small overhead.

4.3   Detecting Collisions in Point-Randomized Pairing Calculations

Our attack is based on the following observation: in Algorithm 3 the mask is applied once to the public parameter and at least once to the secret input. During the first iteration of Miller's loop, the tangent evaluation calculates $(xZ_T^2 - X_T)$, which is in fact $(x\lambda^2 - x_P\lambda^2)$, for which $x\lambda^2$ is computed in the tangent evaluation and $x_P\lambda^2$ is computed in the randomization step.

Thus, if the known input x_P is equal (or "partially equal") to the secret x, then the EM traces are expected to be similar. The data x, x_p are long precision integers, for instance 256-bit integers, and then it is impossible to test all the 2^{256} values for x. However, the targeted operations work on "word representations" of those integers, like for example when implementing the Montgomey multiplication [33]. So, we can consider only one word of each of those integers. Even with this remark, the words are still too long, for instance, a 256-bit integer can be stored in 8 words of 32 bits in an 32-bit architecture. Then "partially equal" denotes the equality of a part of the word such as the least significant byte.

In order to exploit this observation, our proposed attack scheme is the following. We assume that there exist 2^8 points P_j such that the 8 LSBs (Least Significant Bits) of the x coordinate cover all 2^8 possibilities.

$$x_{P_0} = (\star\star\cdots\star\,00000000)_2$$
$$x_{P_1} = (\star\star\cdots\star\,00000001)_2$$
$$\vdots$$
$$x_{P_{255}} = (\star\star\cdots\star\,11111111)_2$$

We then perform a pairing between each P_j and the secret point Q. The λ_j value is chosen at random. For each EM trace, it is necessary to focus on two critical moments: the computations of $x_{P_j}\lambda_j^2$ and $x\lambda_j^2$.

For each of the resulting "pairs of traces", we need to evaluate the similarities between the two signals. These similarities can be estimated through cross correlations for example. The maximum correlation coefficient then yields a candidate for the 8 LSBs of the secret x.

Averaging is necessary in order to reduce the effect of noise on the attack. Obviously, due to the randomness of λ, it is not recommended to average the acquired traces. However, for a fixed input x_{P_j} and x, we computed the cross correlations between traces for $x_{P_j}\lambda^2$ and $x\lambda^2$ computations. We thereby obtain

$c_{P_j}^{(0)}$, and we repeat the process with other unknown λ. We then collect some $c_{P_j}^{(n)}$ coefficients for each key hypothesis and subsequently compute an average correlation coefficient for all hypothetical keys. This number n is further denoted n_P.

We subsequently repeat the method with other values of P_j covering another portion of the data, and the secret is fully recovered.

5   Practical Implementation of the Collision Attack against Point Randomization

In this section, we report the practical results obtained when implementing our collision attack. The experiments were carried in two stages. A first stage consisted in testing the feasibility of detecting collisions, at word level, on our 32-bit target device. In the second stage, we implemented our attack on a Pairings implementation integrating Jacobian point randomisation countermeasure.

5.1   Preliminary Characterization of Collision Detection on Our Target Device

The targeted device is an ARM Cortex M3 processor working on 32-bit registers. We implemented the representative target operations over 32-bit integers:

$$- x_{P_j} \times \lambda^2,$$
$$- x \times \lambda^2.$$

As source of side channel information, we use the ElectroMagnetic (EM) waves emitted by the chip during the targeted calculations. This technique does not need any depackaging of the chip and allowed to have "local" measurements when precisely positioned on top of the die. The electromagnetic emanation (EM) measurements were done using a Langer EMV-Technik LF-U 5 probe equipped with a Langer Amplifier PA303 BNC (30 dB). The curves were collected using a Lecroy WaveRunner 640Zi oscilloscope. The acquisition frequency of the oscilloscope is 10^9 samples per second. The EM measurements acquisition method is recalled by the Algorithm 4, it is similar to Algorithm 3 in paper [20]. As a result, in one EM measurement there are two multiplications. An example of such a trace is given in Fig. 2.

The choice of EM leakages source is justified by the fact that the device under test is not appropriate for acquiring power consumption. Indeed, the device has many power sources and grounds, so if we want to keep the power consumption, the choices of them is not so simple, and can be a combination of several sources/grounds. The other reason is linked to the practical equipment to make the power consumption attack. A resistance should be placed on the source or on the ground, then there is a risk of damaging the circuit. The EM equipment is just a probe to place over the integrated circuit. Furthermore, in the case of our device, it is not necessary to depackage to integrated circuit, then there is no dangerous manipulation of the circuit.

Algorithm 4. EM measurements acquisition procedure.

Data: n_P, the repetition number

Result: A data base of EM measurement $R \in \mathcal{M}_{256,n_P,2t}$, t is the traces length

```
1  for j = 0 to 255 do
2  |    x_j ← (0...0j_7j_6...j_0)_2;    // j = (j_7...j_0)_2 in radix 2 representation
3  |    for i = 0 to n_P − 1 do
4  |    |    λ ← random in {0,...,2^32 − 1};
5  |    |    Execute the routine: computation of x_j × λ², x × λ²;
6  |    |    Store the EM measurement in R[j,i]
7  |    end
8  end
9  return R;
```

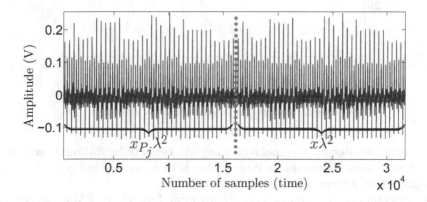

Fig. 2. An example of electromagnetic emanation measurement © [20].

At the end of Sect. 4.3 we introduced the theoretical technique to distinguish the good key when the correlation coefficient is used to detect collisions. This naive method consists in comparing two traces by cross correlation for each couple $x_{P_j} \times \lambda^2$ and $x \times \lambda^2$, and computes a coefficient for each key hypothesis (denoted by x_{P_j}) by averaging the correlation over the n_P repetitions.

We used this method with our EM measurements by using the correlation criterion. The attack succeeds if the maximal value for the collision detection criterion is reached when $x_{P_j} = x$. Then we can classify the key candidates (on 8 bits) according to their criterion values. The keys are now ranked from the most to the least probable, the position of the correct secret key is called the "key ranking". The key ranking is a value between 1 and 256, it is worth 1 if the attack succeeds in recovering the secret's least significant byte.

Figure 3 shows that the key ranking slightly decreases with the number of traces used for the attack.

The method does not provide convincing results with the 256 × 300 traces.

However, the shape of the curve in the Fig. 3 is decreasing. If the decrease is

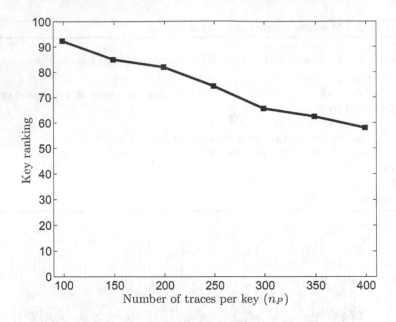

Fig. 3. Results for a naive collision attack.

approximatively linear, the good secret key will begin to be distinguishable from $n_P \approx 1000$ traces. Nevertheless, this number is high, we will see in the following paragraph how we managed to decrease this value.

In this approach the comparison is horizontal. Indeed, the EM measurements C_1 and C_2 are sampled over t points, the returned coefficient is the cross correlation computed with the Pearson coefficient:

$$\rho\left(C_1, C_2\right) = \frac{covariance(C_1, C_2)}{\sigma(C_1)\sigma(C_2)}. \tag{7}$$

The main drawback of this method is the need to perfectly align the traces as the correlation coefficient largely depends on the adjustment of the traces' position. The toy example in Figs. 4 and 5 of EM measurement show the great dependency between the coefficient correlation and the alignment of traces. This small demonstration and our practical experiences convinced us to use another collisions detection techniques.

Due those lukewarm results we investigate another technique for detecting collisions.

Advanced Collisions Detection. The aim this time is to detect if there exists a link in the EM measurements during the two targeted multiplications using "vertical correlations" as initially proposed in [42].

Instead of comparing the traces between each other and giving a coefficient that indicates whether there is a collision, it is a point-to-point comparison (where each point is a temporal instant within each trace).

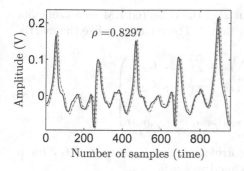 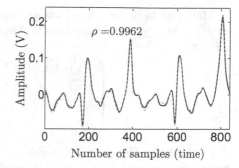

Fig. 4. Traces without retouching © [20].   **Fig. 5.** Shifted traces on 7 points sample © [20].

Figure 6 illustrates this principle. The left pattern corresponds to the multiplication $x_{P_j} \times \lambda^2$ and the other one corresponds to the operation $x \times \lambda^2$. For the sake of have "clear" pictures, Fig. 6 only shows three traces ($n_P = 3$).

The trick proposed by Varchola *et al.* [42] to avoid the synchronization problem consists in the selection of a time instant in the first multiplication, a window in the second one and drag the single vector on the window to compute t correlations.

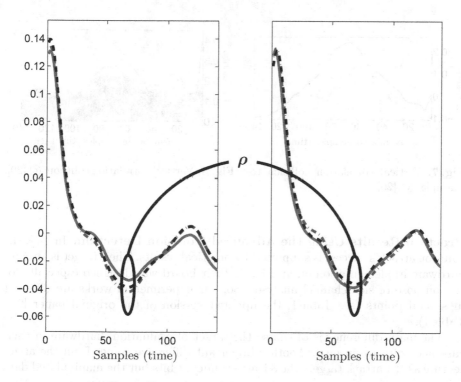

Fig. 6. Vertical correlation collision principle.

More precisely, for a fixed known input x_{P_j}, the collected EM measurements are $R_j \in \mathcal{M}_{n_P, 2t}$ as we have seen in Algorithm 4. The result R is like the matrix in Eq. 8.

$$
R_j =
\begin{pmatrix}
C_{1,1}^{(1)} & C_{1,2}^{(1)} & \cdots & C_{1,t}^{(1)} & C_{2,1}^{(1)} & \cdots & C_{2,t}^{(1)} \\
C_{1,1}^{(2)} & \cdots & & C_{1,t}^{(2)} & C_{2,1}^{(2)} & \cdots & C_{2,t}^{(2)} \\
\vdots & & & \vdots & \vdots & & \vdots \\
C_{1,1}^{(n_P)} & \cdots & & C_{1,t}^{(n_P)} & C_{2,1}^{(n_P)} & \cdots & C_{2,t}^{(n_P)}
\end{pmatrix}.
\tag{8}
$$

From there, the attacker builds a "correlation trace" $corr_j \in \mathcal{M}_{1,t}$ for a chosen time instant t_{interset} with $corr_j$ defined in Eq. 9.

$$
corr_j(i) = \rho\left(
\begin{pmatrix}
C_{1,t_{\text{interest}}}^{(1)} \\
\vdots \\
C_{1,t_{\text{interest}}}^{(n_P)}
\end{pmatrix},
\begin{pmatrix}
C_{2,i}^{(1)} \\
\vdots \\
C_{2,i}^{(n_P)}
\end{pmatrix}
\right), \forall i = 1,\ldots,t
\tag{9}
$$

The Eqs. 8 and 9 are come from the original paper [20], Eqs. 6 and 7.

To illustrate the general shape of such a "correlation trace" we refer the reader to Fig. 7. For this example we make a toy example with $n_P = 100$.

As in classical side-channel attacks, the highest correlation allows to identify the most probable key (the thickest blue curve in Fig. 8, with $n_P = 400$).

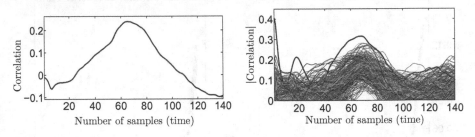

Fig. 7. Vertical correlation collision toy example © [20].   **Fig. 8.** Vertical correlation collision © [20].

Practical Results Using the Advanced Collision Detection. In [42], the collision attack's success is supported by practical results. Their target is an 8-bit hardware implementation on an FPGA, their board was designed especially for the purpose of side-channel analyses. So, our experimental works are different in several points (see Table 1, the updated version of the original paper [21], Table 1).

The main difference is of course the target of evaluation, hardware in their case and software in ours. Another important difference comes from the architecture as the attack targets the 8 least significant bits but the manipulated data

Table 1. Difference between target and set-up.

Settings	Varchola *et al.* [42]	Our case
Device	FPGA	Microcontroller
Architecture size	8-bit	32-bit
Clock frequency	16.384 MHz	24 MHz
Sampling frequency	20 Gsps	10 Gsps
Side-channel source	Power	EM

are on 32 bits with the device producing leakages related to the 32-bit manipulated data. Therefore, unlike [42], our 256 keys hypothesis do not cover all the possible sought secret value.

Hence the question is the following: the traces are from 32-bit manipulated data, will the leakages be sufficiently meaningful to target only 8 bits at a time? Our attack is a chosen plaintext attack because the x_{P_j} have a particular shape, indeed, $x_{P_j} = (00 \ldots 0j_7j_6 \ldots j_0)_2$.

In our experimentation we chose $n_P = 400$ and hence we have the attack results presented in Fig. 9. Each score is obtained by averaging the results for 100 attacks with different traces. These figures show the ranking of the correct key (8 least significant bits) among the 256 possible ones. The guess is correct when the rank equals to one. This ranking decreases with the number of traces in a significant way.

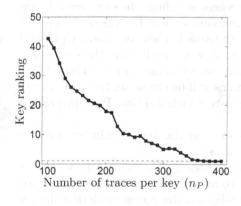

Fig. 9. Byte 1 © [20].

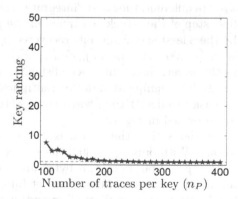

Fig. 10. Byte 2 © [20].

The attack recovers, the 8-bit key when the number of trace per key n_P is close to 400 (i.e. a total of EM measurement close to $n_P \times 2^8 = 400 \times 256 = 102400$). The secret key can be easily discriminated in a small set of candidates, resulting a huge loss of entropy.

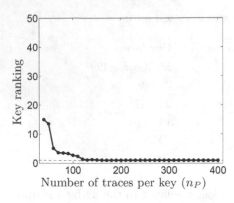

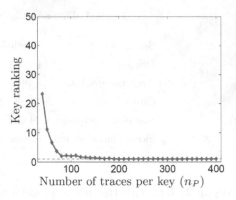

Fig. 11. Byte 3.   **Fig. 12.** Byte 4.

5.2   Recovering the Full 256 Secret Bits Integer with Collisions

In order to recover the full secret point during the Tate pairing calculation that we implemented and that we run on our 32-bit platform, we applied the method described previously to the other bytes, within the same 32-bit word first, and then for the other 32-bit words, in order to recover the full 256-bit secret integer. The used BN curves to implement the Tate pairing are set for $t = 3FC0100000000000$ (in hexadecimal).

Afterwards, the 8 least significant bits are fixed to the recovered byte and we pursue with the following byte. The attack on the other bytes is very similar to what has been described so far in the "advanced" technique. The known inputs x_{P_j} are different: they first "integrate" the 8 least significant bits recovered by the first step of the attack as carried in the previous section. Let $(\widehat{x_7 x_6} \ldots \widehat{x_0})_2 = \widehat{x}$ be the 8 least significant bits recovered by the attack, then the chosen ciphertext is $x_{P_j} = (00 \ldots 0 \boldsymbol{j_7 j_6} \ldots \boldsymbol{j_0} \widehat{x_7 x_6} \ldots \widehat{x_0})_2$. Now, when j will have the same value as the secret, there will be a collision not only on 8 bits but also on 16 bits. When the 16 bits manipulated in the multiplications will be the same, the collision will be easier to detect than when there were only 8 identical bits. Practical results are provided in Fig. 10.

It shows that the attack is easier as soon as the least significant bits are known. With only $n_P = 300$, the attack succeeds.

In the 32-bit word two bytes are still unknown. The same attack method allows us to recover these 32 secret bits. To attack the other words of the integer is not more complicated, everything relies on the proper understanding of the multiplication algorithm. Practical results are provided in Figs. 11 and 12. Efficiency of these attacks is similar when the target is the byte 2. That is about $n_P = 300$.

The Cost of Carrying the Attack. Our targeted Pairings implementations involve 256-bit length integer arithmetic. That is, since there are 8 words of 32-bit integer, then the previous attack needs to be performed 8 times. But, the messages (x_P) are chosen, so we can construct such x_P to recover the 8 words at the same time. It is like a parallel process:

1. Setting the messages $x_{P_j} = [X_{j,7}, X_{j,6}, \ldots, X_{j,0}]$ with the $X_{j,i}$ 32-bit word which are the x_{P_j} of Sect. 5 and capture the side-channel leakages.
2. For each $i = 0, \ldots, 7$ make the attack to recover the 8 LSBs of each X_i.
3. Start again with the second least significant bits of X_i.

Thus, the attack to find the 256 bits does not require 8 times more traces than the one we presented to recover 32 bits. There are 8 independent attacks, but not 8 times more traces.

Thus, the number of traces required to break the x_Q coordinates of the secret input is:

$$E \simeq 2^8 (400 + 3 \times 300) \simeq 3.5 \times 10^5$$

To compare with the attack against the unprotected version, recent results [21] show an attack with an averages of 200 traces to recover one word, so $8 \times 200 = 1600$ for the entire 256-bits secret integer. Then the countermeasure constrains the attacker to achieve 200 times more power measurements. In our experiment, one trace is acquired in an average of 0.4 s. Thus, the collision attack on the protected implementation take 2 days to recover the secret x_Q.

6   Conclusion

Among the recent publications in the field of side-channel attacks against the pairing-based cryptography, there are sometimes some tips for countermeasures. However, none offers real security proofs, both theoretical and practical. We propose a critical analysis of one of the most interesting methods from an efficiency point of view. We propose here to show theoretically and practically how we use a collision-based side-channel attack to defeat the countermeasure based on point randomisation. In order to study the real effectiveness of the countermeasure, we also expose the attack schemes to target an unprotected pairing.

An attack against Ate pairing without protection requires only about 150 traces measurement [21]. With the countermeasure of randomization we mount an attack with 3.5×10^5 traces. The security of protocols based on pairings against side-channel attacks can not be ensured with this countermeasure only. Then, we can therefore recommend to also randomize the secret at the beginning of the pairing. The randomization of Jacobian coordinates of the secret elliptic curve point implies the non-reportion of the operation between the mask and the secret, and thus our comment on the collision is no longer valid. In contrast, Jacobian coordinates randomization of the secret implies to rewrite the line and tangent equations. The Jacobian-Affine combination is no longer possible (Eq. 4). A combination study of coordinate systems which remain effective are proposed in the thesis [19], where the projective-projective system turns out effective at the time when this thesis was published.

Finally, recent papers [4,26,30,31] show new improvements in the algorithms used to solve discrete logarithm, in particular over BN curves. Those latter developments only require the redefinition of the Pairings' parameters and key sizes (parameter t in Eq. 3). However, our attack scenario would still hold as our attack is independent of the choice of the curve parameters.

Acknowledgements. This work was supported in part by the EUREKA Catrene programme under contract CAT208 MobiTrust and by a French DGA-MRIS scholarship.

References

1. Aranha, D.F., Karabina, K., Longa, P., Gebotys, C.H., López, J.: Faster explicit formulas for computing pairings over ordinary curves. In: Paterson, K.G. (ed.) EUROCRYPT 2011. LNCS, vol. 6632, pp. 48–68. Springer, Heidelberg (2011). https://doi.org/10.1007/978-3-642-20465-4_5
2. Bajard, J.C., El Mrabet, N.: Pairing in cryptography: an arithmetic point of view. In: Proceedings of SPIE: ASPAAI (2007)
3. Barbulescu, R., Gaudry, P., Guillevic, A., Morain, F.: Improving NFS for the discrete logarithm problem in non-prime finite fields. In: Oswald, E., Fischlin, M. (eds.) EUROCRYPT 2015, Part I. LNCS, vol. 9056, pp. 129–155. Springer, Heidelberg (2015). https://doi.org/10.1007/978-3-662-46800-5_6
4. Barbulescu, R., Gaudry, P., Kleinjung, T.: The tower number field sieve. In: Iwata, T., Cheon, J.H. (eds.) ASIACRYPT 2015, Part II. LNCS, vol. 9453, pp. 31–55. Springer, Heidelberg (2015). https://doi.org/10.1007/978-3-662-48800-3_2
5. Barreto, P.S.L.M., Naehrig, M.: Pairing-friendly elliptic curves of prime order. In: Preneel, B., Tavares, S. (eds.) SAC 2005. LNCS, vol. 3897, pp. 319–331. Springer, Heidelberg (2006). https://doi.org/10.1007/11693383_22
6. Barreto, P.S.L.M., Kim, H.Y., Lynn, B., Scott, M.: Efficient algorithms for pairing-based cryptosystems. In: Yung, M. (ed.) CRYPTO 2002. LNCS, vol. 2442, pp. 354–369. Springer, Heidelberg (2002). https://doi.org/10.1007/3-540-45708-9_23
7. Bauer, A., Jaulmes, E., Prouff, E., Wild, J.: Horizontal collision correlation attack on elliptic curves. In: Lange, T., Lauter, K., Lisoněk, P. (eds.) SAC 2013. LNCS, vol. 8282, pp. 553–570. Springer, Heidelberg (2014). https://doi.org/10.1007/978-3-662-43414-7_28
8. Beuchat, J.-L., González-Díaz, J.E., Mitsunari, S., Okamoto, E., Rodríguez-Henríquez, F., Teruya, T.: High-speed software implementation of the optimal ate pairing over barreto–naehrig curves. In: Joye, M., Miyaji, A., Otsuka, A. (eds.) Pairing 2010. LNCS, vol. 6487, pp. 21–39. Springer, Heidelberg (2010). https://doi.org/10.1007/978-3-642-17455-1_2
9. Blömer, J., Günther, P., Liske, G.: Improved side channel attacks on pairing based cryptography. In: Prouff, E. (ed.) COSADE 2013. LNCS, vol. 7864, pp. 154–168. Springer, Heidelberg (2013). https://doi.org/10.1007/978-3-642-40026-1_10
10. Boneh, D., Franklin, M.: Identity-based encryption from the weil pairing. In: Kilian, J. (ed.) CRYPTO 2001. LNCS, vol. 2139, pp. 213–229. Springer, Heidelberg (2001). https://doi.org/10.1007/3-540-44647-8_13
11. Coron, J.-S.: Resistance against differential power analysis for elliptic curve cryptosystems. In: Koç, Ç.K., Paar, C. (eds.) CHES 1999. LNCS, vol. 1717, pp. 292–302. Springer, Heidelberg (1999). https://doi.org/10.1007/3-540-48059-5_25

12. Duursma, I., Lee, H.-S.: Tate Pairing Implementation for Hyperelliptic Curves $y^2 = x^p - x + d$. In: Laih, C.-S. (ed.) ASIACRYPT 2003. LNCS, vol. 2894, pp. 111–123. Springer, Heidelberg (2003). https://doi.org/10.1007/978-3-540-40061-5_7

13. Eisenträger, K., Lauter, K., Montgomery, P.L.: Improved weil and tate pairings for elliptic and hyperelliptic curves. In: Buell, D. (ed.) ANTS 2004. LNCS, vol. 3076, pp. 169–183. Springer, Heidelberg (2004). https://doi.org/10.1007/978-3-540-24847-7_12

14. El Mrabet, N., Di Natale, G., Flottes, M.L.: A practical differential power analysis attack against the miller algorithm. In: PRIME, pp. 308–311, July 2009

15. Fouque, P.-A., Valette, F.: The doubling attack – why upwards is better than downwards. In: Walter, C.D., Koç, Ç.K., Paar, C. (eds.) CHES 2003. LNCS, vol. 2779, pp. 269–280. Springer, Heidelberg (2003). https://doi.org/10.1007/978-3-540-45238-6_22

16. Galbraith, S.D., Harrison, K., Soldera, D.: Implementing the tate pairing. In: Fieker, C., Kohel, D.R. (eds.) ANTS 2002. LNCS, vol. 2369, pp. 324–337. Springer, Heidelberg (2002). https://doi.org/10.1007/3-540-45455-1_26

17. Ghosh, S., Roychowdhury, D.: Security of prime field pairing cryptoprocessor against differential power attack. In: Joye, M., Mukhopadhyay, D., Tunstall, M. (eds.) InfoSecHiComNet 2011. LNCS, vol. 7011, pp. 16–29. Springer, Heidelberg (2011). https://doi.org/10.1007/978-3-642-24586-2_4

18. Hutter, M., Medwed, M., Hein, D., Wolkerstorfer, J.: Attacking ECDSA-enabled RFID devices. In: Abdalla, M., Pointcheval, D., Fouque, P.-A., Vergnaud, D. (eds.) ACNS 2009. LNCS, vol. 5536, pp. 519–534. Springer, Heidelberg (2009). https://doi.org/10.1007/978-3-642-01957-9_32

19. Jauvart, D.: Sécurisation des algorithmes de couplages contre les attaques physiques. Ph.D thesis, Université Paris-Saclay (2017)

20. Jauvart, D., Fournier, J.J.A., Goubin, L.: First practical side-channel attack to defeat point randomization in secure implementations of pairing-based cryptography. In: Proceedings of the 14th International Joint Conference on e-Business and Telecommunications - Volume 6: SECRYPT (ICETE 2017), pp. 104–115. INSTICC, SciTePress (2017)

21. Jauvart, D., Fournier, J.J.A., El-Mrabet, N., Goubin, L.: Improving side-channel attacks against pairing-based cryptography. In: Cuppens, F., Cuppens, N., Lanet, J.-L., Legay, A. (eds.) CRiSIS 2016. LNCS, vol. 10158, pp. 199–213. Springer, Cham (2017). https://doi.org/10.1007/978-3-319-54876-0_16

22. Joux, A.: A one round protocol for tripartite Diffie-Hellman. J. Cryptol. **17**, 263–276 (2004)

23. Joux, A., Odlyzko, A., Pierrot, C.: The past, evolving present, and future of the discrete logarithm. In: Koç, Ç.K. (ed.) Open Problems in Mathematics and Computational Science, pp. 5–36. Springer, Cham (2014). https://doi.org/10.1007/978-3-319-10683-0_2

24. Joye, M., Neven, G. (eds).: Identity-Based Cryptography. IOS Press (2008)

25. Kim, T.H., Takagi, T., Han, D.-G., Kim, H.W., Lim, J.: Side channel attacks and countermeasures on pairing based cryptosystems over binary fields. In: Pointcheval, D., Mu, Y., Chen, K. (eds.) CANS 2006. LNCS, vol. 4301, pp. 168–181. Springer, Heidelberg (2006). https://doi.org/10.1007/11935070_11

26. Kim, T., Barbulescu, R.: Extended Tower Number Field Sieve: A New Complexity for the Medium Prime Case. Cryptology ePrint Archive (2015)

27. Koblitz, N., Menezes, A.: Pairing-based cryptography at high security levels. In: Smart, N.P. (ed.) Cryptography and Coding 2005. LNCS, vol. 3796, pp. 13–36. Springer, Heidelberg (2005). https://doi.org/10.1007/11586821_2

28. Koc, C.K., Acar, T., Kaliski, B.S.: Analyzing and comparing montgomery multiplication algorithms. IEEE Micro **16**(3), 26–33 (1996)

29. Kocher, P., Jaffe, J., Jun, B.: Differential power analysis. In: Wiener, M. (ed.) CRYPTO 1999. LNCS, vol. 1666, pp. 388–397. Springer, Heidelberg (1999). https://doi.org/10.1007/3-540-48405-1_25

30. Kusaka, T., et al.: Solving 114-Bit ECDLP for a barreto-naehrig Curve. In: Kim, H., Kim, D.-C. (eds.) ICISC 2017. LNCS, vol. 10779, pp. 231–244. Springer, Cham (2018). https://doi.org/10.1007/978-3-319-78556-1_13

31. Menezes, A., Sarkar, P., Singh, S.: Challenges with Assessing the Impact of NFS Advances on the Security of Pairing-based Cryptography. Cryptology ePrint Archive (2016)

32. Miller, V.S.: Use of elliptic curves in cryptography. In: Williams, H.C. (ed.) CRYPTO 1985. LNCS, vol. 218, pp. 417–426. Springer, Heidelberg (1986). https://doi.org/10.1007/3-540-39799-X_31

33. Montgomery, P.L.: Modular multiplication without trial division. Math. Comput. **44**, 519–519 (1985)

34. Moradi, A., Mischke, O., Eisenbarth, T.: Correlation-enhanced power analysis collision attack. In: Mangard, S., Standaert, F.-X. (eds.) CHES 2010. LNCS, vol. 6225, pp. 125–139. Springer, Heidelberg (2010). https://doi.org/10.1007/978-3-642-15031-9_9

35. Naehrig, M., Niederhagen, R., Schwabe, P.: New software speed records for cryptographic pairings. In: Abdalla, M., Barreto, P.S.L.M. (eds.) LATINCRYPT 2010. LNCS, vol. 6212, pp. 109–123. Springer, Heidelberg (2010). https://doi.org/10.1007/978-3-642-14712-8_7

36. Page, D., Vercauteren, F.: Fault and Side-Channel Attacks on Pairing Based Cryptography. IEEE Trans. Comput. (2004)

37. Pan, W., Marnane, W.P.: A correlation power analysis attack against tate pairing on FPGA. In: Koch, A., Krishnamurthy, R., McAllister, J., Woods, R., El-Ghazawi, T. (eds.) ARC 2011. LNCS, vol. 6578, pp. 340–349. Springer, Heidelberg (2011). https://doi.org/10.1007/978-3-642-19475-7_36

38. Schramm, K., Wollinger, T., Paar, C.: A new class of collision attacks and its application to DES. In: Johansson, T. (ed.) FSE 2003. LNCS, vol. 2887, pp. 206–222. Springer, Heidelberg (2003). https://doi.org/10.1007/978-3-540-39887-5_16

39. Scott, M.: Computing the Tate pairing. CT-RSA, pp. 293–304 (2005)

40. Silverman, J.H.: The Arithmetic of Elliptic Curves. GTM, vol. 106. Springer, New York (2009). https://doi.org/10.1007/978-0-387-09494-6

41. Unterluggauer, T., Wenger, E.: Practical attack on bilinear pairings to disclose the secrets of embedded devices. In: ARES, pp. 69–77 (2014)

42. Varchola, M., Drutarovsky, M., Repka, M., Zajac, P.: Side channel attack on multi-precision multiplier used in protected ECDSA implementation. In: ReConFig, pp. 1–6, December 2015

43. Whelan, C., Scott, M.: Side channel analysis of practical pairing implementations: which path is more secure? In: Nguyen, P.Q. (ed.) VIETCRYPT 2006. LNCS, vol. 4341, pp. 99–114. Springer, Heidelberg (2006). https://doi.org/10.1007/11958239_7

On the Relation Between SIM and IND-RoR Security Models for PAKEs with Forward Secrecy

José Becerra[⊠], Vincenzo Iovino[⊠], Dimiter Ostrev[⊠],
and Marjan Škrobot[⊠]

Interdisciplinary Centre for Security, Reliability and Trust,
University of Luxembourg, 6, Avenue de la Fonte, 4364 Esch-sur-Alzette, Luxembourg
{jose.becerra,vincenzo.iovino,dimiter.ostrev,marjan.skrobot}@uni.lu

Abstract. Password-based Authenticated Key-Exchange (PAKE) protocols allow the establishment of secure communication entirely based on the knowledge of a shared password. Over the last two decades, we have witnessed the debut of a number of prominent security models for PAKE protocols, whose aim is to capture the desired security properties that such protocols must satisfy when executed in the presence of an active adversary. These models are usually classified into (i) indistinguishability-based (IND-based) or (ii) simulation-based (SIM-based). However, the relation between these two security notions is unclear and mentioned as a gap in the literature. In this work, we prove that SIM-BMP security from Boyko et al. (EUROCRYPT 2000) implies IND-RoR security from Abdalla et al. (PKC 2005) and that IND-RoR security is equivalent to a slightly modified version of SIM-BMP security. We also investigate whether IND-RoR security implies (unmodified) SIM-BMP security. The results obtained also hold when forward secrecy is incorporated into the security models in question.

Keywords: Security models · SIM-based security
IND-based security · Password Authenticated Key Exchange
Forward secrecy

1 Introduction

The Password Authenticated Key Exchange (PAKE) problem asks for two entities, who only share a password, to engage in a conversation so that they agree on a *session key*. The established session key can be used to protect their subsequent communication. PAKE protocols play a key role in today's world as they allow for authenticated key exchange to occur without the use of Public-Key Infrastructure (PKI), by using a human-memorable password instead. Theoretically, they are fascinating, because of their ability to use a weak secret – such as a password or a pin – to produce a strong cryptographic key in a provably secure way over a hostile communications network.

© Springer Nature Switzerland AG 2019
M. S. Obaidat and E. Cabello (Eds.): ICETE 2017, CCIS 990, pp. 173–198, 2019.
https://doi.org/10.1007/978-3-030-11039-0_9

The nature of passwords makes PAKE protocols vulnerable to *dictionary attacks*. In such attacks, an adversary tries to break the security of the protocol by exhaustively enumerating all possible passwords until a guess is correct. This strategy might not be very successful on AKE schemes where the legitimate entities share a high-entropy key as long-term secret. However, in the PAKE setting the long-term secrets come from a small set of values, i.e. a dictionary, posing a genuine security threat.

We distinguish between two types of possible dictionary attacks: *offline* and *online* dictionary attacks. In an offline dictionary attack, the adversary uses interaction with the honest parties – or mere eavesdropping – to get information about the password that allows him to launch an exhaustive offline search. In an online dictionary attack, an attacker takes a password from the set of possible passwords, *interacts* with a legitimate party by running the protocol and checks whether the key exchange succeeds for the candidate password or not.

The cryptographic goal when designing PAKE protocols is to ensure that the attacker essentially cannot do better than an online dictionary attack. This goal recognizes that while online dictionary attacks cannot be avoided, offline dictionary attacks can and should be prevented. Numerous PAKE protocols have been designed to meet this goal but have later been found to be flawed [1–3]. Consequently, *security models* for PAKE have been devised to get assurance on the claimed security properties by performing a rigorous analysis.

In this work, we consider the provable security approach, where protocols are analyzed in a complexity-theoretic security model: the goal being that no reasonable algorithm can violate security under various hardness assumptions. The complexity-theoretic security models are classified into indistinguishability-based (IND-based) and simulation-based (SIM-based). In the IND-based approach security means that no probabilistic polynomial-time (PTT) adversary can distinguish an established session key sk from a random string, i.e. it guarantees semantic security on sk. The SIM-based approach defines two worlds: an *ideal world* which is secure by definition and the *real world* which is the real protocol execution against some PPT attacker. In the SIM-based setting, security asks for the indistinguishability between the ideal world and real world executions.

When dealing with formal security modeling of PAKE, the difference between the two previously mentioned approaches, IND and SIM, has practical consequences. It is accepted that IND-based models are easier to work with for protocol designers that wish to prove the security of their protocols. In fact, currently, most of the security proofs for PAKEs are constructed under the IND-based models Find-then-Guess (IND-FtG) from [4] and Real-or-Random (IND-RoR)[1] from [5]. In contrast, constructing security proofs in SIM-based models is considered more challenging. Two SIM-based models for PAKE that have seen wider use are Boyko, MacKenzie and Patel's (BMP) model [6] that is derived from Shoup's SIM-based model for AKE [7] and the Universal Composability (UC) framework of Canetti et al. [8] that follows the UC paradigm of Canetti [9].

---

[1] IND-RoR is a refinement of IND-FtG model in which the adversary has access to multiple test queries instead of a single one.

While complex for constructing proofs of security, it is fair to recognize that SIM-based security (i) offers a more intuitive and natural approach to defining security, (ii) it is simpler to describe and interpret the security properties captured by the model, (iii) SIM-secure protocols are well suited to accommodate secure composition results, and (iv) it is possible to prove security of PAKE protocols even in the case of correlated passwords that may come from arbitrary password distributions.

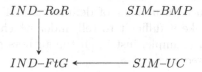

Fig. 1. Known relations between PAKE security definitions [10].

The known relations between PAKE security definitions are summarized in Fig. 1. In particular, to the best of the knowledge of the authors, no work has been done to formally analyze the relation between the IND-RoR and SIM-BMP security notions for PAKE.[2] As we can see in Fig. 1, the only existing result that is known to hold between IND and SIM based definitions is the one from [8]. There, the authors show that their SIM-UC definition implies the IND-FtG definition from [4].

In practical terms, the lack of comparison results between IND-based and SIM-based models for PAKEs means that the security of PAKE protocols, such as SPEKE,[3] that have been studied in the SIM-BMP simulation model of [6] can not be compared with other PAKE protocols that are secure according to the SIM-UC or IND definitions.

Forward Secrecy. Commonly referred as Perfect Forward Secrecy (PFS), it is a security property for Authenticated Key-Exchange (AKE) and PAKE protocols. Roughly speaking, it ensures the protection of session keys – negotiated between two honest participants – even if the underlying long-term secret material (passwords for PAKEs) later gets compromised [15]. It is a highly desirable security property specially for PAKEs as unfortunately, there exist in real life different ways in which the adversary could obtain such password information e.g. via phishing attacks a cheated client could reveal his password to some malicious

---

[2] The result by Shoup [7] on the equivalence between IND-FTG model and SIM model for authenticated key exchange with a high-entropy long-term secret does not carry over to the PAKE setting. The reason for this is that there is a non-negligible upper bound on the advantage of the adversary in IND-based security definitions for PAKE. This, in turn, does not admit loose reductions.

[3] The SPEKE protocol [11] is one of the most well-known PAKE designs. It has been proposed by Jablon in 1996 and proven secure in the SIM-BMP model under the Random Oracle (RO) assumption by MacKenzie [12]. SPEKE is practically relevant as it is specified in the ISO/IEC 11770-4 [13] and IEEE P1363.2 [14] standards.

entity or the data base storing the client's password at the server could get compromised resulting in massive password leakage [16–18]. Therefore, it has been explicitly a design goal in relevant PAKEs [19,20].

The intuition of forward secrecy was first mentioned by Diffie et al. in [15]. It was later formalized and incorporated in AKE [7,21–23] and PAKE [4,24] security models. It is indisputable that this formalization enhanced the understanding of forward secrecy by identifying distinct means in which a principal can get compromised and the information revealed to the adversary in such a case. However, it produced a number of definitions and variations on forward secrecy which might make it difficult to tell under which circumstances protocol "P" is *fs-secure*. For example, just in [4] the authors provide three different definitions for forward secrecy.

1.1   Our Contribution

In this work our contributions can be summarized as follows:

- We first reconcile the syntactic differences between the IND-RoR and SIM-BMP models for PAKE thus allowing honest comparison between them. More specifically, we slightly modify the initialization procedure of the IND-RoR model [5] such that it follows the SIM-BMP model.
- We incorporate forward secrecy into the SIM-BMP and IND-RoR security models. We consider only the *weak corruption model* as defined in [4], which is the most used type of forward secrecy.
- We prove that SIM-BMP security implies IND-RoR security and that IND-RoR security is equivalent to a slightly modified version of SIM-BMP security adapted to the model of [25]. We also investigate whether IND-RoR security implies (unmodified) SIM-BMP security.
- The results in this paper are based on the earlier conference paper [10]. Here, we extend the results obtained earlier and show that they also hold when forward secrecy in the weak corruption model is incorporated into the security models in question.

1.2   Related Work

Authenticated Key Exchange (AKE). The complexity theoretic treatment of security for AKE protocols was initiated by Bellare and Rogaway in 1993 [26]. In their groundbreaking work, they followed the indistinguishability (IND) approach to formalize the notion of security for AKE protocols, using previously established symmetric keys as long-term secrets and considering the realistic scenario of concurrent sessions running on a network under full control of the adversary. In their model, an AKE protocol is secure if, under the allowed adversary actions, the established session key is computationally indistinguishable from a random string. After this initial work, numerous others have appeared studying the cryptographic security for AKE protocols following the IND-based approach [21,22,27–31].

In parallel, the first simulation (SIM) definition for AKE was given by Bellare, Canetti and Krawczyk [32]. In 1999, Shoup proposed another security model for AKE protocols in the SIM-based setting [7] and informally compared his model with the one from [32]. In the same work, the author gave a sketch of a proof arguing that SIM-security against both *static* and *adaptive* adversaries is equivalent to the corresponding IND-security notions of [27]. Canetti and Krawczyk in [33] took SIM definitions further by expanding the composition guarantees of AKE from [7] to arbitrary protocols within the Universal Composability (UC) framework of Canetti [9].

Password Authenticated Key Exchange (PAKE). The idea of PAKE has been first put forward by Bellovin and Meritt in [34]. Their proposal, the EKE protocol, was the first to show that it is possible to design a password authentication mechanism that can withstand offline dictionary attacks. The SPEKE protocol from Jablon [11] soon appeared, following a very different design strategy. However, both of these works included only informal security justifications. The first adequate security models for PAKE appeared in [4] and [6] around the same time. Both models were built upon already existing AKE models. Although the SIM-based model from [6] has been used to prove secure several PAKE protocols (PAK [6], RSA-based SNAPI [35], and SPEKE [12]), it is the IND-FtG model from [4] that has established itself as the model of choice when analyzing PAKEs. Using the IND-FtG model, Katz et al. [36] managed to achieve a breakthrough: they have shown how one can *efficiently* realize PAKE without random oracles, but instead relying on a common reference string (CRS). In more theoretical work, Goldreich and Lindell [25] proposed a PAKE in the plain model[4] that follows the simulation tradition. A few years later, Abdalla et al. [5] showed that a stronger model than IND-FtG is necessary when trying to achieve three-party PAKE. Hence, they proposed a new model, known as the IND-RoR model, which is proven to be stronger than the IND-FtG model in the case of PAKE. Recently, Škrobot and Lancrenon [37] have shown that the IND-FtG model may not be enough when looking at composition between PAKEs and arbitrary symmetric key protocols (SKP). However, on the positive side, they have shown that IND-RoR secure PAKE protocols with weak forward secrecy can be safely composed with arbitrary, higher-level SKPs. For these reasons, the IND-RoR model – enriched to handle forward secrecy – is considered the state-of-the-art model and has been used in the analysis of most recent PAKE protocols [38,39]. Another model which is prominent in PAKE research is the Universal Composability (UC) framework for PAKE of Canetti et al. [8]. This model has been recently extended to treat augmented PAKEs [40] - asymmetric PAKE protocols in which a server holds a hard-to-invert function[5] of the password. For more relevant papers on PAKE, we refer the reader to Pointcheval's survey [41].

---

[4] In the plain model, the security of a cryptosystem is proved using only general complexity assumptions and no trusted setup.

[5] Due to the low entropy of passwords such function can be inverted in practice by applying dictionary attacks.

1.3   Organization

The rest of the paper is organized as follows: In Sect. 2 we describe the Real-or-Random model for PAKE due to Abdalla et al. [5]. Next, in Sect. 3, we introduce the simulation-based model for PAKE from Boyko et al. [6]. We assume some familiarity with the models and refer to the original publications for a full description. Section 4 examines the relation between the Real-Or-Random model of [5] and the simulation-based model of Boyko et al. [6]. Finally, we conclude the paper in Sect. 5.

2   The Real or Random Security Model for PAKE

The Real-or-Random (IND-RoR) security model for 2-party PAKE was introduced by Abdalla, Fouque and Pointcheval in [5]. In this section, we present an augmented version of the original model that allows us to explicitly incorporate the requirement of forward secrecy. Before we recall the IND-RoR model with forward secrecy, we introduce the notation that will used in the paper.

2.1   Notation

Let S be a set with cardinality $|S|$. We write $s \xleftarrow{\$} S$ to denote sampling uniformly at random from S. The output of a probabilistic algorithm D on input x is denoted by $y \leftarrow D(x)$, while $y := D(x, r)$ denotes the (deterministic) output of an algorithm D on input x and fixed random coins r. Adversaries (respectively, challengers) will be denoted $\mathcal{A}$ (resp. $\mathcal{CH}$) in the IND-RoR model and $\mathcal{B}$ (resp. $\mathcal{RM}$) in the SIM model. The directory of passwords is pw, PPT stands for probabilistic polynomial-time and λ is the security parameter. A function $f : \mathbb{N} \to \mathbb{R}_+$ is said to be negligible if it decreases faster than the inverse of any polynomial and the symbol $negl$ designates some unspecified negligible function. We write $A \stackrel{c}{\equiv} B$ to denote two computationally indistinguishable distributions.

2.2   Description of the IND-RoR Model with Forward Secrecy

The so called IND-RoR model of Abdalla et al. [5], defines security via a *game* played between a challenger $\mathcal{CH}$ and some adversary $\mathcal{A}$ whose goal is to distinguish *real* session keys from *random* strings. It follows from the Find-then-Guess (IND-FtG) model of [4], however, the IND-RoR model allows $\mathcal{A}$ to ask *multiple* test queries to different instances while the IND-FtG restricts $\mathcal{A}$ to a single test query. This simple yet important change results in the IND-RoR model being strickly stronger than the IND-FtG model for PAKE. This is in contrast with the AKE scenario in which the two models are considered equivalent.

Recall that in [4], several variants of the IND-FtG model are described: these models can be differentiated depending on the type of forward secrecy they are trying to capture. Nevertheless, the original IND-RoR model from [5] does not include a forward secrecy requirement. In this section, we present an augmented version[6] of the original IND-RoR model to incorporate forward secrecy by following [4,42], which we will simply refer as FS-IND-RoR to differentiate from the original IND-RoR model.

PROTOCOL PARTICIPANTS. Each participant in a two party PAKE protocol is either a client $C \in \mathcal{C}$ or a server S. Let $\mathcal{U} = \mathcal{C} \bigcup S$ denote the set of all (honest) participants. Additionally, each *initialized* participant U is associated with a unique identifier id_U. During the execution of the protocol, there might be several running instances of each participant. A running instance i of some participant $U \in \mathcal{U}$ is called an *oracle instance* and is denoted by Π_U^i.

LONG-TERM SECRETS. Server S holds a password π for each client C, i.e. it holds a vector $L = < \pi_i >_{i \in \mathcal{C}}$. In the opposite direction, client C shares a single password π with server S. For simplicity let π also denote the function assigning passwords to pair of users. We will refer to $\pi[id_C, id_S]$ as the password shared between client C and server S. Note that $\pi[id_C, id_S] = \pi[id_S, id_C]$, while $\pi[id_C, id_C]$ is not allowed in the model. The passwords are assumed to be independent and uniformly distributed.

PROTOCOL EXECUTION. Protocol P is an algorithm that describes how participants behave in response to inputs from their environment. Each participant can run P in parallel with different partners, which is modeled by allowing an unlimited number of *instances* of each participant to be created. We assume the presence of an adversary $\mathcal{A}$ who has full control over the network i.e. she entirely controls the communication between legitimate entities. She can enumerate, off-line, the words of the password directory pw.

SECURITY EXPERIMENT IN FS-IND-ROR MODEL. Security in the IND-RoR model with forward secrecy is defined via a game played between the challenger $\mathcal{CH}$ and adversary $\mathcal{A}$. At the beginning of the experiment, $\mathcal{CH}$ tosses a coin and sets $b \in \{0, 1\}$ outside of $\mathcal{A}$'s view. Then $\mathcal{A}$ is given access to (i) endless supply of user instances Π_U^i and (ii) oracle queries to control them. Oracle queries are answered by the corresponding Π_U^i according to P. $\mathcal{A}$'s goal is to find out the value of the hidden bit b. Next, we summarize the oracle queries $\mathcal{A}$ can access during the security experiment.

– **Initialize user**$(U, id_U, role_U)$. $\mathcal{A}$ assigns the string id_U as identity and $role_U \in \{client, server\}$ to user $U \in \mathcal{U}$, subject to the restriction that id_U has not been already assigned to another user. There are two cases:
  • If $role_U = server$ we simply write S instead of U. Then, for every initialized client $C \in \mathcal{C}$ with id_C, a password is picked uniformly at random from the dictionary pw and assigned to the corresponding pair of client-server, i.e. $\pi[id_C, id_S] \xleftarrow{\$} pw$.

---

[6] Note that, in addition to the treatment of forward secrecy, we will introduce a minor change to the IND-RoR and the SIM-BMP model to allow for meaningful comparison between them. Otherwise, the models would be syntactically incomparable. Whenever possible, we prefer to change the SIM-BMP model rather than IND-RoR since the latter is more widespread.

- In case $role_U = client$ we shall simply write C instead of U. Then, provided that S has already been initialized with id_S, do $\pi[id_C, id_S] \xleftarrow{\$} pw$.
- **Initialize User Instance**$(U, i, role_U^i, pid_U^i)$. An instance $i \in \mathbb{N}$ of initialized user $U \in \mathcal{U}$ is created and denoted by Π_U^i. It is assigned (i) a role $role_U^i \in \{open, connect\}$ and (ii) a partner identity pid_U^i corresponding to the *identity* of some user U' that Π_U^i is supposed to communicate with in the future. The following constraint must hold:
  - $role_U$ and $role_{U'}$ are complementary, i.e. $role_U = server$ and $role_{U'} = client$ or the other way around.

  User instances are modeled as state machines with implicit access to the protocol description P and its corresponding password, i.e. some Π_U^i with $pid_U^i = id_{U'}$ is given access to $\pi[U, pid_U^i]$.
- **Send** (U, i, m). $\mathcal{A}$ sends message m to user instance Π_U^i. The latter behaves according to the protocol description, sends back the response m' to $\mathcal{A}$ (if any) and updates its state as follows:
  - continue: Π_U^i is ready to receive another message.
  - reject: Π_U^i aborts the protocol execution and sets the session key $sk_U^i = \perp$. This can be due to receiving an unexpected message m.
  - accept: Π_U^i holds pid_U^i, session identifier sid_U^i and sk_U^i. However, Π_U^i still expects to receive another message to fulfill the protocol specification.
  - terminate: Π_U^i holds pid_U^i, sid_U^i and sk_U^i. It has completed the protocol execution and will not send nor receive any other message.
- **Execute** (U, i, U', j). The transcript of the execution is returned to $\mathcal{A}$. It models honest execution of the protocol between Π_U^i and $\Pi_{U'}^j$.
- **Corrupt** (U). $\mathcal{A}$ learns the long-term secret information of some initialized user U. If $role_U = client$, then $\mathcal{A}$ gets π_U. Otherwise, if $role_U = server$, then $\mathcal{A}$ receives $L = < \pi_i >_{i \in C}$.
- **Test** (U, i). $\mathcal{A}$ asks for the session key of user instance Π_U^i. Provided that $status_U^i = terminate$, $\mathcal{CH}$ responds as follows[7]:
  - If there was a Corrupt (U^*) query -where U^* can be any user- and a Send query directed to Π_U^i before the sk is computed, then $\mathcal{A}$ gets the real sk of Π_U^i. Otherwise:
  - $\mathcal{CH}$ responds using the bit b. If $b = 1$ then $\mathcal{A}$ gets the real sk of Π_U^i, if $b = 0$ she gets a random string $r \xleftarrow{\$} \{0,1\}^{l_{sk}}$, where l_{sk} denotes the length of session keys. To ensure consistency, whenever $b = 0$ the same random string is returned for test queries asked to two *partnered* instances.

Matching Instances. Two instances, Π_U^i and $\Pi_{U'}^j$, are matching instances if:

- $pid_U^i = id_{U'}$, $pid_{U'}^j = id_U$
- Users have complimentary roles, i.e. one has role *client* and the other has role *server*.
- User instances have complimentary roles, i.e. one instance has the role *open* and the other *connect*.

---

[7] This is commonly referred as *freshness* condition.

Partnering. Two matching instances Π_U^i and $\Pi_{U'}^j$ are *partners* if both instances *accept* – each holding pid_U^i, sid_U^i, sk_U^i and $pid_{U'}^j$, $sid_{U'}^j$, $sk_{U'}^j$ respectively – and the following holds:

- $sid_U^i = sid_{U'}^j$ and $sk_U^i = sk_{U'}^j$,
- No oracle besides Π_U^i and $\Pi_{U'}^j$ accepts with some $sid' = sid_U^i$, except with negligible probability.

Advantage of the Adversary. During the experiment, $\mathcal{A}$ is allowed to ask several test queries directed to different oracle instances Π_U^i in the *terminate* state. All these queries are answered depending on the bit b chosen at the beginning of the experiment with either the real session key if $b = 1$ or a random string otherwise. At the end of the game, $\mathcal{A}$ outputs a bit b' and wins the game if $b' = b$, i.e. if she distinguished real session keys from random strings. The advantage of $\mathcal{A}$ in the FS-IND-RoR security game for protocol P and passwords sampled uniformly at random from dictionary pw is defined as follows:

$$Adv_{P,pw}^{FS-RoR}(\mathcal{A}) := 2 \cdot \Pr\left(b' = b\right) - 1. \tag{1}$$

Definition 1. *Protocol P is FS-IND-RoR secure if*

1. *(Completeness) If protocol messages are faithfully transmitted between two matching instances then both instances accept and compute the same key.*
2. *(Bounded Adversary Advantage) For all PPT adversaries $\mathcal{A}$:*

$$Adv_{P,pw}^{FS-RoR}(\mathcal{A}) \leq \frac{n}{|pw|} + negl(\lambda) , \tag{2}$$

where n is an upper bound on the number of sessions initialized by $\mathcal{A}$ and λ is the security parameter.

Remark 1. As we mentioned before, different flavors of forward secrecy exist in the literature, e.g. just in [4] the authors provide three particular definitions which could either weaken or strengthen the security guaranteed by the model in case of compromise of long term secret information. While the intuition of forward secrecy and the security guarantee that it aims to provide are understood, it is unclear which definition of forward secrecy is *de facto* the right one for PAKE protocols. Therefore, to be explicit, we consider forward secrecy in the *weak corruption model* described in [4], where corruption of some principal leaks only its password to the adversary, i.e. no internal state is revealed.

In the Client-Server setting, it is reasonable to assume that compromise of the server leaks the whole password data file to the adversary, even for *asymmetric* PAKEs. Thus, the model pessimistically renders every instance, whose session key was negotiated after *someone* got corrupted, as *compromised* and no security is guaranteed. Such a case is formalized in the Test query, which is answered with the *real* session key, i.e. *independently* of the bit b, whenever the previously mentioned scenario occurs. We note that it is possible to fine-tune the model by distinguishing compromise of a server from a client's one, however, it will place new cumbersome conditions to the Test query making the analysis more complex and without gaining some significant improvement.

Remark 2. When using passwords as means of authentication, there is a non-negligible probability of an adversary successfully impersonating an honest user by simply guessing its password. This problem is unavoidable and inherent to PAKE protocols. Consequently, the security definition considers a PAKE protocol to be secure if only on-line dictionary attacks are possible i.e. the protocol should not leak any information that allows the adversary to obtain the password in an off-line manner.

3   Security in the Simulation Mode with Forward Secrecy

SIM-based security requires the definition of two scenarios: (i) an *Ideal World* (*IW*) which describes the key exchange *service* that is meant to be provided and (ii) a *Real World* (*RW*) to describe the real interaction between honest protocol participants and an adversary attacking the protocol. The *IW* is designed in such a way that it is secure by definition and follows the desired security properties that a PAKE should satisfy.

When dealing with passwords as long-term secret information for authentication, the security model has to acknowledge the non-negligible probability of an adversary guessing the correct password and successfully impersonating an honest user. There are two ways to incorporate this *defect* due to the low entropy of passwords in the SIM-based security model; the first approach is considered in [6,8] while the second in [25,43]:

1. Incorporate the non-negligible probability of an adversary guessing the password into the ideal world, by explicitly allowing the ideal world adversary to verify the guess of a candidate password. Then one defines a protocol to be secure if the real-world execution is computationally indistinguishable from an execution in the ideal world.
2. Do not allow password guessing in the ideal world but relax the requirement of indistinguishability between the real world and ideal world transcripts. One defines a protocol to be secure as one whose real-world execution is distinguishable from an execution in the ideal world with probability at most $n/|pw| + negl(\lambda)$, where n is the number of active user instances and pw is the dictionary. Keep in mind that we make use of this approach in Sect. 4 when we prove Theorem 3.

For now we consider only the first approach. We augment the original SIM-BMP model of Boyko et al. [6] to account for scenarios where *forward secrecy* is required. For clarity, we refer to the later simulation model with forward secrecy as FS-SIM-BMP to distinguish from the original one. The inclusion of this security property in the SIM-BMP model allows us to provide a fair comparison to the IND-RoR model with forward secrecy as described in Sect. 2, otherwise, the models would be incomparable simply because they aim for different security guarantees. We consider forward secrecy in the *weak corruption model* as described in [4,7] for this task.

3.1   Ideal World

The ideal world (IW) model describes the service that a PAKE aims to provide, i.e. to allow parties to jointly compute a high entropy secret session key, which can be used later in higher level *applications*. In the IW there are no messages flowing around the network nor cryptography. The session keys are chosen at random by a trusted party and delivered out-of-band to the honest users.

Formally, the ideal world involves interaction between a trusted entity called ideal world *Ring Master* and an ideal world adversary, denoted by $\mathcal{RM}^*$ and $\mathcal{B}^*$ respectively. The *ring master* is similar to the *challenger* in the FS-IND-RoR experiment. The details of the ideal world execution follow.

PROTOCOL PARTICIPANTS: As defined in the FS-IND-RoR model.

LONG-TERM SECRETS: The FS-SIM-BMP model does not make any assumption on the password distribution. However, to allow a fair comparison to the FS-IND-RoR model, we assume the passwords to be independent and uniformly distributed.

PROTOCOL EXECUTION: There is no protocol execution in the ideal world. The session key of an instance is generated by the $\mathcal{RM}^*$ when $\mathcal{B}^*$ asks that instance the *start session* query. Additionally $\mathcal{B}^*$ is given access to the following oracles:

- **Initialize User**$(U, id_U, role_U)$. Identical to that in the FS-IND-RoR model.
  [Transcript: ("init. user", $U, role_U$)]
- **Initialize user Instance**$(U, i, role_U^i, pid_U^i)$. Identical to that in the FS-IND-RoR model.
  [Transcript: ("init. inst.",U, i, pid_U^i)][8]
- **Abort user Instance** (U, i). Adversary $\mathcal{B}^*$ asks $\mathcal{RM}^*$ to abort user instance Π_U^i. We say then that Π_U^i is *aborted*.
  [Transcript: ("abort. user inst.",U, i)]
- **Test Instance Password** (U, i, π'). For user instance Π_U^i and password guess π', $\mathcal{B}^*$ queries if π' equals $\pi(U, pid_U^i)$. If this is true, the query is called *successful guess on* $\{U, pid_U^i\}$.
  This query can be asked only once per user instance. The user instance must be initialized and not yet engaged in a session, i.e. no start session operation has been performed for that instance. Note that $\mathcal{B}^*$ is allowed to ask a *test instance password* query to an instance that is *aborted*. This query does not leave any records in the transcript.

---

[8] Note that the original SIM-BMP model [6] also places $role_U^i$ in the transcript, but we have chosen to remove it. This is because in the ideal world, from two partnered instances, the one with the role "open" will always start session first. On the other hand, in the real world, the adversary is free to choose which instance is assigned role "open" and which "connect". Thus, a real world adversary could make an honest execution of a protocol between an instance with role "connect" that terminates first, and an instance with role "open" that terminates second. Such a transcript, which constitutes an honest execution of a protocol, would not be simulatable in the ideal world if the roles "open" and "connect" are placed in the transcript.

- **Corrupt** (U). $\mathcal{B}^*$ learns the long-term secret information of some initialized user U. If $role_U = client$, then $\mathcal{B}^*$ gets π_U. Otherwise, if $role_U = server$, then $\mathcal{B}^*$ receives $L = < \pi_i >_{i \in \mathcal{C}}$.
  [Transcript: ("Corrupt", U, π_U)]
- **Start Session** (U, i). $\mathcal{B}^*$ specifies that a session key for user instance Π_U^i must be generated, by specifying one of the three *connection assigments* available:
  - **open for connection from** (U', j). This operation is allowed if: (c1) $role_U^i = open$ and user instances Π_U^i and $\Pi_{U'}^j$ are *matching instances*, (c2) $\Pi_{U'}^j$ has been *initialized* and not *aborted*, (c3) no other instance is *open for connection* from $\Pi_{U'}^j$, and (c4) no *test instance password* operation has been performed on Π_U^i. Then $\mathcal{RM}^*$ generates session key sk_U^i at random. Then Π_U^i is said to be *open for connection from* $\Pi_{U'}^j$.
  - **connect to** (U', j). This operation is allowed if: (c1) $role_U^i = connect$ and user instances Π_U^i and $\Pi_{U'}^j$ are *matching instances*, (c2) $\Pi_{U'}^j$ has been *initialized* and not *aborted*, (c3) $\Pi_{U'}^j$ was open for connection from Π_U^i after Π_U^i was initialized and $\Pi_{U'}^j$ is still open for connection and (c4) no *test instance password* operation has been performed on Π_U^i. The $\mathcal{RM}^*$ sets $sk_U^i = sk_{U'}^j$ and $\Pi_{U'}^j$ is no longer open for connection.
  - **expose** (U, i, sk). $\mathcal{B}^*$ assigns session key sk of his choice to user instance Π_U^i. This connection assignment is allowed if at least one of the following conditions hold: (i) there has been a successful test instance password on Π_U^i or (ii) there was a Corrupt query, directed to any user, before the *start session* operation.
  [Transcript: ("start session", U, i)]
- **Application** (f, U, i). The adversary specifies an efficiently computable function f and a user instance Π_U^i for which a session key sk_U^i has already been established. It gets back $f(\{sk_U^i\}, R)$, where R is a global random bit string which user instances are given access to. R is not correlated to the established session keys and usually is referred to as the environment.
  [Transcript: ("application", $f, f(sk_U^i, R)$)]
- **Implementation.** This is a do nothing operation. $\mathcal{B}^*$ is allowed to place *implementation* operations without taking any effect in the ideal world. It is needed to allow $\mathcal{B}^*$ to construct *transcripts* that are equivalent to those in the real world.
  [Transcript: ("impl", $cmmt$)]

Transcript. Some of the previously mentioned queries are recorded in a *transcript*. Let IWT^* denote the transcript generated by $\mathcal{B}^*$.

Remark 3. The SIM-BMP model handles on-line dictionary attacks, which are unavoidable and inherent to PAKEs, by introducing the notion of passwords and specifically the *test instance password* query in the ideal world definition. This approach places the fundamental requirement that an active adversary can test at most one password per protocol execution. In fact, provided that the PAKE in question should be deemed SIM-BMP secure, the test instance password allows the simulator to create ideal world transcripts which are computationally indistinguishable from real world ones.

In a more general sense, the *expose* connection assignment is allowed whenever the adversary could compute by his own the session key shared with some instance Π_U^i, e.g. a successful online dictionary attack or a Corrupt query asked before the connection assignment. This is similar to the freshness condition defined for IND-based models, which prevents the adversary from winning the experiment by *trivial* means.

The purpose of running PAKE protocol is to later use the established session keys in higher-level application protocols, e.g. the construction of secure communication channels is their most natural application. However, partial information about the established session key could potentially be leaked to the adversary through the usage of such keys, e.g. cryptanalysis, side channel attacks, etc. The application query models the ability of the adversary to get any information she wishes about the environment and the established session keys. The function f is defined by $\mathcal{B}^*$, the only constraint is that it must be efficiently computable.

3.2   Real World

The real-world (RW) describes the scenario where a PAKE protocol runs. There is a real world Ring Master ($\mathcal{RM}$), whose role is similar to the role of the challenger in the FS-IND-RoR experiment, and a real-world adversary $\mathcal{B}$ who tries to attack the PAKE.

PROTOCOL PARTICIPANTS: Identical to IW.

LONG-TERM SECRETS: Identical to IW.

PROTOCOL EXECUTION: The same as in the FS-IND-RoR model. Also, user instances are defined as state machines with implicit access to id_U, pid_u^i and the corresponding password. The communication between the instances is entirely controlled by $\mathcal{B}$ via the following queries:

- **Initialize User**$(U, id_U, role_U)$. Identical to that in the FS-IND-RoR model.
  [Transcript:("init. user", $U, role_U$)]
- **Initialize User Instance**$(U, i, role_U^i, pid_U^i)$. This is identical to that in the FS-IND-RoR model.
  [Transcript: ("init. inst.", U, i, pid_U^i)]
- **Send** (U, i, m). The same as in the FS-IND-RoR model except that the following is added to the transcript:
  [Transcript: ("impl", "msg", $U, i, m, m', state_U^i$)]. Additionally, the following record is added to the transcript depending on $state_U^i$.
  If $state_U^i$ = "terminate" add ("start session", U, i).
  If $state_U^i$ = "abort" add ("abort", U, i).
- **Corrupt** (U). The same as in IW.
  [Transcript: ("Corrupt", U, π_U)]
- **Application** (f, U, i). The same as in IW.
  [Transcript: ("application", $f, f(sk_U^i, R)$)]

Transcript. Let RWT be the transcript generated by $\mathcal{B}$. This is a sequence of records describing the actions of $\mathcal{B}$ when interacting with the real world protocol. $\mathcal{RM}$ generates $\mathcal{B}$'s random tape and places it in the first record of the transcript. [Transcript: ("impl", "random tape", rt)].

Definition 2. *A protocol is FS-SIM-BMP secure if*

1. *(Completeness) If protocol messages are faithfully transmitted between two matching instances then both instances accept and compute the same key.*
2. *(Simulatability) for every efficient real-world adversary $\mathcal{B}$, there exists an efficient ideal world adversary $\mathcal{B}^*$, such that $RWT \stackrel{c}{\equiv} IWT^*$. Alternatively:*

$$\forall \mathcal{B} \; \exists \mathcal{B}^* \; \forall \mathcal{D}: \; |\Pr[1 \leftarrow \mathcal{D}(RWT)] - \Pr[1 \leftarrow \mathcal{D}(IWT^*)]| \leq negl(\lambda). \quad (3)$$

4   Relations Between FS-IND-RoR and FS-SIM-BMP

In this section, we establish the relations between FS-IND-RoR and FS-SIM-BMP security models for PAKEs. The results obtained follow from earlier conference paper [10]. The difference is that in the present work the considered security models incorporate the notion of forward secrecy as security requirement.

We start by showing that FS-SIM-BMP security implies FS-IND-RoR security.

Table 1. Correspondence of $\mathcal{A}$'s and $\mathcal{B}$'s queries. It follows from Table 1 in the earlier conference paper [10], however, in this work we additionally consider the Corrupt query.

FS-IND-RoR	FS-SIM-BMP
init user	init user
init user instance	init user instance
send	send
execute	send
test	application
corrupt	corrupt

Theorem 1. *(FS-SIM-BMP Security $\Rightarrow$ FS-IND-RoR Security). For any PAKE protocol P secure in the SIM-BMP model with forward secrecy, P is also secure in the IND-RoR model with forward secrecy.*

Proof. We demonstrate that if protocol P satisfies FS-SIM-BMP security, then the advantage of any adversary $\mathcal{A}$ in the FS-IND-RoR experiment is bounded by $n/|pw| + negl(\lambda)$, where n is an upper bound on the number of sessions initialized by $\mathcal{A}$.

For clarity the proof is divided in two parts which we summarize here:

1. First we build a *real-world* adversary $\mathcal{B}^{\mathcal{A}}$ from $\mathcal{A}$. The motivation is to generate a real-world *transcript* RWT according to the FS-SIM-BMP model but following $\mathcal{A}$'s commands. Additionally, since P is FS-SIM-BMP secure, the simulatability definition guarantees the existence of an ideal-world transcript IWT^* that is computationally indistinguishable from the RWT. Additionally, we show that one can use the previously generated RWT to instantiate again $\mathcal{A}$ and obtain *identical executions* of the previously simulated experiment to $\mathcal{A}$. The same reasoning applies when initializing $\mathcal{A}$ according to IWT^*.

2. We build a distinguisher $\mathcal{D}^{\mathcal{A}}$ using $\mathcal{A}$ as a subroutine, whose goal is to tell apart RWT from IWT^* transcripts. The distinguisher looks at whether $\mathcal{A}$ wins his security challenge when initialized with the given transcript. From this, we can bound the advantage of $\mathcal{A}$ in the FS-IND-RoR experiment to at most $n/|pw| + negl(\lambda)$.

Concrete details of Part 1 and Part 2 follow:

Part 1. We construct $\mathcal{B}^{\mathcal{A}}$ using an $\mathcal{A}$ as a subroutine, where $\mathcal{B}^{\mathcal{A}}$ uses his own $\mathcal{RM}$ to answer $\mathcal{A}$'s queries. $\mathcal{B}^{\mathcal{A}}$ can perfectly simulate the FS-IND-RoR experiment to $\mathcal{A}$ (see Table 1). The objective is to generate a transcript RWT from the interaction $\mathcal{RM}$ vs $\mathcal{B}^{\mathcal{A}}$. The resulting transcript will be used in the second part of the proof.

We detail the construction of $\mathcal{B}^{\mathcal{A}}$, however, a reader familiar with FS-SIM-BMP and FS-IND-RoR security models could simply go to Table 1 and notice that $\mathcal{B}^{\mathcal{A}}$ can *perfectly* simulate the FS-IND-RoR experiment to $\mathcal{A}$.

- The interaction $\mathcal{RM}$ vs $\mathcal{B}^{\mathcal{A}}$ starts when the former initializes $\mathcal{B}^{\mathcal{A}}$ with random tape $rt_{\mathcal{B}}$ - as described in Sect. 3. Next $\mathcal{B}^{\mathcal{A}}$, who simulates the challenger $\mathcal{CH}$ in the FS-IND-RoR game, generates a uniformly distributed bit-string $rt_{\mathcal{A}}$ and initializes $\mathcal{A}$ with random tape $rt_{\mathcal{A}}$.

- $\mathcal{B}^{\mathcal{A}}$ sets $b \xleftarrow{\$} \{0,1\}$ outside $\mathcal{A}$'s view.

- $\mathcal{B}^{\mathcal{A}}$ uses his $\mathcal{RM}$ to answer $\mathcal{A}$'s queries: When $\mathcal{A}$ makes *Initialize user, Initialize user instance* or *Send* queries, $\mathcal{B}^{\mathcal{A}}$ simply forwards them to his $\mathcal{RM}$ and its response (if any) is forwarded back to $\mathcal{A}$. *Execute* queries asked by $\mathcal{A}$ are converted into *Send* queries appropriately. See Table 1.

- $\mathcal{B}^{\mathcal{A}}$ answers $\mathcal{A}$'s *Test* query using his *Application* query and the bit b. If there was a *Corrupt* and a *Send* query, then $\mathcal{B}^{\mathcal{A}}$ uses his *Application* query to reveal sk_U^i. Otherwise, if $b = 1$ then $\mathcal{B}^{\mathcal{A}}$ uses his *Application* query to reveal sk_U^i, however, if $b = 0$, then $\mathcal{B}^{\mathcal{A}}$ generates a random string $r \leftarrow \{0,1\}^{l_{sk}}$ and gives it to $\mathcal{A}$. In order to avoid strategies where $\mathcal{A}$ could trivially win the game, whenever $b = 0$ the same r is returned for test queries asked to two *partnered* instances[9].

- The experiment continues and $\mathcal{A}$ is allowed to make more queries as she wishes. Eventually, $\mathcal{A}$ outputs her guess b' and the FS-IND-RoR game finishes.

---

[9] In order to achieve sound simulation, we assume that partnering information is publicly computable [30].

– $\mathcal{B}^{\mathcal{A}}$ makes an application query and writes in the transcript the string "$b, rt_{\mathcal{A}}$".
For the sake of the proof, it is not necessary to write the bit b' in the transcript.

The real-world transcript created is RWT. Furthermore, the FS-SIM-BMP definition guarantees the existence of a corresponding ideal-world transcript IWT^*, i.e. $\forall \mathcal{B} \ \exists \mathcal{B}^*$ such that $RWT \overset{c}{\equiv} IWT^*$.

Remark 4. Given either RWT or IWT^*, it is possible create instances of $\mathcal{A}$ as needed, simulate to $\mathcal{A}$ the FS-IND-RoR experiment and obtain *identical executions* as recorded in the corresponding transcript. The reason is that $\mathcal{A}$ can be initialized with random tape $rt_{\mathcal{A}}$ contained in the transcript, and then $\mathcal{A}$'s behavior is deterministic and known in advance – given the corresponding transcript –. *Rewinding* the adversary to a *specific* state is a standard proof technique [44]. However, our requirement is simpler since we only need to initialize and run $\mathcal{A}$ from the beginning.

Part 2. We use sequence of games and the previously generated transcript to demonstrate that FS-SIM-BMP Security $\Rightarrow$ FS-IND-RoR Security.

Let G_0 be the experiment where $\mathcal{A}$ is initialized according to the real-world transcript RWT, i.e. a real-world adversary $\mathcal{B}^{\mathcal{A}}$ is simulating the FS-IND-RoR experiment to $\mathcal{A}$. Let S_0 be the event where $\mathcal{A}$ outputs $b' = b$ in G_0. It holds that $\Pr[S_0] = \Pr[\mathcal{A} \text{ wins} \mid t = RWT]$.

Let G_1 be the experiment where $\mathcal{A}$ is initialized according to the ideal-world transcript IWT^*. Let S_1 be the event where $\mathcal{A}$ wins his FS-IND-RoR experiment in G_1; then $\Pr[S_1] = \Pr[\mathcal{A} \text{ wins} \mid t = IWT^*]$.

We first analyze the term $\Pr[\mathcal{A} \text{ wins} \mid t = IWT^*]$. Provided that FS-SIM-BMP security holds, we will then show that $\mathcal{A}$ can not notice the transition from G_0 to G_1, and this will give us a bound on the advantage of $\mathcal{A}$ in the FS-IND-RoR experiment.

Assume for now we are in experiment G_1 and consider how the keys in IWT^* were generated. Let γ be the event that at least one sk is generated via *expose* connection assignment as a result of a *test instance password* query that occurs during the execution of $\mathcal{B}^*$ interacting with $\mathcal{RM}^*$, i.e. a successful online dictionary attack. Let β be the complement of γ, i.e. the event that no successful password guess occurred during the interaction of $\mathcal{B}^*$ and $\mathcal{RM}^*$.

Claim 1. $Pr(\gamma) \leq n/|pw|.$[10]

Proof. For a single user instance, by definition of the ideal world, the probability of a successful password guess by $\mathcal{B}^*$ is $1/|pw|$. We apply the union bound, and get that if there are at most n instances, $Pr(\gamma) \leq n/|pw|$. □

---

[10] While these equations looks similar to that of earlier conference paper [10], the interpretation is different. In the present work, the underlying security models incorporate forward secrecy as explicitly requirement.

Claim 2. $Pr(b = b' \mid \beta) = 1/2$. (see Footnote 10)

Proof. Given than β occurs, the session keys placed in IWT^* were generated either by (i) *expose* connection assignment -provided that there was a Corrupt query before the connection assignment- or (ii) *open* or *connect* connection assignment. Then, whenever $\mathcal{A}$ makes a Test query to an instance whose session key was generated via case (i), the simulator answers with the real sk computed at the tested instance, i.e. the answer is independent of the bit b by definition of the FS-IND-RoR experiment. Similarly, whenever $\mathcal{A}$ makes a Test query to an instance whose session key was generated via case (ii), the simulator answers with a random string independent of the bit b. Therefore, the view of $\mathcal{A}$ is independent of the hidden bit b so $Pr(b = b' \mid \beta) = 1/2$. $\square$

Using Claims 1 and 2 we get:

$$\Pr\left[\mathcal{A} \text{ wins} \mid t = IWT^*\right] = \Pr\left[(b' = b) \mid \gamma\right] \cdot \Pr\left[\gamma\right]$$
$$+ \Pr\left[(b' = b) \mid \beta\right] \cdot \Pr\left[\beta\right]$$
$$\Pr\left[\mathcal{A} \text{ wins} \mid t = IWT^*\right] \leq \frac{1}{2} + \frac{n}{2 \cdot |pw|}. \text{ (see Footnote 10)} \tag{4}$$

Equation 4 expresses the observation that, by construction of the ideal-world, an adversary cannot do better than online dictionary attacks.

Now, we build a PPT algorithm $\mathcal{D}^{\mathcal{A}}$ whose aim is to distinguish real-word from ideal-world transcripts. $\mathcal{D}^{\mathcal{A}}$ gets as input a transcript $t \in \{RWT, IWT^*\}$, and uses it to initialize a PPT adversary $\mathcal{A}$ and simulate a FS-IND-RoR experiment to $\mathcal{A}$. The simulation will be either G_0 or G_1. If SIM-security holds, then $\mathcal{D}^{\mathcal{A}}$ cannot distinguish real world and ideal world transcripts, and so $\mathcal{A}$ cannot win his FS-IND-RoR experiment with advantage greater than $n/|pw| + negl(\lambda)$.

In more details, on input some transcript t, $\mathcal{D}^{\mathcal{A}}$ proceeds as follows:

- Look for the last record of the transcript containing the string "$b, rt_{\mathcal{A}}$".
- $\mathcal{D}$ "simulates" the challenger in the FS-IND-RoR experiment and initializes $\mathcal{A}$ on random tape $rt_{\mathcal{A}}$. Since $\mathcal{A}$ is given $rt_{\mathcal{A}}$, she behaves (deterministic) the same way as recorded in the transcript t. Every query asked by $\mathcal{A}$ can be answered by $\mathcal{D}$ by just reading t.
- Eventually $\mathcal{A}$ outputs her guess b' and $\mathcal{D}$ proceeds as follows: If $b = b'$ $\mathcal{D}$ outputs "1" and if $b \neq b'$ it outputs "0". Additionally, when a bad event occurs, e.g. $\mathcal{A}$ cannot be initialized, or her queries cannot be answered by reading t, then $\mathcal{D}$ outputs $\perp$.

$\mathcal{A}$ wins her FS-IND-RoR game whenever she outputs $b' = b$. By construction of $\mathcal{D}$ it holds that:

$$\Pr\left[1 \leftarrow \mathcal{D}(RWT)\right] = \Pr\left[S_0\right]$$

and

$$\Pr\left[1 \leftarrow \mathcal{D}(IWT^*)\right] = \Pr\left[S_1\right].$$

From Eq. 3 of FS-SIM-BMP security we know the following holds:

$$|\Pr[1 \leftarrow \mathcal{D}(RWT)] - \Pr[1 \leftarrow \mathcal{D}(IWT^*)]| \leq negl(\lambda). \text{(see Footnote 10)} \quad (5)$$

Then it holds that $|\Pr[S0] - \Pr[S_1]| \leq negl(\lambda)$. By definition of G_0 and G_1:

$$|\Pr[\mathcal{A} \text{ wins } | t = RWT] - \Pr[\mathcal{A} \text{ wins } | t = IWT^*]| \leq negl(\lambda). \text{(see Footnote 10)} \quad (6)$$

The term $\Pr[\mathcal{A} \text{ wins } | t = RWT]$ is actually the probability of $\mathcal{A}$ winning on a perfectly simulated FS-IND-RoR experiment. We combine with Eq. 4 and get:

$$\Pr[\mathcal{A} \text{ wins } | t = RWT] \leq \frac{1}{2} + \frac{n}{2 \cdot |pw|} + negl(\lambda)$$

We obtain that, if FS-SIM-BMP-security holds, then $\forall$ PPT $\mathcal{A}$ $Adv_{P,pw}^{FS-RoR}(\mathcal{A})$ $\leq n/|pw| + negl(\lambda)$, proving that FS-SIM-BMP $\Rightarrow$ FS-IND-RoR. $\square$

Now we investigate the reverse, i.e. whether FS-IND-RoR security also implies FS-SIM-BMP security. We obtain the following result:

Theorem 2. *If P is not FS-SIM-BMP secure, then $\exists \mathcal{A}$ s.t. $Adv_{P,pw}^{RoR}(\mathcal{A}) > n_A/|pw| + \omega$, where n_A is the number of explicit password guesses of $\mathcal{A}$ and ω is a non-negligible function of the security parameter.*

Proof. We build a FS-IND-RoR adversary $\mathcal{A}^{\mathcal{B}}$, as the sequential composition of two adversaries: $\mathcal{A}_1$ and $\mathcal{A}_2^{\mathcal{B}}$. First, $\mathcal{A}^{\mathcal{B}}$ invokes $\mathcal{A}_1$. $\mathcal{A}_1$ tries a number of online dictionary attacks. If one of these is successful, then $\mathcal{A}^{\mathcal{B}}$ can win the FS-IND-RoR experiment. If none of the online dictionary attacks is successful, then $\mathcal{A}^{\mathcal{B}}$ invokes $\mathcal{A}_2^{\mathcal{B}}$. Next, we describe the details of $\mathcal{A}_1$ and $\mathcal{A}_2^{\mathcal{B}}$.

(i) Construction of $\mathcal{A}_1$. Let $\mathcal{A}_1$ be an adversary who tries to masquerade user U to user V n_A times. Each time, $\mathcal{A}_1$ chooses a new candidate password and runs the protocol with V. If one of the password guesses is successful, then $\mathcal{A}_1$ can win the IND-RoR experiment. By construction,

$$\Pr[\mathcal{A}_1 \ wins] = \frac{n_A}{|pw|}. \text{(see Footnote 10)} \quad (7)$$

(ii) Construction of $\mathcal{A}_2^{\mathcal{B}}$. We have assumed that FS-SIM-BMP security does not hold. Then $\exists \mathcal{B} \ \forall \mathcal{B}^* \ \exists \mathcal{D}$ s.t.:

$$|\Pr[1 \leftarrow \mathcal{D}(RWT)] - \Pr[1 \leftarrow \mathcal{D}(IWT^*)]| > \omega, \text{(see Footnote 10)} \quad (8)$$

where ω is non-negligible term.

Let $\mathcal{A}_2^{\mathcal{B}}$ be an adversary in the FS-IND-RoR experiment which uses $\mathcal{B}$ and $\mathcal{D}$ as subroutine. The game $\mathcal{A}_2^{\mathcal{B}}$ vs $\mathcal{CH}$ proceeds as follows:

- At the beginning of the experiment, $\mathcal{CH}$ chooses a bit b at random and outside $\mathcal{A}_2^{\mathcal{B}}$'s view.

- $\mathcal{A}_2^{\mathcal{B}}$ uses $\mathcal{B}$ as subroutine and answers $\mathcal{B}$'s queries as follows: When $\mathcal{B}$ asks for Initialize user, Initialize user instance, Send or Corrupt queries, $\mathcal{A}_2^{\mathcal{B}}$ simply forwards them to her $\mathcal{CH}$ and its response (if any) is forwarded back to $\mathcal{B}$.
- $\mathcal{A}_2^{\mathcal{B}}$ uses her Test query to answer $\mathcal{B}$'s Application queries. When $\mathcal{B}$ asks for an application of the efficiently computable function f on sk_U^i and a global random string R, $\mathcal{A}_2^{\mathcal{B}}$ asks $\text{Test}(U, i)$ to her $\mathcal{CH}$, obtains sk_U^i, computes $f(sk_U^i, R)$ and sends the result to $\mathcal{B}$.

Claim 3. *The transcript produced by $\mathcal{A}_2^{\mathcal{B}}$ is either RWT or IWT^*.*

Proof. $\mathcal{B}$'s actions produce a transcript t. Consider the following scenario: $\mathcal{B}$ asks an Application query and $\mathcal{A}_2^{\mathcal{B}}$ answers it by asking a Test query to his own challenger. Without loss of generality, let us consider fresh instances, i.e. those where we give credit to the adversary if he answers with $b' = b$: If $b = 1$, $\mathcal{A}_2^{\mathcal{B}}$'s Test queries are answered with real session keys, else if $b = 0$ $\mathcal{A}_2^{\mathcal{B}}$ gets a random string taken from the session key space. Therefore, $\mathcal{A}_2^{\mathcal{B}}$'s answer to $\mathcal{B}$'s application queries is either a function of the real session key or a function of a random string. Looking at the definition of the real and ideal-world transcripts, we conclude that whenever $b = 1$ the transcript generated is real-world while if $b = 0$ the transcript is ideal world. The reason is that in the real-world, the user instances compute their sk's according to the description of the protocol and only such *computed* sk's are placed transcript. However, in the ideal-world, the session keys placed in the transcript are (i) random strings provided that freshness condition is satisfied or (ii) no restriction about sk provided that freshness is not satisfied, i.e. the simulator is given the freedom to specify the session key as he wishes. $\square$

Let $\mathcal{D}$ be the PPT distinguisher whose existence is guaranteed by the negation of FS-SIM-BMP security.[11] Next, $\mathcal{A}_2^{\mathcal{B}}$ invokes $\mathcal{D}(t)$ and simply forwards $\mathcal{D}$'s output to $\mathcal{CH}$. By construction, $\mathcal{A}_2^{\mathcal{B}}$ wins whenever $\mathcal{D}$ is able to distinguish real-world from ideal-world transcripts. Therefore:

$$\Pr\left[\mathcal{A}_2^{\mathcal{B}} \; wins\right] = \Pr\left[b = 1\right] \cdot \Pr\left[1 \leftarrow \mathcal{D}(RWT)\right]$$
$$+ \Pr\left[b = 0\right] \cdot \Pr\left[0 \leftarrow \mathcal{D}(IWT^*)\right],$$

which using Eq. 8 gives:

$$\Pr\left[\mathcal{A}_2^{\mathcal{B}} \; wins\right] > \frac{1}{2} + \omega. \text{(see Footnote 10)} \qquad (9)$$

We build $\mathcal{A}$ as the sequential composition of $\mathcal{A}_1$ and $\mathcal{A}_2^{\mathcal{B}}$. It follows that:

$$\Pr\left[\mathcal{A}^{\mathcal{B}} \; wins\right] = \Pr\left[\mathcal{A}_1 \; wins\right] + \Pr\left[\mathcal{A}_2^{\mathcal{B}} \; wins\right] - \Pr\left[\mathcal{A}_1 \; wins\right] \cdot \Pr\left[\mathcal{A}_2^{\mathcal{B}} \; wins\right],$$

which from Eqs. 7 and 9 yields:

$$\Pr\left[\mathcal{A}^{\mathcal{B}} \; wins\right] > \frac{n_A}{2 \cdot pw} + \frac{1}{2} + \omega$$

---

[11] Without loss of generality, we can assume $\mathcal{D}$ is more likely to output 1 on a real world than on an ideal world transcript; otherwise, flip the output bit of $\mathcal{D}$.

$$Adv_{P,pw}^{FS-RoR}(\mathcal{A}^{\mathcal{B}}) > \frac{n_A}{pw} + \omega, \text{ (see Footnote 10)} \tag{10}$$

where ω is a non-negligible function.   □

Unfortunately, Theorem 2 is not enough to prove that FS-IND-RoR security implies FS-SIM-BMP security. The reason is that the total number of instances initialized by our construction of $\mathcal{A}$ is $n_A + n_B$, where n_A is the number of explicit password guesses of subroutine $\mathcal{A}_1$ and n_B is the number of instances initialized while subroutine $\mathcal{A}_2^{\mathcal{B}}$ is simulating the real world ring master to $\mathcal{B}$. Therefore, proving by contradiction that FS-IND-RoR $\Rightarrow$ FS-SIM-BMP would require $Adv_{P,pw}^{FS-RoR}(\mathcal{A}) > (n_A + n_B)/pw + \omega$.

We recall from Sect. 3 that there are two ways to take account of online dictionary attacks in SIM-based security models for PAKEs:

1. Include a *test instance password* query in *IW* and require computational indistinguishability of *RWT* and *IWT**.
2. Do not include a *test instance password* in *IW* but allow a non-negligible bound on the distinguishability of *RWT* and *IWT**.

The SIM-based model Boyko, MacKenzie and Patel [6] follows the first style. We modify it so it follows the second style. We call the modified model FS-SIM-BMP'. The only changes are the following:

1. Remove the *test instance password* query from *IW* in FS-SIM-BMP.
2. Relax the requirement of indistinguishability between real and ideal world.

FS-SIM-BMP' Security. Protocol P is FS-SIM-BMP' secure if it satisfies completeness and additionally for all *Real World* adversaries $\mathcal{B}$, there exits an *Ideal World* adversary $\mathcal{B}^*$ such that for all distinguishers $\mathcal{D}$:

$$|\Pr[1 \leftarrow \mathcal{D}(RWT)] - \Pr[1 \leftarrow \mathcal{D}(IWT^*)]| \leq \frac{n}{|pw|} + negl(\lambda), \text{ (see Footnote 10)}$$
$$\tag{11}$$

where n is an upper bound on the number of sessions initialized by $\mathcal{B}$.

Next, we show that FS-IND-RoR security implies FS-SIM-BMP' security.

Theorem 3. *(FS-IND-RoR Security $\Rightarrow$ FS-SIM-BMP' Security). If protocol P is secure in the IND-RoR model with forward secrecy, then P is also secure in the SIM-BMP' model with forward secrecy.*

Proof. This is a proof by contradiction and the strategy is similar to the one employed in Theorem 2.

We assume that FS-SIM-BMP' security does not hold. Then $\exists \mathcal{B} \ \forall \mathcal{B}^* \ \exists \mathcal{D}$ s.t.:

$$|\Pr[1 \leftarrow \mathcal{D}(RWT)] - \Pr[1 \leftarrow \mathcal{D}(IWT^*)]| > \frac{n}{|pw|} + \omega, \text{ (see Footnote 10)} \tag{12}$$

where n is an upper bound on the number of sessions initialized and ω is a non-negligible function.

Then, we build an adversary $\mathcal{A}^{\mathcal{B}}$ using $\mathcal{B}$ and $\mathcal{D}$ as subroutines such that $\mathcal{A}$ breaks FS-IND-RoR security. We construct $\mathcal{A}^{\mathcal{B}}$ from $\mathcal{B}$ and $\mathcal{D}$ in exactly the same way as we built $\mathcal{A}_2^{\mathcal{B}}$ from $\mathcal{B}$ and $\mathcal{D}$ in the proof of Theorem 2.

Using the same analysis as in the proof of Theorem 2, we get:

$$\Pr\left[\mathcal{A}^{\mathcal{B}} \ wins\right] = \Pr\left[b = 1\right] \cdot \Pr\left[1 \leftarrow \mathcal{D}(RWT)\right]$$
$$+ \Pr\left[b = 0\right] \cdot \Pr\left[0 \leftarrow \mathcal{D}(IWT^*)\right] ,$$

which using Eq. 12 gives:

$$\Pr\left[\mathcal{A}^{\mathcal{B}} \ wins\right] > \frac{1}{2} + \frac{n}{2 \cdot |pw|} + \omega ,$$

And finally from Eq. 1:

$$Adv_{P,pw}^{FS-RoR}(\mathcal{A}^{\mathcal{B}}) > \frac{n}{|pw|} + \omega, \ (\text{see Footnote 10})$$

but ω is not negligible, a contradiction.   □

Now, we investigate the reverse, i.e. whether FS-SIM-BMP' security implies FS-IND-RoR security. We obtain the following result:

Theorem 4. *(FS-SIM-BMP' Security $\Rightarrow$ FS-IND-RoR Security). If protocol P is SIM-BMP' secure with forward secrecy, then for all PPT $\mathcal{A}$, $Adv_{P,pw}^{FS-RoR}(\mathcal{A}) \le 2 \cdot n/|pw| + negl(\lambda)$.*

Proof. We follow the same argument as in the proof of Theorem 1 up to Eq. 5, which we simply update according to the FS-SIM-BMP' security definition given in Eq. 11. Hence:

$$|\Pr\left[\mathcal{A} \ wins \ | \ t = RWT\right] - \Pr\left[\mathcal{A} \ wins \ | \ t = IWT^*\right]| \qquad (13)$$
$$\le \frac{n}{|pw|} + negl(\lambda). \ (\text{see Footnote 10})$$

It is easy to see that $\Pr\left[\mathcal{A} \ wins \ | \ t = IWT^*\right] = 1/2$ since $\mathcal{A}$ cannot gain any information about the hidden bit b. However, $\Pr\left[\mathcal{A} \ wins \ | \ t = RWT\right] = 1/2 + 1/2 \cdot Adv_{P,pw}^{FS-RoR}(\mathcal{A})$ as result of $\mathcal{A}$ running on a perfectly simulated FS-IND-RoR experiment. Following Eq. 13 we obtain:

$$Adv_{P,pw}^{FS-RoR}(\mathcal{A}) \le \frac{2 \cdot n}{|pw|} + negl(\lambda)$$

□

The guarantee that $\forall \mathcal{A}$, $Adv_{P,pw}^{FS-RoR}(\mathcal{A}) \le 2 \cdot n/|pw| + negl(\lambda)$ means that protocol P satisfies the definition of FS-IND-RoR security (Definition 1) with a degradation factor $c = 2$. A similar constant factor appears in the reduction used in [5] to prove that IND-RoR security implies IND-FtG security.

Using the results of Theorems 1 and 3 from [10], as well as the known relation IND-RoR $\Rightarrow$ IND-FtG [5], we obtain the following corollary:

Corollary 1. *The following relations hold*

- *SIM-BMP Security $\Rightarrow$ IND-FtG Security*
- *SIM-BMP Security $\Rightarrow$ SIM-BMP' Security*

The question of whether SIM-BMP' Security $\Rightarrow$ SIM-BMP Security remains open. Note that SIM-BMP' $\Rightarrow$ SIM-BMP would imply that the three security notions IND-RoR, SIM-BPM and SIM-BMP' are equivalent. A similar reasoning can be applied when considering forward secrecy in the aforementioned security models.

5 Conclusion and Future Work

Although PAKE is a widely studied primitive and found in real-world security protocols, a clear relation between its major security notions (IND and SIM) was missing in the literature. In this work, we aimed at filling this gap. We have summarized the relations obtained in this work in Fig. 2.

During our work on this topic, we identified some delicate definitional issues veiled under the many subtleties of the security notions for PAKE. We recall what we consider the most relevant:

- In IND-based models [4,5] the possible states in which a user instance could be are continue, reject, accept and terminate. Roughly speaking, an instance is in *accept* state whenever it has computed the *sk* but is still waiting to receive another message – typically a confirmation code – to fulfill the protocol specification, while an instance in *terminate* state means that it has computed the *sk*, has finished the protocol execution and is not sending nor receiving any other message. Particularly in the IND-FtG model, a Reveal query can be asked to instances in *accept* state while a Test query can only be directed to instances in *terminate* state. The aforementioned distinction between accept and terminate states does not exist in SIM-based models due to how the ideal world is modeled. The idea is the following:
  - In the SIM-BMP model, the Application query models the leakage of session keys in higher level protocols. The implicit requirement is that the corresponding user instance has *terminated* his protocol execution, which is modeled in the Ideal-World via connection assignments.
  - In IND-FtG model, the Reveal query models (i) the leakage of session keys in higher level protocols and (ii) leakage of session keys before the protocol is finished, i.e. *accept* state.

The aforementioned peculiarity is specially relevant for Corollary 1. In order for the implication SIM-BMP $\Rightarrow$ IND-FtG to hold, we require the Reveal (U, i) query in the IND-FtG model to be legitimate only if the instance Π_U^i is in *terminate* state. It might be a minor difference between IND-based and

SIM-based models, yet we consider it is worth mentioning, specially because it is generally assumed that SIM-based security definitions are stronger than their corresponding IND-based ones. However, as we have just explained, there are technicalities that need to be addressed when formally stating the relation between the security models.

- A more remarkable difference between IND and SIM models for PAKEs is how online dictionary attacks are captured in the security model. In IND-base models, the advantage of an adversary is formulated according to parameter n, which represents the number of active instances created by the adversary in question. Note that such a definition does not specify or take into account the fact that the adversary's strategy is randomized, and thus n may be a randomized function as well. For instance, an adversary could create a large number of instances with negligible probability making the bound on its advantage grow. The difference between models with an explicit formulation of a non-negligible bound on the advantage and models without such an explicit formulation seems to be related to the difficulty in proving IND-RoR $\Rightarrow$ SIM-BMP. Another related issue is about the password distribution and the correlation of passwords between users. We leave the quest for a more precise definition that would take into account the above-mentioned remarks for future work.
- The SIM-BMP model offers a more meaningful security definition by better capturing the capabilities of an attacker against a PAKE protocol, for instance online dictionary attacks. Additionally, the SIM-BMP model does not place any artificial constraints on the passwords distribution, whereas the IND-RoR requires the passwords to be uniformly distributed and independent. The last requirement might be difficult to satisfy in real scenarios. In particular, it is known that certain passwords are more likely to be selected than others and that users tend to choose similar passwords when connecting to different services.

Finally, we demonstrated that the results obtained in [10] are still satisfied when the corresponding security models incorporate forward secrecy as required security property.

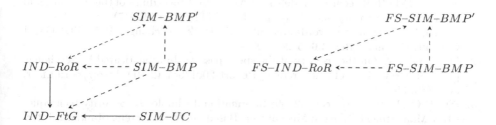

Fig. 2. Relation between PAKE security definitions. In dashed arrows are the results of (i) this paper and (ii) earlier conference paper [10].

Acknowledgements. We are especially grateful to Jean Lancrenon for all his suggestions and fruitful discussions. This work was supported by the Luxembourg National Research Fund (CORE project AToMS and CORE Junior grant no. 11299247).

References

1. Nam, J., Choo, K.R., Paik, J., Won, D.: An offline dictionary attack against a three-party key exchange protocol. IACR Cryptology ePrint Archive 2013, p. 666 (2013). http://eprint.iacr.org/2013/666
2. Clarke, D., Hao, F.: Cryptanalysis of the dragonfly key exchange protocol. IET Inf. Secur. **8**, 283–289 (2014)
3. Becerra, J., Šala, P., Škrobot, M.: An offline dictionary attack against zkPAKE protocol. Cryptology ePrint Archive, Report 2017/961 (2017). https://eprint.iacr.org/2017/961
4. Bellare, M., Pointcheval, D., Rogaway, P.: Authenticated key exchange secure against dictionary attacks. In: Preneel, B. (ed.) EUROCRYPT 2000. LNCS, vol. 1807, pp. 139–155. Springer, Heidelberg (2000). https://doi.org/10.1007/3-540-45539-6_11
5. Abdalla, M., Fouque, P.-A., Pointcheval, D.: Password-based authenticated key exchange in the three-party setting. In: Vaudenay, S. (ed.) PKC 2005. LNCS, vol. 3386, pp. 65–84. Springer, Heidelberg (2005). https://doi.org/10.1007/978-3-540-30580-4_6
6. Boyko, V., MacKenzie, P., Patel, S.: Provably secure password-authenticated key exchange using Diffie-Hellman. In: Preneel, B. (ed.) EUROCRYPT 2000. LNCS, vol. 1807, pp. 156–171. Springer, Heidelberg (2000). https://doi.org/10.1007/3-540-45539-6_12
7. Shoup, V.: On formal models for secure key exchange. Cryptology ePrint Archive, Report 1999/012 (1999). http://eprint.iacr.org/1999/012
8. Canetti, R., Halevi, S., Katz, J., Lindell, Y., MacKenzie, P.: Universally composable password-based key exchange. In: Cramer, R. (ed.) EUROCRYPT 2005. LNCS, vol. 3494, pp. 404–421. Springer, Heidelberg (2005). https://doi.org/10.1007/11426639_24
9. Canetti, R.: Universally composable security: a new paradigm for cryptographic protocols. In: 42nd Annual Symposium on Foundations of Computer Science, FOCS 2001, pp. 136–145. IEEE Computer Society (2001)
10. Lopez Becerra, J.M., Iovino, V., Ostrev, D., Skrobot, M.: On the relation between SIM and IND-RoR security models for PAKEs. In: Proceedings of the International Conference on Security and Cryptography. SCITEPRESS (2017)
11. Jablon, D.P.: Strong password-only authenticated key exchange. ACM SIGCOMM Comput. Commun. Rev. **26**, 5–26 (1996)
12. MacKenzie, P.: On the security of the speke password-authenticated key exchange protocol. Cryptology ePrint Archive, Report 2001/057 (2001). http://eprint.iacr.org/2001/057
13. ISO/IEC 11770–4:2006/cor 1:2009, Information Technology - Security techniques - Key Management - Part 4: Mechanisms Based on Weak Secrets. Standard, International Organization for Standardization, Genève, Switzerland (2009)
14. Standard Specifications for Password-Based Public Key Cryptographic Techniques. Standard, IEEE Standards Association, NJ, USA (2002)
15. Diffie, W., Van Oorschot, P.C., Wiener, M.J.: Authentication and authenticated key exchanges. Des. Codes Crypt. **2**, 107–125 (1992)

16. Cameron, D.: Over 560 million passwords discovered in anonymous online database (2017). https://bit.ly/2vgJqli
17. Perlroth, N., Gelles, D.: Russian hackers amass over a billion internet passwords (2014). https://nyti.ms/2Apak05
18. Ian, P.: Linkedin confirms account passwords hacked (2012). https://bit.ly/2v2qjMh
19. Hao, F., Ryan, P.: J-PAKE: authenticated key exchange without PKI. Trans. Comput. Sci. 11, 192–206 (2010)
20. MacKenzie, P.: The PAK Suite: protocols for password-authenticated key exchange. DIMACS Technical report 2002–46 (2002)
21. LaMacchia, B., Lauter, K., Mityagin, A.: Stronger security of authenticated key exchange. In: Susilo, W., Liu, J.K., Mu, Y. (eds.) ProvSec 2007. LNCS, vol. 4784, pp. 1–16. Springer, Heidelberg (2007). https://doi.org/10.1007/978-3-540-75670-5_1
22. Canetti, R., Krawczyk, H.: Analysis of key-exchange protocols and their use for building secure channels. In: Pfitzmann, B. (ed.) EUROCRYPT 2001. LNCS, vol. 2045, pp. 453–474. Springer, Heidelberg (2001). https://doi.org/10.1007/3-540-44987-6_28
23. Krawczyk, H.: HMQV: a high-performance secure Diffie-Hellman protocol. In: Shoup, V. (ed.) CRYPTO 2005. LNCS, vol. 3621, pp. 546–566. Springer, Heidelberg (2005). https://doi.org/10.1007/11535218_33
24. Katz, J., Ostrovsky, R., Yung, M.: Forward secrecy in password-only key exchange protocols. In: Cimato, S., Persiano, G., Galdi, C. (eds.) SCN 2002. LNCS, vol. 2576, pp. 29–44. Springer, Heidelberg (2003). https://doi.org/10.1007/3-540-36413-7_3
25. Goldreich, O., Lindell, Y.: Session-key generation using human passwords only. In: Kilian, J. (ed.) CRYPTO 2001. LNCS, vol. 2139, pp. 408–432. Springer, Heidelberg (2001). https://doi.org/10.1007/3-540-44647-8_24
26. Bellare, M., Rogaway, P.: Entity authentication and key distribution. In: Stinson, D.R. (ed.) CRYPTO 1993. LNCS, vol. 773, pp. 232–249. Springer, Heidelberg (1994). https://doi.org/10.1007/3-540-48329-2_21
27. Bellare, M., Rogaway, P.: Provably secure session key distribution: the three party case. In: Leighton, F.T., Borodin, A., (eds.) Proceedings of the Twenty-Seventh Annual ACM Symposium on Theory of Computing, STOC 1995, pp. 57–66. ACM (1995)
28. Blake-Wilson, S., Menezes, A.: Entity authentication and authenticated key transport protocols employing asymmetric techniques. In: Christianson, B., Crispo, B., Lomas, M., Roe, M. (eds.) Security Protocols 1997. LNCS, vol. 1361, pp. 137–158. Springer, Heidelberg (1998). https://doi.org/10.1007/BFb0028166
29. Cremers, C.: Examining indistinguishability-based security models for key exchange protocols: the case of CK, CK-HMQV, and eCK. In: Proceedings of the 6th ACM Symposium on Information, Computer and Communications Security, ASIACCS 2011, pp. 80–91. ACM (2011)
30. Brzuska, C., Fischlin, M., Warinschi, B., Williams, S.C.: Composability of bellare-rogaway key exchange protocols. In Chen, Y., Danezis, G., Shmatikov, V., (eds.) Proceedings of the 18th ACM Conference on Computer and Communications Security, CCS 2011, pp. 51–62. ACM (2011)
31. Jager, T., Kohlar, F., Schäge, S., Schwenk, J.: On the security of TLS-DHE in the standard model. In: Safavi-Naini, R., Canetti, R. (eds.) CRYPTO 2012. LNCS, vol. 7417, pp. 273–293. Springer, Heidelberg (2012). https://doi.org/10.1007/978-3-642-32009-5_17

32. Bellare, M., Canetti, R., Krawczyk, H.: A modular approach to the design and analysis of authentication and key exchange protocols. In: Vitter, J.S., (ed.) Proceedings of the Thirtieth Annual ACM Symposium on the Theory of Computing, STOC 1998, pp. 419–428. ACM (1998)
33. Canetti, R., Krawczyk, H.: Universally composable notions of key exchange and secure channels. In: Knudsen, L.R. (ed.) EUROCRYPT 2002. LNCS, vol. 2332, pp. 337–351. Springer, Heidelberg (2002). https://doi.org/10.1007/3-540-46035-7_22
34. Bellovin, S.M., Merritt, M.: Encrypted key exchange: password-based protocols secure against dictionary attacks. In: 1992 IEEE Symposium on Research in Security and Privacy, SP 1992, pp. 72–84 (1992)
35. MacKenzie, P., Patel, S., Swaminathan, R.: Password-authenticated key exchange based on RSA. In: Okamoto, T. (ed.) ASIACRYPT 2000. LNCS, vol. 1976, pp. 599–613. Springer, Heidelberg (2000). https://doi.org/10.1007/3-540-44448-3_46
36. Katz, J., Ostrovsky, R., Yung, M.: Efficient password-authenticated key exchange using human-memorable passwords. In: Pfitzmann, B. (ed.) EUROCRYPT 2001. LNCS, vol. 2045, pp. 475–494. Springer, Heidelberg (2001). https://doi.org/10.1007/3-540-44987-6_29
37. Škrobot, M., Lancrenon, J.: On composability of game-based password authenticated key exchange. In: Piessens, F., Smith, M., (eds.) 3rd IEEE European Symposium on Security and Privacy – EuroS&P 2018. IEEE (2018)
38. Abdalla, M., Benhamouda, F., MacKenzie, P.: Security of the J-PAKE password authenticated key exchange protocol. In: IEEE Symposium on Security and Privacy, SP 2015, pp. 571–587. IEEE Computer Society (2015)
39. Lancrenon, J., Škrobot, M., Tang, Q.: Two more efficient variants of the J-PAKE protocol. In: Manulis, M., Sadeghi, A.-R., Schneider, S. (eds.) ACNS 2016. LNCS, vol. 9696, pp. 58–76. Springer, Cham (2016). https://doi.org/10.1007/978-3-319-39555-5_4
40. Jarecki, S., Krawczyk, H., Xu, J.: OPAQUE: an asymmetric PAKE protocol secure against pre-computation attacks. In: Nielsen, J.B., Rijmen, V. (eds.) EUROCRYPT 2018. LNCS, vol. 10822, pp. 456–486. Springer, Cham (2018). https://doi.org/10.1007/978-3-319-78372-7_15
41. Pointcheval, D.: Password-based authenticated key exchange. In: Fischlin, M., Buchmann, J., Manulis, M. (eds.) PKC 2012. LNCS, vol. 7293, pp. 390–397. Springer, Heidelberg (2012). https://doi.org/10.1007/978-3-642-30057-8_23
42. Kunz-Jacques, S., Pointcheval, D.: About the security of MTI/C0 and MQV. In: De Prisco, R., Yung, M. (eds.) SCN 2006. LNCS, vol. 4116, pp. 156–172. Springer, Heidelberg (2006). https://doi.org/10.1007/11832072_11
43. Nguyen, M., Vadhan, S.P.: Simpler session-key generation from short random passwords. J. Cryptology 21, 52–96 (2008)
44. Canetti, R., Gennaro, R., Jarecki, S., Krawczyk, H., Rabin, T.: Adaptive security for threshold cryptosystems. In: Wiener, M. (ed.) CRYPTO 1999. LNCS, vol. 1666, pp. 98–116. Springer, Heidelberg (1999). https://doi.org/10.1007/3-540-48405-1_7

History-Based Throttling of Distributed Denial-of-Service Attacks

Negar Mosharraf[1], Anura P. Jayasumana[1](✉), Indrakshi Ray[2],
and Bruhadeshwar Bezawada[2]

[1] Department of Electrical and Computer Engineering, Colorado State University,
Fort Collins, CO, USA
negar@engr.colostate.edu, Anura.Jayasumana@colostate.edu
[2] Department of Computer Science, Colorado State University,
Fort Collins, CO, USA
{Indrakshi.Ray,bru.bezawada}@colostate.edu

Abstract. Distributed Denial-of-Service (DDoS) attack has been identified as one of the most serious threats to Internet services. The attack
denies service to legitimate users by flooding and consuming network
resources of the target server. We propose a distributed defense mechanism that filters out malicious traffic and allows significant legitimate
traffic during an actual attack. We investigate the features of network
traffic that can be used to do such filtration and describe a history-
based profiling algorithm to identify legitimate traffic. We use Bloom
filters to efficiently implement the history-based profile model, which
serves to reduce the communication and computation costs. To further
improve communication and computation costs, we describe two optimizations: (a) using only three octets of the IP address to generate the
history profile, and (b) a data structure called Compacted Bloom Filter, which is a modified version of a regular Bloom filter. We use these
notions as building blocks to describe a distributed framework called
Collaborative Filtering for filtering attack traffic as far away as possible
from the target server. The proposed techniques identify a set of nodes
that are best suited for filtering attack traffic, and places the Bloom filters in these locations. The approach is evaluated on different real-world
data sets from Auckland University, CAIDA, and Colorado State University. Under different experimental settings, we demonstrate that 70–95%
attack traffic can be filtered by our approach while allowing the flow of
a similar percentage of legitimate traffic.

Keywords: Distributed Denial-of-Service attack · Flooding attack
Network security · Bloom filter

An earlier version of this work appeared in [1]. This work was partially supported
by NSF I/UCRC Award Number 1650573 and funding from CableLabs. The views
and conclusions contained in this document are those of the authors and should not
be automatically interpreted as representing the official policies, either expressed or
implied of NSF, CableLabs, Furuno Electric Company, SecureNok, and AFRL.

M. S. Obaidat and E. Cabello (Eds.): ICETE 2017, CCIS 990, pp. 199–223, 2019.
https://doi.org/10.1007/978-3-030-11039-0_10

1   Introduction

Internet servers constitute critical infrastructure and they must be protected from Denial-of-Service (DoS) attacks. In recent years, large scale Distributed DoS (DDoS) attacks have been responsible for massive network and service outages [2,3]. The following attacks show that the attacks have increased in volume as well as severity. On February 9, 2000, Yahoo, eBay, Amazon.com, E*trade, ZDnet, buy.com, the FBI and several other websites fell victim to DDoS attacks resulting in millions of dollars in damages [4,5]. In 2014, a record 400 Gbps DDoS attack against CloudFlare was recorded, which was about a 100 Gbps increment compared to the last previously seen DDoS attack [6] up till that time. And, in 2016, the attack against KrebsOnSecurity was estimated to be 620 Gbps [7]. The most intense attack known to date is that on GitHub in 2018, with an incredible 1.35 Tbps at peak [8]. The flooding traffic is large enough to crash the victim by communication buffer overflow, disk exhaustion, or connection link saturation [9]. Despite significant research focusing on countermeasures, DDoS attacks continue to be a major threat [10].

DDoS attacks generated by compromised Internet-of-Things (IoT) devices is an emerging threat. An attack in January 2018 utilized over 13,000 hijacked IoT devices to generate attack an traffic rate of 30 Gbps [11].

In this work, our focus on large scale flooding that is aimed at asphyxiating the links to the target server and denying service to legitimate users. Specifically, we focus on distinguishing normal traffic from attack traffic and throttling the rate of attack traffic in the event of an attack, and to do this closer to the attack sources rather than to the target destinations.

A plethora of DDoS defense and response mechanisms have been suggested in the past, including preventive techniques [12,13], packet filtering [14], flood pushback [15], DDoS detection mechanisms [4,16] and distributed defense mechanisms [17–22]. Preventive techniques aim to solve the problem of IP spoofing but this is a hard problem because attackers can compromise a large number of computers or IoT devices to create zombies. Furthermore, these techniques often penalize legitimate traffic because they are unable to distinguish between attack and legitimate traffic.

In order to continue to provide services under DDoS attacks, it is essential to distinguish attack traffic from legitimate traffic. The challenge is how to detect attack traffic without misclassifying legitimate traffic. An unusually high traffic volume may, in itself, not a good indicator of a DDoS attack, as it can also occur due to flash crowds. Thus, other features that help distinguish attacks from normal traffic have to be considered. We look into multiple features of DDoS attacks and normal traffic to extract characteristics that give information about the occurrence of the DDoS attacks. These features are used to establish a high confidence IP address history that represents the normal traffic profile. Anything outside the normal traffic profile is treated as attack traffic. The IP address history that forms the normal traffic profile must be propagated to the upstream routers so that the attack traffic can be blocked early on close to the source of the attack. However, propagating this IP address history for normal traffic during an attack introduces communication overhead on already congested routes.

To address these problems, we demonstrate how a Bloom filter can be used to store the normal IP address history profile, which is propagated to the routers close to the attack sources. The use of Bloom filter reduces the communication cost and also, minimizes the storage cost at the routers. The effectiveness of our approach is validated using a real dataset collected from Colorado State University (CSU) in 2015 as well as Auckland University Data set coupled with Center for Applied Internet Data Analysis (CAIDA) 2007 attack dataset. To minimize the size of the Bloom filter, we describe two optimizations: (a) first, storing only three octets of an IP address and, (b) using a novel data structure called the *Compacted Bloom Filter*, which is a modified version of an ordinary Bloom filter but of a much smaller size. We demonstrate through experiments the tradeoffs of this approach in allowing legitimate traffic and throttling attack traffic. With either one or a combination of these optimizations, the resulting Bloom filters can be efficiently shared among multiple strategically selected nodes without incurring high communication overhead.

Finally, using these building blocks, we describe a collaborative filtering mechanism where the Bloom filters are maintained by different nodes further away from the target server. We describe algorithms to characterize traffic at various nodes and identify the best possible placement of such filters. We show that even with 25% of possible nodes chosen for filtering we can achieve a high attack detection rate of 90% while allowing a high percentage legitimate traffic.

The rest of this paper is structured as follows. Section 2 describes some related work in this area. Section 3 describes how we distinguish attack traffic from normal traffic. Section 4 describes the compacted Bloom filter data structure. Section 5 describes our collaborative filtering mechanism for filtering attack traffic at multiple collaborating nodes. Section 6 validates our model using Auckland University, CAIDA 2007 and CSU 2015 datasets. Section 7 concludes the paper with pointers to future research.

2   Related Work

Pushback [17] is an earlier technique used to mitigate DDoS attacks using a cooperative mechanism. When a link is heavily utilized, information is sent to the upstream routers to curtail some of the downstream traffic. This approach requires deployment of the mechanism in all the routers. However, this may be unacceptable to some routers because of the high computational and memory overheads. Furthermore, this approach penalizes legitimate traffic as well.

Attack source identification and responsive techniques actively try to mitigate DDoS attacks by filtering or limiting the rate of suspicious flows [4,10,16]. Such schemes have two components: attack detection and packet filtering. The characteristics of attack packets, such as source of IP address or marked IP header values [12,23,24], are often used to detect and filter attack traffic. Note that, packet filtering can be applied either close to the attack source [4,16] or close to the victim server [12,16,23,24]. However, an attacker with the knowledge of the utilized features can develop strategies to bypass it.

Some researchers [9,25–28] use change-point detection theory to detect abnormal Internet traffic caused by DDoS attacks where the schemes are based on abrupt changes in traffic flows. In these approaches, the attacker can bypass the detection mechanism by sending out attack flow to change the statistics of the traffic. Moreover, one often does not have accurate statistics to describe the pre-change and post-change traffic distributions.

Another type of approach is based on flow dis-symmetry [4,29,30] where the attacker may use random spoofed source IP addresses and send out the same amount of SYN packets, and FIN/RST packets that can go unnoticed when compared with legitimate traffic flows. Moreover, discriminating flash crowd traffic from DDoS attack traffic is a major drawback of the proposed approaches.

History-based IP Filtering (HIF) [31] is an efficient approach that was proposed to discriminate legitimate traffic from malicious traffic. This approach is based on monitoring the number of the new source IP addresses instead of the volume of the traffic. HIF keeps a history of the legitimate IP addresses that have appeared before and applies filters in the edge router based on this history. However, an adversary can bypass this mechanism by starting to send packets with its IP address prior to conducting the attack. Thus, a more robust and efficient identification mechanism is needed for discriminating attack traffic while allowing legitimate traffic to pass through during the attack period.

3   Attack Identification Mechanism

We scope our work to flooding attacks [32,33] based on UDP, ICMP, TCP SYN, DNS, VoIP, *etc.*, flooding, which focus on exhausting bandwidth of the victim's network. Attackers use spoofed IP addresses to avoid IP trace-back, thereby, thwarting the discovery of the real sources of the attack.

We begin by describing features for characterizing and classifying normal and attack traffic. We make the observation that, during the DDoS attacks, most of the observed source IP addresses are new to the target server, while a majority of IP addresses in a flash crowd would have been seen previously by the target server. Jung *et al.* [34] state that around 82.9% of all IP addresses involved in flash crowd events have sent prior requests to the server. Peng *et al.* [31] advocate the use of network connection history to distinguish legitimate packets from malicious ones. Many organizations, such as universities and banks, have a large group of users that access their services on a regular basis and they have persistent characteristics. Although the user base fluctuates with additions, deletions, *etc.*, in general such a base changes at a much slower time scale compared to attacks and disruptions. However, if only the presence of the IP address in the past is used as the distinguishing feature, the adversary can bypass this mechanism by communicating with a victim server prior to launching the attack. Therefore, we address this problem by using multiple features to distinguish normal from attack traffic to generate accurate normal traffic signatures. Using this high confidence IP address history, we can defend against DDoS attacks that maximally preserve the service availability and minimize the impact of the attack.

3.1   Identification Features

We enumerate the features for distinguishing attack and normal traffic. We use the parameters mentioned by Lee *et al.* [35] for detecting DDoS attacks. These include source/destination IP address, port number and packet size. The number of features is denoted by K where $K = 3$ in our approach. Based on the observation from [34] that most source IP addresses are new to the victim during DDoS attacks whereas a flash crowd traffic contains previously viewed source IP addresses, we use the frequency of an IP address as a distinguishing feature between attack and normal traffic. Since we create a history based on legitimate and valid IP addresses, we consider only those IP addresses with a successful TCP handshake. Note that, a spoofed IP address will not have a complete three-way handshake [31]. Thus, if the packet type is TCP, we require a three-way handshake to demonstrate legitimacy of traffic.

For each parameter P_i, where $1 \leq i \leq K$, we maintain its frequency of occurrence in a given time window and its cumulative distribution function (CDF). Let the parameter P_i take on M different values. The frequency and CDF within a given time window are defined as follows.

Frequency. Let f_{ij} be the number of packets for which the parameter P_i takes on the value of j in a given time window. Let N be the total number of packets. Thus, from [1]:

$$N = \sum_j f_{ij} \tag{3.1}$$

Consider the case of the source IP address which corresponds to parameter $i = 1$, there are 1000 different IP addresses within the time window making $N = 1000$. If there are a total of 5000 packets and a particular IP address j occurs 30 times, then $f_{1j} = 30$ and $N = 5000$. As a packet contains each parameter value, the summation in Eq. 3.1 is independent of i.

Cumulative Distribution Function (CDF). The CDF $C_X(x)$ measures the probability that the variable X takes on a value less than or equal to x. Now consider the parameter i. Let F_i be defined as the random variable representing f_{ij} for some j then, as shown in [1], CDF of F_i is:

$$C_{F_i}(x) = Prob(F_i \leq x) \tag{3.2}$$

For example, $C_{F_1}(10)$ demonstrates the probability that source IP address frequency is less than or equal to 10.

3.2   History-Based Profile Creation

We use the term *signature* of a feature to denote the statistical presence of a feature in the traffic history of the target server. Using the features in Sect. 3.1, our goal is to estimate a good signature that will make the IP address database accurate, robust and hard to be bypassed by an attacker. A key observation is that the DDoS attacks tend to use randomly spoofed IP addresses [32] and other packet features, such as, port number and size of packet, are also selected randomly. Furthermore, the interactions of these features also exhibit some anomalies when compared to that of the normal traffic. Therefore, we make use of the individual features, and also the interactions and correlations, in defining the signature. The signature is based on the CDF of each parameter's frequency during the training period. This signature assists us in selecting reliable IP addresses during the training period and later filters traffic based on those IP addresses.

The next step is assigning scores to IP addresses in the training period and generating the source IP address history. The score value for each IP address depends on the frequencies and the signatures of the selected features. Frequency threshold α_l, which is a measure of reliability in our model, and the corresponding scores are presented in Table 1. We define four confidence scores, b_1, b_2, b_3, and b_4, that can be assigned to a feature. Depending on the feature frequency with respect to α_l in the related signature, a corresponding b_t score is assigned to the feature. In our model, α_l is chosen from one of 70%, 50%, and 30% to indicate how the selected feature follows the signature of normal traffic conditions. This method allocates highest weight to the top 30% of the IP addresses ($i = 1$), port numbers ($i = 2$) and packet sizes ($i = 3$) that occur most frequently. The value of frequency threshold α_l can be adjusted dynamically for each target victim server depending on other conditions as well. Our selection of particular values for α_l is based on experience with different datasets.

Now, if the selected feature occurs more frequently in normal traffic, as indicated by the signature of normal traffic, we give it a higher weight by assigning score b_4. In contrast, if α_l has value less than 30%, we assign the lowest confidence level factor b_1 to it. Low confidence measure indicates that such a feature value is not a common occurrence in normal traffic and thus dropping such packets will have less impact on the normal traffic. Frequent occurrence of such a value during an attack, therefore, is also considered as a potential threat.

Table 1. The score manager (Ref. [1]).

Case	Frequency	Conclusion	Score
1	$\geq \alpha_1 (=70\%)$	High confidence	$b_4 = 4$
2	$\geq \alpha_2 (=50\%)$	Medium	$b_3 = 3$
3	$\geq \alpha_3 (=30\%)$	Low	$b_2 = 2$
4	$< \alpha_4 (=30\%)$	Potential threat	$b_1 = 1$

For example, consider source IP address 129.1.1.1 with frequency 10000. When $C_{F_1}(10000) \geq 70\%$, it means according to IP address signature in training window, 70% of IP addresses occur with a frequency less than 10000. Thus, this is among the top 30% of occurrence rates of IP addresses and we give a high score for this feature. To summarize, the above procedure allocates weight from the set $\{b_1, \ldots, b_4\}$ to each IP address, each packet size, and each port number. Let the weight b_x, b_y, b_z be allocated for IP address β, port number j, packet size k respectively. We assign a net score S_β for IP address β, which is defined as the score value for each IP address β and is determined according to the frequency f_{ij} and confidence degree b_j in the following equation from [1]:

$$S_\beta = (f_{1\beta} * b_x + Max_{j,k}(f_{2j} * b_y + f_{3k} * b_z))/N \qquad (3.3)$$

Thus, S_β depends on three components. For the above example, the first component of $S_{129.1.1.1}$ is computed for IP address 129.1.1.1, based on $f_{1129.1.1.1}$ we get a score of $b_4 = 4$. The second and third components are selected by taking the maximum value of the sum of corresponding values for port number and size of packet over different packets with this IP address. The IP addresses that have an overall score S_β higher than a threshold ν are selected as legitimate IP addresses based on the given history. For TCP connections, source IP addresses that have established a three-way handshake and have a score higher than ν are selected. This helps us create a signature-based IP address history and this history can be used at routers to perform filtering towards the targeted server. We use Bloom filters [26,36], as described next, to store all such valid IP addresses.

3.3 Bloom Filter Mechanism

Bloom filter [26,36] is a space efficient probabilistic data structure for checking whether an element is a member of a set. A Bloom filter maps a set $S = \{s_1, s_2, \ldots, s_n\}$ of n elements into an array of m bits, which are initialized to 0. The Bloom filter uses k independent hash functions, $h_1, \ldots, h_k$, which when applied to each member of the set S returns a value in the range $\{1, \ldots, m\}$. For each element $s \in S$, the bits $h_i(s)$ in the array are set to 1 for $1 \leq i \leq k$. Note that, a position in the array can be set to 1 multiple times by the various hash functions, but only the first change has an effect. To check if $x \in S$, we check whether all $h_i(x)$ are set to 1. If at least one bit is not 1, then $x \notin S$. If all $h_i(x)$ are set to 1, we consider it to mean that $x \in S$, although there is a probability of a false positive, where it suggests that an element x is in S even though it is not. This is acceptable for many applications if the probability of a false positive is sufficiently small. After all the elements of S are hashed into the Bloom filter, the probability p that a specific bit is still 0 is known to be:

$$p = (1 - \frac{1}{m})^{kn} \approx e^{-k\frac{n}{m}} \qquad (3.4)$$

We let $p = e^{-k\frac{n}{m}}$. The probability of a false positive f is then:

$$f = (1 - (1 - \frac{1}{m})^{kn})^k \approx (1 - e^{-k\frac{n}{m}})^k = (1 - p)^k \qquad (3.5)$$

There are three fundamental performance metrics for Bloom filters: the false positive rate f, size of the Bloom filter array m and the number of hash functions k.

Bloom filters are highly efficient even if $m = c*n$ for a small constant c. Although Bloom filters introduce false positives, their use is justified because of the reduction in the network traffic and overhead. In our analysis, we limit the false positive rate to 10%. In order to achieve this false positive rate, we should set c to 5 in our mechanism, *i.e.*, the Bloom filter array is 5 times the number of IP addresses kept in the history. Furthermore, according to Eq. 3.5, we need 4 hash functions for the Bloom filter that is used to store the IP address history.

One problem with the Bloom filter is that its false positive rate strongly depends on the fill ratio, which is the number of bits that are set to 1 and on average is given by $m * p$. Fill ratio, thus, is a function of n, m, and k. In order to have the optimum number of k and f_p, we must have a lower bound on the size of the memory. Thus, it is not suitable for applications running on systems with limited memory. Towards this end, we propose a Compacted Bloom Filter (CmBF), which requires less memory than a Bloom filter to achieve the same false positive rate f_p. When used in a network application, it helps reduce the transmission cost for distribution and the storage cost at the endpoints.

4   Compacted Bloom Filter

CmBF is a probabilistic data structure that is used to represent a set $S = \{s_1, s_2, \ldots, s_n\}$ of n elements and is derived from a standard Bloom filter with parameters n, m, and k, as defined in Sect. 3.3. We now describe how to construct the corresponding CmBF from the standard Bloom filter representation. The standard Bloom filter is first divided into k_0 blocks, denoted by $block_1, block_2, \ldots, block_{k_0}$. Each block has n bits, the positions of which are denoted by $1, 2, \ldots, n$ as shown in Fig. 1.

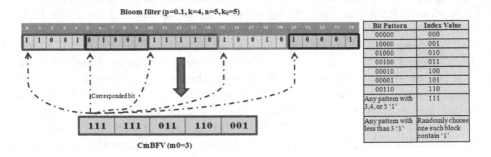

Fig. 1. Compacted Bloom Filter.

A CmBF vector, denoted by CmBFV, is an array of n index values and each index contains m_0 bits, where $\log_2 k_0 = m_0 < k_0$. Note that, for m_0 bits, 2^{m_0} patterns exist in the CmBF vector and the lower bound for m_0 is $\log_2 k_0$ as it is the minimum number of bits required to cover k_0 patterns. Index i in CmBF vector, denoted by CmBFV[i], corresponds to the value of the ith bit positions in $block_1, block_2, \ldots, block_n$ in the standard Bloom filter. For example, the first index in CmBF vector, CmBFV[1], has information pertaining to the first bit of each block in the Bloom filter. We define some rules about how to populate each index based on the bit pattern in the standard Bloom filter.

Consider the set of ith bits in all blocks in the Bloom filter, which we denote as S_i. If there is no '1' in S_i, the ith bit of any block, we set the corresponding bit in CmBF to 0, $i.e.$, CmBFV[i] = 0. If there is exactly one '1' in S_i, which appears in $block_r$, we set CmBFV[i] = r. If all the bits in S_i are '1', we set CmBFV[i] = $2^{m_0} - 1$. If not all bits in S_i are '1', but half or more than half of them are '1's, we set CmBFV[i] = $2^{m_0} - 1$ as well. In this case, some of the ith bits having '0' may be interpreted as '1', thereby introducing more false positives than the standard Bloom filter. If less than half of the bits in S_i are '1', we randomly choose one such block containing '1' in the ith bit position, say $block_s$, and we set CmBFV[i] = s. Thus, all the other blocks that contain a '1' are interpreted as having a '0', thereby increasing the false negative rate compared to the standard Bloom filter. To deal with this issue, as $2^{m_0} - 1$ different index values are available to assign bit patterns in CmBFV, it is more efficient to use all available index values to cover more bit patterns. It reduces the number of bits interpreted as '1' or '0', which in turn decreases the false positive and negative rates. For this reason, one more rule is defined in this structure to cover unused index values. If bit pattern value is less than $2^{m_0} - 1$ and has more than one '1', it means that the bit pattern value is in the range of unused index values. In this case, the index is assigned the bit pattern value. This case occurs in the fourth index value in Fig. 1. Algorithm 1 describes how to assign values to the CmBFV.

Algorithm 1. Generate CmBFV.

Input: Bloom Filter BF: (n, m, k_0, m_0)
Output: $CmBFV$

$COUNT(i)$ counts total number of 1s in location $block[i]$ for all blocks in BF
$BinaryValue(a, b)$ generates the b-bit binary representation of a
$BitPattern(i)$ generates the bit-pattern by concatenating i^{th} bit of each of the n blocks of BF
Let n-bit array $CmBFV$ be initialized to all 0s

for $i=0$ to n do
  if $COUNT(i) == 0$ then
    $CmBFV[i] = BinaryValue(0, m_0)$
  else if $COUNT(i) == 1$ then
    $CmBFV[i] = BinaryValue(i, m_0)$
  else if $BitPattern(i) < BinaryValue(2^{m_0} - 1, m_0)$ then
    $CmBFV[i] = BinaryValue(BitPattern(i), m_0)$
  else if $COUNT(i) < \frac{k_0}{2}$ then
    $CmBFV[i] = s$ where s is a random block such that $block_s[i] = 1$
  else
    $CmBFV[i] = BinaryValue(2^{m_0} - 1, m_0)$
  end if
end for

Querying a given element for the set membership is based on the bit patterns that we defined in constructing the CmBF. The advantage of CmBF is that it reduces the number of bits required and lower false positives are achieved. However, this structure provides some false negatives as well.

5   Collaborative Filtering

In this section, we describe a collaborative filtering mechanism that is able to filter out attack traffic and allow legitimate traffic in the event of a DDoS attack. Our goal is to place such filters as close to the source attack node as possible so that network resources are not wasted in propagating the attack. An algorithm is presented to identify the most effective points where the filter can be placed so as to minimize the attack traffic in the network and maximize legitimate traffic for the target server during the DDoS attack period. The experimental results, presented in Sect. 6, demonstrate that our algorithm accurately selects desirable filtering points where all the filtering routers are selected near the first three routers from attack sources and stop 95% of attack traffic while allowing 77% of legitimate traffic to reach the victim server.

The proposed solution relies on a recently developed technology, typically implemented as Small Form factor Probes (SFP) using FPGAs (Field Programmable Gate Arrays). An SFProbe can plug into any SFP compatible elements such as switches and routers in such a way that it taps into the normal fiber without interfering with the traffic flow. The SFProbe can be programmed, over the network using the same fiber, to do tasks such as counting the number of packets with certain values in header fields and forward information about link traffic to a remote base station. An example of such hardware is JDSU SFProbe [37] and Packet Portal [37]. Packet Portal [37] is a new approach for gathering, distributing and analyzing information from distributed Ethernet ports. The probes connected to the router/switch ports, *e.g.*, JDSU Packet Portals, communicate with a remote base station. It is this feature that we use, as described below, to send the history-based profiles to identify the paths with high intensity of attack traffic. Moreover, the portal base station (PBS) has knowledge about SFProbes attached to the routers throughout the network and can collect data from SFProbes and perform the computations needed for the scheme, obviating the need for routers performing such computations. The portals can be globally time synchronized within a span of one millisecond, thus enabling synchronized measurements that were not previously possible [38]. The proposed approach monitors traffic by SFProbes to efficiently identify routers/switches that are carrying significant volumes of the attack traffic and then applies our packet filtering approach at these selected routers.

First, the target server or network sends the Bloom filter described in Sect. 3.3 to PBS. The PBS sends the Bloom filter to those SFProbes that are plugged into the routers. Each SFProbe starts monitoring the intensity of traffic directed toward the target server in defining time slots. Let, $t_1, t_2, \ldots, t_m$, be discrete time slots and $X(t_m, i)$ be the number of packets received by a router during time slot m at SFProbe i toward the target server. The following equation defines the historical estimate of the average number of packets received by a router where α is a weighted value between 0 and 1.

$$\overline{X}(t_m, i) = (1 - \alpha)\overline{X}(t_{m-1}, i) + \alpha X(t_m, i) \tag{5.1}$$

Let $A_j(t_m, j)$ represent a Boolean variable which equals 1 if the packet P_j is received at router i at time slot t_m and belongs to the corresponding Bloom filter B_v for victim point v and is 0 otherwise.

Let $\overline{W}(t_m, i)$ define the historical estimate of the average number of packets received by the router at SFProbes i during time slot m that match with the Bloom filter. In other words, $\overline{W}(t_m, i)$ shows the average of the number of packets that is considered as the legitimate traffic by the Bloom filter directed towards the targeted server and is given by the following equation where n is the total number of packets flowing towards the targeted server in time slot t_m:

$$\overline{W}(t_m, i) = (1 - \alpha)\overline{W}(t_{m-1}, i) + \alpha \sum_{j=1}^{n} \frac{A_j(t_m, i)}{n} \tag{5.2}$$

During an attack, if there are high number of IP addresses destined to the target that do not match the Bloom filter, then this router is likely to be carrying significant volume of attack traffic. This makes it possible to inform the router to drop packets directed towards the victimized server. We use $R(t_m, i)$, called the Attack Estimation Rate (AER), to determine the average number of packets that do not match the Bloom filter as shown in the following equation:

$$R(t_m, i) = \frac{\overline{X}(t_m, i) - \overline{W}(t_m, i)}{\overline{X}(t_m, i)} \tag{5.3}$$

When the attack starts, SFProbes start monitoring traffic going towards the victim node and sends $R(t_m, i)$ to the PBS. Now, based on the received $R(t_m, i)$ values, the PBS decides the points at which the filters are to be placed. In order to save network resources, the best routers to apply the filtering mechanism must be as far away as possible from the victim node. For instance, if routers with 2 and 3 hop distances have the same attack detection rate, it is more efficient to place the filter on the router which is at hop distance 3 from the victim node instead of the one which is at hop distance 2. We also take into account the volume of potential attack traffic passing through a router when considering the placement of routers. Thus, we use two factors to determine the best routers to place the SFProbes –one is the Attack Estimation Rate $R(t_m, i)$ and the other is the hop distance $H_i(v)$ –that shows how far the ith SFProbe is from the victim node v. For each SFProbe i, the weighted attack estimation rate $S(t_m, i)$ is given by the following equation:

$$S(t_m, i) = \frac{\overline{X}(t_m, i) - \overline{W}(t_m, i)}{\overline{X}(t_m, i)} . H_i(v) \tag{5.4}$$

The routers with higher values of $S(t_m, i)$ will be selected as the more effective routers where the filtering mechanism is to be applied. We evaluated the above approach, which we refer as the Responsive Point's Identification algorithm by considering Hop distance and Attack estimation rate (RPI-HA).

In addition to the hop distance and the volume of attack traffic, other issues must also be considered while placing the filters. One such factor is the number of routers on which filters are placed based on the distribution of the attack traffic. We present a formula that adjusts the number of routers according to the attack traffic distribution that we refer to as the Responsive Point's Identification algorithm by considering Hop distance, Transmission rate, and Attack estimation rate (RPI-HTA). In this scheme, the transmission rate of traffic directed towards the victim node as well as hop distance is considered to determine the best filtering points. SFProbes collect the information of attack estimation rate $R(t_m, i)$ and traffic transmission rate $T(t_m, i)$ during m time slots and send this information to the PBS. To select the filtering points the attack estimation rate $D(t_m, i)$ is computed as follows:

$$D(t_m, i) = \frac{\overline{X}(t_m, i) - \overline{W}(t_m, i)}{\overline{X}(t_m, i)} \cdot \frac{\overline{T}(t_m, i)}{C(v)} \cdot H(v) \tag{5.5}$$

$$\overline{D}(t_m) = (1 - \alpha)\overline{D}(t_m) + \sum_{i=1}^{n} \frac{D(t_m, i)}{n} \tag{5.6}$$

In Eq. 5.5 we consider the distribution of traffic towards the victim node as an important factor that helps determine how the attack is determined by the traffic transmission rate $T(t_m, i)$ and capacity of the victim node $C(v)$. $D(t_m, i)$ determines if the attack is distributed or centralized. Note that, high value of $D(t_m, i)$ indicates that the attack is centralized to a large degree, whereas a low value of $D(t_m, i)$ denotes a distributed attack. If the attack is highly distributed we need to consider more filtering points to stop the attack whereas if the attack is more centralized we apply filters at only a few routers. The average attack estimation rate is given by in Eq. 5.6. We select only those routers whose attack estimation rate $D(t_m, i)$ is higher than average attack estimation rate as filtering points. Thus, in the RPI-HTA algorithm the number of filters to apply depends on traffic transmission rate as well as hop distance.

6   Model Validation

In this section, we used three different sets of data to evaluate the proposed method. For the first data set, we use traces collected at the Colorado State University (CSU). The CSU packet trace contains 4 weeks daily Argus files with flows on a 1 Gbps link from Feb 1st to Feb 28th 2015 where the total compressed data is about 20 GB for each day [39]. The second data set is the packet trace captured at the University of Auckland in New Zealand. The packet trace contains 6.5 weeks IP header traces taken over 155 Mbps Internet links [5]. The total uncompressed data volume is 180 GB and all IP addresses have been mapped into 10.*.*.* using one to one hash mapping for privacy. The Auckland traces record three types of IP traffic (TCP, UDP, ICMP). The third data set is the CAIDA 2007 dataset that contains approximately one hour of anonymized traffic traces from a DDoS attack on August 4, 2007 that contains 359,656,205 attack packets from 9,066 unique IP addresses [40]. We used the CAIDA attack dataset 2007 to create an attack scenario in this experiment as the Auckland trace did not contain any attack data. Finally, we present the results for the two datasets: CSU and Auckland + CAIDA datasets.

Our approach consists of the following three steps:

[**Step 1:**] Create IP address history from the training dataset using the generated signatures and the overall scores.

[**Step 2:**] Construct the Bloom filter using the IP address history created in Step 1.

[**Step 3:**] Identify the collaborative filtering nodes.

Accordingly, for different datasets, we evaluate our the following metrics: (i) History accuracy, (ii) Attack traffic detection rate, and (iii) Normal traffic detection rate. We also present the results of applying our compaction technique for Bloom filter, *i.e.*, CmBF approach. We present the results individually for each dataset as there are several variations across the datasets and the way they are used for the experiments. Finally, we show the results of collaborative filtering for the Auckland + CAIDA dataset only, due to constraints of space.

6.1   Results for CSU Dataset

Approaches for Maintaining IP Address History. There are two different mechanisms to maintain the IP address history: sliding window and history without updating. In the first approach, the IP addresses kept in the history depend only on the specific window length. If the window length is a day, then every day the expired IP addresses are removed from the history and new IP addresses are added to it. In this part of experiment, we set the length of window to be one week. For each day we create a signature-based IP address history based on all IP addresses during this one week period. We build the IP address history using data trace from Feb 1st to Feb 21st and compare it to the trace taken from Feb 8th to Feb 28th. In the second approach, the history is created with a specific length and is not updated during the next two weeks. Due to space constraints, we only show the sliding window results in this work.

Our analysis shows that IP addresses with an occurrence rate above 500 can achieve the highest score as $C_{F_1(500)} \geq 70\%$ and IP addresses with an occurrence rate below 20 get the lowest score. Also, we found that around 10% of IP addresses have a frequency above 2000 and the maximum frequency was around 12000 for a few IP addresses. We report similar analysis for port number and packet size signatures. The IP address history is created based on the overall score and value of threshold ν. In our experiment, ν is determined to be 0.36. In other words, the signature of at least two selected features should have α_l more than 50% and one should have it more than 30% in training time as per Table 1 and Eq. 3.3. However, this value can be fine-tuned as necessary. Determining the value of ν is a tradeoff between history size, history accuracy, and how much protection we have against attack traffic. If we increase the threshold of ν then we are better able to filter attack traffic and, the size of history decreases as well. However, increasing ν also blocks legitimate traffic and so the accuracy of the history for allowing legitimate traffic decreases.

Storage Cost Tradeoffs. We performed the experiment in two variations: the first where we used the entire 4-octets of an IP address, and the second where we used only 3-octets of the IP address. As shown in Table 2, the number of unique IP addresses that were retained in the history is around 3,000,000 for each day. By accepting 10% false positive rate, the size of Bloom filter would be between 1.4 MB to 2.2 MB for each day as shown in Table 2 [1] and Fig. 2. Note that, it is possible to set lower false positive rates but at the cost of increasing the size of the Bloom filter. We accept the false positive rate as 10% and $5n$ for the length of Bloom filter as reasonable values for error rate where n is the number of IP addresses inserted in the Bloom filter.

Furthermore, we can tradeoff between false positive rate, false negative rate and memory reduction by using the CmBF data structure. The size of Bloom filter can be reduced between 20% to 60% with almost similar false positive values compared with those for standard Bloom filter, but accepting 2% to 20% false negative. As shown in Fig. 2, the size of CmBF when entire 4-octet IP address can be in the range of 0.8 MB to 1.8 MB. For the IP address history based on the first three octets of IP address the size of CmBF is between 0.4 MB to 0.8 MB. As the result shows, the size of Bloom filter for each day can vary based on the scheme selected. For instance the maximum size of Bloom filter for Feb 8th is 1800 KB by using the standard Bloom filter and the 4-octet IP address whereas the minimum size is 400 KB by using the CmBF and first three octets of IP address.

History Accuracy. The next step is to evaluate the accuracy of the history, *i.e.*, the percentage of traffic for each day that has already appeared in the history. As shown in Fig. 3, the history accuracy is about 60% to 80% for each day and this confirms that most of the IP addresses that appear in the CSU network under normal conditions have been seen previously and follow the signature of each day's network traffic. The highest history accuracy is 80% for Feb 21st and the lowest one is 60% for Feb 12th. For instance, on Feb 8th the total number of unique IP addresses on packets coming to CSU was 2,709,558 and 1,790,443 of those IP addresses match with the history. We also show the effectiveness of using the first three octets of IP address in Fig. 3. In this case, the accuracy of IP address history improves to around 75% for most of the days while the size of Bloom filter reduces to 50% as shown in Fig. 2.

Table 2. Number of IP addresses in history [1].

Date	Unique IP addresses	Bloom filter size (MB)	Unique first three-octets of IP addresses	Bloom filter size (MB)
8-Feb	3567433	2.22	1549329	0.96
9-Feb	2898726	1.81	1540879	0.96
10-Feb	2993910	1.87	1533835	0.95
11-Feb	3251485	2.03	1573583	0.98
12-Feb	3253085	2.03	1542783	0.96
13-Feb	3214944	2.00	1543112	0.96
14-Feb	3367433	2.10	1506123	0.94
15-Feb	3130830	1.95	1478050	0.92
16-Feb	2986955	1.86	1488892	0.93
17-Feb	3077742	1.92	1465505	0.91
18-Feb	3181456	1.98	1493287	0.93
19-Feb	3086945	1.92	1461922	0.91
20-Feb	3131923	1.95	1486039	0.92
21-Feb	3077169	1.92	1484376	0.92
22-Feb	2957518	1.84	1450000	0.90
23-Feb	3181719	1.98	1522926	0.95
24-Feb	3095821	1.93	1562730	0.97
25-Feb	3095821	1.93	1510018	0.94
26-Feb	2940737	1.83	1541806	0.96
27-Feb	2915739	1.82	1547367	0.96
28-Feb	2303440	1.43	1440457	0.90

The other important parameter to evaluate is how much of the traffic volumes can pass through the Bloom filter and reach the end nodes. As shown in Fig. 4(a), the normal traffic detection rate varies from 68% to 82% using the entire IP address. This demonstrates that the performance of signature-based IP address history is highly reliable for identifying normal traffic and withholding insignificant amount of legitimate traffic. Normal traffic detection rate increases from 80% to 90% if the first three octets of IP addresses are used to generate IP address history.

We investigate the effectiveness of history accuracy and measure how much packet traffic can pass through the Bloom filter. The results are shown in Fig. 5. The x-axis is the traffic volume based on number of packets. From this figure we observe the total traffic received is varying from 160 million to 220 million packets in each day. We note that the external traffic increased suddenly on Feb 10th and Feb 16th whereas the normal traffic, that can pass the history, did not

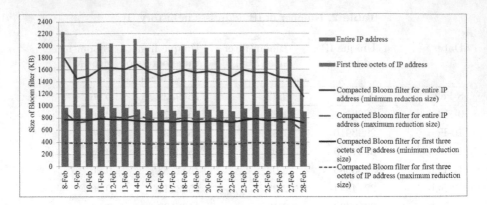

Fig. 2. Bloom filter storage overhead comparison

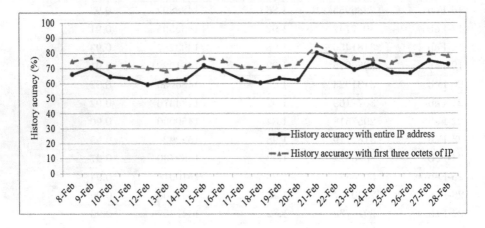

Fig. 3. History accuracy (Ref. [1]).

change by much. It means for those days, part of the incoming traffic to CSU was not seen previously and hence, not included in the history. For almost all the other days the normal traffic that can pass the history has similar behavior. Furthermore, the result shows that the signature-based IP address history with the first three octets can perform better than the history with entire IP address as expected.

We can therefore deduce that by using the first three octets of IP address history, the normal traffic detection rate increases. However, there is a tradeoff between the protection rate and the normal traffic detection rate. When we are using the first three octets of IP address there is some possibility that malicious traffic also share the first three octets of IP addresses that exist in the history and that the signature-based IP address history will not be able filter them. Therefore, the protection rate reduces by using three octets of IP address. On the other hand, by using first three octets of IP address the size of Bloom filter reduces

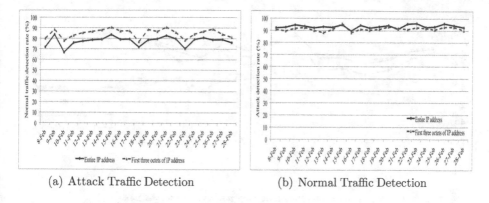

(a) Attack Traffic Detection   (b) Normal Traffic Detection

Fig. 4. Normal and attack traffic detection rates for CSU dataset (Ref. [1]).

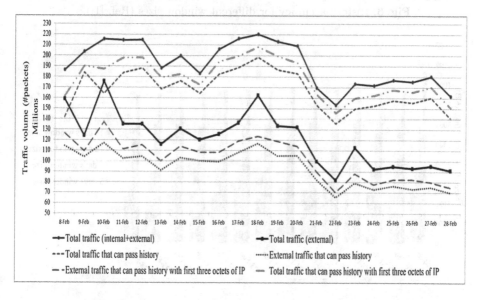

Fig. 5. Traffic volume and number of packets that can pass history (Ref. [1]).

and normal traffic detection rate increases. Therefore, selecting an appropriate approach is based on the size of Bloom filter, history accuracy and protection rate. In general, using the first three octets of IP address gives better history accuracy, normal traffic detection rate, and it reduces the size of Bloom filter, which results in decrease of protection rate. The other important result of this experiment is the attack traffic detection rate shown in Fig. 4(b). CAIDA attack 2007 dataset is used to evaluate this step. The result shows that the Bloom filter with first three octets can perform approximately as well as the Bloom filter with the entire IP addresses. According to Fig. 4(b), we observe almost 95% success with attack detection rate. In fact, our experiment shows that 70% of legitimate traffic can be preserved while filtering out 95% of attack traffic.

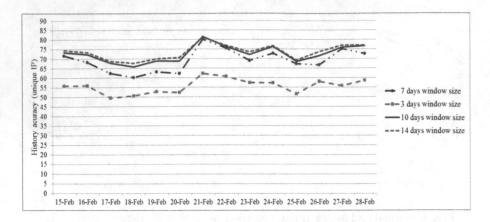

Fig. 6. History accuracy for different window sizes (Ref. [1]).

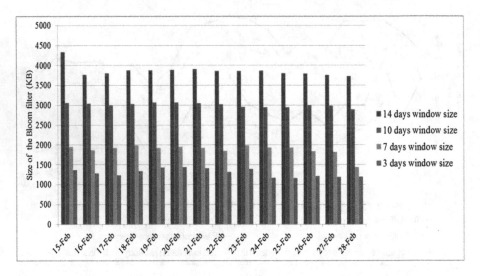

Fig. 7. Size of Bloom filter for different window sizes (Ref. [1]).

Impact of Window Size. We studied the impact of window size by creating history for four different window sizes and measuring the accuracy of the history. We set the window size to 14, 7, 10 and 3 days respectively to create the history and then calculated history accuracy during the period from Feb 15th to Feb 28th as shown in Fig. 6. The number of unique IP addresses that appeared in the history is shown in Table 3. Figure 6 shows that the history accuracy improves as long as we increase the length of window size from 3 to 14 days; however, the interesting observation is that history accuracy does not change significantly after 10 days. In other words, most of the legitimate IP addresses have appeared in the history in the past 10 days and very few other IP addresses have visited CSU only prior to 10 days. The other observation in Fig. 6 is that the largest gap is between window size 3 and 7 days. The history accuracy is around 50% for 3 days window size while this value improves to 65% for 7 days. In fact, this demonstrates that the 3 days window size is too short a period to create a history with high accuracy.

Table 3. Number of unique IP addresses in history with different window sizes (Ref. [1]).

Window size	14 days	10 days	7 days	3 days
15-Feb	6930826	4889103	3130830	2189643
16-Feb	6019868	4858096	2986955	2047126
17-Feb	6080193	4803532	3077742	1987207
18-Feb	6206424	4853005	3181456	2141480
19-Feb	6198630	4910655	3086945	2289896
20-Feb	6224286	4911569	3131923	2308403
21-Feb	6244686	4887286	3077169	2259784
22-Feb	6178677	4832357	2957518	2118029
23-Feb	6166982	4735330	3181719	2239626
24-Feb	6192012	4714798	3095821	1874455
25-Feb	6091122	4717731	3095821	1865488
26-Feb	6069075	4785940	2940737	1944892
27-Feb	6007085	4775288	2915739	1911688
28-Feb	5969252	4628090	2303440	1917622

The other important parameter that impacts history accuracy is size of the Bloom filter. As shown in Table 3 and Fig. 7, enlarging the window size increases the size of history and also improves the history accuracy. According to Fig. 7, size of history increases about 0.7 MB on an average when we change the window size from 10 to 14 days but as shown in Fig. 6 history accuracy is almost similar. Consequently, in choosing between 10 days and 14 days window size, 10 days window size would be a more appropriate selection. Furthermore, from Fig. 7 we also see that size of Bloom filter reduces by 1 MB on an average when the window size changes from 10 to 7 days but the history accuracy decreases by less than 5% because of this reduction. Thus, the 7 days window size is the best choice where we can get good history accuracy with a reasonable size Bloom filter.

6.2   Results for Auckland + CAIDA Dataset

History Accuracy. For this dataset, we use a sliding window of two weeks to keep the IP addresses in the history. We build the history using the data trace from March 12, 2001 to March 25, 2001 and compare the trace taken from March 26 to April 9, 2001 with the previous two weeks trace. As shown in Fig. 8, the history accuracy is about 82–92% for each day and this verifies that most IP addresses that appear in the network under normal conditions have previously appeared in the network. In Fig. 8, we show the effectiveness of using sliding window mechanism and updating history each day. It is interesting to see that the history accuracy drops when we consider the two week history without updating from 12 to 25 March 2001. For instance, the history accuracy drops from 92% to less than 78% in April 7th.

As we have verified, IP address history has good accuracy in terms of capturing legitimate and high confidence IP addresses. The next step is to evaluate efficiency of the Bloom filter that is created using the IP address history for each day. The size of history contained around 420,000 IP addresses for each day.

Attack and Normal Traffic Detection Rate. As shown in Fig. 8(a), normal traffic detection rate is more than 80% each day highlighting the Bloom filter performance. Further, by storing only the first three octets of an IP address, we achieve significant reduction in the number of unique IP addresses and hence, reduction in the size of Bloom filter. The number of unique IP addresses that is kept in the history decreased to less than 0.01 of the previous IP address history. Furthermore, the result shows that the accuracy of the IP address history is increased by this change. That means the most of the normal traffic, which came to the targeted server, shared the first three octets of IP address. As shown in Fig. 8(a), the accuracy of IP address history improved to 95% for most of the days during the two weeks traffic.

The other important result of this experiment is shown in terms of attack traffic detection rate in Fig. 8(b). The result shows that the Bloom filter with the first three octets can perform as well as the Bloom filter with complete IP addresses. In fact, on certain days it works better than the standard Bloom filter. We observe almost 98% of attack traffic detection rate. Our experiment on the Auckland trace traffic shows that we can protect 95% of legitimate traffic with around 0.44 KB of memory. Furthermore, by using only the first three octets, the size of the Bloom filter reduces significantly and filters out about 98% of the attack traffic. As shown in Fig. 8(b), the attack traffic detection rate is around 95% for the entire two week test. For instance, the size of Bloom filter for storing 443, 599 IP addresses is around 34 KB, which can efficiently packed for transferring to the routers.

Collaborative Filtering. Finally, we demonstrate the performance of our collaborative filtering approach using a real network topology from Oregon route-views between March 31 2001 and May 26 2001 and set it up on OPNET. We test the effectiveness of the proposed approach using the DARPA 1998 intrusion detection dataset [41] for this experiment. The dataset contains 7 weeks of training datasets that we use to establish an IP address history and 2 weeks of testing dataset to evaluate our techniques. The training part of the DARPA dataset contains normal traffic as well as labeled attacks, which helped validate our feature selection and imported to the OPNET for simulation. The first step is creating the IP address history from the DARPA training dataset and then create the corresponding Bloom filter. The next step evaluates the responsive defense approach based on the created IP address history in OPNET.

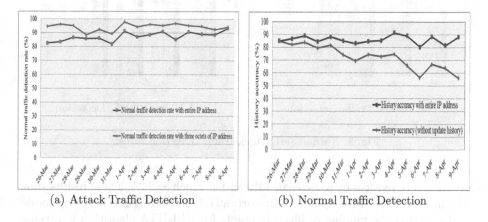

(a) Attack Traffic Detection   (b) Normal Traffic Detection

Fig. 8. Normal and attack traffic detection rates.

The effectiveness of the responsive defense mechanism relies on the collaboration of SFProbes through the network. Increasing the number of SFProbes attached to the routers enables more close monitoring of the network traffic and provides more effective filtering. We look at four different scenarios to validate this. We assume that a different percentage of routers (80% to 25%) have SFProbes attached to them to monitor network traffic. The number of filtering routers is either fixed according to the RPI-HA or variable based on RPI-HTA algorithm. In the RPI-HA algorithm, the number of filtering routers is, 8, 5 and 3, which constitutes, 20%, 12.5% and 7.5%, respectively, of the total routers in the network. We also looked at a fifth scenario where the filters are placed in random locations throughout the network without applying any algorithm to stop the attack traffic. Note that, we considered this scenario in order to explore how the SFProbe can effectively stop attack traffic and also, to evaluate the importance of placing the Bloom filter in the appropriate location.

Figure 9(a), shows the average attack traffic detection rate of 5 runs and the standard deviation. We use a time slot of 60 s. The results demonstrate the effectiveness of using the RPI-HTA algorithm, which considers all the three features: hop distance, transformation rate and attack estimation rate. The RPI-HTA algorithm produces an attack traffic detection rate of 91% when 80% of routers use SFProbes. Note that, even with 25% probes in the network, the RPI-HTA algorithm can stop up to 80% of the attack traffic. This value decreases due to a reduced number of participating SFProbes as expected. Moreover, by applying the random selection to determine placement of filters the attack traffic

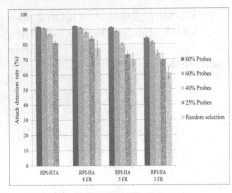

(a) Attack Traffic Detection

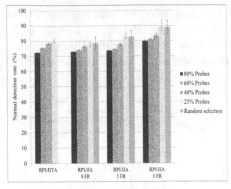

(b) Normal Traffic Detection

Fig. 9. Normal and attack traffic detection rates.

detection rate reduces by more than 14% and as much as 23%. These results show how the location of filters plays an important role in protecting the victim node.

Recall that the number of filtering points for RPI-HTA algorithm is variable and depends on attack distribution, transmission rate, and hop distance. We select 7 filters for networks having 80% and 60% probes and 6 filters for those having 40% and 25% probes according to the RPI-HTA algorithm. As shown in Fig. 9. The attack traffic detection rate for RPI-HTA algorithm for 80% and 60% probes is equal or higher than when RPI-HA algorithm is applied by 8 filtering routers through the network. This means that the RPI-HTA algorithm can provide comparable or better filtering mechanism by using lower number of filtering routers by placing the filters in the appropriate locations.

The other important parameter to evaluate is how many normal packets can reach the victim node. As shown in Fig. 9(b), normal detection rate is around 72% for RPI-HTA algorithm with 80% probes and it increases to around 80% if fewer filters are used to stop attack traffic. False negative rate was only about 3% in this part. Thus, there is a trade off between accuracy of the attack traffic detection rate and the normal traffic detection rate. For instance, by applying RPI-HTA algorithm with 80% probes, we have around 90% attack traffic detection rate and at the same time 72% of normal traffic can pass the Bloom filter and reach the victim node. In contrast, applying RPI-HA algorithm and 3 filtering routers with 25% probes can stop 69% of the attack and permit 90% of normal traffic.

7 Conclusion

We provide a solution for defending against DDoS attacks that looks at the history and uses a rich set of header fields for discriminating attack traffic from normal traffic. We demonstrated how such a differentiation can be done using a Bloom filter. The use of Bloom filter improves the efficiency and reduces the memory requirement at upstream routers participating in mitigation process during the attack time. The efficacy of the proposed approach was validated using multiple real-world datasets. Experiments indicate that for the cases evaluated the proposed filtering model, using a 2 MB Bloom filter, can protect the victim node from 95% of attack traffic while allowing 70% of normal legitimate traffic. In addition, the results show that the size of the Bloom filter can be reduced significantly by creating an IP address history based on the first three octets of IP address while preserving the accuracy of the history and attack detection rate.

The novel Compacted Bloom Filter, provides as good an accuracy as the standard Bloom filter while lowering the storage cost significantly. A collaborative filtering framework was presented to distribute the Bloom filters to routers that are closer to the attack sources. The comprehensive experimental results show very good results in successfully characterizing the network traffic and preserving good traffic with appropriate filtering costs. Our results verify that the proposed signature-based mechanism and the collaborative filtering can be deployed in real networks. Future extensions of this work may involve exploring involves exploring further traffic features and faster implementation of the compacted Bloom filters in hardware.

References

1. Mosharraf, N., Jayasumana, A.P., Ray, I.: Using a history-based profile to detect and respond to DDoS attacks. In: Proceedings of the 14th International Joint Conference on e-Business and Telecommunications (ICETE 2017) - Volume 4: SECRYPT, pp. 175–186 (2017)
2. Steinberger, J., Sperotto, A., Baier, H.: Collaborative attack mitigation and response: a survey. In: IFIP/IEEE International Symposium on IM, pp. 910–913 (2005)
3. Munivara Prasad, K., Rama Mohan Reddy, A., Venugopal Rao, K.: DoS and DDoS attacks: defense, detection and traceback mechanisms - a survey. J. JCST **14**, 15–32 (2014)
4. Gil, T.M., Poletto, T.: MULTOPS: a data-structure for bandwidth attack detection. In: Proceedings of USENIX Security Symposium (2001)
5. Waikato Applied Network Dynamics Research Group: Auckland University data traces (2016). http://wand.cs.waikato.ac.nz/wand/wits/. Accessed 12 Mar 2016
6. Schwartz, M.J.: DDoS attack hits 400 Gbit/s, breaks record (2014). http://www.darkreading.com/attacks-and-breaches/ddos-attack-hits-400-gbit-s-breaks-record/d/d-id/1113787. Accessed 2 Nov 2014
7. https://www.tripwire.com/state-of-security/featured/5-notable-ddos-attacks-2017/
8. DDoS incident report (2018). Accessed 04 Apr 2018
9. Chen, Y., Hwang, K., Ku, W.S.: Collaborative detection of DDoS attacks over multiple network domains. IEEE Trans. Parallel Distrib. Syst. **18**, 1649–1662 (2007)
10. Chen, C., Park, J.M.: Attack diagnosis: throttling distributed denial-of-service attacks close to the attack sources. In: Proceedings of IEEE ICCCN, pp. 275–280 (2005)
11. (2018). Accessed 1 Apr 2018

12. Yaar, Y., Perrig, A., Song, D.: Pi: a path identification mechanism to defend against DDoS attacks. In: Proceedings of IEEE S&P, pp. 93–107 (2003)
13. Wang, H., Jin, C., Shin, K.: Defense against spoofed IP traffic using hop-count filtering. IEEE/ACM Trans. Netw. 15, 40–53 (2007)
14. Kim, Y., Lau, W., Chuah, M., et al.: PacketScore: statistics-based overload control against distributed denial of service attacks. In: Proceedings of INFOCOM, pp. 141–155 (2004)
15. Ioannidis, J., Bellovin, S.: Implementing pushback: router-based defense against DDoS attacks. In: Proceedings of NDSS (2002)
16. Mirkovic, J., Prier, G., Reiher, P.L.: Attacking DDoS at the source. In: Proceedings of IEEE ICNP, pp. 312–321 (2002)
17. Mahajan, R., Bellovin, S.M., Floyd, S., et al.: Controlling high bandwidth aggregates in the network. ACM SIGCOMM 32, 62–73 (2002)
18. Papadopoulos, C., Lindell, R., Mehringer, J., et al.: COSSACK: coordinated suppression of simultaneous attacks. In: Proceedings of Discex III, pp. 94–96 (2003)
19. Francois, J., Aib, I., Boutaba, R.: FireCol: a collaborative protection network for the detection of flooding DDoS attacks. IEEE/ACM Trans. Netw. 20, 1828–1841 (2012)
20. Aghaei Foroushani, Z.H.: TDFA: traceback-based defense against DDoS flooding attacks. In: Proceedings of AINA IEEE, pp. 710–715 (2014)
21. Luo, H., Chen, Z., Li, J., Vasilakos, A.V.: Preventing distributed denial-of-service flooding attacks with dynamic path identifiers. IEEE Trans. Inf. Forensics Secur. 12, 1801–1815 (2017)
22. Hameed, S., Khan, H.A.: SDN based collaborative scheme for mitigation of DDoS attacks. Future Internet 10, 23 (2018)
23. Sung, M., Xu, J.: IP traceback-based intelligent packet filtering: a novel technique for defending against internet DDoS attacks. IEEE Trans. Parallel Distrib. Syst. 14, 861–872 (2003)
24. Yaar, Y., Perrig, A., Song, D.: SIFF: a stateless internet flow filter to mitigate DDoS flooding attacks. In: Proceedings of IEEE S&P, pp. 130–143 (2004)
25. Peng, T., Leckie, C., Ramamohanarao, K.: Detecting distributed denial of service attacks using source IP address monitoring. In: Proceedings of NETWORKS (2004)
26. Wang, H., Zhang, D., Shin, K.: Change-Point monitoring for the detection of DoS attacks. IEEE Trans. Dependable Secure Comput. 1, 193–208 (2004)
27. Manikopoulos, C., Papavassiliou, S.: Network intrusion and fault detection: a statistical anomaly approach. IEEE Commun. Mag. 40, 76–82 (2002)
28. Noh, S., Jung, G., Choi, K., et al.: Compiling network traffic into rules using soft computing methods for the detection of flooding attacks. J. Appl. Soft Comput. 8, 1200–1210 (2008)
29. Mirkovic, J., Reiher, P.: D-WARD: a source-end defense against flooding denial-of-service attacks. IEEE Trans. Dependable Secure Comput. 2, 216–232 (2005)
30. Wang, H., Zhang, D., Shin, K.: Detecting SYN flooding attacks. In: Proceedings of IEEE INFOCOM, pp. 530–1539 (2002)
31. Peng, T., Leckie, C., Ramamohanarao, K.: Protection from distributed denial of service attack using history-based IP filtering. In: Proceedings of IEEE ICC, pp. 482–486 (2003)
32. Peng, T., Leckie, C., Ramamohanarao, K.: Survey of network-based defense mechanisms countering the DoS and DDoS problems. ACM Comput. Surv. 39, 1–42 (2007)
33. RioRey Inc.: Taxonomy DDoS attacks (2012). http://www.riorey.com/xresources/2012/RioRe. Accessed 24 Dec 2015

34. Jung, J., Krishnamurthy, B., Rabinovich, M.: Flash crowds and denial of service attacks: characterization and implications for CDNs and web sites. In: Proceedings of WWW Conference, pp. 293–304 (2002)
35. Lee, K., Kim, J., Kwon, K.H., et al.: DDoS attack detection method using cluster analysis. Expert Syst. Appl. **34**, 1659–1665 (2007)
36. Bloom, B.H.: Space/time trade-offs in hash coding with allowable errors. Commun. ACM **13**, 422–426 (1970)
37. (JDSU)
38. Melander, B., Bjorkman, M., Gunningberg, P.: A new end-to-end probing and analysis method for estimating bandwidth bottlenecks. In: Global Telecommunications Conference, GLOBECOM 2000, vol. 1, pp. 415–420. IEEE (2000)
39. IMPACT Cyber Trust: Colorado state university dataset: FRGPContinuousFlow-Data (2015). Accessed 26 Oct 2016
40. Center for Applied Internet Data Analysis: The CAIDA "DDoS Attack 2007" dataset (2007). http://www.caida.org/data/passive/ddos-20070804-dataset.xml. Accessed 7 May 2016
41. (1998, D.I.D.D.)

LocalPKI: An Interoperable and IoT Friendly PKI

Jean-Guillaume Dumas[1]([✉]), Pascal Lafourcade[2], Francis Melemedjian[3],
Jean-Baptiste Orfila[1], and Pascal Thoniel[3]

[1] Université Grenoble Alpes, CNRS, Laboratoire Jean Kuntzmann,
700 av. centrale, IMAG, CS 40700, 38058 Grenoble cedex 9, France
{Jean-Guillaume.Dumas,Jean-Baptiste.Orfila}@univ-grenoble-alpes.fr
[2] University Clermont Auvergne, LIMOS,
Campus Universitaire des Cézeaux, BP 86, 63172 Aubière Cedex, France
Pascal.Lafourcade@uca.fr
[3] NTX Research SA, 111 Avenue Victor Hugo, 75116 Paris, France
{Francis.Melemedjian,Pascal.Thoniel}@ntx-research.com

Abstract. A public-key infrastructure (PKI) binds public keys to identities of entities. Usually, this binding is established through a process of registration and issuance of certificates by a certificate authority
(CA) where the validation of the registration is performed by a registration authority. In this paper, we propose an alternative scheme, called
LOCALPKI, where the binding is performed by a local authority and the
issuance is left to the end user or to the local authority. The role of a third
entity is then to register this binding and to provide up-to-date status
information on this registration. The idea is that many more local actors
could then take the role of a local authority, thus allowing for an easier
spread of public-key certificates in the population. Moreover, LOCALPKI
represents also an appropriate solution to be deployed in the Internet of
Things context. Our scheme's security is formally proven with the help
of Tamarin, an automatic verification tool for cryptographic protocols.

1 Introduction

The primary goal of a *Public Key Infrastructure* (abbreviated *PKI*) is to bind
a user identity with his public key. They are security architectures that manage
digital certificates, electronic documents used to prove the ownership of a public
key. The current global PKI standard is *PKIX*.

Deploying server certificates is a necessity to bring trust in transactions made
on the Internet. This also mandatory to be able to use electronic signatures,
for authentication, session key transport, authenticated key exchange, or more
generally, any secured communication.

Started near the end of 2015, the Let's Encrypt project goes further and
seeks to democratize the implementation of server certificates. The goal is to
generalize certificates for almost all servers. Why such an initiative? Two constraints have been identified: the cost of certificates and the complexity of their

M. S. Obaidat and E. Cabello (Eds.): ICETE 2017, CCIS 990, pp. 224–252, 2019.
https://doi.org/10.1007/978-3-030-11039-0_11

implementation. Let's Encrypt provides a solution to remove these bottlenecks and as of mid-2018 this has become the choice of more than half of the market shares.

Now, the deployment of certificates for persons (citizen, professional, student, consumer, Internet user) is also a necessity to bring trust in transactions made on the Internet. Despite *PKIX*, this deployment has never really been carried out on a large scale and few of us now possess these certificates. The first goal of LOCALPKI is to democratize the attribution of people certificates, just like Let's Encrypt democratized the attribution of server certificates. The second goal of LOCALPKI is enable an easier deployment of public key certificates in constrained environments like the IOT *Internet of Things*.

Overall, the goal is to generalize certificates for all. How? By removing the three known bottlenecks with *PKIX*: remote delivery, cost of certificates and their complexity of use. LOCALPKI provides a solution on organizational, financial and cryptographic levels (new protocols) in order to eliminate the current, above listed, bottlenecks/issues. For this, the central actors in LOCALPKI will be the Local Registration Authorities (LRA). Those will be established industrial actors, like a bank or a telecom operator for instance, and they will enroll users who are their members or customers thanks to their local network. The Local Registration Authority will remain close to its users, it will have to be the local bank branch office or the next door Telecom agency. Indeed, it is a foremost importance for this actors to deliver to their members or clients certificates that will enable them to authenticate and sign contracts online. Then, to guarantee the security of the system, Electronic Notaries will then be in charge of maintaining the data bases of registered certificates.

Now, for the user, he/she can get a free certificate (with paid options available) near his/her home or work place with the security of face-to-face enrollment (identity verification). The system can also support trust circles. For example, if a user trusts a given financial or telecom player to enroll its customers, then the user will be convinced by the public key authenticity assertion sent by its Digital / Electronic Notary server about one of its customers. Finally, LOCALPKI is not only limited to personal certificates. Tomorrow, the deployment of connected objects certificates will also be a necessity to bring trust in transactions made on the Internet of Things (IOT, Internet of Things). Each manufacturer will become the Registration Authority for its connected objects.

1.1 State of the Art

Over the internet, the main standard is defining the format of public key certificates is X.509, developed by the IETF PKIX working group. This is the most widely used standard in Internet protocols [9]. RFC 5280, which define how to use X.509 in Internet protocols. For instance, almost all major internet players authentify their servers with certificates via the *TLS* (Transport Layer Security) protocol, basis of the *HTTPS* (Hypertext Transfer Protocol Secure). In this paradigm, end entities (users) rely on *Certificate Authorities* (*CA*) which deliver *X*.509 certificates containing, at least, the user's identity and public key and a validity period. These certificates are then signed by the *CA*. Then, before using the public key of another entity, a user verifies the associated certificate: checking validity period, correctness of signature etc. We talk about the *owner* of a certificate and the *user* of a certificate.

Now, in order to be able to use long enough validity periods, a revocation mechanism has then to be set up. Indeed, the burden of renewing one's certificate need not be repeated too often, but a revocation can however be launched in case of unexpected events. The most deployed solutions for this are *Online Certificate Status Protocol* (*OCSP*) [26] and *Certificate Revocation List* (CRL) [9]. In the first case, the user sends a validity query of the owner's certificate to an *OCSP* responder (either maintained by the certificate's issuer, or well known to the user). In the second case, lists of revoked certificates must be regularly updated and published into *CRL Distribution Points* (*CDP*). Users access these *CDP* and check that the owner's certificate is not present inside the list. In the end, depending on the obtained certificate status, the owner is authenticated or not by the user.

On the one hand, in terms of various security and efficiency requirements, mostly depending on the environment where the PKI must be set-up (internet, industrial architecture, power limited devices...), the current state of the art for PKIs is quite substantial. In terms of efficiency, solutions to reduce communication and computation costs of the revocation checks arose, such as *H-OCSP* [22] or *Delta-CRL* [9]. Moreover, the needed trustfulness in the *CA* has been intensively studied in order to reduce the impact of malicious behavior. Indeed, in *PKIX*, a compromised *CA* is able to ruin the entire authentication mechanism by delivering illegitimate certificates. Then, solutions based on public logs of *CA*'s action emerged, with for instance *Certificate Transparency* [18]. In this paradigm, certifications are included in append-only log structures: the log maintainer is able to prove that a specific certificate is present into the structure, and that each new added certificate has only extended the previous structure. The *Accountable Key Infrastructure* [16] exploits public-logs for the certificate management and distributes the trust between several entities. In [25], the authors provide a solution combining public revocation and a more largely distributed trust (using users' browsers) with the *Certificate Issuance and Revocation Transparency*.

On the other hand, more recently, the *Attack Resilient Public-Key Infrastructure* (ARPKI) [4] proposes a PKI where clients choose several authorities (*CAs* and log maintainers) involved into the global process. There, each of these authorities supervises the others' behavior: as a consequence, a single non compromised entity is sufficient to prevent attacks. The solution described in [29] with the *Distributed Transparent Key Infrastructure* (DTKI), provides security even in the case where all these entities are corrupted. Notably, the security of ARPKI and DTKI has been formally proven using the automatic cryptographic protocols verification tool Tamarin [19,27]. Most of these advanced solutions provide enhanced security to the cost of some complexity in the procedures. In a practical set up these solutions involve several authorities, which must be involved in the management of technical services (this is particularly true for the management of worldwide append-only logs). Furthermore, these schemes rely on a *CA*'s signature of certificates in order to guarantee the binding between the public key and the identity.

1.2   Contributions

In this paper, we formally describe and prove the security of a public-key infrastructure called LOCALPKI, based on the *PKI* 2.0 paradigm [6]. The *PKI* 2.0 project and its instances such as LOCALPKI are seeking to democratize the attribution of people certificates, like what *Let's Encrypt* is doing for server certificates. They are essential for secured transactions: authentication, digital signature, confidentiality. LOCALPKI removes three known bottlenecks of *PKIX*: remote delivery, cost of certificates and their complexity of use. The idea is to replace *CA* signed certificates by user self-signed certificates. However, contrary to *PGP* [30], trust is not given by users but by an authority. This authority, a combination of notaries and local actors in our setting, guaranties the binding. Indeed, after registration of a certificate owner by a notary, other users will be able to verify the authenticity of this certificate via a request. For a private verification, a possibility is to send a request to the notary, similar to an *OCSP* procedure: the notary's response depends on the looking up of uniquely recorded legitimate users in his database. For a public verification, a possibility is to provide hashed and signed subsets of the database, similar to NSEC3 [17] (or now NSEC5 [28]) records within DNSSEC [5]. Also, as in *PKIX*, registration and authentication do not need be performed by the same entities. In *PKIX* the former step can be performed by a *Registration Authority*. In LOCALPKI, this entity is a *local* RA, known by the notary and close to the user. It can be a technical service, just like a classical registration authority, but it can also be a local actor or a business service, closer to users. We have in mind banks, postal offices, mobile network operators, delivery points, university offices, for example, and more generally any actor used to check identities. For the user, he can get a free certificate (with possibly paid options available) near his home or work place with the security of face-to-face enrollment (identity verification). For local registration desks, it would often be in its own interest to deliver people certificates to its members or clients. These member/client certificates will enable them to authenticate and perform online operations, for instance securely signing contracts. Moreover, the involved entities, except for the notaries, do not really need any technical knowledge. Overall, our proposition, LOCALPKI, is a first instance of the PKI 2.0 paradigm offering an alternative to *PKIX*. LOCALPKI is able to provide the same services as *PKIX*, from authentication to revocation, via, e.g., cross-certification. But the approach uses instead a user-centric model and does not need a signature by an authority for each certificate. From the simplicity of its setup, we show that LOCALPKI also becomes an interesting solution to deploy a PKI in the *Internet of Things* context. Further, in this paper, we also provide a security analysis of all our protocols, using the formal verification tool Tamarin [19,27]. Finally, we show that the implementation of the LOCALPKI in a practical environment can be effectively realized using existing *PKI* tools: we have deployed a prototype web-based implementation available for testing there: http://hpac.imag.fr/localpki.

1.3 Organization of the Paper

In Sect. 2, we start by defining entities involved in LOCALPKI, and we make a high-level comparison with *PKIX*. Then in Sect. 3, we formally describe all the protocols involved, i.e. the registration, authentication and revocation mechanisms. We also describe a private blockchain based solution to efficiently interoperate multiple instances of LOCALPKI. Section 5 is devoted to the deployment of the architecture, using existing tools and solutions. Finally, in Sect. 6, we define the required security properties and an associated formal model for LOCALPKI. Those enable us to formally prove the security of LOCALPKI, using Tamarin. Finally, in Sect. 7, we show how to deploy LOCALPKI as an Internet of Things PKI.

With respect to the conference version of this paper [11], we describe a complete use case of LOCALPKI in the Internet of Things context (Sect. 7). We also extend the system in order to be able to interoperate multiple instances of LOCALPKI, for instance using a private blockchain (Sect. 4). Finally we add some specifications on the deployment and propose a web-based prototype implementation of LOCALPKI registration (Sect. 5).

2   General Description

In this setting, LOCALPKI is a set of protocols which fulfills all the requirements of a public-key infrastructure (*PKI*): registration of a new user, authentication of registered users, revocation of certificates, renewals, cross-certification, etc.

Informally, the main idea is that users will produce themselves their self-signed certificates, and that notaries will only store the signed hash this certificate and its serial number. The notaries them manage these within a database. Authentication is realized by the notary, just verifying that a given certificate hash is present or not in the database.

In the following, we give more details on the protocols and start by introducing the different entities and their role.

2.1 Entities

There are three different entities in LOCALPKI: the *Electronic Notaries* (*EN*), the *Local Registration Authorities* (*LRA*) and the *users* (or *End Entities*).

The *Electronic Notary* might be seen as the root *CA* in a classical PKI architecture. Actually, he manages the databases containing registered users.

The *Local Registration Authority* represents the intermediate entity between the user and the notary. It is somewhat like a *Registration Authority* in a classical PKI, but in LOCALPKI it is closer to users than to the *CA*. In practice, the *LRA* could be an agency close to the user, such as the user's insurance company, his bank, the postal office, etc. Those agencies usually already have the abilities to check identities. The *LRA* is registered by some *EN*, and the identity checks are performed during the recording of a new user. The multiplicity of Registration Authorities reduces the systemic risk that exists in the event of a Certification Authority compromise.

Finally, *users* represent the entities who want to authenticate or be authenticated by others.

2.2 Comparison with *PKIX*

The main differences between LOCALPKI and *PKIX* are:

- In LOCALPKI registration authorities do not need to be security experts. Therefore they can be closer to users and allow more widespread deployment of the use of certificates in every day life (see Sect. 3.2).
- Certificate creation is done by the *CA* in *PKIX*; in LOCALPKI it is done by the *LRA* while the notaries store and make this decision available (see Sect. 3.2).
- The default authentication mode in *PKIX* is a buffering via the *CRL*; while default authentication mode in LOCALPKI is interactive, somewhat like *OCSP Online-Certificate Status Protocol* (see Sect. 3.3).
- The alternative authentication mode in *PKIX* is *OCSP*, while LOCALPKI can also propose an alternative buffering mechanism called *Certificate Verification Lists* (*CVL*), described in Sect. 3.3.

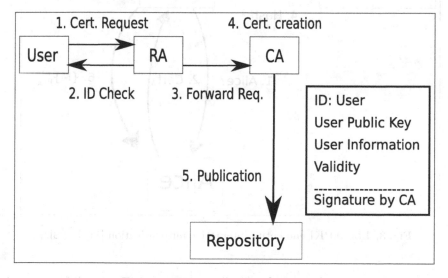

Fig. 1. *PKIX* registration [11, Fig. 2].

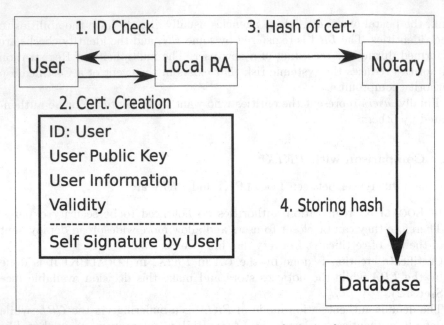

Fig. 2. LOCALPKI registration [11, Fig. 1].

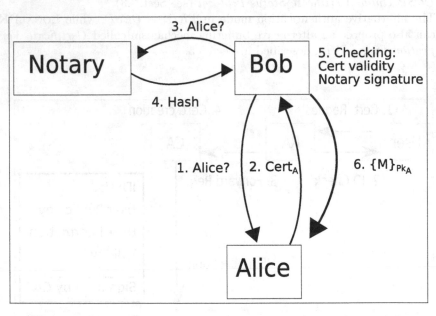

Fig. 3. LOCALPKI end entity interactive authentication [11, Fig. 3].

From a closer look at both protocols execution, the major difference is in the signature of the user's certificate: in *PKIX*, the *CA*'s signature is present whereas in LOCALPKI only the self signature made by the user is required.

As shown in Fig. 2, certificate creation is realized in the 2nd step by the owner instead of the 4th one by the *CA* for *PKIX*, as shown in Fig. 1. Furthermore, the registration authority forwards a certificate request to the *CA*, while the *LRA* only sends the certificate's hash to the notary. Finally, in LOCALPKI certificates are not directly published since the *EN*'s database only contains hashes.

Hence, interactive authentication is also different as shown in Figs. 3 and 4: with LOCALPKI, owners have to provide their certificates to users beforehand, and then the users interact with notaries in order to be convinced of the certificate's validity; with *PKIX* users can recover certificates in a local repository and then interacts with OCSP responders to be convinced of the certificate's validity. The full protocol, in particular the buffering mechanism (the *CVL*, also called public mode within LOCALPKI), is detailed next.

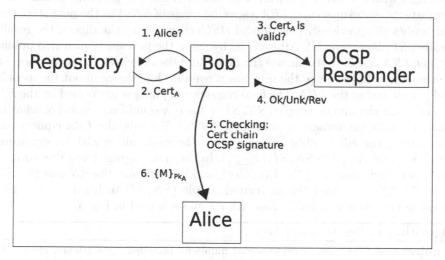

Fig. 4. *PKIX* end entity interactive authentication [11, Fig. 4].

3 Protocol Description

We now give some notations and then formally define the LOCALPKI protocols.

3.1 Notations

The concatenation of two messages m_1 and m_2 is denoted $m_1 \| m_2$. Generally, the notation O_A is used to express the belonging of the object O (e.g., a certificate) to the user A. We denote by Pk_A (resp. Sk_A) the public key (resp. private key) of a user A. We write $\{m\}_{Pk_A}$ (resp. $\{m\}_{Sk_A}$) the action of ciphering (resp. signing) a message m with the public key Pk_A (resp. the private key Sk_A). Hashing a message m is written $H(m)$, with H the hash function. We denote by $X_{509}()$ a function which takes user's information and returns them into the X_{509} certificate format without any signature.

3.2   Registration of a New User

A user first needs to be enrolled into the system: this step is called *registration*.

The phase starts by a new key pair generation by the user. After he interacts with a *LRA* for the registration process. In LOCALPKI the *LRA* should be physically close to the user, so that they can meet in person. The user begins by providing ID proofs according to the established security policy (e.g., a visual check of the ID card). Once the identity check succeeds, the user gives his public key to the *LRA*. Next, the authority generates a field equivalent to the *ToBe-Signed* (TBSCert) in the $X.509$ certificates, containing at least: the user's ID, his public key, a *Serial Number* (SN), a validity period and the URL of the notary associated with the *LRA*. The SN has been obtained by the *LRA* from previous exchanges with the *EN*. The latter is in charge of the SN generation, and communicates to each supervised *LRA* a specific range of SN. For the next step, the user hashes the previously generated $TBSCert$ and signs the digest: the result is called SI (*Signature Id*). Afterwards, by using the previously provided public key, the *LRA* is able to recompute the digest and then to check the correctness of the signature. At this step, the user has proven his knowledge about the associated private key to the *LRA*. The final registration phase is performed by the *EN* who registers the unique couple (SN, SI) (this is a simplified version of what is called a "public key ownership certificate" in [6]). For this, the *LRA* ciphers the couple using the *EN*'s public key, and sends the result along with its signature of this message (i.e., $\{H(SN, SI)\}_{Sk_{LRA}}$). In the end, the registered user owns a certificate $Cert$ containing the $TBSCert$, and in particular the SN and the SI, while the *EN* has added the associated couple (SN, SI) to his database. The complete process is detailed in Algorithm 1 and schemed in Fig. 5.

Algorithm 1. Registration of Alice.

Require: The *LRA* owns *a priori* serial numbers, provided by a trusted electronic notary *EN*.

Ensure: Identity check (by the *LRA*) and registration of Alice into the *EN* database.

1: Alice generates his public key Pk_A.
2: Alice → *LRA*: Pk_A
3: *LRA* checks information and identity of Alice.
4: *LRA* → Alice: Serial number (SN_A), notary URL (URL_{EN}), validity.
5: Alice generates a $X.509$ certificate $TBSCert_A$ (completed with URL_{EN} and SN_A), and computes $SI_A = \{H(TBSCert_A)\}_{Sk_A}$
6: Alice → *LRA*: $TBSCert_A \| SI_A$
7: *LRA* checks SI_A (PoK of the Alice private key).
8: **if** Verification OK **then**
9:    *LRA* → *EN*: $\{SN_A \| SI_A\}_{Pk_{EN}} \| \{H(SN_A \| SI_A)\}_{Sk_{LRA}}$
10: **end if**
11: *EN* decides to add Alice to his database.

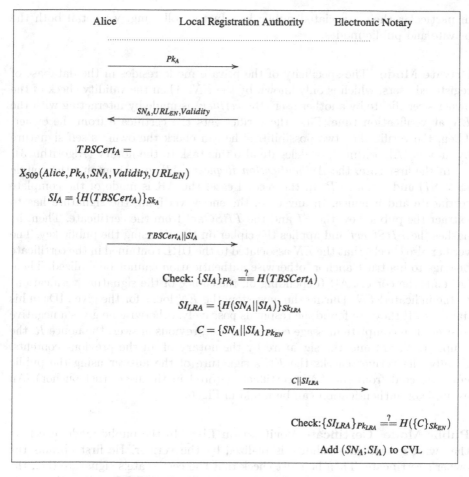

Fig. 5. Registration of Alice [11, Fig. 5].

3.3   Authentication

Once the owner of the certificate has been correctly registered, other users could authenticate him i.e., they are ensured that the used public key is indeed the owner's one. The authentication process in LOCALPKI can be realized in two different ways. First by using a private mode, where only the *EN* knows the full database containing registered users. In this case, the user requests the *EN* about the validity of the owner's certificate, and no more information is revealed. The second possibility is to apply the public mode (also called buffering mode), where the *EN* shares parts of his database with the user, who makes the validity verification by himself. In both cases, the user must be able to first authenticate the *EN* using the URL provided in the certificate. As in *PKIX*, the mechanism used in LOCALPKI is the *trust anchors* [24]. A trust anchor contains certificates of the trusted notaries. Then, users are able to retrieve information on notaries, in particular their associated public key. In the following, we detail both the private and public modes.

Private Mode. The specificity of the private mode resides in the database of registered users, which is only known by the EN. Then the validity check of the owner's certificate by another user (the *verifier*) is made by interacting with the EN at verification time. First the verifier gets the certificate from the owner. Then, the verifier has two possibilities: he can check the owner's self signature by himself (Algorithm 2) or delegate also this task to the notary (Algorithm 3).

In the first case, the *Authentication Request* (AR) only contains the couple (SN, SI) and a nonce R. In the second case, the AR is made of the complete certificate and a nonce. In any case, the entity verifying the signature has to extract the public key, the SI and the $TBSCert$ from the certificate. Then, he hashes the $TBSCert$ and applies the cipher on the SI using the public key. The verifier also checks that the EN associated to the URL contained in the certificate belongs to his trust anchor, otherwise authentication cannot be realized. Then, he sends the correct AR (depending on the choice of the signature verification) to the indicated EN. During the next step, the EN looks for the given IDs in his database. If they are found, he responds positively, otherwise he gives a negative answer. The complete message consists of the previous answer, the nonce R, the couple (SN, SI) and the signature by the notary of all the previous contents. Finally, the verifier checks the EN's signature of the answer using the public key extracted from the EN's certificate (stored in the user trust anchor). An example of authentication can be found in Fig. 6.

Public Mode: Certificate Verification List. In the public mode, checking the owner's certificate validity is realized by the verifier. He first obtains the owner's certificate. Then he must check that the certificate's signature (i.e., the SI) is consistent with the information contained in the $TBSCert$ (i.e., the public key and the SN). After having checked that the EN belongs to his trust anchor, the verifier sends a request to the EN designated by its URL in the certificate. This request asks for the *Certificate Verification List* (CVL) i.e., the content of the database storing the couple (SN, SI) of previously registered users. To exchange the CVL with the user, the EN sends a signature of the CVL in addition to the list itself. This also ensures its integrity. Finally, the verifier checks the signature of the EN, and then verifies that (SN, SI) belongs to the CVL. Of course, just like a CRL, a CVL can be locally stored (buffered) and reused in a certain time interval without any refreshment. Just like for a CRL, a typical refreshment rate for a CVL could be in days. An example of public authentication is given in Fig. 7.

Even if the public mode reduces the number of operation realized by the EN, it implies a non-negligible communication cost. In order to reduce it, the idea is to divide the database into subdomains. Indeed, the EN is in charge of the generation of the SN given to the LRA. Hence, the database is intrinsically divided into LRA subdomains. Then, the verifier could buffer only the CVL

Algorithm 2. Certificate check in private mode (self signature verification).

Require: Alice gets the certificate from Bob. She wants to check the validity of the certificate.

Ensure: Authentication of Bob to Alice if the certificate is correct, failure otherwise.

1: **if** $\{SI_A\}_{Pk_B} \overset{?}{==} H(TBSCert_B)$ **then**
2:    Alice: $R_A \leftarrow^\$$
3:    Alice $\rightarrow URL_{EN}$: AR$=SN_{Bob}\|SI_{Bob}\|R_A$
4:    **if** $(SN_{Bob}; SI_{Bob}) \in$ Database **then**
5:      $Rep = "OK"\|AR$
6:    **else**
7:      $Rep = "Unknown"\|AR$
8:    **end if**
9:    $URL_{EN} \rightarrow$ Alice: $Rep\|\{H(Rep)\}_{Sk_{EN}}$
10:    Alice checks the response signature, and authenticate (or not) Bob.
11: **end if**

Algorithm 3. Certificate check in private mode (delegate signature verification).

Require: Alice gets the certificate from Bob. She wants to check the validity of the certificate.

Ensure: Authentication of Bob to Alice if the certificate is correct, failure otherwise.

1: Alice: $R_A \leftarrow^\$$
2: Alice $\rightarrow URL_{EN}$: AR$=Cert_{Bob}\|R_A$
3: **if** $\{SI_A\}_{Pk_B} \overset{?}{==} H(TBSCert_B)$ **then**
4:    **if** $(SN_{Bob}; SI_{Bob}) \in$ Database **then**
5:      $Rep = "OK"\|AR$
6:    **else**
7:      $Rep = "Unknown"\|AR$
8:    **end if**
9: **else**
10:    $Rep = "Wrong Signature"\|AR$
11: **end if**
12: $URL_{EN} \rightarrow$ Alice: $Rep\|\{H(Rep)\}_{Sk_{EN}}$
13: Alice checks the response signature, and authenticate (or not) Bob.

---

associated to a subdomain, and hence the communication cost between the client and the EN is reduced to this subdomain size.

Comparison Between Public, Private Modes and *PKIX* Mechanisms.
LOCALPKI is designed to be used by default in the private mode, offering a lower communication cost and an always up-to-date database. Nevertheless, the CVL are interesting in the case where an online interaction is not always guaranteed. In comparison with mechanisms used in $PKIX$, the private mode can be assimilated with $OCSP$ and CVL with CRL. Initially, $OCSP$ was not designed to resist against replay attacks. In a later version, a counter-measure has been added to the `responseExtensions` field (see [26, Sect. 4.4.1]). However, as discussed in [26, Sect. 5], this solution is not required by the norm. In the private mode of LOCALPKI, replay attacks are countered by default.

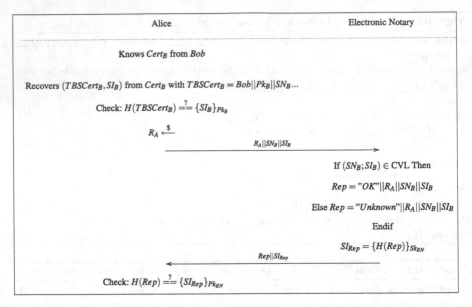

Fig. 6. Authentication of Bob by Alice (in private mode) [11, Fig. 6].

In *PKIX*, the complete list of revoked certificates must be shared. Thus, the communication cost is large. A way to reduce these large broadcasts, on solution can be to use δ-*CRL*'s. Similarly we proposed to allow subdomain CVL's. In the case of the *CVL*, only the subdomain part containing the certificates need to be exchanged to have a correct authentication. But, unlike δ-*CRL*, a subdomain *CVL* is fail-safe. Indeed a user looking only in a partial *CRL* can miss that a certificate has been revoked with another reason, and still use it. On the contrary, if a valid certificate is not present in a subdomain *CVL*, it just cannot be used.

Furthermore, *CRL* based solutions expose users to false positive authentications. Since a *CRL* is not continuously updated, recently revoked certificates could still be considered valid. By using a white-list strategy like *CVL*, verifiers may not succeed in authenticating newly registered users. However, once again, obtaining a false negative is usually a safer fail than a false positive. Besides that, only valid certificates are stored. Then, in case of authentication failure, the verifier cannot know the reason (revocation, unregistered user).

3.4   Revocation

A public key infrastructure should provide a solution to revoke certificates before the end of their validity period. This allows for instance to manage lost or compromised key pairs. In LOCALPKI, a certificate revocation can easily be done by the certificate's owner or by the *LRA*, via a request to the *EN*. In both cases, this request is signed and contains the owner's certificate along with a Revoke message, as shown in Algorithm 4 thereafter. In case of a request from

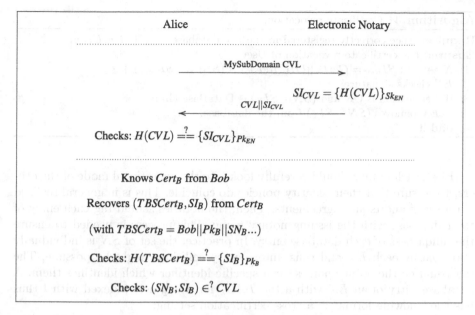

Fig. 7. Authentication of Bob by Alice (in public mode) [11, Fig. 7].

the owner's certificate, the signature acts as a proof of knowledge of the private key. In case of a request by the associated LRA, the notary has anyway to accept registrations from this LRA (for instance within a range of allowed serial number values). This same range can be used to guaranty that the LRA is allowed to revoke this serial number. Hence, in both cases, the EN verifies the signature and if the couple (SN, SI) is present in his database, he simply removes the entry. Thus, an authentication attempt using this revoked couple fails, since the entry has been removed from the EN database. Then the renewal procedure is simple: after the revocation, the user has to enter a new registration process with his LRA.

4   Infrastructures Interoperability

4.1   Cross-Certification Tag

In $PKIX$, cross-certification is a mechanism allowing the interoperability between private PKI. This means that users from a PKI A, are then able to authenticate other users belonging to the PKI B. In practice, the cross-certification consists in the signature of a CA's certificate by another CA. In the end, this creates a trust path between the CAs, which is verified during the authentication process. The cross-certification is generally transparent for the end-users, since the technical checks are realized by the CA. In LOCALPKI, we explain in the following how to define a similar and efficient interoperability system using private blockchain based techniques.

Algorithm 4. Certificate revocation.

Require: Alice correctly registered in the EN database. $X \in \{LRA, User\}$
Ensure: The certificate revocation of User
1: $X \rightarrow EN$: $SI_{Rev} = Cert_X || \{H("Revoke" || (SN_{User}; SI_{User}))\}_{Sk_X}$
2: EN checks signature
3: **if** Verification is OK and $(SN_X; SI_X) \in$ DataBase **then**
4:     EN removes $(SN_X; SI_X)$ from the database.
5: **end if**

First, each notary should carefully look into the operational mode of the others, to be sure that their security policies do coincide. This is in general realized via a set of audits and agreements. Then, the notaries should tag each entry of their database with the issuing notary name. This process is needed to ensure the uniqueness of each database entry. In practice, the set of SN is individually managed by each EN and thus, inter-notary collisions might be possible. The tag could be the notary names, or a specific identifier which identifies them. A database entry of an EN with a tag TAG_k for a end-user indexed with i thus has the following format in a cross-certification setting:

$$TAG_k, SN_i, SI_i$$

4.2   Database Exchange

A first solution ensuring the interoperability between several ENs could be to setup a databases exchange. For instance, the notaries EN_1 and EN_2 agree on a secure exchange protocol, where for instance mutual authentication could be performed out of band. Then, they simply exchange their own signed database, like in the CVL mechanism. In the end, both notaries obtain a shared database. This process could be sufficient when the PKI are locally deployed, e.g, when a company wishes to authenticate users belonging to two distinct subsidiaries, running two instances of LOCALPKI.

This is however inefficient in most cases: indeed, since revoked certificates must be removed from the database and new users can be frequently added, the whole databases would have to be frequently checked and exchanged. We propose an update mechanism that should reduce the communications volume and give the possibility to easily add and remove data from a shared database.

4.3   Private Blockchain Solution

In fact, the problem is quite exactly that of the management of accounts and their balance in the shared state of the *Ethereum* cryptocurrency [7]. There, the solution is based on the use of a structure called a *Merkle PATRICIA Tree* (MPT) [15]. This structure combines that of radix trees [21] with Merkle hash trees [20]. The first ones allow efficient additions or deletions of nodes, whereas the second use the nodes hashes as pointers to the next nodes. In the context of

LOCALPKI, the leafs represent an entry of the *EN* database. Then, to update their mutual databases (which became a shared database thanks to the cross-certification), the notaries have only to update their MPT.

Overall the solution is thus to setup the database as a **private blockchain**, between the notaries involved in the cross certification, using Merkle PATRICIA trees as the underlying data structure.

5   Deployment

LOCALPKI has the advantage to be easily deployed from an existing *PKIX*. Actually, each of these requirements can be satisfied by adapting the current standards of *PKIX*. In the following, we present how to realize it.

Certificate Format. First of all, certificates employed in LOCALPKI can be based on *X.509v3* certificates [9]. Indeed, both PKI, LOCALPKI and *PKIX*, share the same kind of identification data (TBSCert). Then, the *CA*'s signature is replaced by the user's signature and the *SN* can be stored in the serialNumber field.

On-line Authentication Request. The communications with the notaries during authentication in the private mode, Fig. 6, can be set up using the *OCSP* norm [26]. Within the *OCSP* request, the *SN* replaces the current serialNumber in the CertID sequence, and the *SI* is stored in the signature field of the optional Signature sequence. Note that other fields in CertID, such that the issuerNameHash and issuerKeyHash, could be left empty since this information is either irrelevant or redundant with the *SI*. The nonce R_A (see Fig. 6 and Algorithms 2 and 3) can be stored into the *OCSP* requestExtensions.

On-line Authentication Response. Similarly, the notary's answer can also follow the *OCSP* response format, where all the latter fields are also present.

Certificate Validation Lists. In the public mode, Certificate Verification Lists (*CVL*) can be managed just like Certificate Revocation Lists (*CRL*). For example, a *CVL* could be published on the *EN* websites, and can be stored in local repositories. Moreover, if an organization with subdomains is required, e.g., each range of *SN* represents a subdomain, the *Delta-CRL* indicator could used [9], as well as the BaseCRLNumber field which could represent for us an equivalent Base CVL number field.

Revocation. The revocation requests within LOCALPKI and *PKIX* are almost identical. Thus, LOCALPKI may use the *Certificate Management Protocol* [23] directly for revocations.

End-User Authentication. All authentication mechanisms using X.509 certificates, like *Simple Authentication and Security Layer* (SASL) (e.g., via ISO IEC 9798-3), are still enabled with LOCALPKI.

Web of Trust. Similarly, enhancements to the web of trust between authorities like ARPKI [4] or Certificate Transparency [18], which use append only log servers are also applicable to LOCALPKI.

Trust Anchor Stores. Finally, *PKIX* requires trust anchors [24] to be deployed, e.g., within the store of the users' browsers or OS's. Communications between *LRA*s and notaries, also require an anchor mechanism and that of *PKIX* can also be used directly.

Therefore, existing tools like *OpenSSL* allow for all entities to generate keys, certificates, authentication and revocation requests or responses. The technical setup of LOCALPKI is mainly restricted to the management of the databases. This is delegated to the *EN*, who are thus also in charge of maintaining the *PKI* availability. *LRA*s are in charge of communications with the notaries, that is mainly exchanging serial numbers, and of the face to face identity verifications.

Differently, users have several possibilities, depending on their expertise.

- Expert users, first generate themselves their own key pair. Then they request a serial number, *SN*, through the *LRA*, in order to create and sign their certificate. Finally they give the associated *SI* to the *LRA* who will forward it to the notary.
- An intermediate possibility, is for the user to only generate a key pair. The *LRA* will then take charge of the certificate creation and provide means for the user to sign it with his private key (for instance a usb port and a keyboard so as to type the password deciphering the private key stored in a usb device).
- The *LRA* can also create fresh key pairs on the fly and provide everything to the user.

Part or all of the latter two possibilities are easily realized through a dedicated web site. Therefore, the only technical requirement for the *LRA* is the use of tools like *OpenSSL*, in order to help the users registration and the creation of a user-friendly associated API.

We have realized a web-base prototype implementation of the system, available there:

> http://hpac.imag.fr/localpki

This first prototype uses PHP to call some OpenSSL scripts as shown with the capture of Fig. 8.

The main OpenSSL scripts do implement LOCALPKI functions as follows:

- As a LOCALPKI certificate is self signed, `openssl req -new -x509` can be used to generate it (for *PKIX*, it would b a self signed *root CA certificate*).
- To be handled by most web browser, the generated PEM format certificate can then be converted to the PKCS12 format, via `openssl pkcs12`.
- Additionally, `openssl genrsa` can be used to generate the public/private key pair for the user.

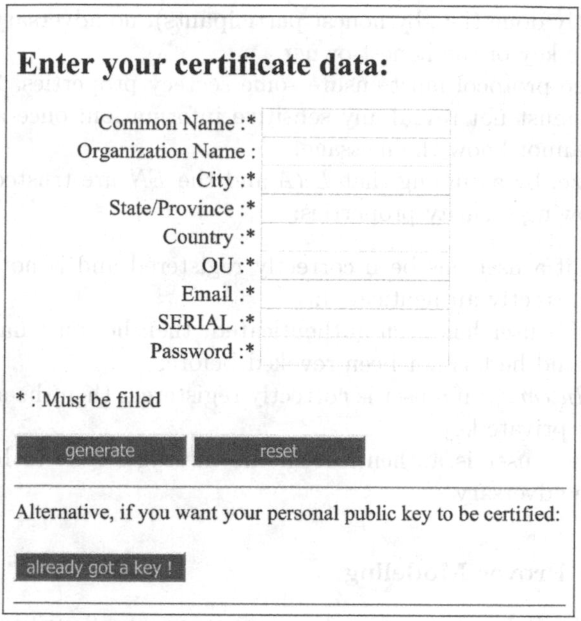

Enter your certificate data:

Common Name :*

Organization Name :

City :*

State/Province :*

Country :*

OU :*

Email :*

SERIAL :*

Password :*

* : Must be filled

generate   reset

Alternative, if you want your personal public key to be certified:

already got a key !

Fig. 8. Web-based prototype implementation of LOCALPKI.

6   Security Analysis

Using asymmetric cryptography, LOCALPKI aims at making authentication of users possible. However, the protocol also provides other security guarantees. In the following, we first define the security properties of LOCALPKI. Then, we use an automatic cryptographic protocols verification tool called *Tamarin Prover*, in order to prove these security properties.

6.1   Security Properties

Firstly the protocol must be *correct*, i.e., if a person has been correctly registered into the database and her certificate is still valid, then he must be correctly authenticated. The underlying property correspond to classical authentication property and is thus about correct identity checks.

Vice versa, an adversary who has not been registered cannot be authenticated. This *soundness property* implies that an adversary cannot forge a certificate considered as valid and cannot impersonate a valid one. A reformulation of the soundness property is that authentication at time i_2 implies a registration at time i_1 with $i_1 < i_2$.

In [4], the authors also defined the *Connection Integrity* as follows: if a user establishes a connection with another one, then the user communicates with the legitimate owner of the private key. In others words, in the case where registration has been correctly done (i.e., by honest participants), no adversary can possibly know the private key of the honest owner.

Moreover, the protocol must ensure some secrecy properties. Indeed, a protocol execution must not reveal any sensitive information: once authenticated, the adversary cannot know the message.

To summarize, by assuming that *LRA* and the *EN* are trusted, LOCALPKI verifies the following security properties:

- *Correctness*: if a user has been correctly registered and is not revoked then he must be correctly authenticated;
- *Soundness*: if a user has been authenticated, then he must have been registered before and he has not been revoked before;
- *Connection Integrity*: if a user is correctly registered, then the adversary does not know his private key.
- *Secrecy*: once a user is authenticated, the messages sent to him cannot be learnt by the adversary.

6.2   Tamarin Prover Modeling

We use *Tamarin Prover* an automatic security protocol verifier [19] to prove these security properties. This tool can verify an unbounded number of sessions. Moreover the intruder follows the Dolev-Yao's intruder model [10]. This means that the intruder extracts all possible information from every exchanged messages on the network. The tool assumes the usual perfect encryption hypothesis (i.e., the adversary cannot learn any information from encrypted messages if he does not know the corresponding secret key). We consider classic equational theories provided by default by Tamarin for the cryptographic operations like encryption or signature. In Tamarin, the protocols are modeled by some multiset rewriting rules. These rules are composed of facts, which model the local knowledge of a participant, such as the reception of a message, or the generation of a fresh number or the emission of a message. Then, each role action is implemented as a `rule`. A rule rewrites a fact into another one, and is eventually labeled in order to trace the realized actions. For example, a rule rewriting a fact composed of a message and key into a message containing the encryption of the message with the key could be labeled as *Cipher*. Facts could be persistent (denoted with a ! before its name), which means that it can be reused arbitrarily often by some rules. Otherwise facts are said to be linear and can be used only once. Once the protocol is modeled by some rules, we model the desired properties as `lemmas`. A lemma is a first-order logic sequence applied on the label of previously defined rules. They contain quantifiers ($\forall$: `All`, $\exists$: `Ex`) and logical connectives (`&`, `|`, `not`, `==>`), along with timepoints (declared with #, and employed with @). For example `Ex sna sia #i. Bob_Auth_Alice(<sna,sia>) @i` means that the event *Bob Authenticates Alice* using variables `<sna,sia>` occurs at time i.

Now, we detail our model and the properties proved. We also show that trust hypothesis on entities are mandatory, just like, e.g., trust hypothesis are required on CAs in *PKIX*, by describing attacks found by the tool if any of these hypothesis is removed.

All the Tamarin source files can be found at: http://hpac.imag.fr/localpki. See the associated *Makefile* for details on how to generate proofs and attacks with Tamarin.

6.3   LocalPKI **Tamarin Model**

According to the result of [8], where the authors prove that for verifying a secrecy property only one intruder is enough and for an authentication property one intruder and at most one honest participant per role is enough, we consider a protocol execution where we have only one notary, one *LRA*, one registered user (Alice) and one verifier (Bob). Our model of this execution comprises the registration of Alice, her authentication by Bob followed by an exchange of a message, and the revocation of her certificate.

In *PKIX* paper, key pair generations are modeled by generic persistent facts, instantiated with different terms. These facts bind the identity of the entity with its public key to represent the trust anchors, i.e., other entities have the correct association between the public key and the identity. Thus, we model the trust anchors of the *LRA* and the *EN* in the same way. In the case of Alice, we need to explicitly define the self-signed certificate described in the Algorithm 1. Moreover, we assume also that the Alice's certificate is public. We have two types of communication channels, depending on the situation:

- a real-life meeting,
- insecure channels.

Since the registration must be realized during a real-life meeting, we assume that it is not subject to any intruder attack. Therefore, our model expresses the information exchanged between the *LRA* and Alice with a private channel (i.e., the adversary is not able to learn or modify any information for this exchange). All others communications are public and then controlled by the intruder and exposed to eventual wiretapping.

The registration of the couple (SN_A, SI_A) in the database is modeled as a state which associate the knowledge of (SN_A, SI_A) to the identity of the *EN*.

Finally, for revocation we have to represent the removal of the certificate from the database. For this we used a tag into a persistent fact to express that the revocation is definitive.

6.4   **Security Properties**

First, we explicit security properties i.e., lemmas, in the case where all entities are supposed honest but in presence of an intruder. As defined in the Sect. 6.1, we have implemented lemmas about correctness, soundness and secrecy of the protocol.

Soundness. The first lemma (**soundness**) proves the soundness of the
LOCALPKI. The couple <sna,sia> represents *SN* the *Serial Number* and
SI the *Signature Id* of Alice. Each label in the lemma represents when
the actual event occurs. The idea is to prove that for all possible cou-
ples <sna,sia> related to the Alice's private key ltkA, if Bob has successfully authenticated Alice at time i (Bob_Auth_Alice()), then it means
that Alice has been previously registered (at time j, by the notary,
EN_Reg_Alice()), and that if the certificate has been revoked
(Cert_Is_Revoked()), then it was at an earlier time k:

```
lemma soundness:
  all-traces
  "All EN B sna sia #i.
  Bob_Auth_Alice(B, <sna,sia>, ltkA) @i
  ==>
  (Ex #j. EN_Reg_Alice(EN, <sna,sia>, ltkA)@j
  & (j<i)) &
  (All #k.
  Cert_Is_Revoked(EN, <sna,sia>, ltkA)@k ==> i<k)"
```

Correctness. The second lemma (**correctness**) ensures that our model is correct, i.e., there exists an execution where Alice is registered, Bob authenticates
Alice and the certificate is not revoked. Thanks to this lemma, we check that
our model realizes the protocol steps in a correct order. Other lemmas in our
modeling also provide sanity checks, for example to show that there exists a
trace where the certificate has been correctly revoked.

```
lemma correctness:
  exists-trace
  "(Ex EN B sna sia ltkA #i #j.
  EN_Reg_Alice_(EN, <sna,sia>, ltkA) @i
  & Bob_Auth_Alice(B,<sna,sia>, ltkA) @j
  & not(Ex EN #l.
  Cert_Is_Revoked(EN, <sna,sia>, ltkA) @l & i<l))"
```

Secrecy. In the secrecy lemma (**secrecy**), we ensure the secrecy of exchanged
messages using a LOCALPKI based authentication. Then, we prove in Tamarin
that the message (denoted x) should not be in the adversary knowledge, written
as K() at any time.

```
lemma secrecy:
  all-traces
  "All x #i. Secret(x) @i ==> not(Ex #j. K(x)@j)"
```

Connection Integrity. Similarly, in the connection integrity lemma
(**connection**), we ensure that the secret key of Alice, ltkA, should not be in
the adversary knowledge neither in the case where Bob authenticates Alice from
her certificate nor in the case where the certificate has been revoked.

```
lemma connection:
  all-traces
  "(All EN sna sia ltkA #i.
    Bob_Auth_Alice(B, <sna,sia>, ltkA)@i
    ==> not(Ex #1. K(ltkA)  @1))
  & (All B sna sia ltkA #i.
    Cert_Is_Revoked(EN, <sna,sia>, ltkA) @i
    ==> not(Ex #1. K(ltkA)  @1))"
```

In other words, whatever subsequent messages sent by any user, Alice's private key remains private.

6.5   Trust Assumptions

Next, we show that our trust assumptions in both the *LRA* and the *EN* are mandatory in order to preserve the security of the protocol (as is the case in *PKIX*). To show this we present attacks on the protocol where one of the entity is malicious i.e. its private key is given to the adversary.

Trust in the EN. In the case where the notary is corrupted, the secrecy is not verified because he is able to add a false key pair to his database. Then after the authentication of Alice by Bob with these keys, a wiretap between communications allows him to retrieve secret exchanged information. Soundness is also falsified: since the adversary has access to the *EN*'s private key, he acts as Alice has been previously registered into the *EN* database whereas she is not. In practice, this attack represents the possibility to the notary of giving to the person of his choice the trust to be authenticated. Concerning the connection integrity property, Tamarin finds an attack as soon as the *EN*'s key is leaked to the adversary. The attack is the following: after its initialization, the *EN* registers himself as Alice. This means that the adversary forges a certificate using Alice's identity, and uses its own private key to sign the certificate. At the next step, Bob authenticates Alice using this certificate, and the adversary knows the associated private key: therefore the connection integrity is broken. First, this attacks highlights the obvious forgery ability of a malicious notary. Second, it shows that the connection integrity property is well-defined. Indeed, such a forgery ruins the integrity, even if the adversary has no knowledge of the Alice's actual private key. This proves that the *EN* should be a trusted entity.

Trust in the LRA. When the *LRA*'s private key is leaked, the tool does not find any attack on the soundness. From a practical point of view, this result makes sense: the *LRA* is only involved into the registration process. Then, even if he provides false information, Alice should be registered before an authentication process. However, by removing the restriction of a unique registration per couple (SN_A, SI_A), the adversary sends a revoked couple to the *EN*, in order to pass over the revocation. In practice, serials numbers are provided by the *EN* so that this attack is easily preventable, by marking the used ones. Secrecy is falsified because the adversary impersonates the *LRA* during the last step of registration, by signing false information (i.e., false key pair). Then, since Bob does not exchange messages with the correct Alice's public key, and a simple wiretap allows the adversary to retrieve secret messages. When the *LRA*'s private key is given to the adversary, the connection integrity is also broken. During this attack, Alice registers herself to the *LRA*. Then the *LRA* modifies Alice's certificate by including its own key pairs: the public one into the certificate, and the private one is used to sign the forged certificate. Then, the fake certificate is sent to the *EN*. Afterwards, suppose that the *EN*, for any reason, decides to revoke this certificate. At this point in time, the *EN* has succeeded in revoking the certificate while the adversary knows the associated private key. Hence, the connection integrity is broken. This attack shows the *LRA* ability to forge certificates. In conclusion, this proves that *LRA* should be a trusted entity.

Trust in Alice. When Alice is corrupted, repercussions on the protocol security are limited. It does not influence soundness property. This result is coherent: even with Alice's private key is given to the adversary, he cannot be authenticated without a previous registering. In practice, a malicious behavior from Alice could be an identity fraud during the registering if the *LRA* has been misled. However, this kind of attacks are out of the Tamarin scope, since ID checking cannot actually be modeled. On secrecy aspects, obviously, if the private key of Alice is leaked, the adversary is able to read the secret messages sent to Alice. This attack could correspond to the Alice's private key theft, where both Alice and the attacker are able to retrieve messages ciphered with the associate public key. Finally, if the private key of Alice is leaked, connection integrity is obviously broken, since the adversary can then use her key. Overall, we conclude that Alice does not need to be a trusted participant.

6.6   Security of the LOCALPKI

From our security analysis, using the Tamarin prover, we have proven the following theorem:

Theorem 1. *If the notary and the local registration authority are not corrupted, then the LOCALPKI security architecture is correct, sound, and preserves confidentiality and integrity.*

Our implementation consists of about 350 source lines of code to describe the model consisting of 20 rules and 4 lemmas. In order to reduce proof timings we have associated each entity to a defined `Role`. Moreover, we have enforced some actions to be unique (denoted as `Only_One`). These constraints are called `axioms` into the code. They avoid generic rewriting of rules either by associating a fixed string to an identity variable or either by implying timepoints equality in case of multiple uses of the same rules. Therefore, using a single core of an *i5 4590@3.50 Ghz* with *8 GB RAM*, we obtain very good performance for the security verification, as shown in Table 1.

Table 1. Timings of Tamarin's proofs of lemmas [11, Tab. 1].

Lemma	CPU time
Correctness:	4.7 s
Soundness:	4.4 s
Connection integrity:	10.9 s
Secrecy:	6.6 s

7 LOCALPKI as an *Internet of Things* PKI

By design, LOCALPKI is made to be deployed into services which are close to end-users. Moreover, this architecture also presents many advantages if used within an highly constrained environments like *Industrial Control Systems* or, more generally, the *Internet of Things* (IoT). IoT is a paradigm where a wide variety of objects, like wireless sensors or mobile phone, are able to interact each others to accomplish a common objective [1,14]. Because of the diversity of the architecture components, reaching security, or at least data integrity and authentication, is arduous. Particularly, this means that no assumption can be made on the computational nor communicating capabilities of the equipment. Another strong constraint of an IoT infrastructure lies into its setup instability: many components are frequently added or removed, and thus the certification process becomes complicated. In the following, we show that using LOCALPKI as a security architecture for the IoT is a solution to some of the previous constraints.

In IoT, we can define a hierarchy: the manufacturer of the objects, the customer, and finally the objects [2]. For instance, one can refer to medical equipment, where the manufacturer sells to the hospital the connected devices. Here, there is a natural analogy with the LOCALPKI actors: the manufacturer is associated with the *EN*, the customer with the *LRA* whereas the *things* represent the end-users, as shown in Fig. 9. Each device is the owner of its own LOCALPKI certificate.

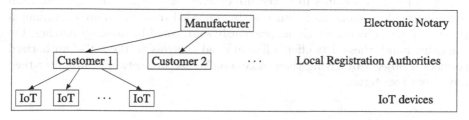

Fig. 9. LOCALPKI as an *Internet of Things* PKI.

The setup works as following: the manufacturer produces his products, and associates to each one of them a *Serial Number*. Then, he sells them to the customer. At this point, the latter is able to generate their certificate according to the protocol 1. Furthermore, the customer (*i.e.* the *LRA*) has the possibility to send by batch all the requests to complete the *EN*'s database. The manufacturer then acts as an Electronic Notary and stores the certificates database. The customers acting as local registration authorities and, potentially with the help of the manufacturer, configure the devices and authorize them onto the network. As already mentioned, then any two devices are able to perform mutual authentication with any challenge-response protocol, like SASL. Note that customers also have the possibility to recover the database and set up their private notary system.

From a practical point of view, this whole scheme allows to generate the certificates out of bands, and then to communicate all the requests at the same time when a connection is available. The global communications volume is quite similar to *PKIX*, but the distribution is different. In LOCALPKI, the majority of the communication is local, *i.e.* it lies between the *LRA* and the end-users, whereas the registration authority of *PKIX* is generally farther. Indeed, before authentication and confidential communication processes, each device sends its public key certificate to each other. For both authentication and confidential communication processes, each device must be sure that the public key of the other device is authentic. To do so, each device can either use the public or private modes of Sect. 3.3.

During the registration process in LOCALPKI, when the end-users and the *LRA* agree on the certificate, the objects are ready to be deployed. On the contrary, with *PKIX* the objects should had to wait for the *Certification Authority* signature. This means that the objects cannot be fully deployed, since they do not have their certificate, until the authority responds to the requests. Here, with LOCALPKI, once the certificate has been created, it is stored into the object, and no more communication with is required between the object and the *EN*. Then, the objects could be immediately distributed. Of course, just like *PKIX*, secure communications are not possible until the *EN* validates the *LRA* requests. The main advantage of LOCALPKI there is thus to be asynchronous.

Furthermore, LOCALPKI provides a more suitable fail-safe system than *PKIX* in IoT. This comes from the use of white lists, which contains the valid certificates. On the one hand, an update is needed to allow secure communications with new objects which, as previously said, could be done by batches. On the other hand, these lists offer a fine-grained controls on the set of authorized connected objects by giving them access on the secure network only after they have been registered.

8 Conclusion

In this paper, we have proposed an alternative public-key infrastructure model, LOCALPKI. This model has been analyzed and its security formally proven using Tamarin. The main feature is that, unlike the *PKIX* standard, here user certificates are self-signed and only the binding of a certificate with an identity is signed by a third-party, a notary in LOCALPKI. Therefore, it is easier for users to use certificates within their local environment. For instance, the registration process can be transferred to the notaries by local businesses, which only have to handle identity verifications. We think that this could foster a wider spread of certificates among everyday end users. For this, notaries just have to maintain an accessible database of fingerprints. Hence, LOCALPKI is an alternative to the *PKIX* solution, providing similar security properties.

Furthermore, we have shown in Sect. 7 that this is particularly well suited to constrained user-environments, such as Industrial Control Systems or, more generally, the Internet of Things. In particular, the asynchronous certification process allows to have an easy and flexible setup. Also, in some cases, the key management of LOCALPKI is better than that of *PKIX*. Another example is for local businesses as a bank, where bank customers have the possibility to look at their account from a website, quite often using a certificate-based authentication. Managing a classical *PKIX* either requires a large internal department or a full delegation of trust to a *PKI* actor. By deploying the LOCALPKI solution, the bank still preserves a local registration, and thus trust and responsibility of its customers, and the technical part of ensuring their authentication is deported to notaries. Overall, the cost and the technical requirements for the company are reduced. Moreover, LOCALPKI also offers to small agencies the possibility to help users for their registration. The economics incentive would be to offer this service only at a moderate cost, where deploying a full *PKI* in every agency should be too expensive.

The main similarities and differences between *PKIX* and LOCALPKI are shown in Table 2:

Table 2. Comparing LOCALPKI and *PKIX*.

	LOCALPKI	*PKIX*
Certificate creation	User & LRA	CA
Certificate signature	User	CA
Certificate registration	EN	/
Default authentication	Interactive (*Private mode*)	Off-line (*CRLs*)
Alternative authentication	Off-line (*Public mode, CVLs*)	Interactive (*OCSP*)
Formal trust	LRA & EN	RA & AC

Finally, as seen in Sect. 5, the overall deployment of LOCALPKI can be made using only existing tools and formats. This facilitates the process, as is demonstrated with our PHP and OpenSSL prototype available implementation: http:// hpac.imag.fr/localpki.

Further work include:

– legal aspect on the shared responsibility of the *LRA* and the *EN* in LOCALPKI should be studied. Indeed, both entities play an important role into the registration and authentication processes. Our first idea is that the *EN* could register the identity of the *LRA* sending information about new users and store this information also within the database. Thus, if this user is recognized as malicious, the *EN* could blame the *LRA*.
– trust enhancement of the authorities, just like for *PKIX*, is also on open problem. Adapting the secure trust computations described in [12] might be easier for LOCALPKI though. There, they compute a global trust by using the trust evaluation of each certification authorities towards the others. This allows to obtain a better hint about the trust given in *CAs*, instead of being based only on the trustfulness given by trust anchors. This method could be relevant to the LOCALPKI architecture, since it is also using the trust anchor mechanism.
– whether this model could also simplify identity-based approaches like certificateless PKI [3,13], for instance using attributes.
– Finally, just like *Let's Encrypt* offers certificates enabling HTTPS (via SSL/TLS) for websites, we have set up a web site offering the possibility to create self-signed LOCALPKI certificates for any user and connected device; we plan to enhance the capabilities of this web-site to manage our other protocols, such as revocation, cross-certification, on-line authentication, database paging, etc.

Acknowledgment. We thank Amaury Huot for his help in implementing the prototype web-based interface to LOCALPKI certificates.

References

1. Atzori, L., Iera, A., Morabito, G.: The internet of things: a survey. Comput. Netw. **54**(15), 2787–2805 (2010). https://doi.org/10.1016/j.comnet.2010.05.010. http://www.sciencedirect.com/science/article/pii/S1389128610001568
2. Badrignans, B., et al.: Security architecture for point-to-point splitting protocols. In: IEEE World Congress on Industrial Control Systems Security, Cambridge, UK, p. 8, December 2017. https://hal.archives-ouvertes.fr/hal-01657605
3. Baek, J., Safavi-Naini, R., Susilo, W.: Certificateless public key encryption without pairing. In: Zhou, J., Lopez, J., Deng, R.H., Bao, F. (eds.) ISC 2005. LNCS, vol. 3650, pp. 134–148. Springer, Heidelberg (2005). https://doi.org/10.1007/11556992_10
4. Basin, D., Cremers, C., Kim, T.H.-J., Perrig, A., Sasse, R., Szalachowski, P.: ARPKI: attack resilient public-key infrastructure. In: Proceedings of the ACM Conference on Computer and Communications Security (CCS), pp. 382–393, November 2014 (2014). https://doi.org/10.1145/2660267.2660298

5. Bau, J., Mitchell, J.C.: A security evaluation of DNSSEC with NSEC3. In: Proceedings of the Network and Distributed System Security Symposium, NDSS 2010, San Diego, California, USA, 28th February–3rd March 2010. The Internet Society (2010). http://www.isoc.org/isoc/conferences/ndss/10/pdf/17.pdf

6. Bouzefrane, S., Garri, K., Thoniel, P.: A user-centric PKI based-protocol to manage FC2 digital identities. IJCSI Int. J. Comput. Sci. Issues 8(1), 74–80 (2011). https://hal.archives-ouvertes.fr/hal-00628633

7. Buterin, V., et al.: Ethereum white paper (2013)

8. Comon-Lundh, H., Cortier, V.: Security properties: two agents are sufficient. Sci. Comput. Program. 50(1–3), 51–71 (2004). https://doi.org/10.1016/j.scico.2003.12.002

9. Cooper, D.: Internet X.509 Public Key Infrastructure Certificate and Certificate Revocation List (CRL) Profile. RFC 5280, May 2008. https://doi.org/10.17487/rfc5280. https://rfc-editor.org/rfc/rfc5280.txt

10. Dolev, D., Yao, A.C.: On the security of public key protocols. In: Proceedings of the 22nd Annual Symposium on Foundations of Computer Science, SFCS 2081, Washington, DC, USA, pp. 350–357. IEEE Computer Society (1981). http://dx.doi.org/10.1109/SFCS.1981.32

11. Dumas, J.-G., Lafourcade, P., Melemedjian, F., Orfila, J.-B., Thoniel, P.: LOCALPKI: a user-centric formally proven alternative to PKIX. In: Proceedings of the 14th International Joint Conference on e-Business and Telecommunications: SECRYPT, (ICETE 2017), vol. 6, pp. 187–199. INSTICC, SciTePress (2017). https://doi.org/10.5220/0006461101870199

12. Dumas, J.-G., Lafourcade, P., Orfila, J.-B., Puys, M.: Private multi-party matrix multiplication and trust computations. In: Proceedings of the 13th International Joint Conference on e-Business and Telecommunications (ICETE 2016), pp. 61–72 (2016). https://doi.org/10.5220/0005957200610072

13. Gentry, C.: Certificate-based encryption and the certificate revocation problem. In: Biham, E. (ed.) EUROCRYPT 2003. LNCS, vol. 2656, pp. 272–293. Springer, Heidelberg (2003). https://doi.org/10.1007/3-540-39200-9_17

14. Giusto, D., Iera, A., Morabito, G., Atzori, L.: The Internet of Things: 20th Tyrrhenian Workshop on Digital Communications. Springer, New York (2010). https://doi.org/10.1007/978-1-4419-1674-7

15. Hall, W.E., Jutla, C.S.: Parallelizable authentication trees. In: Preneel, B., Tavares, S. (eds.) SAC 2005. LNCS, vol. 3897, pp. 95–109. Springer, Heidelberg (2006). https://doi.org/10.1007/11693383_7

16. Kim, T.H.-J., Huang, L.-S., Perrig, A., Jackson, C., Gligor, V.: Accountable key infrastructure (AKI): a proposal for a public-key validation infrastructure. In: Proceedings of the 22nd International Conference on World Wide Web, WWW 2013, New York, NY, USA, pp. 679–690. ACM (2013). http://doi.acm.org/10.1145/2488388.2488448

17. Kolkman, O.M., Mekking, M., Gieben, R.M.: DNSSEC operational practices, Version 2. RFC 6781, December 2012. https://doi.org/10.17487/rfc6781. https://rfc-editor.org/rfc/rfc6781.txt

18. Laurie, B., Langley, A., Kasper, E.: Certificate transparency. RFC 6962, June 2013. https://doi.org/10.17487/RFC6962. https://rfc-editor.org/rfc/rfc6962.txt

19. Meier, S., Schmidt, B., Cremers, C., Basin, D.: The TAMARIN prover for the symbolic analysis of security protocols. In: Sharygina, N., Veith, H. (eds.) CAV 2013. LNCS, vol. 8044, pp. 696–701. Springer, Heidelberg (2013). https://doi.org/10.1007/978-3-642-39799-8_48

20. Merkle, R.C.: A digital signature based on a conventional encryption function. In: Pomerance, C. (ed.) CRYPTO 1987. LNCS, vol. 293, pp. 369–378. Springer, Heidelberg (1988). https://doi.org/10.1007/3-540-48184-2_32

21. Morrison, D.R.: PATRICIA - practical algorithm to retrieve information coded in alphanumeric. J. ACM **15**(4), 514–534 (1968). https://doi.org/10.1145/321479.321481

22. Muñoz, J.L., Esparza, O., Forné, J., Pallares, E.: H-OCSP: a protocol to reduce the processing burden in online certificate status validation. Electron. Commer. Res. **8**(4), 255 (2008). https://doi.org/10.1007/s10660-008-9024-y

23. Peylo, M., Kause, T.: Internet X.509 Public Key Infrastructure - HTTP Transfer for the Certificate Management Protocol (CMP). RFC 6712, September 2012. http://dx.doi.org/10.17487/rfc6712. https://rfc-editor.org/rfc/rfc6712.txt

24. Reddy, R., Wallace, C.: Trust anchor management requirements. RFC 6024, RFC Editor, October 2010. https://rfc-editor.org/rfc/rfc6024.txt

25. Ryan, M.D.: Enhanced certificate transparency and end-to-end encrypted mail. In: 21st Annual Network and Distributed System Security Symposium, NDSS 2014, San Diego, California, USA, 23–26 February 2014. The Internet Society (2014). http://www.internetsociety.org/doc/enhanced-certificate-transparency-and-end-end-encrypted-mail

26. Santesson, S., Ankney, R., Myers, M., Malpani, A., Galperin, S., Adams, D.C.: X.509 Internet Public Key Infrastructure Online Certificate Status Protocol - OCSP. RFC 6960, June 2013. https://doi.org/10.17487/rfc6960. https://rfc-editor.org/rfc/rfc6960.txt

27. Schmidt, B., Meier, S., Cremers, C.J.F., Basin, D.A.: Automated analysis of Diffie-Hellman protocols and advanced security properties. In: Chong, S. (ed.) 25th IEEE Computer Security Foundations Symposium, CSF 2012, Cambridge, MA, USA, 25–27 June 2012, pp. 78–94. IEEE Computer Society (2012). http://dx.doi.org/10.1109/CSF.2012.25

28. Vcelak, J., Goldberg, S., Papadopoulos, D.: NSEC5, DNSSEC Authenticated Denial of Existence. Internet-Draft draft-vcelak-nsec5-03, Internet Engineering Task Force, September 2016 (2016, Work in Progress). https://tools.ietf.org/html/draft-vcelak-nsec5-03

29. Yu, J., Cheval, V., Ryan, M.: DTKI: a new formalized PKI with verifiable trusted parties. Comput. J. **59**(11), 1695–1713 (2016). https://doi.org/10.1093/comjnl/bxw039

30. Zimmermann, P.R.: The Official PGP User's Guide. MIT Press, Cambridge (1995)

No Such Thing as a Small Leak: Leakage-Abuse Attacks Against Symmetric Searchable Encryption

Alexandre Anzala-Yamajako[1], Olivier Bernard[2], Matthieu Giraud[3(✉)], and Pascal Lafourcade[3]

[1] European Patent Office, Munich, Germany
ayamajakoanzala@epo.org
[2] Laboratoire Chiffre, THALES Communications and Security, Gennevilliers, France
olivier.bernard2@thalesgroup.com
[3] Université Clermont Auvergne, LIMOS, Aubière, France
{matthieu.giraud,pascal.lafourcade}@uca.fr

Abstract. *Symmetric Searchable Encryption* (SSE) schemes enable clients to securely outsource their data while maintaining the ability to perform keywords search over it. The security of these schemes is based on an explicit leakage profile [1], has initiated the investigation into how much information could be deduced in practice from this leakage. In this paper, after recalling the leakage hierarchy introduced in 2015 by Cash et al. and the passive attacks of [1] on SSE schemes. We demonstrate the effectiveness of these attacks on a wider set of real-world datasets than previously shown. On the other hand, we show that the attacks are inefficient against some types of datasets. Finally, we used what we learned from the unsuccessful datasets to give insight into future countermeasures.

Keywords: Symmetric Searchable Encryption · Leakage
Passive attacks

1 Introduction

The importance of digital data in everyday life is no longer in doubt. Their handling must be done with care leading to create and manage backups. To have access to those backups from anywhere and from different devices, outsourcing this digital data to a cloud provider is an enticing solution. The character of this data can be sensitive and/or confidential since some of this data are legal documents, banking and medical, industrial patents or emails. However, we host this digital data in all sorts of untrusted environments, potentially with unknown server administrators, OS and hypervisors. The trivial solution for a client is to use symmetric encryption. Indeed, since data is encrypted with a secret key unknown by the cloud provider, data confidentiality is no longer a problem. However, symmetric encryption prevents any server-side processing of the client

© Springer Nature Switzerland AG 2019
M. S. Obaidat and E. Cabello (Eds.): ICETE 2017, CCIS 990, pp. 253–277, 2019.
https://doi.org/10.1007/978-3-030-11039-0_12

data as is the norm on plaintext data. In particular, the processing of search queries by the server sent by the client is no longer possible. Indeed, if the client gives a keyword to the server, the latter cannot retrieves the documents containing that keyword since documents are encrypted. On the other hand, fully homomorphic encryption [2] allows the server to execute directly in the encrypted domain search operation needed to answer search queries. Unfortunately, such an approach would solve our problem only from a theoretical point of view because making a fully homomorphic encryption scheme work in practice remains an open question (as noted e.g., in [2]). *Symmetric Searchable Encryption* (SSE) schemes introduced by Song et al. in [3] aim at retaining this search capability on encrypted data. SSE scheme is a protocol executed between a client and a server. We consider a client owning a sensitive/confidential set of plaintext documents stored in a *DataBase* denoted DB. We assume that this client has limited computational power and storage capacity. On other hand, we consider a server having a large storage space and high processing power. This server is *honest-but-curious* [4], i.e., it is not trusted by the client except for executing correctly the search protocol. First, an SSE scheme creates, from DB, metadata that is protected in an *Encrypted DataBase* (EDB). Then the client outsources EDB on the server along with the encryptions of the documents. After that, the client can send a search token generated from a keyword and her symmetric secret key. With this search token, the server can find the encrypted documents matching the query with the help of EDB. Finally, the corresponding encrypted documents are sent back to the client for decryption. The basic functionality of an SSE scheme is to retrieve the encrypted documents matching one single keyword query. However, there exist SSE schemes allowing the client to add new encrypted documents to the encrypted database while retaining the search capability; these schemes are called *dynamic* SSE [5,6]. Others SSE schemes focus on expanding the expressiveness of the search queries such as Boolean [7] and sub-string search queries [8].

By its nature, a SSE scheme reveals to an observer the *search* pattern, indicating which other queries were also for the considered keyword and representing the fact that SSE scheme sends the same search token when a search is repeated. It also reveals the *access* pattern, showing the identifiers of documents concerned by the search token. This kind of information leaked by a given SSE scheme to the server is formalized by a *leakage function* [6,9]. The security of a SSE scheme is based on this function proving that the scheme does not leak more information than described in the leakage function. However, this leaked information can be used by an honest-but-curious server executing dutifully the scheme to deduce information on the stored documents. For instance, some *inference attacks* [10–12] use these search and access patterns to reconstruct DB. In this paper, we show that it is possible to reconstruct DB without using the search and access pattern leading to passive attacks. We focus on the information revealed by the encrypted database EDB regardless exchanges between the client and the server. We argue that this model is realistic since it allows for the server itself (or any entity having access to the encrypted database, as the server administrator or the OS) to be malicious by manipulating the leaked information. Based on deployed SSE schemes, Cash et al. [11] define four *leakage profiles* L4, L3, L2 and L1 depending on leaked information by the schemes. The L4 profile represents SSE schemes that are the most leaky while the L1 profile represents the least leaky schemes. Commercially available SSE solutions such as CipherCloud[1] and Skyhigh Networks[2] are L4 schemes, while Bitglass[3] (resp. ShadowCrypt[4]) is a L3 scheme (resp. L2 scheme). On the contrary, most SSE schemes proposed in academic research have L1 profile. The advantage of the L4-, L3- and L2-SSE schemes is that they can be set up as a proxy or as extensions in client-side. Indeed, no modification on server-side is necessary. Although these solutions are tempting, it is important to study the practical impacts of these information leaks on the document knowledge of the server. In this paper, we study the impact of a passive attacker (as the server storing EDB).

Our Contributions. We design passive attacks against SSE schemes of L4, L3 and L2 leakage profiles in order to reconstruct as much as possible the database DB. Our attacks do not rely on observing search queries, neither on the access pattern. We assume that the server, storing the encrypted documents and the encrypted database EDB, only knows a small sample of plaintexts. Using this known sample and the leaked information by the scheme on the encrypted database EDB, we start by finding the identifiers in the encrypted database associated to the plain documents of the sample. This first step leads to correspondences between plain documents and their representation in the encrypted database. Then, the adversary considers each correspondence and tries to deduce values of plain keywords in the encrypted database. Since L4-, L3- and L2-SSE schemes replace each plain keywords by the same value, these keywords-values associations are used to recover other documents that are not in the sample known by the adversary. Our attack on L4 schemes uses repetitions and order of keywords in each document, our attack on L3 schemes uses order of shared keywords between documents while our attack on L2 schemes uses only information on shared keywords between documents. We demonstrate that the efficiency and practicality of our three passive attacks depend on the nature of the data set. In fact, when we consider data sets such as mailing-list, emails, or books, we show that an adversary knowing only 1% of plain documents is able to reconstruct between 65% and 90% of the protected data at 80%. On the contrary, when we consider data sets constituted of server logs or of movies descriptions, our attacks are practically inefficient. In fact, if the adversary knows only 1% of plain documents, she is able to reconstruct at most less than 5% of the protected data at 80% for SSE schemes of L4 and L3 leakage profile, while she is not able to do any associations when we consider SSE scheme of L2 leakage profile.

Related Work. Considering an *active* adversary that is able to add chosen documents in the database of the client, Cash et al. [11] present a partial document

---

[1] https://ciphercloud.com/technologies/encryption/.
[2] https://skyhighnetworks.com/product/salesforce-security/.
[3] https://bitglass.com/salesforce-security.
[4] https://shadowcrypt-release.weebly.com/.

recovery attack on L3- and L2-SSE schemes using frequency distribution of keywords hashes. Moreover, Zhang et al. [13] consider an adversary that has the extra ability to issue selected queries and mount a query recovery attack that works on any dynamic SSE scheme. These active attacks are very efficient. They reveal associations between keywords and search tokens with only few injected files. Contrary to these attacks, we consider only a passive adversary who is not able to plant document in the database or to issue particular queries.

An other family of attacks, based on the search pattern and the access pattern have been also proposed and are called *inference attacks*. The first one is the *IKK Attack* and has been proposed by Islam et al. [10]. The goal of their attack is to associate search tokens sent by the client to actual keywords. In order to do that, they exploit the data access pattern revealed by client queries and assume that the adversary has access to a co-occurrence matrix. Each element of the co-occurrence matrix corresponds to the probability that two keywords appear in a randomly chosen document. However, Cash et al. [11] stress that this matrix needs to be so precise for the attack to succeed. This precision legitimates the assumption that the adversary has access to the number of documents in which every keyword appears. With this strong extra knowledge, authors mount a more effective attack named the *Count Attack* [11]. These two attacks target SSE schemes of L1 leakage profile. However, the strength of their assumptions questions their practicality. On the contrary, our attacks do not rely on observing client queries but only assume that the adversary knows the encrypted database, which totally natural when we consider the server as the adversary. In a different way, Abdelraheem et al. [14] proposed an inference attack when a client protect a relational database with a SSE scheme. Exploiting the structural properties of relational databases, the authors show that record-injection attacks mounted on relational databases have worse consequences than their file-injection counterparts on unstructured databases as data sets that we consider.

Cash et al. [11] also proposed a passive attack concerning L3-SSE schemes to partially recover documents when the adversary knows plaintext-ciphertext pairs. Unlike them, our attacks suppose that we do not have any plaintext-ciphertext pairs initially. An other inference attack proposed by Pouliot and Wright in [12] and called *Shadow Nemesis Attack* uses a training data set in order to build a co-occurrence matrix as in [11]. This co-occurrence matrix is then reduced to the problem of matching search tokens to keywords to the combinatorial optimization problem of weighted graph matching. The *Shadow Nemesis Attack* can be performed on L2-SSE schemes as our attacks. While our attacks use a sample of plain documents of the original database DB, their attack can use a training data set instead of a partial knowledge of the original data set in addition of the encrypted database.

Wang et al. [15] also present inference attacks on searchable encryption. As we do, they consider passive attacks where an adversary knows a subset of documents. Authors propose an other leakage model where the one-to-one mapping between keywords and tokens change to a one-to-many mapping (as used in Mimesis aegis [16]), increasing the difficulty of statistical analysis. They algorithms and attacks follow the same idea as our paper [1] then without any surprise they results are similar to our results. Moreover they claim that our attacks cannot be applied to index-based SSE schemes, which is not true at all.

Our article is an extended version of [1]. The main difference is that we selected nine different datasets samples and evaluate the impact of our attacks showing that the efficiency of our passive attacks depends on the nature of the data sets. Indeed, we show that our attacks are very efficient against database containing books, emails or mailing-list. On the contrary, data sets such as server logs or movies descriptions are resistant to such passive attacks. Moreover, we give statistic measures the different data sets, including the number of documents sharing the same length in L4 point of view, the number of documents sharing the same length in the L3 point of view, and the occurrence of each keywords for each data set. We experiment our attacks on these samples as detailed in Sect. 5, and we also add results of our attacks for three datasets in full among the selected samples, namely *Commons*, *Hadoop*, and *Lucene*.

Outline. We start by providing background on SSE schemes and their security recalling notations in Sect. 2. Then we recall in Sect. 3 the leakage hierarchy of SSE schemes presented in [11]. We describe our new passive attacks in Sect. 4 and we demonstrate their effectiveness in Sect. 5 before to conclude in Sect. 6.

2 Symmetric Searchable Encryption

The notations and definitions provided in this section are shorter version of the ones presented in [1]. They have been included here to ease the reader understanding of SSE schemes but the reader is refered to [1] for a more complete presentation.

2.1 Notations

Sequences, Lists and Sets. We define a sequence of elements as an ordered set where repetitions are allowed. A list is therefore an ordered set where all elements are distinct, i.e., there is no repetition. Finally, a set is defined as an unordered bunch of distinct elements. We denote sequences by parenthesis $(\dots)$, lists by square brackets $[\dots]$ and sets by braces $\{\dots\}$. Let E be a set (resp. list or sequence), then we denote the number of elements in E by $\#E$.

Documents and Keywords. Let $\mathsf{DB} = \{d_1, \dots, d_n\}$ be a set of n documents. We recall that DB is called the *data set*. Each document of DB is composed of keyword belonging to a dictionary $\mathsf{W} = \{w_1, \dots, w_m\}$ made of m keywords. Moreover, each document $d_i \in \mathsf{DB}$ is a sequence of length ℓ_i, in other terms $d_i = (w_{i_1}, \dots, w_{i_{\ell_i}}) \in \mathsf{W}^{\ell_i}$. We denote by W_i the set of distinct keywords of the document d_i, i.e., $\mathsf{W}_i = \{[d_i]\}$.

When the same objects are considered on server-side, we describe them by introducing the star superscript. Hence, we denote the set of search tokens associated to the keywords of W by $\mathsf{W}^* = \{w_1^*, \dots, w_m^*\}$. In the same way, we denote the set of ciphertexts of DB by $\mathsf{DB}^* = \{d_1^*, \ldots, d_n^*\}$ where d_i^* is the encryption of d_i. Finally, we denote the set of tokens associated to d_i^* by W_i^*. Since the association between d_i and d_i^* is not known by the server a priori, we use an identifier, denoted id_i, to uniquely represent d_i^*. Moreover, a datastructure EDB is also provided. It contains protected metadata that allows the server to answer search queries sent by the client.

Considering a keyword w, we denote by $\mathsf{DB}(w)$ the list of all the indices i such that $d_i \in \mathsf{DB}$ contains the keyword w. We denote by N, the number of pairs (d, w) where $d \in \mathsf{DB}$ and $w \in d$, i.e. $N = \#\{(d, w) \mid d \in \mathsf{DB}, w \in d\}$. We remark that N corresponds to a lower bound on the size of EDB. Indeed, N can always be computed by the server from EDB. Server-side, the list of the identifiers of all the documents $d_i^* \in \mathsf{DB}^*$ associated to the search token w^* is denoted $\mathsf{EDB}(w^*)$. We stress that this information is not accessible directly from w^* and DB^*, we need the extra protected metadata structure EDB.

2.2 SSE Schemes

The basic definition of a symmetric encryption scheme is given with an algorithm for setup and another for search.

First, the client generates two datastructures denoted DB^* and EDB. As defined above, DB^* is composed of ciphertexts of DB, and EDB contains protected metadata associated to DB. Then the client outsources these two datastructures to the server. Assuming the client wants to search for a specific keyword w, she computes with the help of her secret key the search token w^* associated to w, and sends it to the server. When the server receives the search token w^* from the client, the server uses EDB to return the identifiers of all encrypted documents matching the client's search. From this list of identifiers, the client retrieves the associated ciphertexts and decrypt them in order to obtain the plaintext documents. We stress that the server should not be able to learn anything about the client's query or the returned documents during the process. For further details, see Definition 1.

Definition 1 (Static SSE scheme [9]). *Given a symmetric encryption scheme $(\mathcal{E}.(\cdot), \mathcal{D}.(\cdot))$ we define a static SSE scheme of security parameter λ as a quartet of polynomial-time algorithms $\Pi = (\mathsf{Gen}, \mathsf{Setup}, \mathsf{SearchClient}, \mathsf{SearchServer})$ by:*

$(K, k) \leftarrow \mathsf{Gen}(1^\lambda)$ *is a probabilistic key generation algorithm that is run by the client. It takes as input a security parameter λ, and outputs two symmetric secret keys K and k which are both kept securely by the client.*

$(\mathsf{EDB}, \mathsf{DB}^*) \leftarrow \mathsf{Setup}(K, k, \mathsf{DB}, \mathcal{E}.(\cdot))$ *is an algorithm that is run by the client to set the scheme up. It takes as input secret keys K and k, the database DB and the algorithm $\mathcal{E}.(\cdot)$, and outputs both the protected metadata EDB and the encrypted documents $\mathsf{DB}^* = (\mathcal{E}_k(d_1), \ldots, \mathcal{E}_k(d_n))$.*

$w^* \leftarrow \mathsf{SearchClient}(K, w)$ *is a deterministic algorithm that is run by the client to send a query to the server. It takes as input the secret key K and a keyword queried $w \in \mathsf{W}$, and outputs the search token $w^* \in \mathsf{W}^*$ associated with w. Finally w^* is sent to the server.*

$\mathsf{EDB}(w^*) \leftarrow \mathsf{SearchServer}(\mathsf{EDB}, w^*)$ *is a deterministic algorithm that is run by the server to answer a client-query. It takes as input the protected metadata* EDB *and the client-generated search token* w^* *and outputs* $\mathsf{EDB}(w^*)$: *the identifiers of the encrypted documents containing keyword w. This list is sent back to the client.*

2.3   Security of SSE Schemes

The notion of a *leakage function* of a SSE scheme has been introduced by Curtmola et al. [9]. The leakage function, denoted $\mathcal{L}$, of a SSE scheme is the set of information revealed by the SSE scheme to the server. It formalizes the information leaked to the server by both the encrypted database EDB and by the client queries.

An SSE scheme is said to be $\mathcal{L}$-secure if no information other than what is described by the leakage function is leaked by the SSE scheme to the server. More precisely, the $\mathcal{L}$-security of a SSE scheme proves that any polynomial-time adversary making a sequence of queries, constitued of keywords of W, can successfully tell with only negligible probability whether the protocol is honestly executed or simulated from the leakage function $\mathcal{L}$.

Although the leakage function described a bound of leaked information by the SSE scheme on the stored documents, it does not tell us what this leakage implies *in practice* on the knowledge of the protected data. The objective of [1] was to present algorithms that gave more insight into the practical impact of such leakage for the different leakage profiles presented above. In this work we focus on the difference of effectiveness of those algorithms when faced with different document sets and investigate the reasons for those differences.

3   A Leakage Hierarchy

Similarly as in Sect. 2, this section is a shorter version of the content presented in [1]. It has been included here for the article to be self-contained but the reader is referred to [1] for a more complete presentation.

L4 *Leakage Profile.* Without taking in consideration the meaning of words, a document is described by the number of its words, their order and their occurrence. Moreover, a document can be described by words shared with other documents. L4-SSE schemes reveal this information, so nothing is lost about the plaintext non-semantic structure. So, a SSE scheme of leakage function $\mathcal{L}$ is of class L4 if and only if:
$$\mathcal{L}(\mathsf{EDB}) = \left\{(w^*_{i_1}, \ldots, w^*_{i_{\ell_i}})\right\}_{1 \leqslant i \leqslant n}.$$

L3 *Leakage Profile.* For keyword search purposes, it is not necessary to know the occurrence count of each keyword. L3-SSE schemes of leakage function $\mathcal{L}$ do not reveal this, i.e.:
$$\mathcal{L}(\mathsf{EDB}) = \left\{\mathsf{L3}_{\mathsf{EDB}}(\mathsf{id}_i)\right\}_{1 \leqslant i \leqslant n},$$
where $\mathsf{L3}_{\mathsf{EDB}}(\mathsf{id}_i) = [(w^*_{i_1}, \ldots, w^*_{i_{\ell_i}})].$

L2 *Leakage Profile.* L2-SSE schemes only reveal the set of tokens of a document. The server can however still determine which documents contain a given token. A SSE scheme of leakage function $\mathcal{L}$ is of class L2 if and only if:

$$\mathcal{L}(\mathsf{EDB}) = \left\{ W_i^* \right\}_{1 \leqslant i \leqslant n}.$$

L1 *Leakage Profile.* With no initial search, L1-SSE schemes leak the least possible amount of information, i.e. the number N of document/keyword pairs of the dataset:

$$\mathcal{L}(\mathsf{EDB}) = \{N\}.$$

4   Partial Plaintext Recovery Attacks

The attacks presented in [1] are briefly recalled here. As previously pointed out, a more complete presentation can be found in [1]. We start by recalling the intuition behind the attacks as well some facts regarding their applicability.

These are passive attacks which aim at recovering plaintext information from the sole knowledge of EDB. The only assumption made here is that we know a small sample $\mathcal{S}$ chosen randomly among the set of plaintext documents.

The attacks proceed in two steps. In the first step, each plaintext of $\mathcal{S}$ is associated to its protected information in EDB. This step is performed using statistical properties that can be computed independently from the plaintexts themselves or from the associated leakage given in EDB. The efficiency of the attack heavily depends on the statistic capacity to give unique results over the dataset. In the second step, the keywords of the plaintexts are paired with their tokens. The matching keywords and tokens obtained can be spread back into EDB thus recovering content of the encrypted documents. [1] presented very positive results and the application of these same attacks to different datasets allows to gain more insights into their computational complexity as well as intuition for potential countermeasures. Those results are presented in Sect. 5.

4.1   Mask Attack on L4-SSE Schemes

We introduce the *mask* of a document d_i (resp. id_i), denoted by $\mathsf{mask}(d_i)$ (resp. $\mathsf{mask}(\mathsf{id}_i)$), as the sequence where all keywords (resp. tokens) are replaced by their position of first appearance.

The idea of the attack is intuitive: for each plaintext $d \in \mathcal{S}$, the mask of d is computed; this mask is then compared with all masks of corresponding length computed from EDB. The attack is summarized in Algorithm 1.

4.2   Co-Mask Attack on L3-SSE Schemes

Here, we introduce the *co-resulting mask* of a pair (d_1, d_2) of documents, denoted by $\mathsf{comask}(d_1, d_2)$. Intuitively, it can be viewed as the mask of positions of shared

Algorithm 1. Mask Attack.

Input: EDB, $\mathcal{S} \subseteq$ DB

Output: Set of tokens $W^*_{rec} \subseteq W^*$ associated to their keyword in W

foreach $d \in \mathcal{S}$ **do**

   | $A_d = \{i \mid \ell_i = \#d \text{ and } \mathsf{mask}(id_i) = \mathsf{mask}(d)\}$;

end

return $W^*_{rec} = \{W^*_i \mid \#A_{d_i} = 1\}$

---

keywords in the other document. More formally, if $\mathsf{Pos}(w, d)$ is the position of keyword w in document $[d]$, we define:

$$\mathsf{comask}(d_1, d_2) = \Big(\big(\mathsf{Pos}(d_1[i], d_2)\big)_{1 \le i \le \#W_1}, \ \big(\mathsf{Pos}(d_2[i], d_1)\big)_{1 \le i \le \#W_2} \Big).$$

The co-resulting mask can also be computed directly from every pair of encrypted identifiers so by abuse of notation we denote it denoted by $\mathsf{comask}(id_1, id_2)$.

In practice, instead of randomly searching for matching pairs we iteratively construct a set A_t containing all t-tuples of identifiers such that the co-resulting masks of all pairs in the t-uple match the co-resulting masks of the corresponding pairs in $(d_1, \ldots, d_t) \subseteq \mathcal{S}$. More formally:

$$A_t = \Big\{ (id_{i_1}, \ldots, id_{i_t}) \mid \forall s, u \le t, \ \mathsf{comask}(id_{i_s}, id_{i_u}) = \mathsf{comask}(d_s, d_u) \Big\}.$$

The Co-Mask attack is summarized in Algorithm 2.

Algorithm 2. Co-Mask Attack.

Input: EDB, $\mathcal{S} = \big(d_1, \ldots, d_{\#\mathcal{S}}\big) \subseteq$ DB

Output: Set of tokens $W^*_{rec} \subseteq W^*$ associated to their keyword in W

```
/* Consider the first pair of documents                          */
```
$A_2 = \left\{ (id_{i_1}, id_{i_2}) \mid \begin{array}{l} \#id_{i_1} = \#[d_1], \ \#id_{i_2} = \#[d_2] \\ \text{and } \mathsf{comask}(id_{i_1}, id_{i_2}) = \mathsf{comask}(d_1, d_2) \end{array} \right\}$;
```
/* Construct A_t from A_{t-1} using d_t                           */
```
for $t = 3$ **to** $\#\mathcal{S}$ **do**

     $A_t = A_{t-1} \times \{id \mid \#id = \#[d_t]\}$;

```
    /* A_t will be reduced by considering all new pairs (d_j, d_t)  */
```

     foreach $j < t$ **do**

        $C_{j,t} = \left\{ (id_{i_j}, id_{i_t}) \mid \begin{array}{l} id_{i_j} \in A_t[j], \ id_{i_t} \in A_t[t] \\ \text{and } \mathsf{comask}(id_{i_j}, id_{i_t}) = \mathsf{comask}(d_j, d_t) \end{array} \right\}$;

        $A_t = \{a \in A_t \mid (a[j], a[t]) \in C_{j,t}\}$;   /* Keep consistent t-tuples */

        if $\#A_t = 1$ **then** break

     end

end

return $W^*_{rec} = \{W^*_t \mid \#A_{\#\mathcal{S}}[t] = 1\}$

4.3   PowerSet Attack on L2-SSE Schemes

The loss of keyword-order information under L2 leakage presents us with two new challenges: first, the co-resulting mask cannot be computed and second, even if a document is correctly associated to its identifier, finding the correct association between each keyword and its token is still to be done. The PowerSet Attack addresses both issues.

Associating Documents and Identifiers. We introduce the *power set of order h* of a list of t documents, denoted by $\mathsf{PowerSet}_h^t(d_1, \ldots, d_t)$, and defined as the sequence of the $\binom{t}{h}$ cardinals of all possible intersections of h elements of the t-uple.

More formally:

$$\mathsf{PowerSet}_h^t(d_1, \ldots, d_t) = \left(\# \bigcap_{1 \leq j \leq h} d_{i_j} \right)_{1 \leq i_1 < \cdots < i_h \leq t}.$$

The superscript will be omitted when it is clear from the context and since this sequence can also be computed directly from the list of encrypted identifiers so by abuse of notation we denote it by $\mathsf{PowerSet}_h(\mathsf{id}_1, \ldots, \mathsf{id}_t)$.

We again iteratively construct a set A_t containing all t-tuples of identifiers such that all power sets of order less than t correspond to the power sets of the corresponding documents in $(d_1, \ldots, d_t) \in \mathcal{S}$. When t reaches $\#\mathcal{S}$, all information on $\mathcal{S}$ has been processed and singleton components of $A_{\#\mathcal{S}}$ give a correct association.

Let $A_t^{(h)}$ be the set of compatible t-tuples with all power sets of order up to h:

$$A_t^{(h)} = \left\{ (\mathsf{id}_{i_1}, \ldots, \mathsf{id}_{i_t}) \;\middle|\; \forall s \leq h, \quad \begin{array}{c} \mathsf{PowerSet}_s(d_1, \ldots, d_t) \\ = \mathsf{PowerSet}_s(\mathsf{id}_{i_1}, \ldots, \mathsf{id}_{i_t}) \end{array} \right\}.$$

The algorithm then computes the following decreasing sequence, using the procedure Reduce given in Algorithm 3 to go from $A_t^{(h)}$ to $A_t^{(h+1)}$:

$$A_{t-1} \times \{\mathsf{id} \mid \#\mathsf{id} = \#\{d_t\}\} = A_t^{(1)} \supseteq A_t^{(2)} \supseteq A_t^{(3)} \supseteq \cdots \supseteq A_t^{(t)} = A_t.$$

Algorithm 4 summarizes the first phase of the PowerSet Attack.

Associating Keywords and Tokens. As token order is not preserved under L2 leakage, finding the correct keyword-token associations remains non-trivial.

To solve this problem, we construct the *inverted index* of $\mathcal{S}_0$, denoted by $\mathsf{inv}(\mathcal{S}_0)$, which associates the keywords $w \in \mathcal{S}_0$ and to the identifiers of the documents containing w. This inverted index is then ordered by decreasing number of identifiers to form the *ordered inverted index* $\mathsf{inv}_{\geq}(\mathcal{S}_0)$.

The keyword/token association process is given in Algorithm 5.

Algorithm 3. Reduce procedure: computing $A_t^{(h+1)}$ from $A_t^{(h)}$.

Input: $\mathcal{S}_t = (d_1, \ldots, d_t)$, h-order candidates $A_t^{(h)}$
Output: Set of $(h + 1)$-order candidates $A_t^{(h+1)}$

$B_t = A_t^{(h)}$;
/* Consider each subset of $(h + 1)$ elements containing d_t */
foreach $1 \leq j_1 < \cdots < j_h < t$ **do**

$\quad C_{j,t} = \left\{ \left((\mathrm{id}_{i_j}), \mathrm{id}_{i_t}\right) \mid \begin{array}{l} \mathrm{id}_t \in B_t[t], \ (\mathrm{id}_{i_j}) \in B_t[j], \\ \text{and } \#\left(\mathrm{id}_{i_t} \cap (\mathrm{id}_{i_j})\right) = \#(d_t \cap (d_j)) \end{array} \right\}$;

$\quad B_t = \{b \in B_t \mid ((b[j]), b[t]) \in C_{j,t}\}$;   /* Keep consistent t-tuples */
$\quad$ **if** $\#B_t = 1$ **then** break
end
return $A_t^{(h+1)} = B_t$

Algorithm 4. PowerSet Attack: documents-identifiers association.

Input: EDB, $\mathcal{S} = (d_1, \ldots, d_{\#\mathcal{S}}) \subseteq \mathrm{DB}$
Output: Set of documents $\mathcal{S}_0 \subseteq \mathcal{S}$ associated to their identifiers in EDB

/* Consider the first pair of documents   */
$A_2 = \left\{ \left(\mathrm{id}_{i_1}, \mathrm{id}_{i_2}\right) \mid \begin{array}{l} \#\mathrm{id}_{i_1} = \#\{d_1\}, \ \#\mathrm{id}_{i_2} = \#\{d_2\} \\ \text{and } \mathsf{PowerSet}_2(\mathrm{id}_{i_1}, \mathrm{id}_{i_2}) = \mathsf{PowerSet}_2(d_1, d_2) \end{array} \right\}$;
/* Construct A_t from A_{t-1} using d_t */
for $t = 3$ to $\#\mathcal{S}$ **do**

$\quad A_t^{(1)} = A_{t-1} \times \{\mathrm{id} \mid \#\mathrm{id} = \#\{d_t\}\}$;
$\quad$ /* Consider intersections of increasing order h to reduce A_t */
$\quad$ **for** $h = 2$ to t **do**
$\quad\quad A_t^{(h)} = \mathsf{Reduce}\left(A_t^{(h-1)}\right)$;
$\quad\quad$ **if** $\#A_t^{(h)} = 1$ **then** set $A_t = A_t^{(h)}$ and break
$\quad$ **end**
end
return $\mathcal{S}_0 = \{d_t \mid \#A_{\#\mathcal{S}}[t] = 1\}$

Algorithm 5. PowerSet Attack: keywords-tokens association.

Input: EDB, set $\mathcal{S}_0 \subseteq \mathcal{S}$ of documents associated to their identifiers
Output: Set of tokens $\mathsf{W}^*_{\mathrm{rec}} \subseteq \mathsf{W}^*$ associated to their keyword in W

$\mathsf{W}^*_{\mathrm{ign}} \leftarrow \emptyset$;   /* Contains associated and indistinguishable tokens */
Compute $\mathrm{inv}_{\geq}(\mathcal{S}_0)$;
foreach $w \in \mathrm{inv}_{\geq}(\mathcal{S}_0)$ *taken in decreasing order* **do**

$\quad A_w = \left(\bigcap \{\mathsf{W}^*_i \mid \mathrm{id}_i \in \mathrm{inv}_{\geq}(\mathcal{S}_0)[w]\}\right) \setminus \mathsf{W}^*_{\mathrm{ign}}$;
$\quad \mathsf{W}^*_{\mathrm{ign}} = \mathsf{W}^*_{\mathrm{ign}} \cup A_w$; /* Associated ($\#A_w = 1$) or indistinguishable */
end
return $\mathsf{W}^*_{\mathrm{rec}} = \{A_w \mid \#A_w = 1\}$

---

5 Experimental Results

Before to present the experimental results, we describe the datasets on which we ran the attacks of [1] reintroduced in Sect. 4.

5.1 Real-World Datasets

The attacks presented in Sect. 4 were ran on different real-world datasets to evaluate their practical efficiency. We choose 9 datasets and for each dataset, we select a random sample of 2,000 documents where we apply our attacks. We summarized the different samples in Fig. 1. We recall that #DB is the number of documents in the dataset, #W is the number of distinct keywords in the dataset, and N denotes the number of pairs (d, w) where $d \in$ DB and $w \in d$.

Dataset	Content	#DB	#W	N
Gutenberg	books	2,000	527,999	8,153,007
Commons	mailing list	2,000	40,924	264,554
Hadoop	mailing list	2,000	46,097	343,428
Lucene	mailing list	2,000	38,619	269,718
Subversion	mailing list	1,909	35,190	319,845
Enron	emails	2,000	25,998	184,202
Wikipedia	articles	2,000	60,379	335,620
IMDb	movie database	2,000	5,671	20,457
Nasa	server logs	2,000	2,280	17,971

Fig. 1. Details on selected samples of the datasets.

The first dataset sample is the *Project Gutenberg* dataset [17] containing full texts of public domain books. The next four datasets samples are mailing lists from the *Apache* foundation, namely *Apache Commons* [18], *Apache Hadoop* [19], *Apache Lucene* [20], and *Apache Subversion* [21]. The following dataset sample is the email dataset from the *Enron* corporation, available online [22]. Then, the *Wikipedia* dataset sample is formed of articles coming from the online encyclopedia Wikipedia[5]. The following dataset is *IMDb* [23], it is composed of movies descriptions as an alphanumeric unique identifier of the title, the type/format of the title (e.g. movie, short, video, etc.), the more popular title, the original title, the release and the end years, the primary runtime of the title, and the genre. The final dataset is *Nasa* consisting of server logs of `http` requests to the NASA Kennedy Space Center web server in Florida [24]. They are composed of hostname, timestamp, request, HTTP reply code, and the number of bytes in the reply.

---

[5] https://en.wikipedia.org/.

One email, one book, one message, one article, one movie description, or one log server is considered as one document. For each document, stopwords have been removed and keywords processed using the standard Porter stemming algorithm [25].

Those datasets were chosen for their variety as they are a representative sample of datasets that one might want to protect with SSE schemes. As we will see in the following the efficiency of the attacks varies wildly with the type of dataset considered.

5.2   Foreseeing the Cost of the Attacks

In [1] the computational cost of the attacks sketched by making some assumptions on the statistical properties of the considered dataset. Further experiments have shown that those assumptions, while holding true for the datasets considered in [1], could also be far from the empirical truth when looking at other types of datasets. Therefore, we take a different approach as the one chosen in [1]: instead of deriving formulas for the computational complexity of an attack based on assumptions about the dataset, we measure parameters of the dataset and derive from that the approximate difficulty of running the attack *on this particular dataset*. We believe that this approach is more useful to evaluate the practical security of a given SSE scheme as this can only be evaluated once faced with a dataset. The other advantage of this approach is that it provides insight towards possible counter-measures against the attacks presented above.

The governing parameter for the cost of the mask attack is the number of candidate masks that need to be computed for each plaintext document. This is exactly the number of encrypted documents having the same length as the target plaintext. Therefore, Fig. 2 shows the number of documents having the same length in the view of the L4 leakage profile for our 9 datasets, i.e., we take in account the repetition of keywords in the documents. The y-axis of Fig. 2 represents the number of documents sharing a given length. From the figure we can predict that the mask attack will be extremely efficient on the dataset *Gutenberg* for which there is at most 3 encrypted candidate for each target plaintext. At the other end of the spectrum, all the documents of the *Nasa* dataset have length 10. This effectively means that each target plaintext requires to compute the mask of *all* encrypted documents. This property makes the attack extremely slow and effectively impractical. These results follow the intuition that a dataset of documents of arbitrary length will be far easier to attack that a dataset made of very formatted documents. This intuition is further confirmed by the results of the other 7 datasets: the non-formatted datasets *Commons*, *Hadoop*, *Lucene*, *Subversion*, *Enron*, and *Wikipedia* force the computation of less than 35 masks per target while *IMDb* forces, in most cases, the computation of several hundreds masks. We remark that these datasets have very different original size which confirms that the complexity of the attack is only marginally linked to the total size of the dataset.

Since the governing parameter for the cost of the CoMask attack is also the number of candidate of equal length, we perform a very similar analysis but

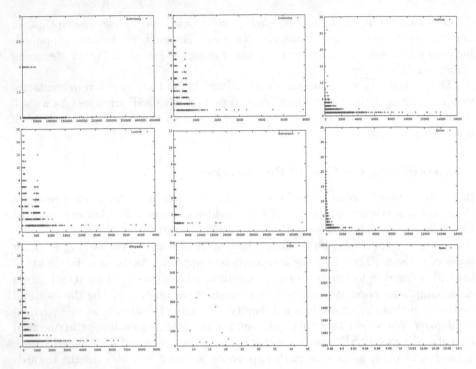

Fig. 2. Number of documents depending on the length with the L4 view.

this time considering the length in view of the L3 leakage profile, i.e., we count the number of different keywords in each document. Since the length under this leakage profile is necessarily smaller than the length in the view of the L4 leakage profile we expect to see similar results with more "collisions" of length. This is indeed what we observe in Fig. 3. Both extremes stay the same: there is at most 4 candidates for each target plaintext on the *Gutenberg* dataset and again almost all documents of the *Nasa* dataset have the same length. In between, *Commons, Hadoop, Lucene, Subversion, Enron,* and *Wikipedia* have at most 40 candidate per target while *IMDb* boasts again several hundreds candidates. We note here that while in the case of the mask attack the cost grows linearly with the number same-length candidates, the cost of the CoMask attack grows like its square (since we compute a pair of matching co-resulting mask). This gives the intuition that the attacks could be made much slower by simply padding all the encrypted documents.

Finally, we measure the occurrence of all keywords present in the sample, i.e., the number of documents containing the considered keyword, starting from the less frequent and ending with the most frequent. Results are presented in Fig. 4 and help to predict the efficiency of the PowerSet attack. In fact, the PowerSet attack is based on the number of keywords shared between documents. Hence, if a dataset has a lot of keywords shared between its documents, then the

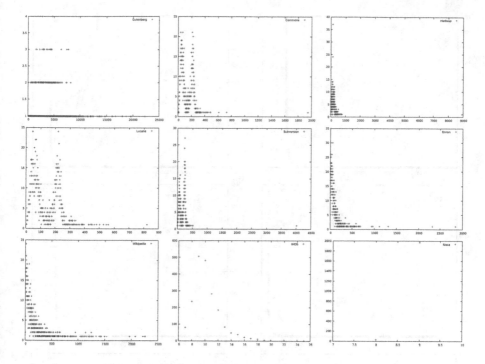

Fig. 3. Number of documents depending on the length with the L3 view.

probability to distinguish documents on their shared documents is higher. We can predict that the PowerSet attack will more efficient on *Gutenberg, Commons, Hadoop, Lucene, Subversion, Enron, Wikipedia* datasets, than on *IMDb* and *Nasa* datasets.

5.3 Efficiency Measures

We ran our attacks for different sizes of S using steps of 1% until 10% then steps of 10% from 10% to 100%. Here 1% is 1% of the pairs (d, w) of the dataset; this allows us to perform a fairer comparison between datasets than the usual per-document measure, as knowing a long document do not have the same impact as knowing a short one.

The measured *success rate* is the ratio of keywords-tokens associations over the set of keywords of S. Then, these correspondences are spread back into EDB in order to evaluate their impact on other documents of the dataset. In particular, we measured the rate of documents of the dataset whose keywords are recovered at 80%, 90% and 100%.

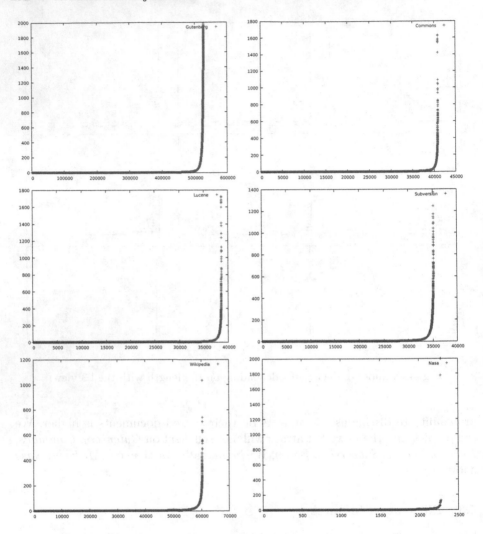

Fig. 4. Occurrence of keywords, from less frequent to more frequent.

5.4   Experimental Results on Datasets Samples

We expose here the results of our attacks on the chosen datasets. All attacks are performed on an Intel® Xeon® using 64 Gb RAM with REDIS[6], an in-memory data structure store.

Experimental Results of the Mask Attack. Results for the Mask attack are presented in Fig. 5. We notice that we have three categories of results.

---

[6] https://redis.io/.

The first category is when the mask attack can associate with a high ratio keywords and tokens. As shown in Fig. 7, this is the case for *Gutenberg, Commons, Hadoop, Lucene, Subversion, Enron, Wikipedia* datasets. In fact, for each percentage of knowledge, the adversary can associate with a ratio equals to 1, keywords that it knows to their corresponding tokens. Hence, we can observe that the Mask attack is ravaging for mailing list, emails, articles, and books datasets.

Second, very few associations between keywords and tokens can be done. As exposed in Fig. 5, the Mask attack result on dataset *IMDb* is in this category. As we can see in Fig. 2, a lot of documents have the same length. This is due to the structure of the dataset. In fact, movies descriptions are very similar since each keyword has a specific set of possible values. However, the number of keywords composing the title of the movie can be discriminant that is why we can associate some documents with the Mask attack. However, the adversary can at most associate 10% of the keywords that it knows to their corresponding tokens.

Finally, no association between keywords and tokens can be performed whatever the part of knowledge over the dataset. As we can see in Fig. 5, results of the Mask attack on the *Nasa* dataset is in this category. Each server log is composed of the same number of keywords, hence mask of server logs cannot be distinguishable by the length (Fig. 2). Moreover, each keyword in a server log has a specific role, for instance: client IP address, request date/time, page requested, HTTP code, bytes served, then the probability to have repetitions in the masks (for example, hostname equals to the timestamp or to the number of bytes served) is very low. Hence, masks of server logs are always the same, i.e., $(1, \ldots, \ell)$ where ℓ is the fixed number of keywords in server logs. This is why our mask attack is inefficient against server logs dataset, i.e., the adversary can not associate keywords that it knows to their corresponding tokens.

Experimental Results of the CoMask Attack. Results for the CoMask attack are presented in Fig. 6. We notice that we have two categories of results.

The first category is where the ratio of association between keywords and tokens is high for each percentage of known dataset. As shown in Fig. 6, datasets *Gutenberg, Commons, Hadoop, Lucene, Subversion, Enron* and *Wikipedia* are in this category since the adversary can associate almost 100% of the keywords in the known dataset to their corresponding tokens. Their common particularity is that they have a lot of frequent keywords (Fig. 4). In fact, the CoMask attack uses the shared keywords between documents to distinguish computed comask. Hence, we argue that datasets having a such distribution of frequent keywords are less resistant against the CoMask attack since the documents pairs can be more distinguishable.

The second category concerns *Nasa* and *IMDb* datasets. As we can see in Fig. 6, the ratio of keyword-token associations is very low (3% for the *Nasa* dataset, and 10% for the *IMDb* dataset). With Fig. 4, we see that these two datasets have very few frequent keywords. Hence, computed comask from the

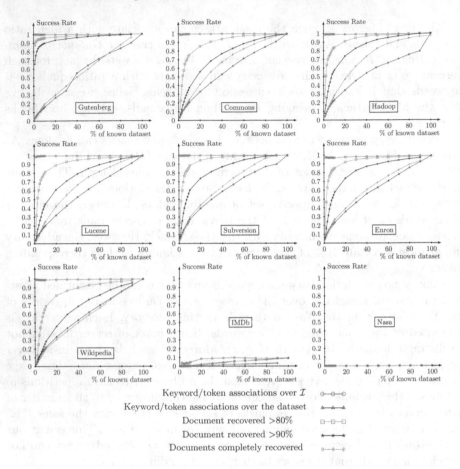

Keyword/token associations over $\mathcal{I}$ ⊖—⊖—⊖
Keyword/token associations over the dataset   ▲—▲—▲
Document recovered >80%   □—□—□
Document recovered >90%   ✱—✱—✱
Documents completely recovered   ◇—◇—◇

Fig. 5. Efficiency of our *Mask* attack depending on the knowledge rate of the server.

percentage of known dataset do not discriminate. We assume that a dataset having very few shared frequent keywords is resistant to the CoMask attack.

Experimental Results of the PowerSet Attack. Results for the PowerSet attack are presented in Fig. 7. We notice that we have four categories of results.

First, the ratio of association between keywords and tokens is always high whatever the part of knowledge of the dataset. It is the case for the PowerSet attack applied to the *Gutenberg* dataset as shown in Fig. 7 where an adversary can always associate keywords to their corresponding tokens whatever the percentage of known dataset. As shown in Fig. 4, the occurrence of frequent keywords is much bigger in the *Gutenberg* dataset, i.e., a lot of documents in the dataset share different keywords. In the context of the PowerSet attack, this fact helps to match known documents to their representation in the encrypted documents, and to recover keywords.

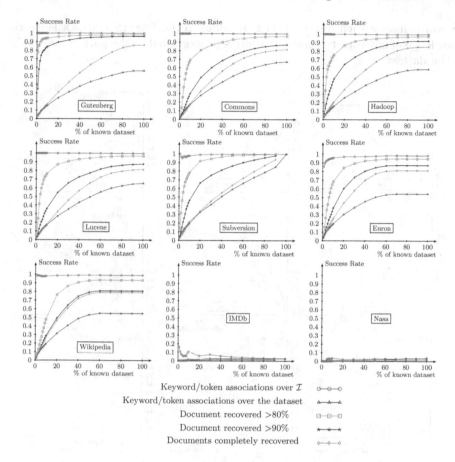

Keyword/token associations over $\mathcal{I}$ ⊖—⊖—⊖

Keyword/token associations over the dataset   ▲—▲—▲

Document recovered >80%   ⊟—⊟—⊟

Document recovered >90%   ⋆—⋆—⋆

Documents completely recovered   ◇—◇—◇

Fig. 6. Efficiency of our *CoMask* attack depending on the knowledge rate of the server.

The second category of results is illustrated in Fig. 7 by *Commons, Hadoop, Lucene,* and *Subversion* datasets. In this case, the association between keywords and tokens depending of the part of knowledge of the dataset is relatively of a constant order. As shown in Fig. 4, the most frequent keywords of these four datasets are present in a quarter of the documents while the most frequent keywords are present up to five times per document. We assume that a dataset with a such distribution for keywords occurrences is sensible to the PowerSet attack.

Third, the association between keywords and tokens is progressive depending the part of knowledge of the dataset. We see in Fig. 7 that results of the PowerSet attack on *Enron* and *Wikipedia* datasets are in this category. The similarity between these two datasets lies in the distribution of the mots frequent keywords. As we can see in Fig. 4, frequent keywords are present in a quarter of documents while the most frequent keyword is in all the documents or twice. Due to the nature of the PowerSet attack, we assume that a dataset where most frequent keywords have a such distribution is sensible to the PowerSet attack since the knowledge of keyword-token association is proportional to the part of knowledge of the dataset.

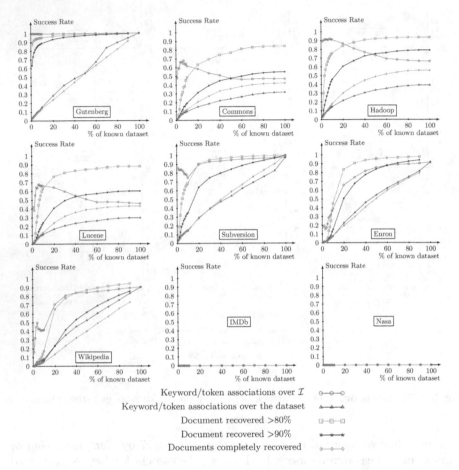

Fig. 7. Efficiency of our *PowerSet* attack depending on the knowledge rate of the server.

Finally, no association between keywords and tokens can be performed, and this whatever the part of knowledge over the dataset. As we can see in Fig. 7, results of the PowerSet attack on *Nasa* and *IMDb* datasets are of this type since an adversary can not associate keywords to their corresponding tokens. These two datasets have a small keywords space: 2,280 for *Nasa* dataset and 5,671 for *IMDb* dataset. Moreover, we see in Fig. 4 that keywords occurrences in these datasets are more homogeneous than in the other datasets. Since, the PowerSet attack deals with the number of shared keywords between documents, we deduce empirically that a dataset with a small keywords space and with a homogeneous distribution of keywords occurrences is resistant against the PowerSet attack.

Remark. As noted in [11], this reconstruction allows to reveal sensitive information even if the order of keywords is not preserved. Human inspection of the output of our attacks gives a clear idea of the sense of each document.

5.5   Scaling Up: Experimental Results on Full Datasets

In order to get a more complete picture of the practicality of the attacks, we present in this section results of the Mask, CoMask, and PowerSet attacks on three full datasets: *Commons, Lucene,* and *Hadoop.* The results of the attack themselves are very close to the ones presented in the previous section: the details on these datasets are given in Fig. 8. The benefit of running the attacks on the full datasets was the impact of low probability events (only observable on large documents sets) on the running time of the attacks. In particular two phenomenon slowed down the attacks majorly and had to be dealt with in a specific way. The first of these phenomenons was the presence of duplicates in the original datasets. If not handled specifically, duplicates documents actually prevent "early-abort" in both the CoMask and the Powerset attacks. Unfortunately at high orders (several hundreds of documents) one cannot afford to not quickly eliminate candidates. This has the practical consequence that duplicates need to be removed before the elimination procedure which incurs a cost that grows like the square of the number of same-length candidate. The second phenomenon is similar but worse in its consequences. There are documents that are indistinguishable in the sense that they are almost identical but their difference appear in the same documents. Actually, the case most often encountered is documents that are equal up to 2 words (one in each document) but that those 2 words do not appear anywhere else in the dataset. That means that the two documents are not equal (and therefore would not be filtered out by the procedure outline above) but they are effectively equivalent through the leakage profile. Dealing with those documents during the attacks incurs a very high cost even in comparison to the task of eliminating duplicates.

Dataset	Content	#DB	#W	N
Commons	mailing list	28,997	230,893	3,910,562
Lucene	mailing list	58,884	394,481	7,952,794
Hadoop	mailing list	21,312	206,315	3,655,222

Fig. 8. Details on selected full datasets.

Results of the Mask attack are presented in Fig. 9, results of the CoMask attack in Fig. 10, and results of the PowerSet attack are exposed in Fig. 11.

5.6   Further Protecting Your Datasets

The previous sections have given some intuition as to what would constitute the most promising avenue for efficient countermeasures against leakage-abuse

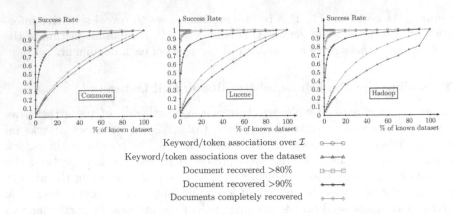

Fig. 9. Efficiency of our *Mask* attack depending on the knowledge rate of the server.

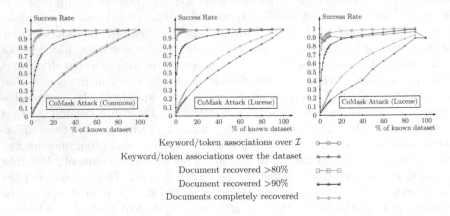

Fig. 10. Efficiency of our *CoMask* attack depending on the knowledge rate of the server.

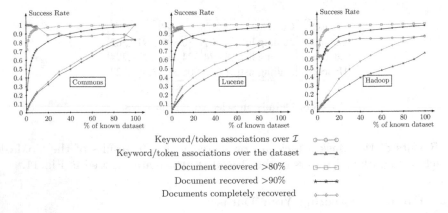

Fig. 11. Efficiency of our *PowerSet* attack depending on the knowledge rate of the server.

attacks. We leave as future work the analysis of the cost/benefit ratio of those countermeasures but any practical use of SSE scheme should consider implementing the following counter-measures.

Length Padding. The owner of the dataset should make sure that all of the documents in the datasets have a least $t - 1$ other documents of the same length with t being large enough that t^2 calculations of co-resulting masks (respectively, powersets of order 2) is considered prohibitive.

Ghost Twin Insertion. The owner of the dataset should insert "ghost twin documents" in the dataset. The "ghost twin" of a document d is a document d' that is indistinguishable from d through L2 leakage profile. The easiest method for creating ghost twins is to start from the inverted index with a keyword w that only appears in one document d. The ghost twin of d is the document d where all the occurrences of w have been replaced by $\tilde{w}$ and where $\tilde{w}$ does not appear anywhere else in the dataset.

6   Conclusion

SSE schemes are known to be insecure considering an adversary who is able to perform file-injections. In fact, Zhang et al. [13] shown that only few injected files can reveal to an adversary associations between keywords and search tokens. Moreover, SSE schemes are also vulnerable to passive observations of search tokens since they reveal the underlying searched keyword when the data set is completely known as shown in [10–12].

In this paper, we focus on the impact of passive attacks on SSE schemes of profiles L4, L3 and L2, i.e., families of SSE schemes that are currently used as commercially solutions [26–28]. We consider an adversary who has access to the encrypted database (stored by the server) and knows a sample of plaintexts having generated this encrypted database. As we shown first in [1], our attacks are devastating on most real-world datasets that we used, namely mailing-list, emails, and books datasets. Indeed, regardless of the leakage profile and knowing a mere 1% of the original documents in data set, we are able to recover 80% of the content of 90% of the documents. However, the efficiency of our attacks depends on the nature of the considered data set. In fact, as we shown in this paper, an adversary performing our attacks on encrypted databases generated from datasets composed of very formatted data like server logs or of movies descriptions extracts not much information on original documents. In the best case, she can recover 80% of the content of only 5% of the documents. In fact, such documents are very structured and contain very few shared words, preventing the retrieval of information to associate keywords and tokens, thus avoiding the retrieval of the content of the documents. Finally we gave insight into interesting techniques for further protecting encrypted databases based on the knowledge acquired during our experiments.

To conclude, the results in this paper does cast doubt on the legitimacy of SSE schemes and help us to better understand the practical security of SSE schemes. Relying on the experimental results of our attacks on the server logs and movies descriptions data sets, it will be interesting to further investigate the cost/benefit ratio of countermeasures to these attacks.

Acknowledgments. This research was conducted with the support of the FEDER program of 2014-2020, the region council of Auvergne-Rhône-Alpes, the support of the "Digital Trust" Chair from the University of Auvergne Foundation, the Indo-French Centre for the Promotion of Advanced Research (IFCPAR) and the Center Franco-Indien Pour La Promotion De La Recherche Avancée (CEFIPRA) through the project DST/CNRS 2015-03 under DST-INRIA-CNRS Targeted Programme.

References

1. Giraud, M., Anzala-Yamajako, A., Bernard, O., Lafourcade, P.: Practical passive leakage-abuse attacks against symmetric searchable encryption. In: Proceedings of the 14th International Joint Conference on e-Business and Telecommunications (ICETE 2017) - Volume 4: SECRYPT, Madrid, Spain, 24–26 July, 2017, pp. 200–211 (2017)
2. Gentry, C.: Fully homomorphic encryption using ideal lattices. In: Proceedings of the Forty-First Annual ACM Symposium on Theory of Computing, STOC 2009, pp. 169–178. ACM, New York (2009)
3. Song, D.X., Wagner, D., Perrig, A.: Practical techniques for searches on encrypted data. In: Proceedings of the 2000 IEEE Symposium on Security and Privacy, SP 2000, p. 44. IEEE Computer Society, Washington, DC (2000)
4. Goldreich, O.: Secure Multi-party Computation, Working Draft (1998)
5. Cash, D., et al.: Dynamic searchable encryption in very-large databases: data structures and implementation. In: 21st Annual Network and Distributed System Security Symposium, NDSS 2014, San Diego, California, USA, 23–26 February, 2014 (2014)
6. Kamara, S., Papamanthou, C., Roeder, T.: Dynamic searchable symmetric encryption. In: Proceedings of the 2012 ACM Conference on Computer and Communications Security, CCS 2012, pp. 965–976. ACM, New York (2012)
7. Cash, D., Jarecki, S., Jutla, C., Krawczyk, H., Roşu, M.-C., Steiner, M.: Highly-scalable searchable symmetric encryption with support for boolean queries. In: Canetti, R., Garay, J.A. (eds.) CRYPTO 2013. LNCS, vol. 8042, pp. 353–373. Springer, Heidelberg (2013). https://doi.org/10.1007/978-3-642-40041-4_20
8. Faber, S., Jarecki, S., Krawczyk, H., Nguyen, Q., Rosu, M., Steiner, M.: Rich queries on encrypted data: beyond exact matches. In: Pernul, G., Ryan, P.Y.A., Weippl, E. (eds.) ESORICS 2015. LNCS, vol. 9327, pp. 123–145. Springer, Cham (2015). https://doi.org/10.1007/978-3-319-24177-7_7
9. Curtmola, R., Garay, J., Kamara, S., Ostrovsky, R.: Searchable symmetric encryption: improved definitions and efficient constructions. In: Proceedings of the 13th ACM Conference on Computer and Communications Security, CCS 2006, pp. 79–88. ACM, New York (2006)
10. Islam, M.S., Kuzu, M., Kantarcioglu, M.: Access pattern disclosure on searchable encryption: ramification, attack and mitigation. In: 19th Annual Network and Distributed System Security Symposium, NDSS 2012, San Diego, California, USA, 5–8 February, 2012 (2012)

11. Cash, D., Grubbs, P., Perry, J., Ristenpart, T.: Leakage-abuse attacks against searchable encryption. In: Proceedings of the 22nd ACM SIGSAC Conference on Computer and Communications Security, CCS 2015, pp. 668–679. ACM, New York (2015)

12. Pouliot, D., Wright, C.V.: The shadow nemesis: inference attacks on efficiently deployable, efficiently searchable encryption. In: Proceedings of the 2016 ACM SIGSAC Conference on Computer and Communications Security, Vienna, Austria, 24–28 October, 2016, pp. 1341–1352 (2016)

13. Zhang, Y., Katz, J., Papamanthou, C.: All Your Queries Are Belong to Us: The Power of File-Injection Attacks on Searchable Encryption. Cryptology ePrint Archive, Report 2016/172 (2016) http://eprint.iacr.org/2016/172

14. Abdelraheem, M.A., Andersson, T., Gehrmann, C., Glackin, C.: Practical attacks on relational databases protected via searchable encryption. IACR Cryptology ePrint Archive 2018, p. 715 (2018)

15. Wang, G., et al.: Leakage models and inference attacks on searchable encryption for cyber-physical social systems. IEEE Access 6, 21828–21839 (2018)

16. Lau, B., Chung, S.P., Song, C., Jang, Y., Lee, W., Boldyreva, A.: Mimesis aegis: a mimicry privacy shield-a system's approach to data privacy on public cloud. In: Proceedings of the 23rd USENIX Security Symposium, San Diego, CA, USA, 20–22 August, 2014, pp. 33–48 (2014)

17. Project Gutenberg. http://www.gutenberg.org/wiki/Main_Page. Accessed Mar 2016

18. Apache Commons email dataset. http://mail-archives.apache.org/mod_mbox/commons-user/. Accessed Mar 2016

19. Apache Hadoop email dataset. http://mail-archives.apache.org/mod_mbox/hadoop-user/. Accessed Mar 2018

20. Apache Lucene email dataset. http://mail-archives.apache.org/mod_mbox/lucene-java-user/. Accessed Apr 2016

21. Apache Subversion email dataset. http://mail-archives.apache.org/mod_mbox/subversion-users/. Accessed Mar 2018

22. Enron email dataset. http://www.cs.cmu.edu/~./enron/. Accessed Apr 2016

23. IMDb dataset. https://www.imdb.com/interfaces/. Accessed Mar 2018

24. Nasa-HTTP server logs. http://ita.ee.lbl.gov/html/contrib/NASA-HTTP.html. Accessed Mar 2018

25. Porter, M.F.: An algorithm for suffix striping. Program 14, 130–137 (1980)

26. CipherCloud. Cloud Data Encryption. https://www.ciphercloud.com/technologies/encryption/. Accessed 18 Jan 2017

27. Bitglass. Security, Compliance, and Encryption. http://www.bitglass.com/salesforce-security. Accessed 18 Jan 2017

28. Skyhigh Networds. Skyhigh for Salesforce. https://www.skyhighnetworks.com/product/salesforce-security/. Accessed 18 Jan 2017

Computer-Based Analysis of Tomatis Listening Test System Audio Data

Félix Buendía-García[1]([⊠]), Manuel Agustí-Melchor[1], and Cristina Pérez-Guillot[2]

[1] Computing Engineering Department,
Universitat Politècnica de València, Valencia, Spain
fbuendia@disca.upv.es
[2] Applied Linguistic Department,
Universitat Politècnica de València, Valencia, Spain

Abstract. Audio information can be represented in a wide range of formats that need to be further processed. This is the case of data which are obtained from devices addressed to measure human listening levels. The current paper describes the computer-based analysis of different types of data related to the listening level measures coming from TLTS (Tomatis Listening Test System) devices. Such data can be classified into several formats such as images displaying listening graphical curves or spreadsheets collecting digitized values from those device measurements. In the first case, image analysis techniques were used to process listening curves gathered through the TLTS tests in the context of a collaboration project with the Isora Solutions company where the proposed system was applied. In the case of the spreadsheet data, a web-based tool was developed to complement the information processing of listening data sources which were gathered from the TLTS devices. The obtained results show the suitability of the implemented software tools to analyze different kind of information associated to the measurement of listening levels in the TLTS.

Keywords: Listening levels · Image processing
Web-based spreadsheet tools · Tomatis Listening Test System

1 Introduction

Audio information is a key component in many processes that need to measure the hearing acuity of individuals or their listening levels. Such processes can be based on objective measurements coming from physical or acoustic signals, or relying on subjective user responses. Moreover, audio data can be represented in a wide range of formats that introduce an additional layer of analysis complexity. The current work is addressed to describe the computer-based analysis of several data sources that are interpreted from the user responses in the TLTS (Tomatis Listening Test System). This system is able to gather listening level responses from individuals who are involved in tests conducted by experts in the topic. The data collected from these responses can be represented by means of different formats such as images displaying listening graphical curves or spreadsheets collecting digitized values from measurement returned by TLTS devices. The main aim of the research work deals with the analysis of such data and the tools developed to this end.

© Springer Nature Switzerland AG 2019
M. S. Obaidat and E. Cabello (Eds.): ICETE 2017, CCIS 990, pp. 278–291, 2019.
https://doi.org/10.1007/978-3-030-11039-0_13

There are multiple types of tests that can be addressed in a hearing context such as Pure Tone Audiometry (PTA), Masking Level Difference (MLD) or Speech analysis. Each test is able to produce different data types to be processed. The computer-based analysis proposed in this work intends to combine and integrate data sources coming from TLTS measurements. Such integration will enable a more comprehensive and holistic view of listening level outcomes in a context of auditory stimulations to improve this kind of hearing skills. Computers have been quite useful to help the hearing analysis when several multimedia signal sources are combined. For example, Mackersie et al., [1] presented the evaluation of speech perception through a computers-assisted test called CASPA (Computer Assisted Speech Perception Assessment). This work was extended in the system CasperSent [2] as a multimedia program whose main purpose was sentence-level speech-perception training and test-ing. A set of auditory assessment tests based on integrating phonetic discrimination and word recognition were described in [3]. Fernandez et al., [4] used detection of eye gesture reactions as a response to sounds in order to provide computer aided hearing assessment. Therefore, such combination of data sources is essential to obtain a detailed view of the specific auditory or listening scenario.

Another interesting aspect to consider during the analysis of these listening audio data is related to the intervention of experts in the test process. Automated tests have been developed to check hearing issues using air conduction tests [5]. In this sense, there is a systematic review of works [6] that check the validity of automated threshold analysis compared with the gold standard of manual threshold analysis. That demonstrates a need to allow human experts to participate in this process by providing them with several listening data sources and enabling their analysis. The current work presents a set of tools capable to process listening curves together with collected spreadsheets in order to extract information which can be extremely useful to analyze subject's hearing levels from a global perspective. The remainder of the paper is structured in the following sections. The second section shows the work context in which the proposed analysis has been applied. A set of tools to support such analysis is described in the third section. Section 4 deals with a case study that exemplifies how these tools have contributed to the analysis of listening level measurements. Finally, some Conclusions and further works are drawn.

2 Work Context

The context of the current work lies in a collaboration project [7] between the Universitat Politècnica de València and Isora Solutions addressed to test the neu-rosensorial stimulation for the improvement of listening skills in English language. This kind of collaboration tries to understand the effects of some neural stimulation experiments in those processes related to the understanding of English as a foreign language. Thereby, there is need to carry out such experiments and to analyze their results concerning several listening levels of those users who participated in the project. One first step about the proposed analysis deals with the methods and tools used to measure the subject's hearing capability according to different sound frequencies. There are several methods to measure this capability and they can be divided into subjective and objective categories. Mendel [8] emphasized on the need for both subjective and objective documentation of hearing aid outcomes. In the current context, subjective measures have been performed to gather listening level information by means of specific hearing tests. Pure tone audiometry (PTA) is usually measured in dB HL (Hearing Level) and this value is used to identify the hearing threshold level of an individual. This level represents the higher intensity of sound to be perceived by a subject, compared with people who have a normal hearing level. For this work, a device called TLTS (Tomatis Listening Test System) has been deployed, which is based on the use of de SPL (Sound Pressure Level) values as the difference between the pressure produced by a sound wave and the barometric pressure.

TLTS was designed by Dr. Alfred Tomatis [9] using a curve of absolute hearing threshold values and it is used for performing a specific listening test that registers hearing levels once these are almost inaudible. The listening test evaluates an individual's auditory thresholds in terms of frequency, ability to identify the source of sounds, ability to discriminate between frequencies, and auditory laterality. The analysis of the resulting curves helps to determine the person's quality of listening and from this to induce a psychological profile. This kind of tests has been performed by professionals of Isora Solutions as part of the aforementioned collaboration project and there are several types of actions which can be carried out to determine subject's listening levels in this context. Next subsections describe such actions and the obtained outcomes to be further processed and analyzed.

2.1 Listening Tests

Listening is a key skill when learning a foreign language since communication is only possible being able to understand what you hear. Sometimes, users have problems to listen correctly because they are unable to process certain audio signals. The aim of those tests proposed to evaluate the users' listening levels consists of processing different hearing parameters related to:

- Thresholds
- Laterality
- Selectivity

Threshold of hearing is the minimum sound of level that a human ear can perceive in a certain frequency band and it is considered as a measure of hearing sensitivity. This kind of sensitivity can be represented using a chart that displays the audible threshold intensity for standardized frequencies. Figure 1 shows an example of line chart that represents intensity thresholds measured using dB SPL values (displayed on the vertical axis), which change as frequency ranges from 250 to 8000 Hz (horizontal axis). In this chart, blue lines are associated to the air conduction while red line symbols refer to the bone conduction and the green line to the availability features.

Both via air and via bone conduction (using a vibrator placed on the top of the head) are the main data sources in the TLTS tests. It is important to remark the difference in the sound speed of the two mediums since the travelling time of the bone conduction to the brain is assumed to be faster that the air conduction. According to Dr. Tomatis, the bone conducted sound serves as a wakeup call to prepare the brain for incoming sound. Then, the delay between bone and air-conducted sound has to be measured.

The second test is based on checking laterality, which is only obtained from a TLTS device, as a measure to observe how humans focus their hearing on one ear. Laterality, also called Lateralization, was studied by Broca [10] and Wernicke [11] who introduced the concept of unilateral left hemispheric control of language functions. It is widely accepted that language is predominantly a left-hemispheric function and there

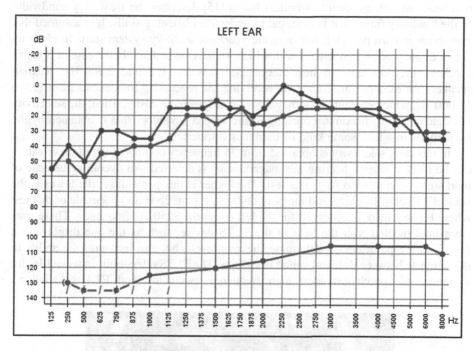

Fig. 1. Sample of TLTS chart to display threshold curves.

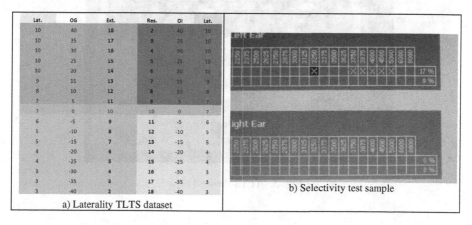

a) Laterality TLTS dataset

b) Selectivity test sample

Fig. 2. Listening test configuration [14].

are several references to its impact in related skills [12, 13]. The TLTS measurement is based on two main values called Extraction (Ext.) and Resistance (Res.) representing the laterality profile. Figure 2a shows a table that displays the matching between these two values and the laterality levels.

Selectivity refers to the ability to differentiate the pitch of sounds in relation to each other, but also the direction of variation in pitch. In the context of audiology and psychoacoustics the concept of critical bands [15] describes the frequency bandwidth of the "auditory filter" that is essential to understand listening skills. It is assumed that everybody is born polyglot, but over the years our auditory system starts to close up and does not process frequencies with which we have no contact. In the case of Spanish speakers, they are able to hear frequencies between 125 and 2,500 Hz; Russian speakers, for example, are capable of receiving and processing frequencies from 125 to 11,000 Hz, which explains why they learn languages more easily. Then, the selectivity test determines the maximum opening of the subject's auditory that is obtained by the frequencies in which some kind of barrier is detected.

In this case, selectivity is obtained from 35 frequency options. Each of these values can be marked when a hearing misunderstanding is detected. An overall percentage of marks can be computed from this test. The higher is this percentage, the lower is the subject's level of listening and memory abilities. Figure 2b shows a sample of this test where barriers mark is observed for the left ear in the 3250 Hz frequency. These tests were implemented with the help of the TLTS device, such as the one displayed on Fig. 3. This type of device determines hearing levels, but also measures the ability to discriminate between different sound intensities. The TLTS offers built-in wave files for a variety of speech extended high frequency evaluation and PTA calculations.

Fig. 3. TLTS device [14].

It provides features to process speech information through live voice, mp3 recordings and wave files as well as word recognition capabilities. For tone analysis, several air conduction and bone condition mechanisms are addressed, and the possibility to manage masking information. Outcomes produced by this kind of device are divided in two categories: image files and spreadsheets documents. Next section describes those software tools developed to analyze such outcomes.

3 Computer-Based Analysis of Listening Tests

The processing and analysis of the data sources produced by the TLTS devices required the development of some specific tools. Intensity thresholds and availability were represented by means of listening curve charts such as the one shown on Fig. 1. On the other hand, laterality and selectivity data were stored on spreadsheets documents in a tabular format such those displayed on Fig. 4. Both types of data were difficult to manage and analyze and a framework [14] was proposed to deal with this variety of information. Figure 5 shows an overview of the framework functionality that is structured in two main flows: the first one (on the left) addressed to process the curve images and the second one in charge of processing spreadsheet data.

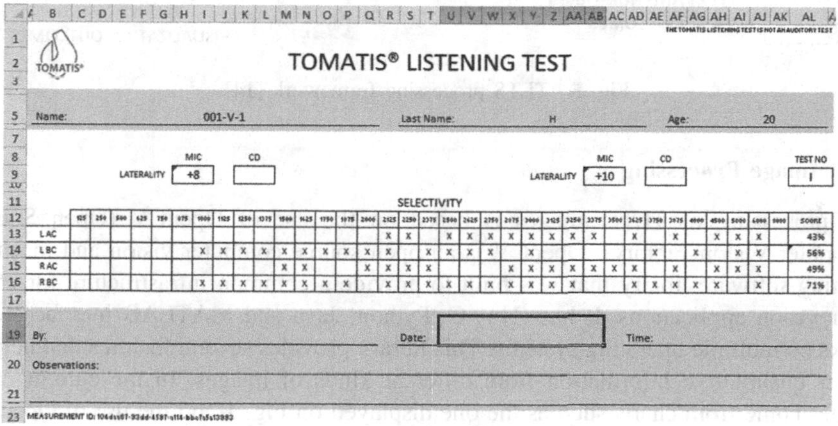

Fig. 4. Listening test spreadsheet format.

The results of both flows were integrated in order to process, analyze and interpret them from different perspectives ranging from the generation of new documents and data sets in several formats (e.g. CSV or XML) to enable an advanced analysis based on the extraction of statistics and graphics displaying the listening test outcomes.

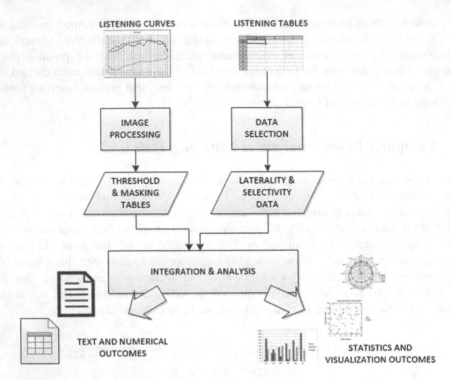

Fig. 5. TLTS processing framework [14].

3.1 Image Processing

The processing of TLTS images is based on the use of OpenCV (Open Source Computer Vision Library). OpenCV is an open source computer vision and machine learning software library that was built to provide a common infrastructure for computer vision applications. It has C++, C, Python, Java and MATLAB interfaces and works on multiple operating systems. This library provides several features that help to gather quantitative information from different kinds of images. In the current case, images come from charts such as the one displayed on Fig. 1 and the use of OpenCV enables to get the locations of points that compose the listening curve lines. These locations assign values of intensity thresholds (measured in dB) for each frequency value in the horizontal axis. Original images are bitmaps of resolution 1200 × 850 pixels. A first processing step consists in identifying each of the lines by color, and segmenting it from the rest of the image.

The second step is about computing the measured values of each point of a segmented line. Checked points for each of the values of the frequencies can be located from the analysis of the labels in the horizontal axis, providing a frequency value in Hz. By projecting these point locations in the vertical axis, the dB value can be computed. In order to find such points, a template matching process is performed to detect the point shapes. The coordinates of the center of mass of these shapes are returned using an iterative sequence over the curve color lines. Figure 6a shows a part of the image in

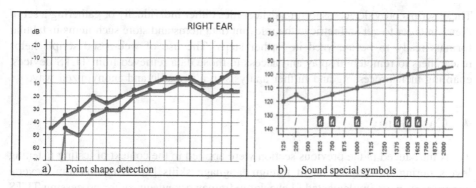

a)   Point shape detection   b)   Sound special symbols

Fig. 6. TLTS image segmentation [14].

which the detected points are marked. A similar matching procedure is used to filter the symbols as they are displayed on the lower part of Fig. 6b, in which "?" characters are marked within red squares representing special sound issues. At the end of the image processing, tabular formats with the collected data are produced and converted to text files (e.g. CSV documents).

3.2   Spreadsheet Processing

The process of gathering information from spreadsheets is based on the use of PHP scripts which allow researchers to get a web view of listening audio data. Figure 7 shows an example of screenshot that displays Laterality values from a selected dataset.

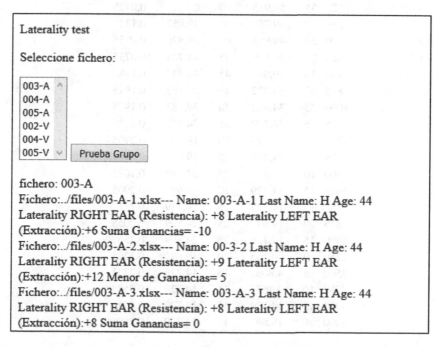

Fig. 7. Script outcomes for selecting laterality data items [14].

These scripts provide access to spreadsheet files either individually or gathering a set of them, in order to get and retrieve the relevant data items and store such items in tabular formats ready to be analyzed in further steps. The use of web-based scripts helps researchers to remotely display and access to those data retrieved from TLTS devices, enabling their processing and further analysis in a versatile and anonymized way.

4   Case Study

Tools introduced in the previous section were applied in the context of testing listening levels during the acquisition of foreign language skills [7]. With this aim, several experiments were implemented to check the framework adequacy for processing TLTS signals. These experiments represent different measures of listening level tests that were available in a tabular format after the framework application [14]. A first evaluation consisted in comparing values obtained from processing listening curves with the original tabular values. Table 1 shows a list of threshold values coming from audio conduction tests for a specific subject whose listening curves were processed using the mentioned framework. These values are structured into several columns that display the listening frequency, the threshold data for the Left ear on Air Conduction (LAC), or Bone Conduction (LBC), the extracted points (Ext.) from both graph charts, and the Average difference between these data. Such list of values was based on a sample of

Table 1. List of threshold values (measured and extracted).

Freq.	LAC	Extracted	LBC	Extracted	Avg. Dif.
125	55	54,915	0	0	0,0425
250	40	39,783	50	49,953	0,132
500	50	49,953	60	59,876	0,0855
625	30	30,109	45	44,744	0,0735
750	30	29,86	45	44,744	0,198
875	35	34,822	40	39,783	0,1975
1000	35	34,822	40	39,783	0,1975
1125	15	14,729	35	34,822	0,2245
1250	15	14,729	20	19,69	0,2905
1375	15	14,729	20	19,69	0,2905
1500	10	9,767	25	24,899	0,167
1625	15	14,729	20	19,69	0,2905
1750	15	14,729	15	14,729	0,271
1875	20	19,69	25	24,899	0,2055
2000	15	14,729	25	24,899	0,186
2250	0	−0,155	20	19,69	0,2325
2500	5	4,806	15	14,729	0,2325
2750	10	9,767	15	14,729	0,252
3000	15	14,729	15	14,729	0,271
4000	20	19,69	15	14,729	0,2905

listening chart and the average difference was less than 0.3 in every processed data item either for air or bone conduction. This pilot experience was a first test and the obtained results reinforced the suitability of the image processing as a powerful data source to analyze threshold values in listening curves.

Selectivity information was also analyzed using the spreadsheet documents collected from the TLTS devices. In this case, a group of 120 users was selected to test their listening levels. These users were divided in three groups (*Blue*, *Orange* and *Green*) receiving each one a different stimulation program. More specifically, the *Blue* group received a complete Neurosensory Stimulation (NS) program, while the Orange was partially stimulated and no stimulation was provided to the *Green* group. There were approximately, 40 participants per group distributed by gender (50% Male + 50% female). Four listening tests using the TLTS devices were carried out by Isora consultants and after these tests their results were collected and stored in a Web server. A PHP script was implemented to allow researchers to access remotely the spreadsheet data and to obtain selectivity results. Figure 8 shows part of the selectivity results for a selection of users in the *Blue* group, displaying X symbols for those frequencies in which these participants had some type of listening barrier. Using a Web access was right for a first contact of researchers with the listening test results, checking their values but they were difficult to manage in a systematic manner. Thereby, a CSV document was produced to enable a detailed processing, as it is shown in Fig. 9 with a bar chart displaying frequencies associated to air sound conduction in the left ear (LAC) and the right ear (RAC). These measures were compared with those produced via bone sound conduction (LBC and RBC, respectively).

```
Pruebas Selectivity

Seleccione fichero:

003-A
004-A
005-A
002-V
004-V
005-V        Prueba Grupo

004-A-1, 125, 250, 500, 625, 750, 875, 1000, 1125, 1250, 1375, 1500, 1625, 1750, 1875, 2000, 2125, 2250, 2375,
2500, 2625, 2750, 2875, 3000, 3125, 3230, 3375, 3500, 3625, 3750, 3875, 4000, 4500, 5000, 6000, 8000,
LAC,..............,X, X, X, X, X, X, X, X, X, X, X, X, X, X, X, X, X, X, X, X, X,,
LBC,.....................,X, X, X,.,.., X, X, X, X, X,,
RAC,................,X, X,.,., X, X, X, X, X, X, X, X, X, X, X, X,,
RBC,....................,X,.,.., X,....., X, X,,
004-A-2, 125, 250, 500, 625, 750, 875, 1000, 1125, 1250, 1375, 1500, 1625, 1750, 1875, 2000, 2125, 2250, 2375,
2500, 2625, 2750, 2875, 3000, 3125, 3250, 3375, 3500, 3625, 3750, 3875, 4000, 4500, 5000, 6000, 8000,
LAC,....................................
LBC,....................................
RAC,....................................
RBC,.............................., X,,
004-A-3, 125, 250, 500, 625, 750, 875, 1000, 1125, 1250, 1375, 1500, 1625, 1750, 1875, 2000, 2125, 2250, 2375,
2500, 2625, 2750, 2875, 3000, 3125, 3250, 3375, 3500, 3625, 3750, 3875, 4000, 4500, 5000, 6000, 8000,
LAC,....................................
LBC,....................................
RAC,....................................
RBC,....................................
```

Fig. 8. Script outcomes displaying the collection of selectivity data items [14].

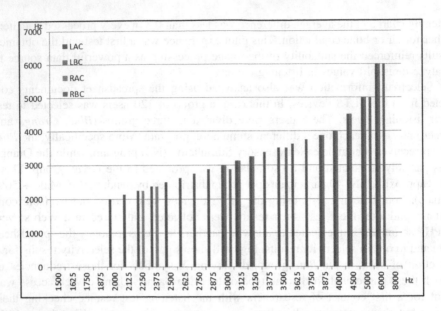

Fig. 9. Graphic chart to display selectivity distribution of listening frequencies [14].

A further analysis was performed to compare the application of the NS program [7] in different times of the experience. This comparison allowed researchers to check the evolution of the participants and the effectiveness of the stimulation received by them. Figure 10 shows a set of boxplot charts displaying the distribution of selectivity frequencies in three different tests for the *Blue* and Green experiment groups. These boxplots represent in the horizontal axis the types of sound conduction, either for Air in the left ear (LAC) and the right ear (RAC), or Bone conduction (LBC and RBC) while the vertical axis shows the distribution of frequencies in the range from 0 to 6000 Hz, in which some barriers were detected. In the first case, boxplots associated with the *Blue* group (upper images in Fig. 10) display a shift in the range of selectivity frequencies, mainly in the transition from the Test1 to Test2. For example, mid-values moved from 3375 Hz to 3625 Hz (LAC), from 2875 Hz to 3625 Hz (LBC), from 3375 Hz to 3875 Hz (RAC), or from 3125 Hz to 3875 Hz (RBC). That means an average increment of 18% in the range of these frequencies that together with the decrement of blocked frequencies (from 1099 in Test1 to 364 in Test2) represent a significant improvement in the listening capabilities of the tested users. However, in the *Orange* case that served as control group with neutral stimulation (lower area images in Fig. 10) the shift in the range of selectivity frequencies was about an 8% with a decrement to about 70% in the blocked frequencies compared to 33% in the *Blue* group. These were some samples to show the usefulness of the information provided by the developed analysis tools and their application to the mentioned experiments.

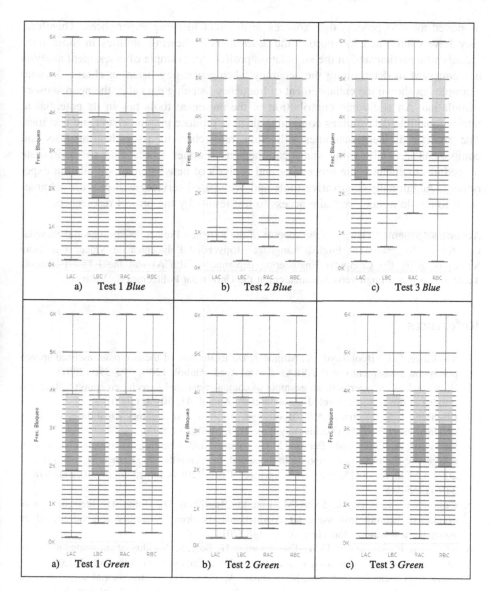

Fig. 10. Selectivity analysis for the *Blue* and *Green* groups. (Color figure online)

5   Conclusions

The current work has presented a computer-based set of tools addressed to process and analyze listening audio data coming from several data sources. These data items have been represented by images and spreadsheet files produced by the TLTS devices in the context of specific hearing tests developed in a neurosensory stimulation project. Outcomes collected during these tests show the wide range of possibilities of the proposed tools to process data sources in different listening experiences. Therefore, they have contributed to improve the assessment of hearing abilities in those individuals who participated in the stimulation project. An example of assessment analysis has consisted in determining the accuracy when processing listening charts. Another example has shown the enhancement of frequency listening data after the neurosensory stimulation. An additional contribution of the presented tools lies in its potential to retrieve multiple data sources combining them to produce graphic charts and text files. The analysis of these outcomes will allow researchers to assess hearing tests and compare their results using statistical methods. Further works plan to incorporate procedures to enhance the processing and analysis of new listening stimulation experiences. Additionally, innovative tools and Web-based services will provide a framework to enable a more versatile access to test results by the project researchers.

Acknowledgements. Thanks to the support of the Research Project "Neurosensorial Stimulation for the Integration of English Language" Universitat Politècnica de València & Isora Solutions, 2016, the Computer Engineering department (DISCA) and the ETSINF (Escola Tècnica Superior d'Enginyeria Informàtica) at the Universitat Politècnica de València.

References

1. Mackersie, C.L., Boothroyd, A., Minniear, D.: Evaluation of the computer-assisted speech perception assessment test (CASPA). J. Am. Acad. Audiol. **12**(8), 390–396 (2001)
2. Boothroyd, A.: CasperSent: an example of computer-assisted speech perception testing and training at the sentence level. J. Acad. Rehab. Audiol. **41**, 30–50 (2006)
3. Eisenberg, L.S., Martinez, A.S., Boothroyd, A.: Assessing auditory capabilities in young children. Int. J. Pediatr. Otorhinolaryngol. **71**, 1339–1350 (2007)
4. Fernández, A., Ortega, M., Penedo, M.G.: computer aided hearing assessment: detection of eye gesture reactions as a response to the sound. In: Campilho, A., Kamel, M. (eds.) ICIAR 2014. LNCS, vol. 8815, pp. 39–47. Springer, Cham (2014). https://doi.org/10.1007/978-3-319-11755-3_5
5. Convery, E., Keidser, G., Seeto, M., Freeston, K., Zhou, D., Dillon, H.: Identification of conductive hearing loss using air conduction tests alone: reliability and validity of an automatic test battery. Ear Hear. **35**(1), 1–8 (2014)
6. Mahomed, F., Swanepoel, D.W., Eikelboom, R.H., Soer, S.: Validity of automated threshold audiometry: a systematic review and meta-analysis. Ear Hear. **34**, 745–752 (2013)
7. Perez, C., Garcia, C., Conejero, M., Capitán, A., Cerna, H.: Neurosensorial stimulation for the integration of English language. http://www.tomatis.com/es/el-metodo-tomatis/actualidad/neurosensorial-stimulation-for-the-integration-of-english-language-en.html. Last Accessed 31 Feb 2018
8. Mendel, L.L.: Objective and subjective hearing aid assessment outcomes. Am. J. Audiol. **16**, 118–129 (2007)
9. Tomatis, A.: The Ear and Language. Moulin Publishing, Norval (1996)
10. Broca, P.: Remarques sur le siege de la faculte du langage articule; suivies d'une observation d'aphemie. Bull. Soc. Anat. Paris **6**, 398–407 (1861)

11. Wernicke, C.: The symptom of complex aphasia. In: Church, A.E. (ed.) Diseases of the nervous system, pp. 265–324. Appleton, New York (1911)
12. Deppe, M., et al.: Assessment of hemispheric language lateralization: a comparison between fMRI and fTCD. J. Cereb. Blood Flow Metab. **20**(2), 263–268 (2000)
13. Szaflarski, J.P., Holland, S.K., Schmithorst, V.J., Byars, A.W.: fMRI study of language lateralization in children and adults. Hum. Brain Mapp. **27**(3), 202–212 (2006)
14. Buendía-García, F., Agustí-Melchor, M., Pérez-Guillot, C., Cerna, H. Capitán, A.: A Computer-based framework to process audiometric signals using the tomatis listening test system. In: Proceedings of SIGMAP/International Joint Conference on e-Business and Telecommunications, pp. 25–34 Madrid, Spain (2017)
15. Fletcher, H.: Auditory patterns. Rev. Mod. Phys. **12**(1), 47 (1940)

Optimising Link Quality for Throughput Enhancement in Wireless Sensor Networks

Evangelos D. Spyrou[✉]

School of Electrical and Computer Engineering, Aristotle University of Thessaloniki,
Egnatia Street, Thessaloniki, Greece
evang_spyrou@eng.auth.gr

Abstract. End-to-end throughput is a major concern in wireless networks. One key approach for enhancing throughput is the optimisation
of link quality. This can be efficiently done via power control. Link quality metrics, such as the Expected Transmission Count (ETX), promotes
throughput maximisation, since it employs bidirectional links and it is
additive by nature. This means that the ETX from the basestation to a
node is the sum of all the ETX values across the route. Definitely, nodes
behave selfishly, in most cases, in order to satisfy their benefits from
their strategies. The methodology that describes this kind of behaviour
more accurately is game theory. Thus, we consider nodes to be individual players that operate to maximise their utilities. In this paper, we
propose a distributed game-theoretic algorithm, which attempts to keep
the reliability of transmission to high standards, while reducing energy
consumption. The actions of the nodes are transmission power levels that
reside on a finite space; hence, we proceed with majorisation properties
and the concavity of the utility function to indicate convergence. Furthermore, we employ the Fictitious Play learning methodology, which is
a very well-known learning algorithm for game theoretic approaches, to
show some learning properties of our approach. We provide simulations
to highlight the efficiency of our approach.

1 Introduction

End-to-end throughput [21] is a major issue in Wireless Sensor Networks
(WSN)s. A WSN comprises a set of links formed by nodes that transmit their
packets, in order to reach a basestation. However, nodes experience interference
during their transmission, thereby making the transmission difficult. Furthermore, the delay of the transmission of the packet increases, since the interfered
node has to do an exponential backoff [9] and retransmit the packet. At the same
time, this node may be receiving packets, making its link quality with the sender
to increase. Thereafter, the messages enter a queue and need to be serviced with
the minimum delay, thus impacting the capacity of the link [17].

One approach to increase throughput is to enhance the link quality between
nodes forming links. This can be done via power control, whereby we enhance

© Springer Nature Switzerland AG 2019
M. S. Obaidat and E. Cabello (Eds.): ICETE 2017, CCIS 990, pp. 292–312, 2019.
https://doi.org/10.1007/978-3-030-11039-0_14

the network's reliability of communication by increasing the radio transmission power level, in order to strengthen the signal strength. Link quality is directly related to throughput, as we can see in the novel paper presenting the Expected Transmission Count (ETX) metric [12]. However, raising the transmission power may result in packets being lost due to the complexities of the wireless channel. An increase in transmission power might cause an increase in interference and collisions, decreasing the number of packets received; hence, the end-to-end throughput of the network. On the other hand, as we see in [38], if the distance between the transmitter-receiver and interferer-receiver is difference by approximately a factor of 2, interference does not cause packet loss. This indicates that a node may select a high transmission power level, in order to strengthen its signal, without suffering from packet loss. Moreover, packets using different transmission powers may result in their packets simultaneously transmitted successfully, depending on their distance and transmission power level [28].

There is a sweet spot in ETX related to transmission power levels that can keep throughput to a high level, while not using a larger transmission power level than necessary. The transmission power also affects the energy consumption of the node, directly influencing the lifetime of the WSN [3]. In order to handle this trade-off, we present a finite strategy distributed game-theoretic approach that maximizes each node's end-to-end throughput, while using the optimal transmission power from an optimisation point of view, as it is shown in [39]. Specifically, we focus on the trade-offs between energy consumption and ETX. We use non-cooperative game theory, since it can appropriately describe the behavior of selfish nodes and find an optimal solution in a distributed manner. Moreover, we highlight cross-layer considerations by discussing the relationship between ETX and delay, capacity, contention and topology control. Modeling systems with selfish algorithms have been shown to provide efficient solutions that improve network performance [45]. We propose a game-theoretic model of the end-to-end throughput optimisation algorithm and we call this algorithm Game-theoretic End-to-End Throughput Optimisation Algorithm (GETOA).

The contributions in this paper are the following:

- We aim to solve the end-to-end throughput by utilising the additive ETX value.
- We show the relationship between ETX with capacity and delay.
- We show the relationship between ETX and contention.
- We provide information regarding the link of power control and ETX with topology control.
- We formulate a game theoretic model with finite strategies and show that it is a potential game. This means that it converges to a Nash Equilibrium.
- We show that it reaches the global optimum.
- We prove that the Nash Equilibrium is Lyapunov stable.

This paper is structured as follows: Sect. 2 provides the related work, Sect. 3 gives a brief description of game theory and potential games, Sect. 4 gives the system model, Sect. 5 provides our game-theoretic algorithm, Sect. 6 gives the results of our approach and Sect. 7 presents the conclusions and the future work.

2   Related Work

Power control is a well-known method to provide energy efficiency, connectivity and network communication reliability [20,37]. Nowadays, there is a debate on its use and efficiency, since the new generation of wireless networks are able to handle interference in a different way, such as the LTE networks. However, inter-cell interference between LTE stations can be still handled with power control [5]. Furthermore, the increase in Internet of Things (IoT) devices and the mobility in the services may create a problem of the orthogonality in LTE systems. Hence, the research community has started doing work on Non Orthogonal Multiple Access (NOMA) systems, where power control is evidently useful [7]. In traditional wireless networks, such as Zibgee and Wi-Fi, power control is a major issue for interference management and communication reliability.

To the end of solving the end-to-end throughput issue, there has been a plethora of approaches that dealt with the Medium Access Control (MAC) layer [1,2,32,40]. However, in this work we are addressing the problem in the network layer and we are providing the reader with necessary information regarding the relationship of capacity and delay with ETX. There are practical works in the literature that implicitly show enhancement of throughput by adjusting transmission power and relate it to link quality [15,23,36]. Here, we are focusing on an approach that attempts to enhance end-to-end throughput further up the stack from the MAC layer.

Zeng et al. [47] studied opportunistic routing, which may cope with poor link reliability by taking advantage of the broadcast nature and spatial diversity of the wireless medium. The authors target scenarios with multiple rates, interference, candidate selection and prioritisation on the maximum end-to-end throughput or capacity of opportunistic routing. By carefully considering wireless interference, transmitter conflict graphs are composed, in order to introduce concurrent transmitter sets as constraints related to the transmission conflicts or opportunistic routing. Thereafter, the maximisation of the end-to-end throughput is formulated as a maximum-flow linear programming problem subject to the transmission conflict constraints. Moreover, a rate selection method is proposed to perform a comparison of multiple rate scenarios against single rate ones. The results given in the paper provide evidence that end-to-end throughput can be enhanced as well as that the multiple rate scenario improves throughput as well.

Choi et al. [8] address the multi-hop link property of link selection, where the increase in the rate of link may be the reason for the decrease of another link's rate. The end-to-end throughput in a multi-hop network is restricted by the lowest rate of a link. This suggests that the max-min fair allocation of the link rates constitutes an optimal strategy that maximises end-to-end-throughput. The authors suggest an approach that makes all link rates equal, thus having the max-min fair allocation property, using a transmission power control algorithm. In particular, this distributed algorithm operates by a node averaging the link rates close to it and adjusts its transmission power to accomplish the average rate. Thereafter, it repeats this operation until all rates are equalised. The results shown in the paper maximizes end-to-end throughput while enhancing energy efficiency of multi-hop nodes.

Yu et al. [46] addressed the problem of network capacity performance in the presence of interference in a multi-hop wireless network, when nodes are competing for the channel medium. In this work, the minimisation of interference power, in order to maximise network capacity is discussed. To this end, the authors propose a consensus power control algorithm that maximises end-to-end throughput. This algorithm adjusts the transmission powers of the nodes to maximize the average end-to-end throughput with a consensus coefficient. Results in this work show that maximum average end-to-end throughput is achieved for all traffic flows and energy efficiency is accomplished. The drawback of this approach lies in the use of the algorithm in dense wireless network deployments.

Incel et al. [16] studied the information collection in tree based sensor network deployments. Hence, they evaluate methodologies that belong to the family of many-to-one communication scheme, known as convergecast. The authors consider time scheduling on a channel with and without transmission power control settings. The former targets the minimisation of the required time slots to achieve convergecast. The latter employs power control to reduce schedule length using multiple frequencies. The authors provide lower bounds on the schedule length when interference diminishes, and suggest approaches that ensure the achievement of such bounds. Furthermore, performance of a number of channel assignment methods suggest that multi-frequency scheduling is enough to eliminate most of the interference. The finding is that data rate is not only dependent on interference; thus, spanning trees are constructed that result in the improvement of scheduling performance using a number of deployment densities.

Chantzis et al. [6], suggests a scheme that aims to provide information regarding the local network throughput impact on topological properties, such as maintenance of neighbourhoods and load balancing. To this end, the authors propose a protocol that adaptively tunes transmission power with low throughput settings where nodes accomplish a degree of symmetric and coherent links. Furthermore, the network throughput is maximised provided that degree is satisfied. Results show that link quality and symmetry as well as links degree satisfaction can be regulated appropriately by transmission power and adaptive throughput control.

3   Game Theory and Potential Games

Game theory studies mathematical models of conflict and cooperation [44], between players. Therefore, our meaning of the term game corresponds to any form of social interaction between two or more nodes. The rationality of a node is satisfied if it pursuits the satisfaction of its preferences through the selection of appropriate strategies. The preferences of a node need to satisfy general rationality axioms, then its behavior can be described by a utility function. Utility functions provide a quantitative description of the node's preferences and the main objective is therefore the maximization of its utility function.

In this work, we focus on strategic non-cooperative games, since we consider nodes to act as selfish players that want to preserve their interests. The intuition behind this is that the nodes will reach an optimal state, without having to pay a price to maximize their payoffs. The Nash equilibrium [29] is the most important equilibrium in non-cooperative strategic form games. It is defined as the point where no node will increase its utility by unilaterally changing its strategy.

In 2008, Daskalakis proved that finding a Nash equilibrium is PPAD-complete [10]. Polynomial Parity Arguments on Directed graphs (PPAD) is a class of total search problems [31] for which solutions have been proven to exist; however, finding a specific solution is difficult if not intractable. This development drove the community to 'Potential Games', since they guarantee the convergence to pure Nash equilibria and best response dynamics.

This class of games consists of the exact and ordinal potential games. This work employs exact potential games and refer the reader to [27] for details on the methodology. In order to use exact potential games, it is essential to have a potential function that has the same behavior as the individual utility function, when a player unilaterally deviates.

More formally:

A game $G\langle N, A, u \rangle$, with N players, A strategy profiles and u the payoff function, is an exact potential game if there exists a potential function

$$V : A \to \mathbb{R} \tag{1}$$

subject to

$$\forall i \in N, \forall \sigma_{-i} \in A_{-i}, \forall \sigma_i, \sigma_i' \in A_i \tag{2}$$

where σ_i is the strategy of player i, σ_i' is the deviation of player i, σ_{-i} is the set of strategies followed by all the players except player i and A_{-i} is the set of strategy profiles of all players except i such as

$$V(\sigma_i, \sigma_{-i}) - V(\sigma_i', \sigma_{-i}) = u_i(\sigma_i, \sigma_{-i}) - u_i(\sigma_i', \sigma_{-i}) \tag{3}$$

4   System Model

We consider a wireless network that consists of a number of nodes that transmit their data in a wireless fashion. The network is essentially an undirected graph G which has V number of vertices and E number of edges $G = (V, E)$. Link asymmetry is considered, thereby the network nodes send data and acknowledgment packets to each other.

One of the key issues of the wireless links, is the number of link layer transmissions of a packet. This is a good metric that aims to increase throughput of a link as well as the network, by minimising transmissions and, of course, retransmissions of packets. Thus, the metric ETX emerged, which is the average number of transmissions of data and ACK packets. A node calculates ETX by obtaining the frame loss ratio of a wireless link l with each of its neighbouring nodes in the data direction, denoted as PRR_{frwd}. Thereafter it continues by repeating the aforementioned procedure in the opposite direction, denoted as PRR_{bkwd}. ETX is widely known as the inverse of the probability of Packet Success Delivery given as

$$ETX_l = \frac{1}{PRR_{frwd} * PRR_{bkwd}} \tag{4}$$

As it is clear from Eq. (4) a link is perfect if its ETX value is 1. Moreover, the route ETX is the sum of the ETX of every link in the route. Hence, a two-hop route of perfect links has an ETX of 2. As we can see, the larger the ETX value the less reliable the links. ETX has several significant features, such as that it affects throughput, since it depends on delivery ratios. Also, it detects link asymmetry by employing bidirectional ratios, uses precise link loss ratio measurements, and penalizes routes with more hops, which have lower throughput due to interference between different hops of the same path [21]. In addition, ETX may implicitly lower the energy consumption per packet, as each transmission or retransmission may increase a node's energy consumption.

At this point we will provide the relationship of ETX with transmission power of each node. Note that we consider a Rayleigh channel [33]. For a wireless link (i, j), the Packet Reception Ratio $PRR_{i,j}$ is defined as the ratio of the number of packets received by node j over the number of packets sent by node i. This is the PRR_{frwd} and similarly, $PRR_{j,i}$ is the PRR_{bkwd}. It can be expressed by approximation as

$$PRR_{i,j} = (1 - \xi)^l \tag{5}$$

where l is the packet length in bits. The Bit Error Rate (BER), which we denote as $\xi_{i,j}$, is given by the following formula [13]

$$\xi_{i,j} = \frac{1}{2}\left(1 - \sqrt{\frac{\gamma_{i,j}}{1 + \gamma_{i,j}}}\right) \tag{6}$$

where $\gamma_{i,j}$ is the Signal-to-Interference-plus-Noise Ratio (SINR) of the transmission from node i to node j. $\gamma_{i,j}$ is given by

$$\gamma_{i,j} = \frac{H_{i,j}p_i}{\displaystyle\sum_{t \neq i, t \neq j} p_t H_{t,j} + N_0} \tag{7}$$

We model the wireless channel as a log-distance shadowing path loss channel, defined as

$$PL(d) = PL(d_0) + 10\eta log(\frac{d}{d_0}) + X_\sigma \tag{8}$$

where $PL(d)$ is the path loss at distance d, $PL(d_0)$ is the path loss, which is known, at reference distance d_0, η is the path loss exponent and X_σ is the zero-mean Gaussian random variable with standard deviation σ. Our setting is based on a dynamic environment, possibly indoor, where the nodes transmit or receive in a multipath manner. This setting is equivalent to node mobility. Shadow fading and distance based attenuation vary; hence, the instant value of the magnitude of the received signal is a random variable with Rayleigh probability density function. Here, we assume that the channel coefficients are constant for a code-word, but there are independent and identically distributed (i.i.d) for different blocks. For a set of different links, the channel fading coefficients are statistically i.i.d., which is a reasonable assumption, since nodes are spatially deployed [35].

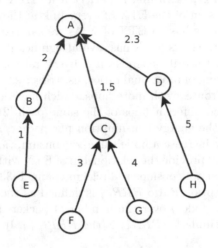

Fig. 1. ETX valued network [39].

State-of-the-art wireless routing protocols, such as CTP [14], use ETX to encapsulate the routes' packet reception quality by making it additive. An example can be seen in Fig. 1. As we can see, the ETX values of the links originating at the basestation are being added as the network goes downwards away from the basestation. Each node selects its parent node that it transmits to depending on the link quality of the available parents. For instance, node G has an ETX value of 5.5 to reach node A, which is the basestation. This implicitly provides us substantial information regarding the hop-count of the nodes in the network. Throughput of the network may be optimised, since we can attempt to optimise the link quality in entire routes.

Hence, we consider the additive route ETX that we call AETX, which is given in Eq. (9). We denote R is the set of nodes that create the links of a route to the basestation for every node $i \in R$.

$$AETX = \sum_{i=1}^{R} ETX_i \qquad (9)$$

4.1 Relationship Between AETX and Capacity

We know that the capacity of the link is given by the Shannon's formula, which is a function of the SINR between nodes i, j in Eq. (7) as

$$f(\gamma_{i,j}) = W \log_2(1 + \gamma_{i,j}) \tag{10}$$

We can derive from Eq. (10) that the capacity of the link is maximised when the SINR of the link is maximum. From Eq. (5), it is straightforward to see that when SINR increases PRR increases as well, except when interference is too large, whereby the node has its maximum PRR by using a transmission power level lower than the maximum value [15]. From Eq. (4) we can derive that the smaller the value of AETX, the larger the capacity of the wireless link. Furthermore, it is intuitive that we have a sweet spot of ETX that maximises the capacity between the two nodes by using one of the finite set of available transmission power levels. Furthermore, we see that in a status of competition for the wireless medium there is a value of the transmission power that is able to maximise the end-to-end throughput of the nodes route to the basestation given in Eq. (9) and maximise capacity at the same time.

Additionally, we are required to show the relationship between the AETX with the delay of the packet transmission due to interference, which will present in the following part of this paper. Our aim is to show that the selection of the most appropriate transmission power level will increase throughput and minimise the delay of packet transmission as well.

4.2 Relationship Between AETX and Delay

In our network scenario we wish to satisfy certain QoS requirements, such as keeping the transmission and queuing delay smaller than an upper bound. We denote the upper bound of the delay as d. We assume that the incoming traffic in our network is Poisson distributed with average packet arrival rate λ_i and packet length of N bits. Thus, we have the rate of the source, which is given by $r_i = M\lambda_i$. We assume that the packets are queued in a FIFO queue. The time required for each packet transmission is given by

$$t_i = \frac{M}{R_i} \tag{11}$$

where R_i is the transmission rate of the queued packets.

We encapsulate a similar approach with Meshkati et al. [25] in our model, to indicate the relationship of the transmission delay with AETX and provide a QoS constraint. We consider an M/G/1 queue with Poisson traffic with the aforementioned parameter λ_i and service time s_i. We transform AETX to be normalised to $[0, 1]$, in order to make it resemble with AETX probability. To this end, the formula of AETX, which we denote as $AETX_i^{norm}$ is given by

$$AETX_i^{norm} = \frac{1}{1 - AETX_{max}} * AETX - \frac{AETX_{max}}{1 - AETX_{max}} \tag{12}$$

where $AETX_{max}$ is the maximum value that $AETX$ can take give the hops that node i exists away from the basestation. Hence, we have the Probability Mass Function (PMF)

$$Pr\{s_i = mt_i\} = AETX_i^{norm}(1 - AETX_i^{norm})^{m-1} \qquad \text{for } m = 1, 2...$$

Thereafter, the service rate μ_i can be given by

$$\mu_i = \frac{AETX_i^{norm}}{t_i} \tag{13}$$

and the load is given by $\rho_i = \frac{\lambda_i t_i}{AETX_i^{norm}}$

The average packet delay as given by Meshkati is given by

$$\bar{d} = t_i \left(\frac{1 - \frac{\lambda_i t_i}{2}}{AETX_i^{norm} - \lambda_i t_i} \right) AETX_i^{norm} > \lambda_i t_i \tag{14}$$

From Eq. (14), we can see that a larger $AETX_i^{norm}$ leads to smaller delay. Hence, a smaller $AETX$ offers as quicker transmission of our packets. Thus, we find that we can define a utility function to create a game-theoretic algorithm that will aim to optimise the end-to-end throughput in a hierarchically routed network.

4.3   Impact of Transmission Power on Contention

Transmission Power is the major reason for the increase of contention on the wireless medium. This is the case, since the number of neighbors of each node increases resulting in a competition of the wireless medium acquisition. A wireless device senses the wireless channel to check its availability using Clear Channel Assessment (CCA). If it finds it free, it transmits the packet. However, if the wireless channel is occupied the device performs an exponential backoff and attempts to retransmit the packet. Hence, we may experience a number of packet retransmissions before a packet is successfully forwarded, unless the maximum retransmissions limit is reached; then, the packet is dropped.

By incorporating AETX in our approach, we attempt to minimise the packet retransmissions while the optimal transmission power level is utilised. As such, contention is minimised and the quality of transmission and the throughput implicitly is enhanced. In particular, if we utilise a state of the art routing protocol, we may accomplish near-optimal link quality due to the hierarchical transmission scheme [14]. Other protocols penalise routes with high ETX [26]; hence, we can see that reducing the transmission power may result in more available links, due to interference mitigation. We can see transmission power contention reduction in [37].

4.4   Other Cross-Layer Considerations

There are other cross-layer consideration related to link quality and power control. The transmission power playes a key role to establishing the degree of each node and preserving network connectivity as we can in [22] and references therein. Hence, we can consider power control with link quality and a topology control (TC) mechanism that optimises network transmission reliability, while the network remains connected.

We can consider TC as a different layer in the wireless sensor device stack. The TC layer is located between the MAC and routing layers. The parameters TC utilises to determine the final topology come from three layers, as it can be seen in Fig. 2. The MAC layer triggers the TC operations when it detects high contention based on the number of neighbors or when a failure/addition of node occurs. Thereafter, the TC collects the neighbors information with their respective link quality estimations (ETX and AETX) from the routing layer. The core layer provides the power with which a packet is received. The TC layer sends the topology update to the MAC and routing layers, in order to continue their operations.

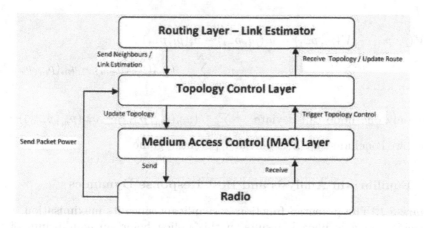

Fig. 2. Parameters that impact decisions of topology control.

In this way, we can further enhance the device stack into optimising several parameters that reside across multiple layers.

5   GETOA

We consider a game-theoretic formulation of the network $Z = (N, A, u)$, where N is the number of players/nodes, A is the set of available strategies to a player and u represent the utility functions of the players.

We define the strategies of the players $A = p_1, ...p_A$ as a set of finite values that correspond to the transmission power settings of a wireless module. Furthermore, we define the utility function of a player i as

$$u_i = -AETX + c_i p_i \tag{15}$$

This a common definition of a utility function that utilises pricing, in order to make the game more efficient [42]. We transform the utility function of (15) in the following manner. We use the negative AETX to the power of two, in order to make the first term concave. The second term includes the variable $c_i > 0$, which is the cost of using the transmission power p_i and is assumed to be set to 1.

$$u_i = -(AETX)^2 + c_i p_i \tag{16}$$

We formulate our game as an exact potential game as shown below

Lemma 1. *The game Z described above with utility functions as in (16) is an exact potential game and its potential function is given by* $V = -\sum_i^N (AETX)^2 + \sum_i^N c_i p_i.$

Proof.

$$V(p_i, p_{-i}) - V(p'_i, p_{-i}) = u_i(p_i, p_{-i}) - u_i(p'_i, p_{-i})$$
$$+ \sum_{m \in N, m \neq i}^N (u_m(p_m, p_{-m}) - u_m(p'_m, p_{-m}))$$

Since only one node can deviate $\sum_{m \in N, m \neq i}^N (u_m(p_m, p_{-m}) - u_m(p'_m, p_{-m})) = 0.$
Hence, we conclude that Z is an exact potential game. $\square$

5.1   Equilibrium Analysis and Best Response Dynamics

Remark 3.1. The potential function is significant since its maximisation, when a specific policy is played, results in this policy being an equilibrium of the designed game.

Since we have a finite strategy set, the potential function needs to satisfy the Larger Midpoint Property (LMP) [43]. The converse is true as well; As such, if a policy is an equilibrium, it maximises the potential function. Our function in Eq. (16) is concave. Thus, Schur concavity is ensured and specific majorisation properties are satisfied [30]. We will show that in the next part of this section.

We consider two n-dimensional vectors $\delta(1), \delta(2)$.

Definition 1 ([24]): A vector $\delta(2)$ majorises $\delta(1)$, which we denote as $\delta(1) \prec \delta(2)$, if $\delta(2)$ is more "unregular" in the following fashion:

$$\begin{cases} \sum_{i=1}^k \delta_{[i]}(1) \leq \sum_{i=1}^k \delta_{[i]}(2), k = 1, 2, ..., n-1 \\ \sum_{i=1}^k \delta_{[i]}(1) = \sum_{i=1}^k \delta_{[i]}(2) \end{cases} \tag{17}$$

where $\delta_{[i]}(m)$ is a permutation of $\delta_i(m)$ satisfying the condition $\delta_{[1]}(m) \geq \delta_{[2]}(m) \geq ... \geq \delta_{[n]}(m), m = 1, 2$.

From Eq. (16) we can derive that the largest element of $\delta(2)$ is larger than the largest element of $\delta(1)$. Similarly, the smallest element of $\delta(2)$ is smaller than the smallest element of $\delta(1)$. Thereafter, we proceed in showing that we can accomplish the global optimum by investigating the Schur convexity properties of majorisation.

Definition 2: A function $f : \mathbb{R}^n \rightarrow \mathbb{R}$ is Schur concave if $\delta(1) \prec \delta(2)$ suggests $f(\delta(1)) \geq f(\delta(2))$.

Definition 1 dictates that there is strong majorisation; Proposition $C.2$ of [24] suggests that a function $f : \mathbb{R}^n \rightarrow \mathbb{R}$ is Schur-concave if it is symmetric and concave. In the next part we will show that the potential function V is Schur-concave.

Lemma 2. *Function V is concave in $\mathbb{R}^n$, where we denote $\mathbb{R}^n$ as a finite set of real numbers with 1-decimal points, min = p_1 and max = p_3*

Proof. The fact that V is concave can be concluded since if the second derivative of the potential function includes two terms, of which the first a concave term and the second will be set to 0 [39]. However, this can serve as an approximation of a continuous function. In order to prove concavity we need to show

$$V(p - 1) + V(p + 1) \leq 2V(p) \tag{18}$$

From Eq. (18) have the following

$$- \sum_i^N (AETX(p_{i-1}))^2 + \sum_i^N c_2 p_{i-1} - \sum_i^N (AETX(p_{i+1}))^2 + \sum_i^N c_3 p_{i+1}$$

$$\leq -2(\sum_i^N (AETX(p_i))^2 + \sum_i^N c_2 p_i) \tag{19}$$

The variables c_1, c_2 and c_3 are set to 1. We can see by the definition of ETX that when the transmission power is increasing the AETX value decreases. Hence, the function V is non-decreasing. Then by definition of Eq. (18), function V is concave.   □

Proposition 1. *If the function $V(p)$ is concave then the function $V(p)$ is Schur concave.*

Proof. The proof is given by using the following corollary from [24].   □

Corollary 1. *Let $\phi(x) = \sum_{i=1}^n g(x)$ where g is concave. Then ϕ is Schur-concave*

Theorem 1. *The GETOA algorithm reaches the global optimum*

Proof. These majorisation properties can be utilised to show that our function follows LMP. Since our function is Schur concave the global optimum p^* majorises another potential p'^*. Since $V(p)$ is Schur concave it follows by definition that $V(p'^*) \geq V(p^*)$. Since, p^* maximises the potential, this is only possible when $V(p'^*) = V(p^*)$. Hence, p^* is the global optimum. $\qquad\square$

In our non-cooperative game formulation we introduce the class of best-response dynamics, in which every node updates its strategy, in order to maximise its utility, given the strategies of the other nodes. We denote the best-response dynamics with β_i for the ith node, which satisfies

$$\beta_i(\mathbf{p}_i) = \arg \max_{p_i \in P_i} u_i(p_i, \mathbf{p}_{-i}) \tag{20}$$

We are investigating finite actions for the nodes' strategies; hence, the best response dynamics may be addressed using the discrete-time fictitious play (DTFP) [4,34]. Fictitious play has been proven to converge in finite potential games [27]. As we can see in the lecture of Johari [18], under the DFTP the nodes move simultaneously. Furthermore, the game starts via the arbitrary selection of a pure strategy p_i^0 and initial beliefs. Hence, we denote as v_i^0 the initial distribution providing the expectations of the other nodes about the strategy that node i will play at time $t = 0$. At each time $t \geq 0$ we select

$$p_i^t \in \beta(\mathbf{v}_{-i}^t) \tag{21}$$

and we let

$$v_i^t = \frac{(F_i^t + v_i^0)}{t+1} \tag{22}$$

where he term F_i^t for a strategy is the empirical frequency of node i's playing strategy and is given by

$$F_i^t(p_i) = \sum_{\tau=0}^{t-1} I\{p_i^\tau = p_i\} \tag{23}$$

The term $I\{A\}$ is the indicator function of A.

Note that with this formulation, v_i^0 is therefore a mixed strategy played at node i at time $t = -1$. Moreover, we provide the formulation of the empirical distribution v_i^t's play up to time t, which is given by

$$v_i^t(p_i) = \frac{F_i^t(p_i)}{t} \tag{24}$$

The update rule of v_i^t can be though of in Bayesian sense. Also, we suppose that nodes beliefs about the probability that player i will play the mixed strategy m_i is given by

$$\mathbb{P}(m_i) = \frac{1}{\prod_{p_i \in A_i} \Gamma(v_i^t(p_i))} \prod_{p_i \in A_i} m_i(p_i)^{v_i^t(p_i)-1} \tag{25}$$

where Γ is the gamma function. Thus it is easy to see that the value of $m_i(p_i)$ is $v_i^t(p_i)$. Furthermore, we can see that the conditional distribution of m_i when node i played p_i^t is a Dirichlet distribution with parameter vector v_i^{t+1}. Finally, when we utilise DFTP, we assume that nodes put equal weight on every strategy they played at the past. The extreme case, where

$$v_i^t(p_i^{t-1}) = 1 \text{ and } v_i^t(p_i) = 0 \tag{26}$$

for all other p_i is called the best response dynamic.

Furthermore, in this paper, we are concentrating in the study of the dynamical properties of our potential game. To this end, we wish to show that the Nash Equilibrium that our approach is converging to is Lyapunov stable [19].

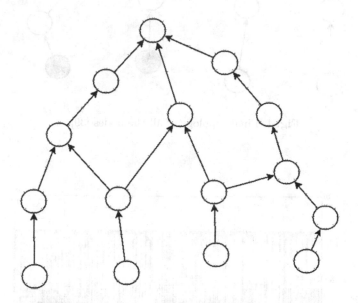

Fig. 3. Initial topology of all the nodes [39].

To prove Lyapunov stability, we provide the following theorem

Theorem 2. *Let* $\Phi = V_{max} - V_{min}$ *with respect to* p *a Lyapunov function. The Nash Equilibrium that our algorithm converges to is globally asymptotically stable.*

Proof. We need to show the following:

- $\Phi(0) = 0$ and $\Phi(p) > 0, \forall x \neq 0$
- $\Delta V(p(k)) \triangleq \Phi(p(k)) - \Phi(p(k-1)) < 0, \forall x(k) \in D$
- $\| p \| \to \infty \Rightarrow \Phi(p) \to \infty$

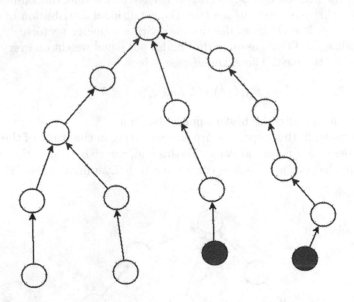

Fig. 4. Final topology of all the nodes [39].

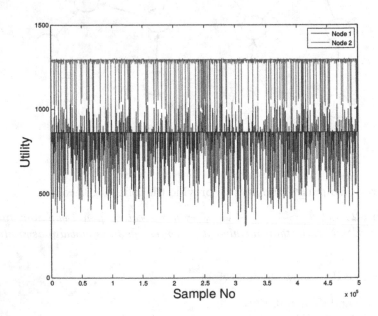

Fig. 5. Utilities of blue nodes. (Color figure online)

where $D \to \mathbb{R}^n$ and indices k instead of the more precise one of kTs, with Ts being the period.

For the first requirement if we set $p_{min} = p_{max} = 0$, then we have $V_{max} = V(0)$ and $V_{min} = V(0)$, which gives us $\Phi(0) = 0$. Furthermore, as the function is non-decreasing we have $V_{max} - V_{min} > 0$.

In order to satisfy the second requirement, if we consider our Lyapunov function to evolve over time period, then the V_{min}, which we denote as $V(p(k))_{min}$ will be larger from $V(p(k-1))_{min}$ in the next state, since we are considering k to be a period of changing transmission power when attempting to maximise the potential function. Also, $V(p(k))_{max} = V(p(k-1))_{max}$ As such, in the next period a node will deviate to maximise its utility, which means that potential function will approach V_{max}. Hence we have

$$\Phi(p(k)) - \Phi(p(k-1)) =$$
$$V(p(k))_{max} - V(p(k))_{min} - V(p(k-1))_{max} + V(p(k-1))_{min}$$
$$= -V(p(k))_{min} + V(p(k-1))_{min} < 0 \quad (27)$$

Regarding the third requirement, as $\parallel p \parallel \to \inf$ then the first term of Φ, V_{max} will be set to infinity, since the function is non-decreasing with the values of p.   □

6   Results

We consider the network of 15 nodes, which is shown in Fig. 3. The arrows represent that the wireless nodes operate in a hierarchical routing mode, where each node unicasts its data to its selected parent. Moreover, the parent selection process is undertaken by evaluation the ETX values of each node's neighbours and choosing the one with the least ETX value. After the formation of the network and the operation of GETOA, the final topology is shown in Fig. 4. We can see that a route towards the basestation has been formed for every mode based on the ETX values of the upstream nodes.

The transmission power values that are selected as strategies of the nodes come from the CC2020 datasheet [11] and are given in Table 1. The reason behind the selection is the fact that want to see the operation of our algorithm in the gray areas as identified in [36]. The operation of GETOA initiates by selecting a random transmission power level and then starts to perform the fictitious play part. We can see the utility function over time of the blue nodes in Fig. 5. Specifically, we can see that Node 1, denoted as the blue node in the right, fluctuates significantly, while it utility seems to get maximised; however, its utility is still not very high, since we assume that this node has the most significant problems and suffers from maximum interference. Thus, as we see in Fig. 7 its ETX value is not very good. On the other hand, node 2 has a high utility accomplishing low ETX values as we can see in Figs. 5 and 7. Its ETX value fluctuates close to the value of 4; thus, if we check the route we can see that its value is close to optimal.

The transmission power used by the nodes come from the beliefs of the strategies that the other nodes will play. We highlight the fact the beliefs of the node do not always result in the highest possible utility, since their forecasting under DFTP might not be the best, even though updating is. In our experiment, node 1 always plays the dominant strategy, which corresponds to the value of 15.2 μA; We omit graph illustration of the transmission power fluctuations. However, we show the beliefs of node 1 strategies in Fig. 6. We see that the dominant belief is that of belief 2, which effectively corresponds to the pure strategy player by node 1.

On the other hand, node 2 shows fluctuation, since its dominant strategy changes. Specifically, it sometimes fluctuates to all three transmission power levels; however, It's dominant strategy is the transmission power level of 17.4 μA. This is explained by checking its utility function values. Node 2 does not suffer from high interference; hence, it raises its transmission power value to accomplish a higher utility, by achieving a higher SINR value.

Table 1. Tx power strategies [39].

Tx power levels	p_1	p_2	p_3
Values	13.9	15.2	17.4

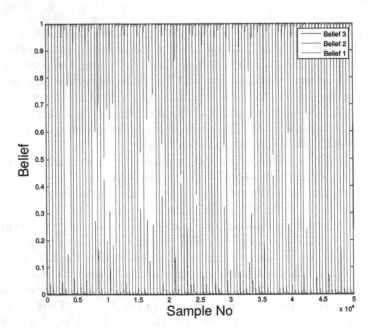

Fig. 6. Belief values of node 1.

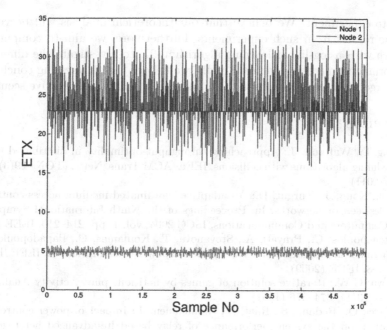

Fig. 7. ETX values of blue nodes. (Color figure online)

7   Conclusions

In this paper, we addressed the end-to-end throughput optimisation using game theory. We established a utility function based on the additive ETX from the sink to each node and we priced it with a price utilising the transmission power used for data transmission. We showed that there is a relationship between ETX with capacity, packet transmission delay contention and topology control. Furthermore, we formulated our game theoretic model with finite strategies and showed that it is a potential game. Moreover, we proved that the Nash equilibrium we located is the global optimum as well, using Schur concavity. Finally, we proved that the Nash equilibrium our GETOA algorithm approached to is Lyapunov stable.

The demonstration of our approach consisted of a network of 15 nodes. We analysed the two blue nodes that exist further down the network to check their behavior under our GETOA algorithm. We found that Node 1 fluctuates due to high interference keeping the same transmission power level. Node 2, increases its utility function, while its ETX value is close to optimal. Since the assumption was that this node suffers from low interference, the result is reasonable. Furthermore, the second node changes its transmission power in the algorithm run to further maximise its utility.

Our future work includes the packet transmission delay as a constraint to our utility function. Also, contention measurements will further strengthen our approach. To this end, we need to utilise network simulators, such as TOSSIM or ns3 to experiment. We believe that our theoretical analysis will be verified with the results from such experiments. Furthermore, we aim to compare our approach with a log-linear learning algorithm [27] to investigate the differences in performance and convergence. Finally, we believe that interesting conclusions will emerge with the comparison of this approach with a cooperative scenario.

References

1. Jiang, L., Walrand, J.: Approaching throughput-optimality in distributed CSMA scheduling algorithms with collisions. IEEE/ACM Trans. Netw. (TON) **19**(3), 816–829 (2011)
2. Ai, J., Kong, J., Turgut, D.: An adaptive coordinated medium access control for wireless sensor networks. In: Proceedings of the Ninth International Symposium on Computers and Communications, ISCC 2004, vol. 1, pp. 214–219. IEEE (2004)
3. Antonopoulos, C., Prayati, A., Stoyanova, T., Koulamas, C., Papadopoulos, G.: Experimental evaluation of a WSN platform power consumption. In: IEEE IPDPS, pp. 1–8. IEEE (2009)
4. Brown, G.W.: Iterative solution of games by fictitious play. Activity Anal. Prod. Alloc. **13**(1), 374–376 (1951)
5. Bulakci, Ö., Redana, S., Raaf, B., Hämäläinen, J.: Impact of power control optimization on the system performance of relay based lte-advanced heterogeneous networks. J. Commun. Netw. **13**(4), 345–359 (2011)
6. Chantzis, K., Amaxilatis, D., Chatzigiannakis, I., Rolim, J.: Symmetric coherent link degree, adaptive throughput-transmission power for wireless sensor networks. In: IEEE International Conference on Distributed Computing in Sensor Systems, pp. 26–34. IEEE (2014)
7. Choi, J.: Effective capacity of noma and a suboptimal power control policy with delay QoS. IEEE Trans. Commun. **65**(4), 1849–1858 (2017)
8. Choi, H.-H., Lee, J.-R.: Distributed transmit power control for maximizing end-to-end throughput in wireless multi-hop networks. Wirel. Pers. Commun. **74**(3), 1033–1044 (2014)
9. ICSLMS Committee: Wireless LAN medium access control (MAC) and physical layer (PHY) specifications (1997)
10. Daskalakis, C., Goldberg, P.W., Papadimitriou, C.H.: The complexity of computing a nash equilibrium. SIAM J. Comput. **39**(1), 195–259 (2009)
11. Chipcon, Products from Texas Instruments: CC2420 data sheet, 2.4 GHz IEEE 802.15. 4/Zigbee-ready RF transceiver (2006)
12. De Couto, D.S., Aguayo, D., Bicket, J., Morris, R.: A high-throughput path metric for multi-hop wireless routing. Wirel. Netw. **11**(4), 419–434 (2005)
13. Fu, Y., Sha, M., Hackmann, G., Lu, C.: Practical control of transmission power for wireless sensor networks. In: 20th IEEE International Conference on Network Protocols (ICNP), pp. 1–10. IEEE (2012)
14. Gnawali, O., Fonseca, R., Jamieson, K., Moss, D., Levis, P.: Collection tree protocol. In: ACM SenSys, pp. 1–14 (2009)
15. Hackmann, G., Chipara, O., Lu, C.: Robust topology control for indoor wireless sensor networks. In: Proceedings of the 6th ACM Conference on Embedded Network Sensor Systems, pp. 57–70. ACM (2008)
16. Incel, O.D., Ghosh, A., Krishnamachari, B., Chintalapudi, K.: Fast data collection in tree-based wireless sensor networks. IEEE Trans. Mob. Comput. **11**(1), 86–99 (2012)

17. Jun, J., Sichitiu, M.L.: The nominal capacity of wireless mesh networks. IEEE Wirel. Commun. **10**(5), 8–14 (2003)
18. Johari, R.: Lecture 6: Fictitious Play. MS&E 336: Dynamics and Learning in Games, Lecture Notes, Stanford University (2007)
19. Khalil, H.K., Grizzle, J.: Nonlinear Systems, vol. 3. Prentice Hall, New Jersey (1996)
20. Komali, R., MacKenzie, A., Gilles, R.: Effect of selfish node behavior on efficient topology design. IEEE Tran. Mob. Comput. **7**(9), 1057–1070 (2008)
21. Li, J., Blake, C., De Couto, D.S., Lee, H.I., Morris, R.: Capacity of ad hoc wireless networks. In: Proceedings of the 7th Annual International Conference on Mobile Computing and Networking, pp. 61–69. ACM (2001)
22. Li, M., Li, Z., Vasilakos, A.V.: A survey on topology control in wireless sensor networks: taxonomy, comparative study, and open issues. Proc. IEEE **101**(12), 2538–2557 (2013)
23. Lin, S., Miao, F., Zhang, J., Zhou, G., Gu, L., He, T., Stankovic, J.A., Son, S., Pappas, G.J.: ATPC: adaptive transmission power control for wireless sensor networks. ACM Trans. Sens. Netw. (TOSN) **12**(1), 6 (2016)
24. Marshall, A.W., Olkin, I., Arnold, B.: Inequalities: Theory of Majorization and Its Applications. Springer, New York (2011). https://doi.org/10.1007/978-0-387-68276-1
25. Meshkati, F., Poor, H.V., Schwartz, S.C., Balan, R.V.: Energy-efficient power and rate control with QoS constraints: a game-theoretic approach. In: Proceedings of the 2006 International Conference on Wireless Communications and Mobile Computing, pp. 1435–1440. ACM (2006)
26. Moeller, S., Sridharan, A., Krishnamachari, B., Gnawali, O.: Routing without routes: the backpressure collection protocol. In: Proceedings of the 9th ACM/IEEE International Conference on Information Processing in Sensor Networks, pp. 279–290. ACM, April 2010
27. Monderer, D., Shapley, L.S.: Potential games. Games Econ. Behav. **14**(1), 124–143 (1996)
28. Moscibroda, T., Wattenhofer, R., Weber, Y.: Protocol design beyond graph-based models. In: Proceedings of the ACM Workshop on Hot Topics in Networks (HotNets-V), pp. 25–30 (2006)
29. Nash Jr., J.: The bargaining problem. Econom. J. Econom. Soc. **18**(2), 155–162 (1950)
30. Olkin, I., Marshall, A.W.: Inequalities: Theory of Majorization and Its Applications, vol. 143. Academic Press, New York (2016)
31. Papadimitriou, C.H.: On the complexity of the parity argument and other inefficient proofs of existence. J. Comput. Syst. Sci. **48**(3), 498–532 (1994)
32. Rajendran, V., Obraczka, K., Garcia-Luna-Aceves, J.J.: Energy-efficient, collision-free medium access control for wireless sensor networks. Wirel. Netw. **12**(1), 63–78 (2006)
33. Rappaport, T.S., et al.: Wireless Communications: Principles and Practice, vol. 2. Prentice Hall PTR, New Jersey (1996)
34. Robinson, J.: An iterative method of solving a game. Ann. Math. **54**(2), 296–301 (1951)
35. Sadek, A.K., Yu, W., Liu, K.: When does cooperation have better performance in sensor networks? In: 3rd Annual IEEE Communications Society on Sensor and Ad Hoc Communications and Networks, SECON 2006, vol. 1, pp. 188–197. IEEE (2006)

36. Son, D., Krishnamachari, B., Heidemann, J.: Experimental study of the effects of transmission power control and blacklisting in wireless sensor networks. In: First Annual IEEE Communications Society Conference on Sensor and Ad Hoc Communications and Networks, SECON 2004, pp. 289–298. IEEE (2004)

37. Spyrou, E.D., Yang, S., Mitrakos, D.K.: Game-theoretic optimal power-link quality topology control in wireless sensor networks. Sens. Transducers **212**(5), 1 (2017)

38. Spyrou, E.D., Mitrakos, D.K.: On the homogeneous transmission power under the SINR model. In: 4th International Conference on Telecommunications and Remote Sensing, ICTRS 2015 (2015)

39. Spyrou, E.D., Mitrakos, D.K.: Game-theoretic end-to-end throughput optimisation in wireless sensor networks. In: Proceedings of the 14th International Joint Conference on e-Business and Telecommunications - Volume 2: WINSYS, (ICETE 2017) (2017)

40. Sun, F., Li, L., Jiang, Y.: Impact of duty cycle on end-to-end performance in a wireless sensor network. In: IEEE Wireless Communications and Networking Conference (WCNC), pp. 1906–1911. IEEE (2015)

41. Tarighati, A., Jaldn, J.: Optimality of rate balancing in wireless sensor networks. IEEE Trans. Signal Process. **64**(14), 3735–3749 (2016)

42. Tsiropoulou, E.E., Katsinis, G.K., Papavassiliou, S.: Distributed uplink power control in multiservice wireless networks via a game theoretic approach with convex pricing. IEEE Trans. Parallel Distrib. Syst. **23**(1), 61–68 (2012)

43. Ui, T.: Discrete concavity for potential games. Int. Game Theor. Rev. **10**(01), 137–143 (2008)

44. Von Neumann, J., Morgenstern, O., Rubinstein, A., Kuhn, H.: Theory of Games and Economic Behavior. Princeton University Press, Princeton (2007)

45. Yeung, M., Kwok, Y.: A game theoretic approach to power aware wireless data access. IEEE Trans. Mob. Comput. **5**(8), 1057–1073 (2006)

46. Yu, Y., Shah, S., Tan, Y., Lim, Y.: End-to-end throughput evaluation of consensus TPC algorithm in multihop wireless networks. In: International Wireless Communications and Mobile Computing Conference (IWCMC), pp. 941–946. IEEE (2015)

47. Zeng, K., Lou, W., Zhai, H.: On end-to-end throughput of opportunistic routing in multirate and multihop wireless networks. In: INFOCOM 2008: The 27th Conference on Computer Communications. IEEE (2008)

BiPS – A Real-Time-Capable Protocol Framework for Wireless Networked Control Systems and Its Application

Markus Engel[1(✉)], Christopher Kramer[1], Tobias Braun[2], Dennis Christmann[1], and Reinhard Gotzhein[1]

[1] Technische Universität Kaiserslautern, Kaiserslautern, Germany
{engel,kramer,christma,gotzhein}@cs.uni-kl.de
[2] Fraunhofer IESE, Kaiserslautern, Germany
tobias.braun@iese.fraunhofer.de

Abstract. In wireless networked control systems (WNCS), sensors, controllers, and actuators exchange data to solve control tasks. Operation of WNCS usually occurs under real-time constraints, in particular regarding synchronicity of value sampling, transmission latencies, and packet losses. This calls for deterministic protocols as well as for real-time-capable implementations of these protocols. In this paper, we present the protocol framework BiPS (Black-burst integrated Protocol Stack), which provides real-time protocol and operating system functionalities, and its implementation on the Imote 2 hardware platform hosting the transceiver CC 2420. Furthermore, we present the application and deployment of BiPS in an industrial environment.

Keywords: Real-time · Wireless networks · Communication protocols Operating systems

1 Introduction

Wireless networked control systems (WNCS) are a class of networked control systems where sensors, controllers, and actuators exchange data over a wireless digital communication network [17] (see Fig. 1). The use of wireless communication technologies for flexible networking is crucial for the operation of these systems. Typically, WNCS have real-time requirements, in particular regarding synchronicity of value sampling, transmission latencies, and packet losses. This calls for deterministic protocols, i.e. protocols with predictable properties regarding, e.g., maximal tick offset, collision-free transmission, and worst-case packet latencies. Furthermore, the implementation of these protocols has to preserve their real-time capabilities, which places demands on operating system (OS) support.

In a previous paper [5], we have introduced the BiPS (Black-burst integrated Protocol Stack) framework. We have outlined BiPS protocols and operating

© Springer Nature Switzerland AG 2019
M. S. Obaidat and E. Cabello (Eds.): ICETE 2017, CCIS 990, pp. 313–336, 2019.
https://doi.org/10.1007/978-3-030-11039-0_15

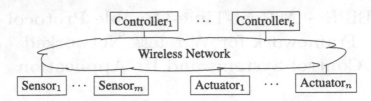

Fig. 1. Wireless networked control system.

system functionalities, and have provided a comparative evaluation with the operating systems TinyOS and RIOT. In this paper, we extend this work. First, we provide more detailed information about BiPS protocols. In particular, we address real-time synchronization, the concept of virtual slot regions, techniques to achieve predictable medium access, and a new protocol for topology discovery. We also report on extensions of the framework concerning real-time application scheduling and on details of nesting another operating system into BiPS. Finally, we present the application and deployment of the BiPS framework in an industrial context.

To achieve highly accurate timing, the BiPS framework runs on top of the Imote 2 hardware platform [24], without further operating system (OS). Therefore, all typical OS functionalities, such as real-time schedulers (time-, event-driven) and hardware drivers are incorporated into the BiPS framework. Thus, BiPS does not only consist of a set of protocols, but also constitutes a light-weight, customized, and layered OS [11].

The paper is structured as follows. In Sect. 2, we outline the BiPS framework and present details of several BiPS protocols. Section 3 is concerned with operating system functionalities of BiPS, in particular, scheduling of protocols and applications, and multiplexing of MAC protocols. In Sect. 4, we present the adaptation and deployment of BiPS in a networked production environment. Section 5 reports on related work. Conclusions are drawn in Sect. 6.

2   The BiPS Framework

BiPS is a protocol framework for wireless networked control systems specialized for the Imote 2 platform [24]. This platform is based on an Intel XScale PXA 270 controller with 256 KiB SRAM, 32 MiB SDRAM, and 32 MiB FLASH. It supports clock rates up to 416 MHz and integrates the widely used IEEE 802.15.4-compliant CC 2420 transceiver [30].

2.1   Overview of the BiPS Framework

The architecture of the BiPS framework is shown in Fig. 2. Shaded parts of the figure show the functionality covered by BiPS. Other parts are to be added before deploying the framework (see Sect. 4). The overall structure of BiPS follows a layered approach, where higher layers abstract from the realization of lower layers by providing abstract interfaces.

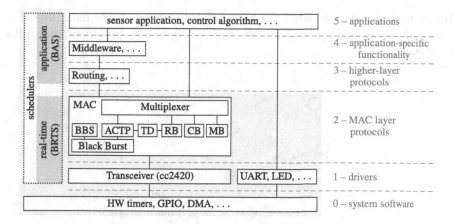

Fig. 2. Architecture of the BiPS framework.

- Layer 0 implements low level functionality to interact with hardware components, such as hardware timers or GPIO pins.
- Layer 1 comprises hardware drivers for peripheral devices, in particular an optimized driver for the CC 2420 transceiver using DMA (Direct Memory Access).
- Layer 2 consists of the synchronization protocol BBS providing network-wide synchronization in multi-hop networks, virtual slot region establishment, four MAC protocols, and topology discovery (see Sects. 2.2 to 2.5). In addition, a multiplexer provides a unique interface to the upper layers (see Sect. 2.6).
- Layer 3 hosts higher-level protocols, e.g. routing protocols (see Sect. 4.2).
- On layer 4, application-specific functionality is located. For WNCS, a customized middleware providing time- and event-triggered services and their location can be conceived (see Sect. 4.1).
- Layer 5 comprises applications, e.g. control algorithms.

In addition, two schedulers form part of the BiPS framework (see Sect. 3):

- The BiPS real-time scheduler (BRTS) controls execution of MAC layer protocols and real-time applications in their assigned time regions.
- The BiPS application scheduler (BAS) is responsible for the execution of non-real-time applications and higher-level functionality.

2.2   Tick and Time Synchronization with BBS

Tick synchronization establishes network-wide reference points in time. This is needed, in particular, to structure time by creating virtual slot regions (see Sect. 2.3), to be exclusively assigned to different communication functionalities and medium access schemes. For instance, it is possible to reserve time slots exclusively for communication among nodes, thereby avoiding collisions.

Time synchronization, in addition, adjusts local clocks to a common time. This is needed to timestamp measurements of sensors, and to synchronize value sampling.

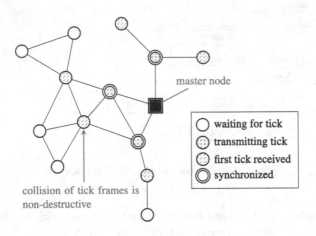

Fig. 3. Operation of BBS.

For tick and time synchronization, BiPS incorporates BBS (Black Burst Synchronization [14]). BBS is well-suited for wireless multi-hop networks and provides network-wide synchronization with low and bounded offset and convergence delay. In further work [9], we have identified several delays when using the Imote 2 platform including its CC 2420 transceiver and derived upper bounds by measuring these delays. Furthermore, we have optimized our implementation in order to keep variable delays as low as possible and thereby achieved a maximum offset of 129 µs per hop.

After initial tick synchronization, BBS performs periodical resynchronization, to mitigate the effects of relative clock skew and clock drift. A master node (see Fig. 3) starts resynchronization by sending a tick frame containing a round number set to 1. When nodes in range receive the tick frame, they resynchronize and broadcast a tick frame with the round number incremented by 1. This is repeated until the maximum network diameter has been reached.

With BBS, tick frames of the same round are sent (almost) simultaneously and therefore may collide (see Fig. 3). To protect them against destruction, they are encoded by sequences of black bursts, i.e. by busy tones of defined length. Thus, overlapping tick frames are not destroyed. This has the advantage that the duration of a synchronization phase is defined by the constant duration of each round – basically the transmission time of a tick frame – multiplied by the maximum network diameter. Furthermore, resynchronization is robust against topology changes caused, e.g., by mobility or failure of nodes.

2.3   Virtual Slot Regions

Based on tick synchronization (see Sect. 2.2), time can be structured network-wide into time slots. In BiPS, this is done in two steps. First, physical time slotting is performed, on top of which virtual time slots are defined.

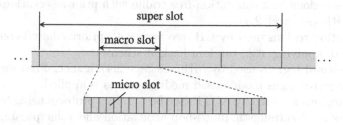

Fig. 4. Physical time slotting.

Physical time slotting divides time into a sequence of super slots consisting of macro slots, which in turn are decomposed into micro slots (see Fig. 4). Note that for a given BiPS deployment, the lengths of time slots are configurable, but fixed. The rationale behind this time structure is as follows:

– The duration of a super slot depends on the sampling periods of the application. To keep bandwidth waste small, sampling and synchronization periods should be chosen such that they can be arranged as a harmonic chain, with the longest period defining the duration of a super slot.
– The duration of a macro slot reflects the (maximal) resynchronization period that is needed to keep offsets sufficiently small.
– Micro slots are the time units combined into virtual slots regions, and are therefore very short, to keep bandwidth waste small. They are consecutively numbered within a super slot.

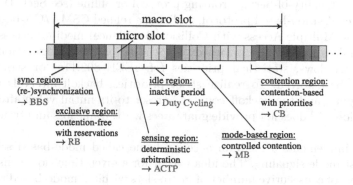

Fig. 5. Virtual time slotting.

Virtual time slotting combines consecutive micro slots into virtual slot regions of configurable lengths, serving different purposes (see Fig. 5):

- Sync regions are formed for (re-)synchronization purposes, placed at the beginning of each macro slot, and used by BBS (see Sect. 2.2). The length of a sync region is derived from the duration of a resynchronization phase.
- Exclusive regions host contention-free traffic with prior reservations, and are used by RB (see Sect. 2.4).
- In contention regions used by CB (see Sect. 2.4), priority-based contention is performed, applying, e.g., random backoff schemes.
- In mode-based regions used by MB (see Sect. 2.4), a specialized form of contention referred to as mode-based medium access is applied.
- Sensing regions are used by ACTP (see Sect. 2.4), a protocol using black-burst encodings for deterministic multi-hop arbitration and value passing.
- Idle regions represent inactive periods that can be used for energy saving (see Sects. 2.7 and 3.2).

Note that in a super slot, virtual slot regions of different types and sizes can be placed in a very flexible manner (see, e.g., Fig. 5). This placement is then repeated for all super slots, reflecting both system level (e.g. synchronization) and application level (e.g. value sampling) requirements.

2.4   Medium Access Control with RB, CB, MB and ACTP

The BiPS framework currently supports three medium access control (MAC) schemes for regular frames: reservation-based, contention-based, and mode-based, implemented by the protocols RB, CB, and MB, respectively.

- RB is a TDMA-based (Time Division Multiple Access) protocol with exclusive reservation, hence enabling deterministic guarantees. BiPS offers an interface to locally (de-)register slot assignments within exclusive regions, distinguishing between transmission and reception. However, the actual reservation and coordination of slot assignments is outside the scope of BiPS, and typically done by a Quality-of-Service routing protocol or offline (see Sect. 4).
- CB is a contention-based protocol, realizing a refined CSMA/CA-based (Carrier Sense Multiple Access with Collision Avoidance) medium access scheme with random backoff and priorities. Depending on the configuration of contention windows, statistical priorities (cf. IEEE 802.11e) or strict priorities can be enforced. To realize strict priorities, backoff intervals are non-overlapping, and the backoff counter is reset to its initial value after loss of contention. CB does not provide guarantees w.r.t. frame loss and transmission latency.
- MB [4] implements a medium access scheme called mode-based scheduling with fast mode signaling. The idea is that for a given time slot (consisting of a number of consecutive number of micro slots within a mode-based region), a defined set of messages may be ready for transmission. Each of these messages is associated with a mode, for which a slot-specific unique priority is defined.

With fast mode signaling, the priorities of messages competing in the same slot are then signaled in a highly efficient way over one hop. Since priorities are unique, there will be one winning node, which is then entitled to transmit. For the message with the highest priority and single-hop transfers without hidden stations, this is equivalent to RB. If that message is a sporadic one, other messages may win, too, thereby improving bandwidth usage while still providing some guarantees, especially if messages scheduled for the same slot are mutually exclusive.

- ACTP (Arbitrating and Cooperative Transfer Protocol [6]) is a so-called binary countdown protocol for wireless multi-hop networks. It provides deterministic priority-based medium arbitration with configurable arbitration radius and (network-wide) transmissions of values with maximum delays. As BBS, ACTP uses black-burst encodings to protect transmissions against collisions. Since these encodings are substantially less efficient than regular frame encodings, only a small amount of data can be exchanged. However, once medium arbitration has been performed, the winning node can switch to regular transmission to transmit more data. This idea has, e.g., been applied in the realization of Try-Once-Discard, a protocol proposed for networked control systems, and its application to an unstable batch reactor [7].

Selection of the best MAC scheme depends on the concrete application scenario and its message characteristics regarding timing and determinism. In case of hard real-time requirements, strictly periodic messages should use RB, while sporadic messages should be transmitted with MB with highest priority.

2.5 Topology Discovery with TD

Due to the limited transmission range of the nodes used, WNCS often form multi-hop networks. Therefore, routing and/or clustering is necessary to exchange data within the network. As they require topology information, routing and clustering protocols typically include functionality to detect communication links. However, we consider topology discovery a basic functionality of a multi-hop network, as it is required by multiple protocols. Therefore, we separate topology discovery functionality from other protocols, and design it as a functionality provided by layer 2, which is available to any higher layer protocols, such as routing or clustering.

TDMA MAC schemes like the RB scheme in BiPS allow exclusive reservations of time slots (see Sect. 2.4). In a multi-hop network, TDMA can be combined with space division multiple access (SDMA) to increase efficiency, as done in WirelessHART. However, one slot may only be reserved for two transmissions at the same time if this does not cause loss or corruption due to interference. To decide whether two concurrent transmissions interfere, it is not enough to know the communication topology. Manual configuration as in WirelessHART is very cumbersome and error-prone. Thus, topology discovery also needs to detect the *interference topology* of the network.

The Black Burst encoding used by BiPS protocols like BBS and ACTP encodes data based on the medium energy level. Energy transmitted by a node can be sensed over a long distance, even if both nodes cannot communicate using the normal encoding. The topology discovery in BiPS therefore also detects the *sensing topology*.

To detect these topologies, the Automatic Topology Discovery Protocol [22] (referred here as TD) is integrated into BiPS. It is executed when the nodes are powered up and before normal operation starts. In this topology discovery phase, BBS synchronization is operational and provides tick synchronization. All other micro slots of the super slot are merged into virtual slots assigned to topology discovery. TD exclusively assigns virtual slots (see Sect. 2.3) to potentially existing nodes. The virtual slot n_{slot} is assigned to a potentially existing node with node number k as follows:

$$k = n_{slot} \bmod N_{nodesMax} \tag{1}$$

As the configuration parameter $N_{nodesMax}$ is known by all nodes, the exclusive reservations are known at startup across the network. Each node then sends a *MEASURE* message in each virtual slot assigned to it. Other nodes listen on the medium. A *MEASURE* message received correctly by node r in a virtual slot assigned to node k indicates that a communication link from k to node r exists. In case a corrupt message is received, it can still be assumed that it has been sent by node k, as no other node is allowed to send in this virtual slot. However, the reception of a corrupt message indicates that k is in interference range of r. The same is true if no message is received, but the energy on the medium during the virtual slot assigned to node k is above a certain threshold. Even sensing links can be detected by analyzing the energy on the medium during exclusively assigned virtual slots. Only if no or very little energy is sensed, it indicates that no link from node k to r exists. As a single observation is not enough, TD checks if the classification of a link stays stable over a defined number of observations. In case the classification keeps changing, TD will eventually classify it as the worst case, i.e. as an interference link. *MEASURE* messages are not only used to detect links, but also to distribute the topology information gathered so far. This way, the detected topology is distributed without additional overhead across the network.

TD terminates when all links are classified as stable and all topology information has been propagated across the network. To this end, a distributed termination decision is done using ACTP at the beginning of each super slot. Once all nodes vote for termination, the protocol terminates and the normal operation phase of the network starts.

As a result of the topology discovery phase, all nodes know the communication, interference and sensing topology of the entire network. This information greatly simplifies the operation of higher layer protocols like routing and clustering.

2.6   Access to MAC Protocols

The lower part of Fig. 6 shows an example of a super slot configuration for three nodes V_a, V_b and V_c. There are three macro slots in one super slot and

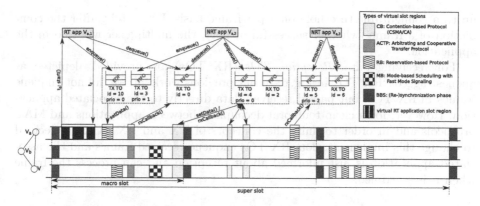

Fig. 6. Configuration of virtual slot regions of three nodes and associated transmission opportunities for node V_a.

each of the nodes has its individual virtual slot configuration. Of course these configurations have overlaps with neighboring nodes, such that communication is possible, but not all stations have to participate in every communication region. Slot regions are assigned to different MAC protocols, which fit the needs of the communication requirements.

Access of applications to MAC protocols in individual slot regions is provided by so called *Transmission Opportunities* (TOs), located in the multiplexer of BiPS (see Fig. 2). We have integrated common MAC functionalities, such as queuing, into the multiplexer, thereby facilitating development of applications and integration of new MAC protocols. The multiplexer also provides a homogeneous interface to pass data between application and different protocols, although meta-data such as addressing schemes might differ among the protocols. To that extent, the multiplexer offers temporal decoupling between real-time communication and application.

For sending data, the multiplexer offers *Sending TOs* (TX TOs), which are depicted as queues tagged "TX TO" in Fig. 6. An application enqueues data into a TX TO via a method call. Whenever a MAC protocol is running in a virtual region and requesting data to be sent, the frame with highest priority is dequeued from TX TO associated with the current region. The priority of a frame is determined by several rules: First, a TX TO can contain more than one TX queue, each with an assigned priority. Of these, the first non-empty queue with the highest priority is selected. After that, the queue's order strategy is taken into account: A FIFO queue selects the oldest frame, whereas an EDF queue selects the frame with the earliest deadline. These concepts offer flexible composition, which can e.g. implement a priority queuing scheme with several traffic classes.

TX TOs are directly interacting with the MAC protocol, i.e. the MAC protocol is informed when a transmission is completed and signaled about the success. In case of failures, the TX TO can automatically reinsert the frame into its queue up to a configurable threshold on a per-frame basis. Ultimately, after the completion of a frame (whether successful or not), the multiplexer will inform the application.

For receiving data, *Reception TOs* (RX TOs) are provided, depicted as queues tagged "RX TO" in Fig. 6. In our previous work [5], we did not enqueue frames in RX TOs, but passed received data directly to the associated application. However, for a clean temporal decoupling between applications and MAC protocols and in order to unify the concepts of TX and RX TOs, we decided to change this implementation. RX TOs enqueue received frames and the associated application is just informed about reception and can process the frame when it is scheduled.

2.7   Application Scheduling and Duty Cycling

Besides scheduling real-time communication, BiPS is also responsible for scheduling applications. We distinguish between two types of applications: *real-time* and *non-real-time*, referred to as RT and NRT applications.

RT applications are, very much like communication slots, scheduled by BRTS (see Sect. 3.1) via the super slot configuration as *virtual real-time application slots*. Since nodes are synchronized, RT applications provide an easy way to establish tick synchronized sampling points across nodes. Using RT applications, we can furthermore assure that data dispatched by these applications is actually available for sending in an upcoming communication slot.

NRT applications are scheduled whenever the RT scheduler is idle, which applies in two cases: First, if the current slot is not belonging to any virtual communication or RT application region, and second, even if a MAC protocol is running, there is still CPU time left, when e.g. idle-listening to the medium or waiting for a timer to expire.

Neighboring micro slots which are not used for communication are joined into *idle regions*. Since all communication, and thus transceiver usage, is coordinated by BiPS, it is able to decide when to power down the transceiver for saving energy. Thereby, BiPS also offers duty-cycling transparent to the application.

3   Operating System Functionalities of BiPS

To run real-time-capable protocols and applications, time-critical functionality must be executed on time and with predictable delays. BiPS therefore runs directly on top of the hardware, without any underlying OS. In state-of-the-practice operating systems, MAC protocols are running in the same conceptual domain as less time-critical functionalities of the control application. Even when using a real-time capable OS, it is still hard to define a schedule that covers all aspects of real-time communication, such as synchronization uncertainties and hardware delays. Here, BiPS provides a subset of OS functionalities and focuses on the needs of real-time-capable protocols.

The design of BiPS strictly distinguishes between real-time functionalities and components with lower requirements w.r.t. timeliness (see also Sect. 2.7). For that, BiPS incorporates two schedulers: The *BiPS Real-Time Scheduler* (BRTS, see Sect. 3.1), responsible for the execution of time-critical components (MAC protocols, Real-Time tasks, core functions of BiPS), and the *BiPS Application Scheduler* (BAS, see Sect. 3.2), executing applications and higher-layer protocols. If for more complex control applications, the limited capabilities of BAS are insufficient, they can be replaced by another OS, such as FreeRTOS by basically virtualizing it (see Sect. 3.3).

3.1   The BiPS Real Time Scheduler (BRTS)

The BiPS Real Time Scheduler is responsible for executing the schedule given by the configuration of virtual slot regions of a node. As explained in Sect. 2.6, we distinguish two different virtual slot region types that are handled by BRTS: First, for *virtual communication slot regions* of the schedule, BRTS has to activate and deactivate the associated MAC protocol at the start and end of the region, respectively. Second, for *virtual RT application slot regions*, it has to transfer control to the associated application. All tasks of BRTS are uninterruptible and have a higher priority than non-real-time parts of the application, which are scheduled by a subordinate scheduler (see Sects. 3.2 and 3.3).

In Fig. 7, the general and protocol-independent structure of a virtual slot region is shown. At local time t_0, the slot region starts by calling the `configure` method of a MAC protocol and by executing the multiplexer, named MPX in the figure, which (if applicable) passes data to be sent to the protocol. The protocol may already begin to transfer data to the transceiver's queue, such that the transmission can begin at t_1 without further delay. The upper bound of the duration needed to do all configuration steps is called d_{maxCfg} in the following. The time we allow for configuration is denoted as d_{start}, which is defined as $d_{\mathrm{start}} := \max\{d_{\mathrm{maxOffset}}, d_{\mathrm{maxCfg}}\}$. On one hand, incorporating the maximum synchronization offset assures that all nodes in their local clock domains reached the start of the same slot region by no later than t_1. On the other hand, by also regarding the maximum delay needed to configure the protocol, we assure that the configuration is indeed completed by t_1. As all maximum delays are known at deployment time, d_{start} is fixed and known by all nodes. At t_1, BiPS calls the `start` method of the protocol, which may start transmissions now.

The duration of the region $d_{\mathrm{slotDuration}}$ can be directly deduced from the duration of the virtual slot region as configured in the slot configuration. While the protocol is in control during the slot duration, it may request further data from the multiplexer for more transmissions and also push received data to the multiplexer, which will notify the application about these events.

At t_2, BRTS switches the transceiver back to reception mode to ensure that all nodes are able to perceive transmissions within the bounds of the assigned virtual slot region. Because of this, all MAC protocols are required to finish their last transmission by t_2. To that end, they are assisted by BiPS, which provides

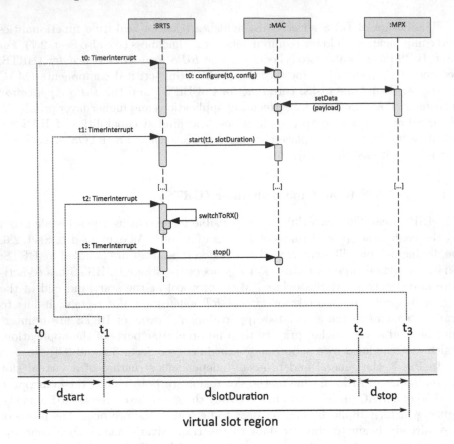

Fig. 7. Structure of virtual slot regions and activation of a MAC protocol by the BRTS.

functions to check whether a certain transmission still fits in the current region, thereby obeying all involved delays imposed by hardware.

The locally perceived end of the slot region is denoted by t_3. The guard time d_{stop} between t_2 and t_3 is defined as $d_{\text{stop}} := \max\{d_{\text{maxOffset}}, d_{\text{TX}\to\text{RX}}^{\text{CC2420}}\}$. By incorporating the worst-case synchronization offset $d_{\text{maxOffset}}$, we guarantee that each node can participate in a transmission. Without doing so, an early receiving node could already perceive the end of the slot before it actually ends and thus miss a transmission. By also taking the transceiver's switching delay $d_{\text{TX}\to\text{RX}}^{\text{CC2420}}$ from TX to RX mode into account, we further guarantee that a late node is capable of receiving new frames right at the start of a subsequent virtual slot region.

When scheduling an RT application in a virtual region, the time structure is very similar to that of a communication slot region. As major difference, there is no interaction between nodes, thus we can safely ignore the guard time d_{start} at the start of a virtual slot region and omit t_1 in this respect. Thus, at t_0, control is handed off to the application. It is required that the application returns control back to BRTS by no later than t_2 since BRTS might have to power up the transceiver again at that point in time. Figure 6 shows an example of three applications executed by node V_a. The applications $v_{a,2}$ and $v_{a,3}$ are non-real-time applications, which are executed during idle regions and one real-time application $v_{a,1}$. This real-time application is executed by the BRTS without preemption upon the start of the virtual RT application slot region in the first macro slot of the super slot.

Besides executing MAC protocols and RT applications, BRTS is also responsible for configuring the power states of the transceiver. From the schedule given by the user, it can derive idle slots and power down the transceiver for power saving during these unused slots. By also knowing about the transceiver's delays to switch power modes, BRTS can set a timer for putting the transceiver back into RX mode before an upcoming communication slot is starting.

3.2 The BiPS Application Scheduler (BAS)

The BiPS Application Scheduler (BAS) is responsible for executing non-real-time (NRT) applications, such as higher layer protocols. It can be classified as cooperative, event-based and non-preemptive. In order to be scheduled by BAS, the application has to register events, such as the reception of data by the multiplexer or a timer expiration, during run-time (normally done at startup). At its core, BAS consists of a loop, constantly checking for events and passing control to the component whose event has been emitted. There is no preemption, thus a component runs until it returns control to the scheduler.

The main point in separating the two schedulers is that all applications scheduled by BAS can be interrupted by BRTS, thereby giving real-time-capable MAC protocols and RT applications a higher priority over the rest of the application.

The only interaction primitive provided by BAS between NRT applications is emitting events. Other synchronization primitives such as mutexes are not needed, since BAS tasks work cooperatively and their execution can only be interrupted by hardware interrupts. There are, however, critical sections in which a component needs to interact with low level functions, e.g., if transmitting messages via UART (Universal Asynchronous Receiver Transmitter) or exchanging data between the application and the multiplexer. In these cases, access to data structures has to be exclusive to prevent data races. In other state-of-the-practice operating systems, this is accomplished by temporarily disabling interrupts, which, on the downside also means that BRTS would be delayed by the duration of the exclusive access. We mitigate this effect by two measures:

- As a first step, we distinguish between those hardware interrupts that are used by BRTS or any RT component (e.g. a hardware timer dedicated for the execution of BRTS components) and those that are not used BRTS at all (e.g. UART). We then use nested interrupts on two levels, which is assisted by the core hardware of the PXA 270 processor. Using this scheme, disabling any or even all non-BRTS interrupts will not affect BRTS, which may thus even interrupt other interrupt handlers of lower priority.

– This is, however, not applicable in all cases. Especially, when data is exchanged with the multiplexer, we still need to prevent BRTS from running concurrently to prevent data races by disabling BRTS interrupts, too. In order to meet all deadlines, we first measured the worst-case processing delay $d_{\text{crit}}^{\max}$ of these critical sections. Then, whenever a time-critical event (such as an expected reception) is about to happen, we let BRTS take over control $d_{\text{crit}}^{\max}$ before that event. BRTS then enters a busy-waiting loop, effectively waiting for the time-critical event to happen. After the event is handled, the busy-waiting loop is exited, and control is returned to BAS.

If neither BRTS nor BAS have to run some task, we may also put the CPU into sleep mode in order to save battery power. However, some caution must be taken: depending on the sleep state, the PXA 270 CPU takes more time to wake up again, i.e. to time to respond to an interrupt, thereby delaying execution of time-critical code. In order to account for the higher delay, BRTS may reschedule its timer before the CPU is set to sleep mode. Thus, although BAS chooses to save energy in the first place, it still lets BRTS decide, so BRTS can reschedule its timers and select a power saving mode in order to wake up early enough when the next scheduled RT task is coming up.

3.3 Nesting Foreign Operating Systems

For more complex applications, the features of BAS might be insufficient – especially, the absence of tasks and preemption might be a limiting factor. For example, consider an application which incorporates a long running calculation, then we would have to split the calculation into several smaller tasks and return control to BAS from time to time such that other events do not suffer from starvation.

In BiPS, BAS can be completely removed and replaced by another operating system (called *nested OS*) which can be ported to the Imote 2 platform in general. It is then possible to use all capabilities of the nested OS, such as multi-tasking, priority scheduling and process interaction.

When porting an operating system to a target platform, the programmer must provide adaptions, such that the more generic code of the OS can interact with the specialized hardware. When nesting an OS into BiPS, similar steps have to be taken. In addition to our previous port of FreeRTOS, which we already mentioned in [5], we also ported RIOT [15] into BiPS. Both are classical real-time OS with support for tasks, task priorities, synchronization primitives, and task preemption. We will now compare typical porting steps and give some details on our ports of FreeRTOS and RIOT:

– When starting up, *initialization code* for setting up the hardware and runtime environment has to be run, such that the OS will find itself in a predefined state. Since initialization is already done by BiPS, the code required to finally start the nested OS is reduced to some function calls into the BiPS core.

FreeRTOS needs an implementation for its `xPortStartScheduler` stub, which is responsible for configuring and starting a periodic timer (see below), as well as to jump into the first task. The code we provided for nesting FreeR-TOS was no different from code we wrote for a standalone port of FreeRTOS, except we could some functions provided by BiPS, e.g. to setup the system timer. Similar considerations apply for our port of RIOT and, in fact, we could even reuse some code we already employed for FreeRTOS. We could therefore extract common code, suitable for both operating systems and integrated them into BiPS. In the actual ports, we could therefore implement the required stubs without going on assembler level. Note, however, that this might be different when considering other OS's.

- Code for *managing interrupts* has to be provided, in order to register and handle interrupts, but also to disable and re-enable them whenever the OS needs to run uninterruptible code. Using BiPS, this translates into calls to the BiPS core. Especially, requesting BiPS to disable interrupts will not disable *all* interrupts, but leave the BiPS-related interrupts enabled, as described for BAS (see Sect. 3.2) already. In consequence, BiPS can not only interrupt the processes but even interrupt core functions of the nested OS kernel, such as switching tasks.

  In both ports, we could implement the required function mostly by function calls into BiPS.

- Code for *manipulating a system timer* is required for scheduling purposes of the OS. Since BiPS provides an interface for manipulating timers, this also translates into calling BiPS functions. Especially on the Imote 2 platform, there are 9 hardware timers, of which we reserved one for the nested OS.

  As already noted, we could use the BiPS timer subsystem to manipulate the timer in our ports.

- Code for *context switching* is required for the OS to switch tasks, e.g. if a task with a higher priority is runnable or a tasks time slice expires. Likewise, *task initialization* code is required for task creation.

  The code must save and restore the hardware-specific part (CPU registers and flags) and runtime-specific parts (such as libc's `_impure_ptr` to support reentrancy of libc functions) of the tasks state. Although BiPS offers some helper functions for that, it also depends on the nested OS on how and what to store. Therefore, some tailoring is still required for implementing context switching.

  For FreeRTOS and RIOT, however, by using the provided helper functions, we could again provide implementations without using additional assembler code. For task initialization, we also modified parts of FreeRTOS, since in it's original version, it allocates a stack for a newly created task using `malloc` with a preconfigured size. The problem with such implementation is, that the tasks' stacks are not separated from their heaps (more precisely: stacks and heaps of multiple tasks are intertwined) and stack overflows go undetected, except for abnormal application behaviour. Since the system software layer of BiPS provides memory management and offers an interface to allocate stacks explicitly, we made subtle adaptions on FreeRTOS to call this function instead of `malloc`. The stack memory returned by BiPS is sufficiently guarded at its bottom, such that stack overflows can be detected reliably.

– *Device drivers* allow accessing hardware components, such as UART. Since we have already implemented a number of device drivers for the Imote 2 platform, device drivers for the nested OS mostly consist of wrappers, translating the concepts of the nested OS into calls to BiPS and vice-versa.

FreeRTOS does not provide drivers – instead, tasks (and IRQ handlers) can communicate using queues. We added an adaption layer, such that frames, received by a MAC protocol are transferred from the multiplexer's queue to FreeRTOS queues. Tasks waiting on such queues are then blocked until frames are received.

Nesting an OS into BiPS can be seen like a virtualization: instead of interacting with hardware directly, the nested OS interacts with BiPS. Since BiPS controls the execution of the inner OS, timeliness and prioritization of MAC protocols and RT applications are guaranteed. On the other hand, if the nested OS is a real-time capable OS (such as FreeRTOS), real-time capability is limited: deadlines of the nested OS are delayed whenever BiPS takes over control to run a protocol or a real-time task.

4   Application and Deployment of BiPS

Industry 4.0 is said to be the next big evolution in production: By making factories smart, production processes become more efficient regarding costs, resources, administration and maintenance efforts. This requires that the production process is continuously monitored using sensors and controlled based on the collected data. Such closed-loop control of a production process often entails deterministic real-time requirements on the underlying communication system. Traditionally, communication systems used for production automation like HART used wires to meet these requirements. However, with a WNCS like BiPS that offers deterministic guarantees, it is possible to use wireless communication between sensors, actuators and controllers. This opens many advantages compared to wired solutions: Wireless nodes are more flexible, can be placed more easily on moving machinery like robots, and do not require cables that are costly to install and maintain in harsh production environments [1].

As BiPS is a well-suited framework for production environments, it was chosen by an Industry 4.0 project [3] that was part of SINNODIUM (Software Innovations for the Digital Enterprise), a large project funded by the German Federal Ministry of Education and Research. In this project, a BiPS-based WNCS called ProNet-W (Production Network – Wireless) [3] was developed and deployed in a production plant bottling liquid soap (see Fig. 8). Several sensors have been installed to monitor the status of the production, e.g. a sensor monitoring the status of a pump, as well as temperature and gas sensors. Other sensors are placed on a robot that moves autonomously throughout the production plant and is used for remote maintenance tasks. All sensors are connected to Imote 2 nodes that run the BiPS-based ProNet-W. The data collected by these sensors is sent over the multi-hop WNCS to an *aggregated server* that acts as a gateway to the enterprise network, providing the data via OPC UA (OPC Unified Architecture). This way, the proALPHA ERP (Enterprise Resource Planning) system can subscribe and process the data according to the defined business logic workflow.

Fig. 8. Imote 2 nodes running BiPS deployed in a production plant bottling liquid soap [23].

4.1 QoS-Capable Service-Oriented Middleware

As part of ProNet-W, BiPS has been extended with ProMid-W (Production Middleware - Wireless), a service-oriented QoS-capable middleware for production environments [3]. Sensor nodes can provide their sensor values as services that are registered in a service registry, where controllers can look them up and subscribe to them. Similarly, actuators provide services that can be used by controllers. Both event-triggered and time-triggered services are supported. The QoS level that a service can provide can be defined by the service provider, e.g. the interval in which a sensor value can be provided. Similarly, service users define the QoS level they require, e.g. a controller can define the needed interval and maximum delay in which it requires a sensor value. As the middleware knows the QoS requirement of the service user, it can take appropriate measures to meet the requirements. Most importantly, this includes finding a route that satisfies the QoS requirements and allocating exclusive TDMA slots along the route as needed. Even though exclusive TDMA reservations eliminate collisions within the network, external interference, node failures, etc., can cause unpredictable loss and delays. Therefore, the middleware monitors whether the QoS requirements of the service user are being satisfied, and notifies it in case they are being violated. The action taken in this case depends on the application. For example, if the current temperature of a pump has not been received for over a minute, the pump might need to be stopped or slowed down.

The service registry of ProMid-W is distributed and partly replicated. The communication topology discovered by TD (see Sect. 2.5) is used as a basis for the decision which nodes act as service registry nodes. Next, a clustering algorithm is used that forms a 3-hop connected dominating set, with the cluster heads selected as service registry nodes (see Fig. 9). Thus, this overlay topology ensures that each node is either a service registry node itself, or has a direct neighbor that is one. The details of the clustering algorithm are explained in [23]. The replication level can be configured with a parameter: Services are being replicated n hops around the service provider node. The assumption is that in a production plant, controllers are usually installed close to the sensors and actuators they require. However, services that are more than k hops away can be found as well, but they require a more costly search along all service registry nodes.

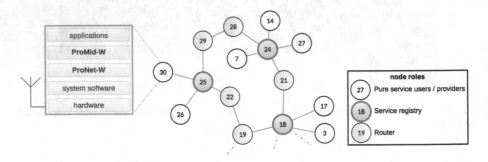

Fig. 9. Network topology with overlay topology of ProMid-W [3].

4.2 QoS Multicast Routing

The ProMid-W middleware also includes QoS routing and reservation of suitable exclusive time slots along the route. As one service (e.g. of one sensor node) can be subscribed by multiple service users (e.g. controllers), the transmission to both service users can usually be (partly) combined to save time slots. This means that the service provider multicasts to all the service users.

To do this efficiently, a QoS multicast routing scheme has been specifically developed for ProMid-W [12]. Especially, this routing scheme supports partially mobile wireless networks. A partially mobile network is a network in which the majority of nodes is stationary (like the nodes installed on a fixed place in the production plant), but a defined subset of the nodes is allowed to move (like the robot that can autonomously move in the production plant). The stationary nodes form a mesh network, i.e. relay frames for other nodes. Mobile nodes, on the other hand, are free to move, and do not relay data for other nodes. However, each mobile node must stay in range of at least one node out of a predefined set of *access nodes*. To ensure deterministic transmissions to mobile nodes, the routing scheme multicasts each transmission to a mobile node to all of its access nodes, which then relay the data to the mobile node if it is in range. The transmission from the mobile node to a stationary node works the other way round (see Fig. 10): The mobile node (M) sends to its currently connected access node (f). The routing scheme reserves transmissions from all access nodes (b and f) to a predefined stationary *distributor node* (g). As only the path from one access node to the distributor node is used at a time, the reservations of these paths are allowed to use the same slots, even if in interference range. We call this a *concast tree*. From the distributor node, transmissions continue the same way as from any other stationary node (in the example, a multicast to the destinations e and j).

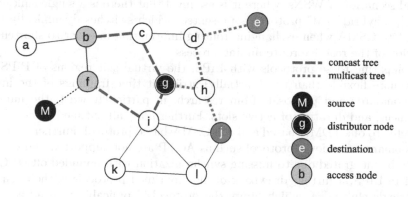

Fig. 10. Route from mobile node M to stationary nodes e and j, consisting of a concast tree from access nodes b and f to the distributor node g and a multicast tree [12].

5   Related Work

Up to our knowledge, there is no related work, that presents a similar flexible framework of (real-time) protocols and includes a detailed discussion of the protocols' implementation with consideration of timing constraints and hardware delays. Therefore, we will address two partial issues of BiPS in this chapter: First, we investigate the protocol aspect, i.e., we survey protocols for WSNs with multi-MAC support. Second, we compare the run-time engine aspect of BiPS by providing an outline of other operating systems for WSNs.

Communication protocols with more than one MAC scheme can be found both in industrial standards and research, and usually comprises a contention-based protocol with CSMA/CA and TDMA.

The most prominent representative from industry is probably IEEE 802.15.4 [21]. In the beacon-enabled mode, IEEE 802.15.4 establishes superframes that are composed of one contention access period, one contention-free period with so-called Guaranteed Time Slots (GTS), and one idle period. In WirelessHART [19], another example from the industry, time is also subdivided into superframes, which – different from IEEE 802.15.4 – consist of time slots of fixed length (10 ms), which are either assigned exclusively to one node or are shared by several nodes running CSMA/CA. The same applies to the ISA 100.11a [20] standard, which, however, allows time slots with configurable length.

In research, several proposals combining CSMA-based MAC protocols with TDMA can be found and are often called hybrid MACs [25]. They all try to combine the benefits of TDMA (e.g., more efficient duty cycling and prevention of collisions) and CSMA/CA (e.g., shorter average delays). Examples are [13] that proposes an extension of IEEE 802.15.4 to mitigate the drawback of the rigid superframe structures, Z-MAC [27], and EE-MAC [26]. ER-MAC [29] addresses typical scenarios of WSNs, where it is assumed that there is a single sink node. In [18], a hybrid MAC protocol is presented, which switches dynamically from TDMA to CSMA when exchanging routing information in order to shorten the duration of the reactive route finding process.

Comparing these protocols with BiPS, the virtual slot regions of BiPS are much more flexible than the (partially) stringent time framings of the industrial standards and proposals from research; in particular w.r.t. the number, placement, and duration of active slots. Furthermore, all outlined protocols are restricted to one TDMA-based and one CSMA-based protocol. Further protocols like a binary countdown protocol such as ACTP are not supported and can not simply be integrated due to missing synchronization with bounded offset. Compared to BiPS, a further drawback of most outlined protocols is their reliance on a single sink node, which limits the protocols' applicability in ad-hoc networks and, in many cases, also implies a topology-dependent slot assignment for TDMA. To assign time slots for TDMA, all protocols either run slot assignment algorithms based on detected communication links or require manual effort to find interference-free schedules. A distinction between communication and interference topology as performed by TD is not made.

Though several evaluations can be found in literature (e.g., in [2,16,28]) showing that the behavior and performance of a protocol highly-depends on the implementation, many related work does not include a detailed discussion of this topic.[1] Instead, most protocol implementations rely on general OS's like Contiki or TinyOS [11] to execute the protocol in an appropriate and timely manner. Particularly, the handling of concurrency of tasks is often not scrutinized but can affect the behavior adversely. Thus, it is often unclear – in particular, if a protocol

---

[1] Some of the related work is not even implemented, but evaluated by analyses or simulations only.

is announced to support real-time guarantees, e.g., due to the incorporation of TDMA – how timing constraints of the protocol are satisfied and if provided prioritization measures are actually sufficient to preserve a protocol's real-time capability.

The most common OS for WSNs is probably TinyOS, an event-driven OS, where tasks are scheduled cooperatively in FIFO or EDF order. Though tasks are not preempted by other tasks, interrupt handlers, commands, and events can preempt them. Since version 2, there is also support for full multi-threading and synchronization primitives, yet w.r.t. the Imote 2 platform, some features like MMU and data caches are no longer used. TinyOS does not offer a mechanism to run the communication stack in a privileged context, such that protocols with stringent timing constraints are not easy to implement. Additionally, the modular structure of TinyOS, yet enabling extensions very flexibly, increases the amount and variance of execution delays. Applications for TinyOS are written in a specialized C dialect, called nesC, rendering the learning curve steeper for C/C++ programmers.

Another well-known OS in this area is Contiki [8], with a special focus on heavily resource-constrained devices. Though the scheduling in Contiki is basically cooperatively, there are also extensions for light-weight multi-threading (so-called Protothreads) and full multi-threading support. To execute time-critical code, Contiki provides real-time tasks, which can preempt any low-priority process. Though Contiki subdivides system execution into tasks, memory protection has never been a goal of Contiki. Programs for Contiki are written in constrained C with a heavy use of C macros.

Different from TinyOS and Contiki, Nano-RK was developed with a special focus on real-time communication [10]. It is designed for classical multi-hop sensor networks, in which nodes are energy-limited and resource-constrained and send sensor values to a sink periodically. The scheduling with Nano-RK is priority-based and preemptive, with additional support of task synchronization. Nano-RK is stated as static design-time framework, thereby enabling offline real-time schedulability analyses to the detriment of runtime flexibility. It follows a reservation paradigm, i.e., tasks can reserve any kind of resource (CPU, network bandwidth, sensors/actuators). Though particular communication protocols are not in the focus of the developers, a basic CSMA/CA template is provided in conjunction with a infrastructure for the integration of custom MAC and routing protocols. The programming language for Nano-RK applications is C.

RIOT is another OS with support of real-time communication [15]. It comes with full multi-threading support and uses IPC (Inter-Process Communication) to pass messages between modules, thereby enabling a better decoupling of tasks. Memory protection or advanced measures on fault detection are not provided by RIOT, and the implementation of time-critical protocols still demands some programming tricks. Like BiPS, applications in RIOT are written in C/C++. Though there is no native port of RIOT for the Imote 2, it can run on this platform in the context of the BAS of BiPS. Thus, higher-level applications running on the Imote 2 with BiPS can benefit from both worlds: The flexible execution of tasks in BAS/RIOT and the real-time communication in BRTS.

FireKernel is also a real-time OS for WSNs [31]. But different from Nano-RK and RIOT, it is designed as micro kernel to minimize resource usage, i.e., it only provides functionalities regarding scheduling, IPC, and synchronization of tasks. Device drivers or even communication protocols have been omitted deliberately. The scheduling of tasks in FireKernel is priority-based and preemptive. Different from Nano-RK, the message-based IPC is mandatory for inter-task communication, thereby simplifying the exchangeability of modules.

Compared to all outlined state-of-the-practice OS's, BiPS is protocol-centric, i.e., the communication protocols are an inherent part of the system architecture (see Fig. 2). Thereby, BiPS can guarantee real-time capabilities of the implemented protocols by design. W.r.t. typical OS functionalities – like scheduling of generic tasks, preemption, and IPC – BiPS itself provides less support compared to all of the discussed OS's. However, this drawback has been eliminated by the integration of FreeRTOS and RIOT on top of BiPS.

6 Conclusion

In this paper, we have presented the Black-burst integrated Protocol Stack (BiPS), an extendable real-time capable protocol framework for wireless networked control systems, its implementation on the Imote 2 hardware platform, and its adaptation and deployment in a production environment. We have elaborated on BiPS protocols for tick and time synchronization, flexible structuring of time into virtual slot regions, supported MAC schemes, duty cycling, and a protocol for automatic detection of communication, interference, and sensing topologies. Furthermore, we have addressed operating system functionalities provided by BiPS, focusing on the BiPS real time scheduler and the application scheduler, and have explained the integration of other (real-time) operating systems. Finally, we have shown how BiPS was successfully adapted to an application in an experimental production plant bottling liquid soap – by adding QoS-capable middleware functionality for the provision, lookup, and subscription of time- and event-triggered services, a QoS multicast routing protocol for partially mobile wireless networks, and application functionality – deployed, and operated.

A key objective of BiPS has been the design of a flexible and extendable framework for real-time communication. This has been achieved by a very flexible structuring of time into physical slots and virtual slot regions, and by the conception of deterministic protocols and the support of a variety of MAC schemes. Another key concern has been the implementation of BiPS that complies with the real-time constraints imposed by the structuring of time. This has been achieved by implementing BiPS on bare hardware, and by providing rigorous protocol-centric operating system support, in particular the BiPS Real Time Scheduler.

References

1. Åkerberg, J., Gidlund, M., Björkman, M.: Future research challenges in wireless sensor and actuator networks targeting industrial automation. In: 2011 9th IEEE International Conference on Industrial Informatics (INDIN), pp. 410–415. IEEE (2011)
2. Basmer, T., Schomann, H., Peter, S.: Implementation analysis of the IEEE 802.15.4 MAC for wireless sensor networks. In: International Conference on Selected Topics in Mobile and Wireless Networking (iCOST) (2011). https://doi.org/10.1109/iCOST.2011.6085840
3. Christmann, D., et al.: Vertical integration and adaptive services in networked production environments. In: Felderer, M., Piazolo, F., Ortner, W., Brehm, L., Hof, H.-J. (eds.) ERP 2015. LNBIP, vol. 245, pp. 147–162. Springer, Cham (2016). https://doi.org/10.1007/978-3-319-32799-0_12
4. Braun, T., Gotzhein, R., Kuhn, T.: Mode-based scheduling with fast mode-signaling - a method for efficient usage of network time slots. J. Adv. Comput. Netw. (JACN) **2**, 48–57 (2014)
5. Christmann, D., Braun, T., Engel, M., Gotzhein, R.: BiPS – a real-time-capable protocol framework for wireless sensor networks. In: Proceedings of the 6th International Joint Conference on Pervasive and Embedded Computing and Communication Systems, pp. 17–27. SciTePress - Science and Technology Publications (2016). https://doi.org/10.5220/0005938300170027
6. Christmann, D., Gotzhein, R., Rohr, S.: The arbitrating value transfer protocol (AVTP) - deterministic binary countdown in wireless multi-hop networks. In: 21st International Conference on Computer Communications and Networks (ICCCN) (2012). https://doi.org/10.1109/ICCCN.2012.6289227
7. Christmann, D., Gotzhein, R., Siegmund, S., Wirth, F.: Realization of try-once-discard in wireless multi-hop networks. IEEE Trans. Industr. Inf. **10**(1), 17–26 (2014). https://doi.org/10.1109/TII.2013.2281511
8. Dunkels, A., Gronvall, B., Voigt, T.: Contiki - a lightweight and flexible operating system for tiny networked sensors. In: 29th Annual IEEE International Conference on Local Computer Networks, pp. 455–462 (2004). https://doi.org/10.1109/LCN.2004.38
9. Engel, M., Christmann, D., Gotzhein, R.: Implementation and experimental validation of timing constraints of BBS. In: Krishnamachari, B., Murphy, A.L., Trigoni, N. (eds.) EWSN 2014. LNCS, vol. 8354, pp. 84–99. Springer, Cham (2014). https://doi.org/10.1007/978-3-319-04651-8_6
10. Eswaran, A., Rowe, A., Rajkumar, R.: Nano-RK: an energy-aware resource-centric RTOS for sensor networks. In: 26th IEEE International Real-Time Systems Symposium (RTSS 2005), pp. 10 pp.-265 (2005). https://doi.org/10.1109/RTSS.2005.30
11. Farooq, M.O., Kunz, T.: Operating systems for wireless sensor networks: a survey. Sensors **11**(6), 5900–5930 (2011)
12. Gebhardt, J., Gotzhein, R., Igel, A., Kramer, C.: QoS multicast routing in partially mobile wireless TDMA networks. In: 2015 IEEE Global Communications Conference (GLOBECOM), pp. 1–7. IEEE (2015)
13. Gilani, M.H.S., Sarrafi, I., Abbaspour, M.: An adaptive CSMA/TDMA Hybrid-MAC for energy and throughput improvement of wireless sensor networks. Ad Hoc Netw. **11**(4), 1297–1304 (2013). https://doi.org/10.1016/j.adhoc.2011.01.005

14. Gotzhein, R., Kuhn, T.: Black burst synchronization (BBS) - a protocol for deterministic tick and time synchronization in wireless networks. Comput. Netw. **55**(13), 3015–3031 (2011)
15. Hahm, O., Baccelli, E., Günes, M., Wählisch, M., Schmidt, T.C.: RIOT OS: towards an OS for the Internet of Things. In: 32nd IEEE International Conference on Computer Communications (INFOCOM), Poster Session (2013)
16. Harvan, M., Schönwälder, J.: TinyOS motes on the internet: IPv6 over 802.15.4 (6lowpan). Praxis der Informationsverarbeitung und Kommunikation **31**(4), 244–251 (2008). https://doi.org/10.1515/piko.2008.0042
17. Haupt, A., et al.: Wireless networking for control. In: Lunze, J. (ed.) Control Theory of Digitally Networked Dynamic Systems, pp. 325–362. Springer, Heidelberg (2014). https://doi.org/10.1007/978-3-319-01131-8_7
18. Hsieh, T.H., Lin, K.Y., Wang, P.C.: A hybrid MAC protocol for wireless sensor networks. In: 2015 IEEE 12th International Conference on Networking, Sensing and Control, pp. 93–98 (2015). https://doi.org/10.1109/ICNSC.2015.7116016
19. IEC: Industrial Communication Networks - Wireless Communication Network and Communication Profiles - WirelessHART (IEC 62591 ed 1.0) (2010)
20. IEC: Industrial Communication Networks - Wireless Communication Network and Communication Profiles - ISA 100.11a (IEC 62734 ed 1.0) (2012)
21. IEEE: IEEE Standard 802 Part 15.4: Low-Rate Wireless Personal Area Networks (LR-WPANs). IEEE Computer Society, New York (2011). http://standards.ieee.org/getieee802/download/802.15.4-2011.pdf
22. Kramer, C., Christmann, D., Gotzhein, R.: Automatic topology discovery in TDMA-based ad hoc networks. In: International Wireless Communications and Mobile Computing Conference, IWCMC 2015, Dubrovnik, Croatia, August 24–28, 2015, pp. 634–639. IEEE (2015). https://doi.org/10.1109/IWCMC.2015.7289157
23. Kramer, C., Christmann, D., Gotzhein, R.: A clustering algorithm for distributed service registries in heterogeneous wireless networks. In: Wireless Days (WD), pp. 1–7. IEEE (2016)
24. MEMSIC Inc.: Imote2 datasheet (2013)
25. Olempia, K.J., Pandeeswaran, C., Natarajan, P.: A survey on energy efficient contention based and hybrid MAC protocols for wireless sensor networks. Indian J. Sci. Technol. **9**(12) (2016)
26. Priya, B., Manohar, S.S.: EE-MAC: energy efficient hybrid MAC for WSN. Int. J. Distrib. Sensor Netw. **9**(12), 526383 (2013). https://doi.org/10.1155/2013/526383
27. Rhee, I., Warrier, A., Aia, M., Min, J., Sichitiu, M.L.: Z-MAC: a hybrid MAC for wireless sensor networks. IEEE/ACM Trans. Netw. **16**(3), 511–524 (2008)
28. Silva, R., Silva, J.S., Boavida, F.: Evaluating 6LowPAN implementations in WSNs. In: Proceedings of 9th Conferncia sobre Redes de Computadores Oeiras, Portugal 21 (2009)
29. Sitanayah, L., Sreenan, C.J., Brown, K.N.: Emergency response MAC protocol (ER-MAC) for wireless sensor networks. In: Abdelzaher, T.F., Voigt, T., Wolisz, A. (eds.) Proceedings of the 9th International Conference on Information Processing in Sensor Networks, IPSN, Stockholm, Sweden. ACM (2010). https://doi.org/10.1145/1791212.1791256
30. TI: CC2420 Datasheet, Revision SWRS041c (2013). http://www.ti.com/lit/ds/symlink/cc2420.pdf
31. Will, H., Schleiser, K., Schiller, J.: A real-time kernel for wireless sensor networks employed in rescue scenarios. In: 2009 IEEE 34th Conference on Local Computer Networks, pp. 834–841 (2009). https://doi.org/10.1109/LCN.2009.5355049

Using Risk Assessments to Assess Insurability in the Context of Cyber Insurance

David Nicolas Bartolini[1], Cesar Benavente-Peces[1(✉)], and Andreas Ahrens[2]

[1] Universidad Politecnica de Madrid, Ctra. Valencia. Km. 7, 28031 Madrid, Spain
Davidnicolas.bartolini@alumnos.upm.es, cesar.benavente@upm.es
[2] Hochschule Wismar, University of Applied Sciences - Technology,
Business and Design, Philipp-Müller-Straße 14, 23966 Wismar, Germany
andreas.ahrens@hs-wismar.de
http://www.upm.es

Abstract. In the current globalisation framework where electronic transactions and data sharing is a common activity, cyber-risks analysis, protection and avoidance have become a key aspect which must be book and prioritised on the business agenda in companies. Nevertheless, this issue is difficult to analyse given the dimension of the problem and the company units and individuals and infrastructures which are involved. In consequence, cyber-insurance is considered as the appropriate mean to avoid financial losses caused by information technologics infrastructures and procedures security breaches. This paper analyses and describes how costumers and their cyber-risks should be assessed by an insurance company in order to establish the company status and implement the required actions to fix the issue. This work describes the three phases required to complete a full cyber-risk assessment and the risks evaluation. Furthermore, the paper highlights the resources that the insurer should keep in its road-map to implement the risk assessment and, thus, to determine the company *insurability*, and the requirements to reach such condition. After the risk analysis completion at the customer's premises, it must be evaluated subsequently at all levels. Among other factors, this evaluation is based on 63 question criteria. In the risk assessment criteria weights are not uniformly distributed and weighting is applied according to the relevance. In particular, criteria that should receive a special attention are referred to as *showstoppers*.

Keywords: Cyber risk management · Cyber insurance
Information security · Data protection

1 Introduction

Currently, information and communication technology, social networks (Facebook, LinkedIn, Research Gate, ...) and Internet (electronic) transactions and

© Springer Nature Switzerland AG 2019
M. S. Obaidat and E. Cabello (Eds.): ICETE 2017, CCIS 990, pp. 337–345, 2019.
https://doi.org/10.1007/978-3-030-11039-0_16

data sharing take a key role in the industry, management, governance and commerce given that most institutions and organizations complete business and communicate with real and possible customers. Besides, these resources act as a 'gateway' to intruders and potential cyber-attacks which can seriously affect institution and individual security and privacy. Independently of the individual(s) or organization initiating an attack (e.g., hackers, criminal gangs, governments), cyber-attacks can happen and if so, it will cause losses difficult to quantify for large and SME (Small and Medium size Enterprises).

In consequence, institutions, organizations and companies, in their risk management roadmap, must take decisions about the tolerance to cyber risks by categorizing them and establish the appropriate protocols and actions, i.e., avoiding, accepting, controlling or transferring it. In this last case is when cyber insurance makes sense and plays a relevant role given the liability of cyber-damages.

Nevertheless, data breaches and cyber-criminal activities (among others) have become to happen very often in the last decades. Analysing these activities in the last five years we find that data breaches have produced high loses and expenses and reputation drop.

Cyber insurance policies, which is also known as cyber risk insurance or cyber liability insurance coverage, are aimed at supporting organizations or companies to avoid or decrease the risk exposure. This investigation highlights the resources that the insurer company should schedule in its road-map to implement the risk assessment and, as result, to determine the company insurability level, and the required improvements to reach such condition.

A cyber insurance policy, also referred to as cyber risk insurance or cyber liability insurance coverage (CLIC), is designed to help an organization mitigate risk exposure by compensating the expenses produced in recovering them system to its normal operation after suffering a cyber-related security breach or other security risk issue. Hence, robust cyber insurance policies would support companies and organizations on their businesses and trades when a data breach, attack or network security failure has occurred.

What makes relevant the investigation shown in this paper is that many companies and organizations are not aware of the advantages that an appropriate cyber insurance policy can provide in the potential, but likely, case a network security failure happens, which also has pushed to widen its scope over the past five years. Although many cyber insurers are knowing their customers and various insurance contracts have existed for several years, the cyber risk management of the companies to be insured is not well known. This situation is not different for new customers. For this reason, distinct methods are used in the context of the risk identification in the interaction with the customer to analyse both the risk and the need for protection. Against this background, the focus of this paper is the presentation of the risk assessment process of a leading insurance company. Which this assessment the insurer can analyse the individual cyber risk. The remaining part of this paper is structured as follows: In Sect. 2 the 3 Phases of Risk Assessment is explained, which include the questionnaire about the customer company and the conduct of the insurability test by the security experts in cooperation with, for example, the underwriters of the insurers. The questionnaire used is often based on the ISO/IEC 27001 standard [10]. Section 3 introduces to the evaluation of the risk assessment questionnaire results and the insurers risk evaluation methods, which includes the final report. Section 4 gives a brief introduction to the relevant *showstopper* questions of the questionnaire. Finally, some concluding remarks are provided in Sect. 5.

2   The 3 Phases of Risk Assessments

First, a workshop is organized at the customer company. The focus is on the customer's advice and less on the sale of the insurance product. This workshop's intention is customer sensitization to cyber risk management. This workshop enables the insurer and his underwriters to make a risk and price assessment, which is in the interest and within the framework of the insurance customers, thus enabling a healthy risk portfolio. In return, the prospective customer company receives an objective overview of its cyber risks, which is included in the workshop catalogue and presented in the final risk assessment dialogue. By doing so, the customer has an indication of how these risks can be adequately treated.

A questionnaire as well as check-lists are called a collection method for risk identification. On the other hand, Delphi methods for the method of creativity and Failure Mode and Effects Analysis (FMEA) belong to the analytical methods [17].

The workshop is part of the risk identification in the context of the insurer's cyber insurance, since it has been established that more complex customer companies can be investigated in more detail and that the underwriter can make a better decision.

This also applies as a valid approach since the cyber risk of a company changes with every change in the business model or business process, as well as with advancing technological development. Furthermore, this is because cyber risk is heavily dependent on soft and hard IT and security management factors [2].

The workshop's approach works in two directions. On the one hand, the insurer must know and understand his risk to offer the customer the best possible premium. On the other hand, the insurer is interested in the fact that the customer himself understands his risk and can use it sensibly.

The cyber risk depends on many factors. Therefore, it is important to know the value of the customer. What these values are and the information they contain, plays a key role for the insurer. Therefore, many business units are investigated. It must be ascertained how the control of the IT operation works, since this is an elementary prerequisite for reliable Information Technology.

Furthermore, the company's safety measures must be ascertained. In this case, questioned how segments are arranged and separated from one another, or what possibilities are used to monitor the networks. It is also questioned, for example, whether the data centres are physically and adequately equipped by the supply devices.

The company is also asked about its preparation against cyber-attacks. Therefore, contact persons from business and industrial IT, management reporting, contract management, risk management, business continuity management, information security management, and IT service management will be interviewed to assess the overall risk.

Furthermore, it is essential that the participants of the customer company come from different departments, since cyber-risks are cross-departmental risks [1]. The Chief Financial Officer is particularly important as she is involved in the management of information security from the business point of view and she is usually responsible for corporate risk management.

Next, the Chief Information Security Officer (CISO) and the Chief Information Officer (CIO) are needed as part of the risk management at the operational level, as they must implement most of the measures.

Since the dependency on suppliers and service providers is sufficient, the head of purchasing department is also an important partner in this workshop.

In this context, the legal department is often involved. This is usually also the point of contact when dealing with questions of the liability of the company in the context of cyber incidents against customers.

During the workshop, the questionnaire is developed in cooperation with the responsible customer. The questionnaire contains questions about the company and closes with the instruction on the pre-contractual obligation to provide information.

Such a questionnaire was developed by the insurer Cyber Risk Management Team (experts) and is based on the ISO/IEC 27001 standard [10].

The questionnaire includes the following areas: The company, its business areas and the company's key figures are dealt with in several points to obtain a quantitative risk approach.

Within a further section, corporate guidelines and procedures are highlighted, and the impact of these guidelines on the company employees.

The specialist also questions whether the company allows cashless payments. This has, inter alia, an impact on possible claims under the payment card industry data security standard [16] requirements.

A next area of concern is the company's cooperation with external service providers. Furthermore, the customer company is asked if a crisis management plan exists and how the company behaves in case of a crisis.

The next question group deals with questions about pre-claims within the scope of insurance protection and whether known facts have been made available to the customers' representative.

Finally, after the company's data are summarized, the desired insurance sums, deductibles and sub-limit are treated.

The customers know that cyber risk is of concern for every business. Thus, they have also agreed to the workshop and have provided their own investments in the form of several resources conducting the workshop.

Therefore, the companies appreciate professional exchange with the experts. The workshops are helpful to understand their own cyber risks and to further perform more effective action. Corporate management is given transparency over cyber risks. This, in turn, helps the IT to gain the necessary attention and acceptance as an important department in the fight against cyber-risks and not to be considered any longer as a cost centre.

The evaluation of the customer portfolio and the conduct of the insurability test are carried out by the experts in conjunction with the underwriters of the insurer after the workshop.

3   Risk Evaluation

The threatened objects are identified, such as the values that affect infrastructure, hardware, buildings as well as software and information. This includes intangible assets, such as the reputation of the company, its employees and, in turn, their knowledge of the threatened objects must also be recorded. With this complete risk knowledge, the value analysis can be done [21].

The values to be protected are evaluated in the value analysis. For this purpose, it is important to measure the interdependencies between the objects. The individual assessment is carried out on both quantitative and qualitative levels. The value of the assets is as much important as the classification (low, medium, high) of it [20].

The threat analysis considers the threats that could affect the objects to be protected. For this purpose, entrance probabilities and damage, which can occur in an event must be estimated. Threats can be caused by technical failure, force majeure, human error, or precautionary action. Organizational deficiencies are also a major part of threat analysis (RFC 2828, 2000).

In classic risk analysis, the individual values should be assessed and a meticulous and comprehensive assessment is to be presented [18]. For each individual object, a strength, weaknesses, opportunity, threat analysis (SWOT analysis) must be conducted. It is necessary to determine who the attackers are and which motives they have. The value or the potential quantitative impact must then be estimated. An assessment (low, medium, high) helps to find an adequately way to protect the most important resources.

Vulnerabilities are like objects. Both have a natural interdependence, and vulnerabilities thus impact objects. Therefore, the objects must be protected because a vulnerability of the input channel is a threat [7].

For an insurance, quantifiability is a key premise to calculate the insurance premiums [19]. Therefore, an insurance company needs more stochastic values than other companies. For this reason, the questionnaire is oriented to the international standard ISO/IEC 27000 not only as already mentioned, but also by its insurance factors.

The analysis also identifies the current insurance situation. It is important for the insurer that there was no reason for another insurer to neglect the cyber insurance. The information technology incident history is also investigated. Whether business interruption occurred during the last five years. It could be an interesting for the insurer, for example, whether the customer experiences a major disruption incident twice a year, for example in the context of Storage

System (RAID 5) failures and limitations of the solid-state disk availability or if information technology failures and cyber-attack occurred. The risk management structure, including the threat and risk modelling and vulnerability management of the customer company, based on the answered questions as well on the public annual reports is carried out.

In addition, the company will be analyzed by means of specific questions as to how the company is positioned within the framework of the Business Continuity Plan. If systems are identified as bottle necks, the experts must check whether the customer can counteract a possible failure, for example by clusters and high availability platforms.

It is also important for the risk assessment to ascertain whether the customer has certified his company according to standards such as ISO 20000 [9], ISO/IEC 27001 [10] or PCI DSS [16].

As human factor in IT security is a key factor, questions about this area are also important and form the end of the evaluation of the questionnaire. For example, the customer is asked whether awareness training and security training are implemented annually.

4   Leading Showstopper Questions

In general, the questionnaire is structured according to the following domains and maturity levels of the respective customer:

- Existing certifications
- IT security Organisation (IT security and risk management)
- Awareness for information security
- Use of external service providers and contract management
- Protection of IT systems
- Network protection
- Detection of attacks
- Data management and storage
- Access and access protection
- Physical security

Each domain and maturity level have many characteristics that are classified according to valuation factors. Statements are categorized to better assess the customer's situation and track common areas across all maturity levels. The components are groups of similar statements to facilitate or comprehensively organize the handling of the assessment. Based on a total of 38 questions (according to NIST, ISO 27001 [10], ISACA [8] etc.), the findings from the risk dialogue can be systematically entered the questionnaire by the risk engineer. This questionnaire is evaluated by the Cyber Risk Engineer as an assessment. This assessment provides the insurer, and the risk engineer, with a repeatable, reproducible and measurable process to inform underwriters of the client's risks and to assist in verifying the insurability of cyber security. The cybersecurity maturity level includes domains, valuation factors, components and individual implementations of measures across the four levels of responsiveness to identify specific controls and practices. Each maturity level contains a descriptive characteristic or characteristic. Instructions describing the customer's behaviour. The practices and processes of a customer consistently lead to the final overall result. The assessment combines information security relevant standards such as ISO 27001 [10], NIST [11–15], BSI Standard, Cobit etc. and thus enables cyber security assessment. NIST defines cybersecurity as the process of protecting information through prevention? Cyber events can have financial, operational, legal and reputation implications. Cyber incidents can have a significant impact on corporate capital. Costs may include forensic investigations, PR campaigns, legal fees and court fees, consumer credit monitoring, technology changes and comprehensive recovery measures [4,6] Cybersecurity therefore needs to be integrated across the enterprise as part of corporate governance processes, information security, business continuity and third-party risk management. Cybersecurity roles and processes referred to in the assessment may be separate roles within the security group (or outsourced) or may be part of broader roles within the institution. Each of the questions contains four different answer options, which correspond to the respective risk situation of the customer. The Risk Engineer determines which category best suits the client's current practices. All statements in each domain and in all included levels must be answered and classified qualitatively to achieve the best possible maturity of this domain. The Risk Engineer can determine the maturity level of the customer in each area, but the assessment is not intended to determine a general maturity level of cyber security only based on these 38 questions in an equally weighted form. On the one hand, domains must be excluded which do not apply to the respective customer, for example if outsourcing is not carried out. Questions or domains that are not applicable to the respective customer have no influence on the determination of the specific insurance capability. In principle, however, an equivalent quantification of the rating can be made from 38 of the above-mentioned questions. The questionnaire is logically staggered so that a rating can be made based on the respective maturity of the answers (between 1 = weak maturity and 4 = strong maturity). If the minimum rating value (>2.00) is reached, the company is generally insurable. However, the risk engineers have incorporated an exception to this fundamental weighting in the risk assessment, since there are 11 show stopper topics within the questions or domains, which must be considered separately. The inherent risk profile and maturity of a company may change over time as threats, vulnerabilities and operating environments change, but fundamental domains and levels of maturity are a prerequisite for a company's cybersecurity, which is categorized as a showstopper. For instance, one of the showstopper questions relates to the security organization. Since the customer must take a holistic approach to cyber security, it is necessary that basic roles within a security organization must be named. The entrepreneur is therefore responsible for the organization of IT security in his company, but he cannot manage the task alone: the development of an IT security organization is necessary (Harris, 2016). Depending on the size of the company, there are distinctive characteristics that can be considered. In a small company with 10 to 20 employees, it is hardly possible to create jobs that deal exclusively with the topic of IT security. Medium-sized companies may have the financial means and the need for one or two full-time IT security jobs. International corporations can't do without an extensive IT security organization. In general, IT security must be exemplified. Management must make the decisions, set precise targets and, of course, set a good example for implementation. In addition, IT security must be carried to all areas of the company, and it must be made clear that every employee is part of the IT security organization. An IT security officer should be appointed, even if not required by law [3]. This can be an own employee or an external service provider. For core tasks, suitable employees must be appointed and equipped with sufficient skills. This is the only way to enforce the guidelines. It goes without saying that the responsible employee must be given the necessary freedom to perform his or her duties adequately. Separation of functions is essential. For example, the IT administrator may not be responsible for creating IT security policies at the same time [10]. All employees and executives (including management) must be regularly informed of the importance of compliance with guidelines (e.g. [5]). This can be done through training, but better through advanced training or even small IT security competitions. Further work will describe detailed information regarding the 11 showstopper questions.

5   Conclusions

Cyber risks are still difficult for insurance companies to assess and appropriate methodologies must be develop and implemented. On the one hand, engineers skilled in IT security are needed to determine the individual customer situation and cyber-risk level. As shown in this investigation, this is done comprehensively by means of risk dialogues and questionnaire-based risk assessment on a multi-stage process. As soon as the respective company has been evaluated, the questionnaire must be analysed. What is relevant for insurance companies is that depending on the result of this evaluation, a customer can be insured or not, as result of the level of cyber-risk determined. This represents an important step in the insurance process, i.e., the acceptance of that risk by the insurer. However, just a certain value obtained during the risk assessment does not yet lead to an acceptance. Therefore, in the further steps of the work it is examined how likely damage events and their probability affect the insurance acceptance process. This phase of risk assessment procedures is carried out by using machine learning techniques and in further research various algorithms are investigated.

References

1. Aguilar, L.A.: Boards of directors, corporate governance and cyber-risks: sharpening the focus (2014). https://www.sec.gov/news/speech/2014-spch061014laa
2. Anderson, R.: Why information security is hard - an economic perspective. In: Seventeenth Annual Computer Security Applications Conference, pp. 358–365 (2001). https://doi.org/10.1109/ACSAC.2001.991552

3. BSI: Bundesamt für sicherheit in der informationstechnik (BSI), 2017. leitfaden zur basis-absicherung nach IT-Grundschutz (2017). https://www.bsi.bund.de
4. Allianz Global Corporate & Specialty: Allianz risk barometer (2016). http://www.agcs.allianz.com/insights/white-papers-and-case-studies/allianz-risk-barometer-2016
5. COSO: The committee of sponsoring organizations of the treadway commission (1992). https://www.coso.org/Pages/erm-integratedframework.aspx
6. Eckert, C.: Concepts, Procedures and Protocols, DE GRUYTER OLDENBOURG (2014)
7. Foreman, P.: Vulnerability Management. CRC Press, Boca Raton (2009)
8. ISACA: Cobit 5 framework (2012). https://www.isaca.org/COBIT/Pages/COBIT-5-Framework-product-page.aspx
9. ISO: ISO/IEC 20000–1. Information technology – service management (2011). https://www.iso.org/standard/51986.html
10. ISO: ISO/IEC 27001: Information technology - security techniques - information security management systems – requirements (2013). https://www.iso.org/standard/54534.html
11. NIST: NIST 800–45: Guideline on electronic mail security (2007). https://nvlpubs.nist.gov/nistpubs/legacy/sp/nistspecialpublication800-45ver2.pdf
12. NIST: NIST 800–123: Guide to general server security (2008). https://nvlpubs.nist.gov/nistpubs/legacy/sp/nistspecialpublication800-123.pdf
13. NIST: NIST 500–291: NIST cloud computing standards roadmap (2013). https://www.nist.gov/publications/nist-sp-500-291-nist-cloud-computing-standards-roadmap
14. NIST: NIST 800–40: Guide to enterprise patch management technologies (2013). https://csrc.nist.gov/publications/detail/sp/800-40/rev-3/final
15. NIST: NIST 800–53: Security and privacy controls for federal information systems and organizations (2013). https://nvd.nist.gov/800-53
16. PCI Security Standards Council: Data security standard (2016). https://cayan.com/getattachment/Developers/Knowledge-Base/Documents-Samples/PCI-Documents/PCI-DSS-v3-2-AOC-Cayan-FINAL2.pdf
17. Rausand, M., Høyland, A.: System Reliability Theory: Models, Statistical Methods, and Applications, Second Edition. Wiley, Hoboken (2004). https://doi.org/10.1002/9780470316900
18. Rausand, M.: Risk Assessment: Theory, Methods, and Applications. Wiley, New York (2011)
19. Rolski, T., Schmidli, H., Schmidt, V., Teugels, J.: Stochastic processes for insurance and finance, p. 68 (2001)
20. Salter, C., Saydjari, O.S., Schneier, B., Wallner, J.: Toward a secure system engineering methodolgy. In: Proceedings of the 1998 Workshop on New Security Paradigms, NSPW 1998, pp. 2–10. ACM, New York (1998). https://doi.org/10.1145/310889.310900
21. Turner II, B.L., et al.: Science and technology for sustainable development special feature: a framework for vulnerability analysis in sustainability science. Proc. Natl. Acad Sci. **100**, 8074–8079 (2003)

Reliability, Fault Tolerance and Other Critical Components for Survivability in Information Warfare

Peter Stavroulakis[1(✉)], Maryna Kolisnyk[5], Vyacheslav Kharchenko[2],
Nikolaos Doukas[3], Oleksandr P. Markovskyi[4],
and Nikolaos G. Bardis[3]

[1] Department of Electronic and Computer Engineering,
Technical University of Crete (TUC), Chania, Greece
pete_tsi@yahoo.gr
[2] Department of Computer Systems and Networks,
National Aerospace University "KhAI", Kharkiv, Ukraine
v.kharchenko@csn.khai.edu
[3] Hellenic Army Academy, Varis – Koropiou Avenue, 116 72 Vari, Greece
nd@ieee.org, nbardis@sse.gr
[4] Department of Computer Engineering,
National Technical University of Ukraine,
(Igor Sikorsky Kyiv Polytechnic Institute), Kiev, Ukraine
markovskyy@i.ua
[5] Department of Automation and Control in Technical Systems,
National Technical University, "KPI", Kharkiv, Ukraine

Abstract. The information revolution has caused many aspects of human activity to critically depend on a wide variety of physically existing or virtual technological achievements such as electronic devices, computer systems, algorithms, cloud resources, artificial intelligence hardware and software entities etc. Many of these systems are used in highly sensitive contexts, such as military applications. This implies the existence of an increasing number of unintentional disturbances or malicious attacks. Successful operation requires qualities such as robustness, fault tolerance, reliability, availability and security. All these may be summarized by the title of survivability. Survivability of critical systems working for sensitive applications involves the ability to provide uninterrupted operation under severe disturbances, gracefully degrade when limiting conditions are reached and maintain the ability to resume normal service once the disturbances have been removed. Survivability is an important, even - though non – functional, lifecycle property of many engineering systems. Further desirable elements of survivability include the ability of systems to recognize and resist attacks or accidents, adapt in order to avoid them and modify their behavior in order to diminish the effects of similar future occurrences. This chapter presents a quantitative approach to assessing survivability and an account of survivability in military systems. A scheme for survivability via replica diversity in the implementation of the AES algorithm is then presented.

© Springer Nature Switzerland AG 2019
M. S. Obaidat and E. Cabello (Eds.): ICETE 2017, CCIS 990, pp. 346–370, 2019.
https://doi.org/10.1007/978-3-030-11039-0_17

Following that, an algorithm for adaptive attack aversion in user authentication systems is presented that is based on Boolean transformations. An approach for increased survivability in Internet of Things (IoT) systems is then presented. Finally, an algorithm for secure data storage in cloud resources is presented that allows attack detection and avoidance.

1 Introduction

Having lived through two previous revolutions, the Industrial and electronics now the world society is living through the information revolution. The information revolution is based on advancements in software, microelectronics, storage, quantum, cloud and soft computing that drive the field of Artificial Intelligence and will soon be powered by nanotechnology.

Technological advancement however did not keep in pace with the requirements of critical network systems, as encountered e.g. in military applications, and left some gaps in the fault tolerance, availability, reliability and security areas requiring measurable and implementable results. It is then natural to raise the question: Can system designs of quantifiable survivability close the gap?

The operational environment of engineering systems is characterized by increasing number of disturbances or attacks [1]. As the interdependence of large-scale distributed systems has grown since the advent of modern telecommunications, so too has the risk from disturbances that rapidly propagate within networks, damage critical infrastructure, and trigger catastrophic failures of systems-of-systems. Survivability is a nonfunctional yet critical lifecycle property of engineering systems which must be robust to disturbances and thus survivable. Given their network structure, systems-of-systems are particularly robust to certain disturbances and particularly sensitive to others. Risks are exacerbated by emergence of new sources of disturbances including both physical and electronic terrorism such as cyber-attacks. Research needed to understand the role of survivability as an attribute in engineering system design.

The issue of survivability has already been extensively studied [2–6] in the past in the context critical networks systems. When talking about survivability of critical network systems, reference is always made to cases where the uninterrupted operation of the system under consideration is of paramount importance independent of any type of attack. Many efforts, however, have been devoted to deriving quantitative survivability parameters leading to specific metrics. This has not been possible because, as demonstrated in subsequent sections survivability is a multidimensional quantity and each component has different weight in the direction of uninterrupted operation depending of the type of the critical system studied.

Survivability as a concept has its origin in the military context and the mainly the air-force and nuclear reactors. It is also used for network systems as it regards the offering and the delivering of critical services and includes the element of time. It is defined thus, as we have seen before, as the capability of system to fulfill its mission in a timely manner, and in the presence of attacks malicious or not, failures, or accidents of any kind. Under survivability, services should have the capacity to recognize and resist attacks, adapt and recover in their presence, in order to diminish the effectiveness of future attacks. Since the network system in question may provide non-essential services as well, it is necessary to have a clear understanding and immediate identification and response to essential services under attack. The survivability strategy must then be set up in four steps: protection, detection, response, and recovery. If the attack is catastrophic, survivability attributes must be able to keep the system operational long enough, regarding at least essential services, before breaking down. To face this reality, survivability design principles have been divided depending on the problem under consideration into two categories: passive and active. Passive design is subdivided into (1) hardness resistance of a system to deformation with the purpose to increase the cost to attacker, (2) stealth which refers to the ability of a system to conceal itself within its operating environment, (3) redundancy referring to duplication of critical system components to increase reliability and (4) diversity to increase variation in the range of systems within an architecture so that an attack not to be able to create a serial damaging event. Active design is subdivided in to (1) regeneration referring to restoration of capability through repair and replacement activities, (2) evolution of the system modification to maintain and possibly extend capability (3) relocation for movement in position and (4) retaliation for provision of negative consequences to origin of disturbance (deterrence). With these designs it has not been possible to derive quantifiable measures that will lead to survivability metrics which so important to have when we are talking about warfare systems as we shall see in the following sections.

2   Quantifiable Survivability Definition

Survivability is defined as the capability of a system to fulfill its mission, in a timely manner, in the presence of attacks, failures, or accidents. The term system is used in the broadest possible sense, including networks and large-scale systems of systems.

The term mission refers to a set of very high-level (i.e., abstract) requirements or goals [1].

Missions are not limited to military settings since any successful organization or project must have a vision of its objectives whether expressed implicitly or as a formal mission statement. Assessment as to whether or not a mission has been successfully fulfilled is typically made in the context of external conditions that may affect the achievement of that mission. For example, assume that a financial system shuts down for 12 h during a period of widespread power outages caused by a hurricane. If the system preserves the integrity and confidentiality of its data and resumes its essential services after the period of environmental stress is over, the system can reasonably be judged to have fulfilled its mission. However, if the same system shuts down unexpectedly for 12 h under normal conditions (or under relatively minor environmental stress) and deprives its users of essential financial services, the system can reasonably be judged to have failed its mission, even if data integrity and confidentiality are preserved.

Timeliness is a critical factor that is typically included in (or implied by) the very high-level requirements that define a mission. However, timeliness is such an important factor that it is included explicitly in the definition of survivability.

The terms attack, failure, and accident are meant to include all potentially damaging events; but these terms do not partition such events into mutually exclusive or even distinguishable sets. It is often difficult to determine if a particular detrimental event is the result of a malicious attack, a failure of a component, or an accident. Even if the cause is eventually determined, the critical immediate response cannot depend on such speculative future knowledge.

Attacks are potentially damaging events orchestrated by an intelligent adversary. Attacks include intrusions, probes, and denial of service. Moreover, the threat of an attack may have as severe an impact on a system as an actual occurrence. A system that assumes a defensive position because of the threat of an attack may reduce its functionality and divert additional resources to monitoring the environment and protecting system assets.

Failures and accidents are included as part of survivability. Failures are potentially damaging events caused by deficiencies in the system or in an external element on which the system depends. Failures may be due to software design errors, hardware degradation, human errors, or corrupted data. Accidents describe the broad range of randomly occurring and potentially damaging events such as natural disasters. Accidents are conceived as externally generated events (i.e., outside the system) and failures as internally generated events.

With respect to system survivability, a distinction between a failure and an accident is less important than the impact of the event. Nor is it often possible to distinguish between intelligently orchestrated attacks and unintentional or randomly occurring detrimental events. The approach used in this chapter concentrates on the effect of a potentially damaging event. Typically, for a system to survive, it must react to (and recover from) a damaging effect (e.g., the integrity of a database is compromised) long before the underlying cause is identified. In fact, the reaction and recovery must be successful whether or not the cause is ever determined.

Finally, it is important to recognize that it is the mission fulfillment that must survive, not any particular subsystem or system component. Central to the notion of survivability is the capability of a system to fulfill its mission, even if significant portions of the system are damaged or destroyed. The term survivable system will be sometimes used as a less than perfectly precise shorthand for a system with the capability to fulfill a specified mission in the face of attacks, failures, or accidents. Again, it is the mission, not a particular portion of the system, that must survive.

An alternative definition supposes a measure of interest M has the value M_o just before a failure occurs. The survivability behavior can be depicted by the following attributes [5]: M_a is the value of M just after the failure occurs; M_u is the maximum difference between the value of M and M_a after the failure; M_r is the restored value of M after some time tv; and tr is the relaxation time for the system to restore the value of M (Fig. 1).

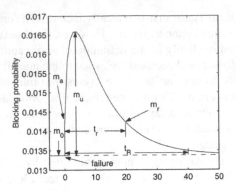

Fig. 1. Survivability after first failure.

For the case of Information Warfare Systems, the notion of survivability of Critical Information Systems must be introduced due to the criticality of the system functioning in the context of real military operations [6]. For many applications regarding Information Systems, reliability satisfies the requirements of the specific system operations, but for critical information systems reliability alone does not address adequately the needs of Critical Information systems, since they do not include the notion of degraded service as an explicit requirement. What is needed is a precise notion of what forms of degraded service are acceptable to users, under what circumstances each form is most useful, and the fraction of time such degraded service levels are acceptable. The notion of survivability that is needed must have three essential characteristics. Firstly, it must be broad enough to encompass various types of damage to the system. Additionally, it must include alternate forms of service, each achieving an effective tradeoff between the benefits of a given level of function and the cost of providing it, under the range of operating conditions for which it is defined. Third, it should model the probability that each of these services must be available for use, as a function of the conditions that the system is expected to encounter. Furthermore, the definition in the case of quantifiable survivability must be precise and unambiguous enough to support an engineering approach to the specification, design, and analysis of critical information systems. If a precise definition of the term survivable is not given, sufficiency of a given system regarding its real requirements cannot be determined. This is not merely an academic point. The owners and users of a system need to be able to determine that, with reasonable quantifiable assurance, the system will perform adequately in its environment. It now remains to detail precisely how the individual aspects of quantifiable survivability fit into this framework to complete a definition that can be put into practice and tested against real engineering needs of information warfare systems as seen in the next subsection.

A modern Battle Management System protecting a nation's defended assets in a theatre of war from varied threats, at strategic, operational and tactical levels, demands faster reaction and quick commander response. Threats of different severities could approach from geographical areas different from the areas where the weapons are deployed. Thus, for defending assets, the nation states need to be networked to gather intelligence about the threats for the central command and control in order to decide on the type and the number of weapons to be engaged to neutralize the threats, assigning weapons to prioritized threats and finally assessing the battle damage, all in real-time. Information superiority and decision dominance are the key factors of modern warfare. A problem faced by the defense-planners is how to design nationwide Central Information Grid (CIG) and software, which will be inter – operable, sustainable and scalable and can still provide the robustness and time critical decisions. In order to be real-time compliant, the overall system should allow decentralized decision-making, which may be overridden by centralized command and control depending on the demand of the situation. The diversity and volume of online data overwhelms the cognitive capabilities of human commanders, which necessitate the use of a Decision Support System (DSS) which will be based on the quantifiable results of the survivability.

3 Survivability of Information Warfare Systems

Information warfare (IW) is a concept involving the battlespace use and management of information and communication technology in pursuit of a competitive advantage over an opponent. The current world is highly connected, but it doesn't take much to tip over into instability or even chaos. Information warfare systems combine electronic warfare, cyberwarfare and psychological operations into a single fighting stance with the aim of paralyzing decision making, and this stance will be central to all information warfare systems: this is also known as 'hybrid warfare'. As such it is divided into Command and Control Warfare, Intelligence-Based Warfare, Electronic Warfare, and Cyberwarfare. Other aspects which could be considered to belong to Information Warfare such as Psychological Warfare, Hacker Warfare, Economic Information Warfare will not be addressed in this chapter.

Survivability must provide essential services but a measurable level of performance must exist in order to maintain an acceptable and quantifiable level of functioning of these essential services.

Survivability necessarily depends on the attributes of Availability, Reliability, Fault Tolerance and Security which are only measured probabilistically and the same is true for Survivability.

4 Replica Diversity in Cryptographic Systems

An important aspect of survivability is concerned with systems that, due to the nature of their operation, have to function in contexts where the hardware used is available to any potential attacker. A characteristic example of this case are smartcards that are up to a certain level open to any intervention by their users. Additionally, in military systems one can envisage crypto devices being captured by the enemy. This section summarizes a method that has been proposed [7] in order to boost survivability in such cases and deals with Power Analysis Attacks.

Power analysis is performed on equipment available to the attacker. This attack attempts to derive encryption keys, access codes and other parameters of the implementation of security equipment based on measurements of the power required by the circuit during its operation [7, 8]. There are two distinct forms of this type of analysis: Simple Power Analysis (SPA) and Differential Power Analysis (DPA). Current measurement techniques allow the completion of the analysis with the execution of an instruction required at the particular level of power. The Advanced Encryption Standard (AES) algorithm, that is based on the Rijndael algorithm and is widely recognized as providing the baseline level of cryptographic security, is particularly susceptible to this type of attack when implemented in dedicated hardware such as smart-cards.

Several forms of countermeasures for this kind of attack exist [7] that randomize the execution of the algorithm, creating stochastic polymorphism. The effectiveness of stochastic polymorphism in the implementation of programs depends on the magnitude of the time variable when each instruction is implemented and the consumption of resources for this. Research [9] shows that the solution of the polymorphic algorithm implementation exercise in the general case, is difficult enough and is connected to the complexity of the analysis of the graphs that model the execution of instructions on the data. An investigation of the Rijndael algorithm was proposed [7] from the point of view of the possibility for stochastic reconfiguration of the calculation and the processing of a method for an effective polymorphic implementation in terminal network devices, microcontrollers and smart cards.

4.1 Analysis of the Calculations of the Rijndael Algorithm

For a polymorphic implementation of the Rijndael algorithm, it is important to study the computational complexity of the temporary relocation of the instructions. It will hence be feasible to impede the possibility of algorithmic analysis based on power consumption comparisons, while minimizing the computational resource expenses necessary for the implementation of polymorphism. For a polymorphic implementation it is therefore necessary to perform:

- An analysis of the correlation of the implemented instruction sequence to the data
- A stochastic generation of the instruction sequence to be executed based, taking into consideration the correlation determined earlier on.

For the class of symmetric packet algorithms, into which the Rijndael algorithm belongs, the correlation of instructions with the data may be established in a relatively simple and precise manner. This is due to the fact that this class of algorithms does not contain conditional instructions.

The fundamental characteristic of a time-domain variation of the execution of the ith instruction ($i \in \{1, .., N\}$, where N is the total number of instructions in the program) is the time interval v_i between an time instance t_{li} and the previous time instance t_{ei} of the execution of the particular command: $v_i = t_{li} - t_{ei}$.

The general characteristics of the time variations in the execution of the algorithm are the average variation in the time T_a of the variation of the execution instance of the instructions and the minimum time T_m of the execution time instance of the instructions.

$$T_a = \frac{1}{N} \cdot \sum_{i=1}^{N} v_i$$
$$T_m = \min_{i=1,..,N} v \tag{1}$$

For the analysis of the possibilities of changing the execution time, it is necessary to investigate the structure of the implementations of the Rijndael algorithm in micro-controllers and smart cards. For this class of computing devices, instructions are in their majority of single byte length. Since the forward and the inverse transformation are of similar nature, only the investigation of the structure of the forward transformation will be presented. The inverse transformation may be dealt with in a similar manner.

The Rijndael algorithm is capable of processing data packets of size 128, 192 or 256 bits, with corresponding state matrix sizes of 4 rows and 4, 6 or 8 columns and the execution of the algorithm involving 10, 12 or 14 iterations, a quantity that depends on the size of the data packet and the size of the key. From the initial packet of keys an independent process will determine the number of circular keys that will be required to be used for each one of the cycles.

The basic cycle of the Rijndael algorithm includes XOR operations with the key (XK) and byte substitutions (BS), operations that are executed independently of all the bytes of the current state table. It also includes line rotations (LR) and row mixing (RM).

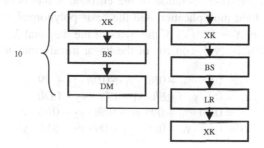

Fig. 2. Block diagram of the Rijndael transformation.

The line rotation operations may be eliminated under the condition that the column mixing changes the arrangement of the diagonal elements (diagonal mix – DM), by assigning the result in the column of the new table. Based on thin fact, the Rijndael calculation procedure consists of 10 identical cycles and a final transformation as shown in Fig. 2. The last part has two additional characteristics: the execution of the line rotation together with the diagonal mix, as well as the final XOR operation involving the key. In summary, the four fundamental operations used in the Rijndael calculation are forward and backward byte substitution, circular displacement of the rows of the state table, column mixups, XOR-ing of the current state matrices with the corresponding matrices of the extended key.

The byte substitution operation in the forward transformation is performed on the Galois field G and uses operations to obtain the multiplicative inverse byte $R = G^{-1}$ mod $p(x)$ and formulates the polynomial $p(x) = x^8 + x^3 + x + 1$, with the subsequent linear transformation of the reversal R. This is done by multiplying the constant table M_d and the XOR sum with the constant byte $B = \{01100011\} : D = S(G) = (M_d \times R) \oplus B$.

Hence, the inverse replacement of the byte D consists of the execution of the inverse linear transformation, using the table $M_r : G = S^{-1}(D) = (M_r \times (D \oplus B))^{-1}$ mod $p(x)$.

The byte replacement operation mentioned above, is a system of non linear Boolean functions of 8 variables and in most implementations, it is completed by using the previously obtained matrices of size 256 (8 × 8), that are stored in non − volatile memory [1]. For the implementation of both the forward and the inverse transformation, two separate tables are required.

The byte rearrangement operation on the diagonal of the state matrix (DM) consists of the transformations $Y = P(X)$ of the bytes of the diagonal $X = \{x_0, x_1, x_2, x_3\}$:

$$
\begin{aligned}
y_0 &= 2 \cdot x_0 \oplus 3 \cdot x_1 \oplus x_2 \oplus x_3 \\
y_1 &= x_0 \oplus 2 \cdot x_1 \oplus 3 \cdot x_2 \oplus x_3 \\
y_2 &= x_0 \oplus x_1 \oplus 2 \cdot x_2 \oplus 3 \cdot x_3 \\
y_3 &= 3 \cdot x_0 \oplus x_1 \oplus x_2 \oplus 2 \cdot x_3
\end{aligned}
\tag{2}
$$

where $Y = \{y_0, \ldots, y_3\}$ is the resulting column of the state matrix, y_0, y_1, y_2, y_3 are state bytes, and the multiplication operation of the encoded 8 bits is performed using the rules of the Galois field multiplication and the basis polynomial $x^8 + x^4 + x^2 + x + 1$. The restore operation, $X = P^{-1}(Y)$ of the bytes of the diagonal $X = \{x_0, x_1, x_2, x_3\}$ to the encoding $Y = \{y_0, \ldots, y_3\}$, consists of the linear transformation:

$$
\begin{aligned}
x_0 &= 0Eh \cdot y_0 + 0Bh \cdot y_1 + 0Dh \cdot y_2 + 09 \cdot y_3 \\
x_1 &= 09 \cdot y_0 + 0Eh \cdot y_1 + 0Bh \cdot y_2 + 0Dh \cdot y_3 \\
x_2 &= 0Dh \cdot y_0 + 09 \cdot y_1 + 0Eh \cdot y_2 + 0Bh \cdot y_3 \\
x_3 &= 0Bh \cdot y_0 + 0Dh \cdot y_1 + 09 \cdot y_2 + 0Eh \cdot y_3
\end{aligned}
\tag{3}
$$

In this fashion, each one of the iterations consists of $4 - \alpha$ independent packets for the processing of the diagonal. The diagonal processing packets involve operations that are performed on 4 bytes of the diagonal of the state matrix. The structure of these operations is shown in Fig. 3.

In this figure, N2 and M3 denote the byte multiplication operations. These operations are performed according to the principle of the Galois field multiplication with basis polynomial $x^8 + x^4 + x^2 + x + 1$.

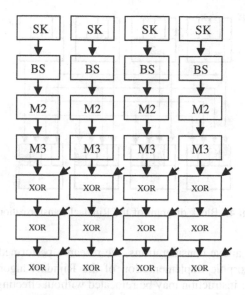

Fig. 3. Operations on the diagonal.

The final XOR operation implements the byte rearrangement on the diagonal and is illustrated in Fig. 3. The arrow in the XOR operation implies that in order to obtain the byte of the result it is necessary to implicitly XOR all the bytes of the diagonal or their multiplication in 2 and 3. The multiplication operations in 2 and 3 may be implemented either by shifts, branch conditions on the C bits and XOR operations, or by using lookup tables.

The total number of operations of each packet is equal to 28. Assuming that the average time for the execution of one instruction is equal to τ, then the maximum case of the time v for the execution of the instructions XK is calculated as $3 \cdot 6 \cdot \tau = 18 \cdot \tau$. Indeed, the execution time for the instructions of XK for the i-th byte of the diagonal, $i \in \{1, \ldots, 4\}$, is defined in terms of the time for the processing of the 3 different bytes of the diagonal without the final XOR operation that uses as an operand the result of the ith byte.

The processing of the packets in the context of an iteration of the Rijndael algorithm is accelerated independently. However, with the transfer to the subsequent cycle, there arises a need for the exchange of the results of the processing of two distinct iterations of the Rijndael algorithm, as shown in Fig. 4. From this Figure it may be deduced that as far as the availability of all necessary previous results is concerned, during the processing of the jth iteration packet, the processing may start in each one of the bytes of the subsequent $(j+1)^{th}$ iteration.

This enables the possibility to unify (in a pipeline fashion and using time division multiplexing) the calculations that concern the jth and the $(j+1)^{th}$ iteration. Of course, the packets of the $(j+1)^{th}$ iteration may not be fully processed, until the processing of the packets of the jth iteration has been completed. It is hence evident that the possibility for parallel processing is feasible only between two consecutive iterations.

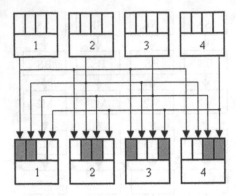

Fig. 4. Block diagram of the Rijndael transformation.

According to the above considerations, the research performed has shown that by means of the polymorphic implementation of the Rijndael algorithm the execution instant for a particular instruction may be relocated without effecting the total execution time for the transformations.

The embodiment of this capability with minimal consequences on the computational resources required, suitable methods for stochastic polymorphic implementation in both an algorithmic form and as program implementation.

The results of this research suggest that the proposed method for the stochastic polymorphic implementation of the Rijndael algorithm is suitable for application in microcontrollers and smart cards. This method permits the reconfigurable sequential implementation of program instructions at the initiation of every program execution, that provides adequate response to the danger of constant data reconstruction by DPCA technology based attacks. The analysis performed on the Rijndael algorithm procedures allows the study of the theoretically feasible limits of the polymorphic implementation of the program and the reduction of the additional time overhead required for the polymorphism. The organization of the stochastically polymorphic implementation of a variation of the algorithm in the location of the instructions is 85%. Experimentally, it was shown that the increase in the time overhead required for the implementation, due to the introduction of the stochastic polymorphism, does not exceed 76%. The application of the above method enables a significant increase in the survivability of critical encryption systems, such as smartcards that have to operate in conditions where potential attackers have uninhibited access without risk.

5 Survivable User Authentication

The efficiency and hence the survivability of information security algorithms is defined based on two factors: the level of security and the amount of computational resources required for the implementation of the security functions. User Authentication is a particular case where lack of computational resources may prohibit the implementation of survivable algorithms, while an attacker may stage denial of service attacks based on overloading the system. This section reviews a scheme that has been presented for user authentication based on Boolean functions [10] and presents high survivability under such conditions.

At the basis of all information security algorithms lies an analytically insoluble mathematical problem. In practice, such problems are one way transformations of the form $Y = F(X)$. For such one way transformations, the forward transformation $F(X)$ is defined such that there is no analytic way of deriving the inverse transformation $\Phi(Y)$ of the known function $F(X)$ such that $X = \Phi(Y)$. The only way to accomplish such a task, i.e. the determination of a value X for a given value Y such that $Y = F(X)$, is to tabulate all possible values of X. The largest part of the problems that do not have an analytic solution and form the basis of cryptographic algorithms, originate from the Boolean algebra and Number Theory. Especially for number theory, problems are related to discrete logarithm calculations and are the basis of most asymmetric cryptographic algorithms (public key encryption algorithms). Well known algorithms belong in this class, such as RSA or El-Gamal, as well as digital signature algorithms like DSS [1]. The basis of another broad class of cryptographic algorithms, lies the difficult to solve Boolean algebra problem of finding the roots of a system of non-linear Boolean functions. In this class belong all symmetric encryption algorithms such as DES, IDEA, Rijndael, as well as a significant proportion of hash algorithms, the most known of which are RC-5, SHA and RIPEMD-160 [11, 12].

The basic advantage of algorithms based on number theory problems that cannot be solved analytically, is the existence of multiple keys. This can be illustrated in the cases of RSA, El-Gamal, EEC where the keys for the forward and backward transformation are diffcrent. Hence, when there exist multiple keys, some of them may be used for decryption and some of them may be used for encryption. This enables more efficient information security schemes to be created on this basis, that permit a more efficient organization of information resources, compared to algorithms based on a single key.

This observation was the motivating force for the creation of the public key encryption algorithm RSA in 1978, the basis of which was the one-way transformation $F(X) = A^X \bmod M$ [12]. From a theoretical point of view, the existence of multiple keys in cryptographic transformations is necessary so as to create multiple solutions, i.e. there exist at least two keys X_1 and X_2, such that $F(X_1) = F(X_2)$. The basic drawback of algorithms based on the principle of the difficult to solve number theory problems, is the low speed of implementation that arises from the high computational complexity of the operations of modular exponentiation in numbers whose size is of the order of several thousand bits.

This drawback is eliminated with information security algorithms that are based on difficult to solve Boolean algebra problems. The recursive computation of a system of Boolean equations may be organized efficiently enough, via software in general purpose processors or on special computational hardware. As far as evaluation is concerned, the speed of an implementation of a Boolean function base algorithm and that of a modulo arithmetic based algorithm, differ by about a factor of 2–3 orders of magnitude [13]. However, algorithms based on Boolean transformations have fewer functional possibilities that do not permit the creation of efficient information security protocols, similarly to those based on analytically impossible to solve number theory problems. More specifically, the use of Boolean transformation does not permit the implementation of asymmetric cryptography, a very significant principle of modern cryptography, the encoding of digital signatures and the identification based on the basis of a "zero knowledge" scheme. One of the factors that contribute to the limitation of the functional capabilities of Boolean transformations, is the uniqueness of Boolean transformations [13].

One of the most promising research areas of current information security technologies is the extension of the functional capabilities of Boolean algebra based algorithms [12]. On the basis of such algorithms, the design of efficient information security protocols will be enabled. Such efficient information security protocols require significantly less computational resources and may hence be executed at speeds that are several orders of magnitude faster than the corresponding ones for modular arithmetic based problems.

Towards the realization of this direction of modern information security technology, an important goal is the development of a methodology for the design of one way Boolean transformations that possess the non-single-value property [13]. Such algorithms may be efficiently used in protocols for the "zero knowledge" based identification of remote subscribers in multi user systems [14].

Previous work on the front of remote subscriber identification was focused on improving efficiency and increasing the level of security by reducing the need for storage and communications [15–19]. The aim of this research is the development of a method for designing Boolean functions that have the necessary one way properties and present non-single-value during the inverse transformation.

In its general form, the idea of the use of Boolean transformations for the implementation of identification based on the principle of zero knowledge, consists of the following steps [10, 20]. Subscriber A produces via a pre-defined procedure a Boolean transformation $F_A(X)$ such that there exists a finite set Ω_A of m incoming vectors $\Omega_A = \{X_{A1}, X_{A2}, \ldots, X_{Am}\}$, for which the transformation $F_A(X)$ assumes the same values $U_A : \forall Q, G \in \Omega_A, Q \neq G : F_A(Q) = F_A(G) = U$. The set Ω_A practically contains a list of session passwords of subscriber A, that are known only to subscriber A. For this reason it may be said that, the set Ω_A is considered to be the private key of subscriber A. The function $F_A(X)$ and the password U_A, are considered to be the public key of subscriber A and during the registration of the subscriber, it is communicated to the system. During access to the system, the subscriber chooses a sequential password G that belongs to the set Ω_A and sends it to the system. The system calculates $F_A(G)$ and compares it to U_A. If $F_A(G) = U_A$, then the subscriber A is considered to have been successfully identified. The proposed identification scheme base on the zero knowledge principle is designed for identification in m sessions. After that, a new registration is required. Taking into account the non-reversibility of $F_A(X)$, the system may not in any other way acquire the passwords that compose the set Ω_A.

Consequently, the transformation $F_A(X)$ and the code U_A are not considered to be secret. Since in every registration cycle of subscriber A, a new entry password is used that belongs to the set Ω_A, the system may easily block all previous passwords. This prohibits the access of an unauthorized third party via the capture of the password of subscriber A.

5.1   Establishment of a Boolean Transformation for Identification

For the implementation of user identification, it is necessary to establish Boolean transformations $F(X)$, such that possess the following properties:

1. The inverse transformation of $F(X)$, $\Phi(X)$ must be a one to many mapping (not unique). This means that there is a set Ω of incoming vectors for which $F(X)$ acquires unique values: $\forall Q, G \in \Omega, Q \neq G : F(Q) = F(G) = U$.
2. Establishment of passwords for the given function $F(X)$ must require the use of computational resources. Essentially, the amount of resources required from the intruder, significantly exceeds the amount of resources required by legitimate subscribers.

It is hence necessary to establish a Boolean transformation $F(X)$, defined in the set of the 2^n values of the n-bit incoming binary vector of $X = \{x_1, x_2, \ldots, x_n\}$, $\forall i \in \{1, \ldots, n\} : x_i \in \{0, 1\}$, giving an n-bit outgoing vector $Y = F(X)$, $Y = \{y_1, y_2, \ldots, y_n\}$, $\forall i \in \{1, \ldots, n\} : y_i \in \{0, 1\}$. Every i^{th} binary component y_i of the outgoing vector Y, may be observed like the value of the Boolean function $f_i(X)$, which is defined on the range of values X. On this basis, it may be stated that the transformation $F(X)$, consists of n Boolean functions $f_1(X), f_2(X), \ldots, f_n(X) : F(X) = \{f_1(X), f_2(X), \ldots, f_n(X)\}$. For this reason and for establishing the transformation $F(X)$, it is necessary that each one of the functions $f_1(X), f_2(X), \ldots, f_n(X)$ is non-linear and depends on all n incoming variables $X = \{x_1, x_2, \ldots, x_n\}$.

As it is commonly known, Boolean transformations may be represented in three forms:

- as a truth table
- as an algebraic canonical form
- as a procedure, i.e. as an algorithm for the calculation of the outgoing vector Y, given the value of the incoming vector X.

When information security procedures are concerned, the third of the above options is commonly used. This is due to the fact that the number of variables defined by such transformations may range to several hundreds. It is hence recommended that such transformations are best described in the form of a procedure.

As the basis of the procedure for calculating transformations $F(X)$, the scheme presented in Fig. 5 is proposed.

The method described in [10] leads to a procedural form for formulating non-linear Boolean functional transformations, whose inverses are not one-to-one. Such transformations may be used in several applications instead of modulo operations on large numbers, thereby giving significant benefits in terms of efficiency (by 2 to 3 orders of magnitude). The relation between the parameters of the procedural form and the characteristics of the Boolean transformations may be determined. The method developed supports the formulation of Boolean functional transformations, the application of which enables the increase of the speed of implementation of security algorithms and of schemes for identification and authentication of remote users.

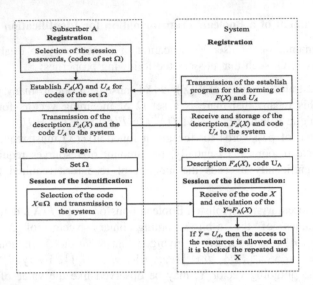

Fig. 5. Identification diagram of subscribers based on the concept zero knowledge with the use of the Boolean functional transformations.

6 IoT Survivability: Architecture and Markov Model

Internet of Things (IoT) Technologies and Big Data, are expected to be increasingly deployed in urban centers, with systems consisting of a large number of devices. Individual survivability of each device does not imply overall system survivability. This section reviews a method that has been developed to quantitatively assess the survivability of IoT entities in a systematic way [21]. At the moment, there are already about 300 million IoT systems that use SIM-card as well as an increasing number of connected devices using low-power network with low bandwidth [22]. IoT is a paradigm that involves ubiquitous presence in the environment of different things/objects that are using wireless and wire networks and unique addressing scheme are able to interact with each other and with other things/objects to create new applications/services to achieve purposes [23]. They are becoming more diverse, and embedding in the micro- and nano-scale physical systems, not only to create a distributed cybernetic system, but also a new concept for computing and communications paradigm of creative self-organized spaces that may occur in real time. IoT interconnects people, devices and systems, and represents the pinnacle of current developments in the field of information technology [24].

IoT widens the internet's scope from people-operated computers towards autonomous intelligent smart devices [25]. Typically, these devices are connected to the Internet for remote monitoring and diagnosis, leading to significant cost savings. IoT can be divided into three parts: mobile; domestic; industrial [26].

The model currently includes over fifty use cases, covering many service categories such as [27, 28]: Smart metering (electricity, gas and water); Facility management services; Intruder alarms & fire alarms for homes & commercial properties;

Connected personal appliances measuring health parameters; Tracking of persons, animals or objects Agriculture; Health Care/E-Health; Retail Safety and Security Automotive & Logistics Energy & Utilities Manufacturing; Smart City; Smart Home; Smart city infrastructure such as street lamps or dustbins; Smart office; Smart hotel; Connected industrial appliances such as welding machines or air compressors.

The concept and architecture of the Smart Business Center (SBC) has already been analyzed [21]. This section describes possible types of software vulnerabilities objects of this system and the development of Markov network model for researching system's SBC reliability indicators. Last section concludes and discusses future research steps.

6.1   Analysis of SBC Network Survivability

Each device of the SBC is a potential entry point for a network attack [29] by insiders, hackers, or criminals. When security is insufficient in even seemingly harmless household appliances, or other IoT products, it presents endemic vulnerabilities and risks [30]. Internet of Things is based on using a variety of sensors and control units. SBC system gives staff complete control over their offices, but, at the same time, there are new dangers and threats due to the fact that the new computer technology with an internet connection, provide possibility of hackers to connect to the system. The IOActive IoT Security Survey, conducted in March 2016, revealed that nearly half (47%) of all respondents felt that less than 10% of all IoT products on the market are designed with adequate security. A staggering 85% believe that less than half of IoT products are secure [31].

As written at [32], the IoT facilities, available by the Internet, may disclose personal user data to another people. Lack of data security IOT brings to detection of vulnerable devices by criminals to gain access to him or other IOT facilities. The attacks report by Kaspersky Lab shows, that IP-cameras are connected wirelessly to the Internet are not necessarily secure: here is the potential for cybercriminals to passively monitor the cameras for the implementation of the code in the network, thereby replacing the image in the camera channel communication to fake shots, or put the system in offline mode. If the data packets are transmitted via a data network, it has not been encrypted, an attacker can create their own version of the software and data processing for controlling the IoT [33]. Physical security - notification of suspicious activity at the moment, which is found near the IoT-device. Alerts come with surveillance cameras, physical access control, and other sensors to detect movement and other [28, 33]. Security and privacy are important requirements for the IoT due to the inherent heterogeneity of the Internet connected objects and the ability to monitor and control physical objects.

6.2   SBS Dependability Modeling

IoT systems combined with their high-availability requirements means that these systems are more at risk of unintended, non-malicious downtime. When designing SBC, it is necessary to provide the security of the operation and the reliability of hardware and software components of the system. Understanding new communication protocols, hardware types, and obscure operating systems is difficult, making IoT security an incredible challenge.

In the network equipment that used for the organization of systems SBC, according to statistics, more and more vulnerabilities found in software code. When exposed to hacker attacks via these vulnerabilities can be stolen proprietary information of the company, and making failure of the software and hardware components of network devices and servers. Manufacturers proposes decisions on the release of patch, redundancy of components to reduce the risks of vulnerabilities of network equipment in IoT. However, vulnerabilities are discovered again and again, and the attacks translates them inoperable technical condition. In order to provide network Dependability of IoT, which includes providing a high reliability and high safety at the required level, it is necessary to develop a mathematical model for a more accurate quantification.

Assumptions in the development of the model:

- stream hardware failures of the system obey the Poisson distribution;
- the flow of failures of subsystems is subject to Poisson for-grabs, as the results of monitoring and diagnostics, anti-virus software testing corrected secondary error (the result of the accumulation of the effects of primary errors and defects, book-marks), and to fix a malfunction or failure of software, eliminating or the conse-quences of software bookmarks and code vulnerabilities, DOS - and DDOS - attacks, the number of primary software defects permanently. Therefore, the assumption is true, that the flow of software failures obeys Poisson distribution, the failure rate is constant;
- the model does not take into account that eliminating software vulnerabilities and design faults changes the parameters of the flow of failures (and recovering). To investigate the dependability SBC use the theory of Markov models, as the failure rates of hardware and software and the availability of software vulnerabilities is constant.

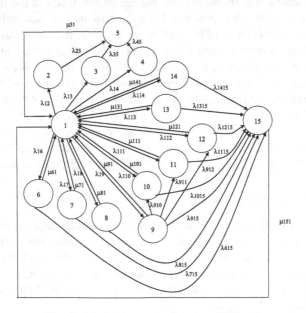

Fig. 6. Markov's graph of system SBC states.

Figure 6 is a Markov graph of functioning of the main subsystems SBC, λ - the intensity of failure or attack, μ - the intensity of the recovery system.

The basic state of the system: (1) Normal condition (up-state) system; (2) Failure due to faulty feeder from the stationary power supply (220 V); (3) Failure due to a malfunction of the second feeder (a solar battery); (4) Failure of the battery in the UPS; (5) Reconfigure the power subsystem; (6) Failure of the cable connecting the Router and Server; (7) Failure of the cable connecting the UPS and Switch, and/or the Router, and/or Server; (8) Failure of the cable connecting the Router and Switch; (9) Firewall Denial; (10) Refusal Server due to a fault server components, or exposure to attacks on the code server system software with vulnerabilities; (11) Failure Router as a result of failure of the router components, or the impact of the attacks on the code of the router operating system vulnerabilities; (12) Switch Failure due to a fault switch components, or exposure to an attack on the system software code switch with the presence of vulnerabilities; (13) Partial failure of the system due to the failure of cable connecting any or multiple sensors and IP cameras; (14) Partial failure of the system due to the failure of any one or more sensors and IP cameras; (15) Failure of the system.

System availability function AC(t) is defined as the sum of the probabilities of staying the system in an up-states: $AC(t) = P_1(t) + P_5(t)$.

Solving the system of Kolmogorov-Chapman equations, we can get the value of the availability function components and SBS network, the number of network failures due to software vulnerabilities, and how and with what intensity the system is restored after such failures. It follows that service availability, service continuity, cyber security, data integrity, resilience and high dependability of software and hardware should be inherent in IoT networks.

7 Data Survivability in Distributed Data Storage Systems

The rapid development of telecommunication devices and data transmission means have led to the wide – spread use of distributed data processing and storage systems, leading to the Cloud Storage paradigm. A significant advantage of distributed information storage and processing systems is their ability to provide high levels of reliability and long operational lives (survival periods). This advantage is particularly important for distributed information storage and processing systems destined for military applications. This section describes a scheme that has been proposed [34] for scalable, secure cloud storage. Information is stored in distributed form in cloud storage units, without being disclosed to potential attacks. The low cost of cloud storage units implies that such a storage system may be scaled in order to provide the required survivability level. System availability is maintained even though access may have been lost several servers up to a maximum number which is a design parameter determined by the system operator.

7.1 Analysis of Existing Data Recovery Methods

The problem of data recovery during or after loss of access to one or more storage nodes of a distributed information storage system, appeared immediately with the appearance such distributed systems for data storage and processing.

Fundamental criteria for judging the efficiency of data recovery means from storage nodes to which access has been lost are:

- the number q of the storage nodes from which data may be recovered
- the number k of redundant storage nodes
- the time required in order to recover the data to which access has been lost.

The value of the last parameter depends on the computational complexity of the data recovery process and the number m of the storage nodes to which access is necessary in order to recover the data. Currently, the fundamental means for data recovery are:

- Backup copies
- Use of correction codes
- Use of erasure codes

The backup copies of data stored in distributed systems ensure the rapid recovery times for lost data. Apart from this fact, the copying of data does not impose limits on the number m of nodes to which access may be re-established. The disadvantage for copying data that immediately becomes apparent is the high level of redundancy that arises as a result and the independence of the possibility for loss of access both to the principle as well as to the redundant storage nodes. In other words, with backup copies it is possible that access will be lost to both the principle and the redundant nodes and the data will be lost.

The use of correction codes [35, 36] allows in principle to recover the information from any number of nodes where the data is stored. Fundamental drawbacks of correction codes are the high level of redundancy required; for most correction codes, this is calculated as $k = 2 \cdot q$ and the fact that recovery time increases rapidly with q.

The best characteristics of redundancy rates $(k = 1.2 \cdot q \ldots 1.5 \cdot q)$ can be achieved by the application of erasure codes [37–39] which, contrary to correction codes, do not solve the problem of lost data localization, but only recovering the data. In [6] the problem of communicating agents is discussed. In particular, the agents store information which broadcast to neighbors using the connections of a given wired infrastructure. The algorithm of average consensus is proved to always exist in bidirectional and connected networks whereas minimum hops convergence is investigated.

Existing erasure codes are oriented towards recovering the data from data stores nodes and are consequently a viable solution only when access to 1–2 data stores nodes is lost [39]. In military systems, the number of storage nodes where data is stored and to which access may be lost for different reasons (e.g. malfunction due to enemy activity, loss of confidentiality etc.) is large. Hence the use of erasure codes in this case will, in general, not solve the problem of recovering the data.

Following the above reasoning, existing means of recovering data in distributed systems do not enable the efficient recovery of data for the particular case of military applications of distributed systems. This situation calls for the development of innovative methods and means for the recovery of data and more specifically methods that will be able to answer to the particularities of the data recovery exercise for this case.

Currently, data backing up schemes are actively used and being constantly developed, for the remote, distributed storage cloud technology. However, denial of access in such systems is a rare occurrence and the related schemes to recover the data are based on the assumption that access has been lost only to a small number of storage node.

The aim of this research is the proposition of methods and schemes for the data recovery in military applications of distributed systems. The resulting algorithms must be capable of providing a solution to the problem, when access has been lost to a relatively large number of data storage nodes, while using the minimum number of redundant storage nodes necessary. As it may be concluded from the above considerations, research work into the development of efficient methods for the creation of information backup and recovery schemes in distributed storage systems, that will be able to operate when access to a large number of storage nodes is lost, is of critical importance to military applications.

7.2   Proposed Scheme

The model considered for this research may be described as follows. An information system that is available to multiple subscribers operates based on m distributed storage nodes. Without loss of generality, it may be considered that the volume of the packets of data stored in each one of the storage nodes is the same. The packets of data stored in each one of the m storage nodes is denoted as $B_1, B_2, \ldots, B_m$. Each packet is composed of n fragments, i.e. each packet $B_j, j(j = 1, \ldots, m)$ may be represented as a set of fragments, $B_j = \{a_{j,1}, a_{j,2}, \ldots, a_{j,n}\}$.

An efficient method for the creation of backup codes to be stored in a distributed information system, that permits the recovery of data during the loss of access to any q storage nodes, via the use of q additional redundant storage nodes. This scheme is hence a scheme that permits the attainment of the theoretically minimum redundancy.

The method is based on the analysis of the representation of the data in distributed systems in the form of a matrix A, with m rows that correspond to the storage nodes and n columns, corresponding to the fragments of the data packets stored in the corresponding storage nodes:

$$A = \begin{Vmatrix} a_{1,1} & a_{1,2} & \cdots & a_{1,n} \\ a_{2,1} & a_{2,2} & \cdots & a_{2,n} \\ & \vdots & & \\ a_{m,1} & a_{m,2} & \cdots & a_{m,n} \end{Vmatrix} \tag{4}$$

1. The backup codes used for the recovery of the data to which access has been lost, are formed as XOR sums of the elements of the columns of the matrix A, as well as of elements located at different angles above and below the diagonal of the matrix.
2. The codes for the q backup storage nodes used for the recovery of the data to which access has been lost, are formed as XOR sums of the elements of the columns of the matrix A and elements of matrix diagonal which have angles $\pm arctg\left(\frac{1}{d}\right)$, where $d = 1, 2, \ldots, \frac{q-1}{2}$ for odd q.
3. For example, for $q = 7$ the use of 7 backup nodes is required, with the corresponding packets being formulated as the sums of the packets of the packets of the principle nodes, located at the columns of matrix A, on the diagonal of matrix A with angles $+45(arctg 1)$, $-45(-arctg 1)$, $+25.56(arctg \frac{1}{2})$, $-25.56(arctg \frac{1}{2})$, $+18.43(arctg \frac{1}{3})$. $-18.43(arctg \frac{1}{3})$.
4. The fundamental idea of the proposed recovery procedure is based on the fact that the numbers corresponding to the q nodes, to which access has temporarily or permanently been lost, are known: $w_1, w_2, \ldots, w_q$, with $w_1 < w_2 < \ldots < w_q$. Consequently, this is necessary for the recovery of q in the corresponding rows of matrix A. For the recovery, the XOR sums of the rows and the diagonals spanning angles $\pm\alpha_1, \pm\alpha_2, \ldots, \pm\alpha_u$, where $u = (q-1)/2$ may be used.

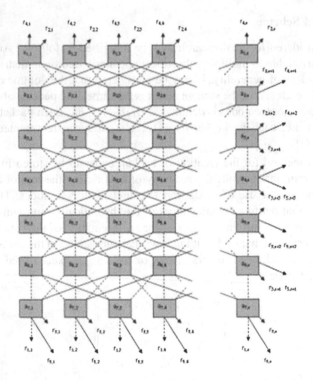

Fig. 7. Architecture for the formulation of the data fragments for the redundant information storage nodes with $m = 7$.

5. Generally, the proposed scheme for the recovery of the data of q nodes, to which access has temporarily or permanently been lost, consists of two levels:

6. (1) For $j = 1, \ldots, u$ sequentially perform restoration of h_j elements of the row w_j of matrix A, using the sum of the elements of the diagonal with angle α_{u-j-1}, which do not intersect row w_{j+1}. For $i = q, q-1, \ldots, u-2$ sequentially perform restoration of h_i elements of the row w_i of matrix A using the sum of the elements of the diagonal $-\alpha_{u-i-1}$, that do not intersect with row w_{i-1}. The restoration of element $a_{u+1,0}$ of matrix A is performed using the XOR sum of the first row of matrix A.

(2) Sequential restoration of the elements of row w_1, w_2, $\ldots$, w_q of matrix A: for $j = 2, \ldots, n$: restoration of the u element a_{w_1,h_1+j}, $a_{w_2,h_2+j}, \ldots, a_{w_u,h_u+j}$ using the sum of the diagonal spanning angles $+\alpha_u$, $+\alpha_{u-1}, \ldots, +\alpha_1$ respectively. Restoration of the u element a_{w_q,h_q+j}, $a_{w_{q-1},h_{q-1}+j}, \ldots, a_{w_{u+2},h_{u+2}+j}$ using the sum of the diagonals spanning angles $-\alpha_u$, $-\alpha_{u-1}, \ldots, -\alpha_{1n}$ respectively; Restoration of the element $a_{u+1,j}$ of matrix A using the XOR sum of j rows of matrix A.

The structure for the formulation of the data fragments for the redundant information storage nodes for $m = 7$ is presented in Fig. 7.

8 Conclusions

In this chapter it was analyzed that usual engineering requirements such as robustness, reliability, robustness, availability, fault – tolerance and security may be integrated as the non – functional requirement of the lifecycle property of survivability. A definition of survivability in the context of critical military systems and systems of systems was given. This definition included the ability to detect attacks and adapt in order to avoid them, the provision of uninterrupted service in the presence of instantaneous or continuous attacks or accidental disturbances or occurrences, the graceful degradation from the operational to the non – operational state without loss of data and the ability for complete recovery once the cause of the disturbance has been removed or eliminated. A method for quantifying the survivability level was presented. Hence, a series of schemes and algorithms for increased survivability were reviewed that have been proposed by the authors. Firstly, a scheme for the implementation of the widely recommended and used AES algorithm that presents algorithm replica diversity and averts power analysis attacks when equipment is captured or exposed to enemy agents. Following that, a scheme for a user authentication scheme that is based on Boolean transformations and presents time diversity by using continuously varying access codes. An approach for achieving high survivability in internet of things systems was then analyzed that permits a quantitative calculation of the level of survivability. Finally, a scheme for data storage in distributed cloud equipment is presented that may be scaled to detect and recover from the required number of storage unit failures or destructions. These schemes provide a toolbox for increased military system survivability design.

References

1. Stavroulakis, P.: Reliability, Survivability and Quality of Large Scale Telecommunication Systems. Wiley, London (2003)
2. Ellison, R.J., et al.: Survivable network system: an emerging discipline. Technical report, CMU/SEI-97- TR-013. Pittsburgh, PA: Software Engineering Institute, Carnegie Mellon University, November 1997
3. Dou, B.-L., Wang, X.-G., Zhang, S.-Y.: Research on survivability of networked information system. In: 2009 International Conference on Signal Processing Systems (2009)
4. Liu, Y., Trivedi, K.S.: Survivability quantification: the analytical modeling approach. Int. J. Performability Eng. **2**(1), 29–44 (2006)
5. Heegaard, P.E., Trivedi, K.S.: Survivability quantification of communication services. In: International Conference on Dependable Systems & Networks: Anchorage, Alaska (2008)
6. Knight, J.C., Strunk, E.A., Sullivan, K.J.: Towards a rigorous definition of information system survivability. In: 2003 Proceedings DARPA Information Survivability, Conference and Exposition (2003)
7. Bardis, N.G., Doukas, N., Markovskyi, O.P.: Organization of the polymorphic implementation of Rijndael on microcontrollers and smart cards. In: MILCOM 2010 Military Communications Conference. IEEE (2010)
8. Kocher, P., Jaffe, J., Jun, B.: Differential power analysis. In: Wiener, M. (ed.) CRYPTO 1999. LNCS, vol. 1666, pp. 388–397. Springer, Heidelberg (1999). https://doi.org/10.1007/3-540-48405-1_25
9. Akkar, M.-L., Giraud, C.: An implementation of DES and AES, secure against some attacks. In: Koç, Ç.K., Naccache, D., Paar, C. (eds.) CHES 2001. LNCS, vol. 2162, pp. 309–318. Springer, Heidelberg (2001). https://doi.org/10.1007/3-540-44709-1_26
10. Stavroulakis, P., Markovskyi, O.P., Bardis, N.G., Doukas, N.: Efficient zero—knowledge identification based on one way Boolean transformations. In: 2011 IEEE GLOBECOM Workshops, pp. 275–280. IEEE (2011)
11. Schneier, B.: Applied Cryptography: Protocols, Algorithms and Source codes in C, 758 p. Wiley, New York (1995)
12. Kurosawa, K., Yoshida, T.: Strongly universal hashing and identification codes via channels. IEEE Trans. Inf. Theory **45**(6), 2091–2095 (1999)
13. Seberry, J., et al.: Nonlinearity and propagation characteristics of balanced Boolean functions. Inf. Comput. **119**(1), 1–13 (1995)
14. Feige, U., Fiat, A., Shamir, A.: Zero knowledge proofs of identity. J. Cryptol. **1**(2), 77–94 (1987)
15. Bardis, N.G., Polymenopoulos, A., Bardis, E.G., Markovskyy, A.P.: Methods for increasing the efficiency of the remote user authentication in integrated systems. Trends Comput. Sci. **12**(1), 99–107 (2003). ISBN 1-59454-065-9
16. Braz, C., Robert, J.M.: Security and usability: the case of the user authentication methods. In: Proceedings of the 18th International Conference of the Association Francophone d'Interaction Homme-Machine, pp. 199–203 (2006)
17. Wang, H., Sheng, B, Tan, C., Qun, L.: Comparing symmetric-key and public-key based security schemes in sensor networks: a case study of user access control. In: Proceedings of the 28th International Conference on Distributed Computing Systems, pp. 11–18 (2008)
18. Tsai, J.-L.: Efficient multi-server authentication scheme based on one-way hash function without verification table. Comput. Secur. **27**(3–4), 115–121 (2008)

19. Bardis, N.G., Doukas, N., Markovskyi, O.: Two level efficient user authentication scheme. In: Proceedings of the 4th IEEE International Conference on Digital Ecosystems and Technology, 12–15 April 2010, Knowledge Village, Dubai, UAE (2010)
20. Bardis, N., Doukas, N., Markovskyi, O.: Fast subscriber identification based on the zero knowledge principle for multimedia content distribution. Int. J. Multimed. Intell. Secur. (2010)
21. Kharchenko, V., Kolisnyk, M., Piskachova, I., Bardis, N.: Reliability and security issues for IoT-based smart business center: architecture and Markov model. In: 2016 Third International Conference on Mathematics and Computers in Sciences and in Industry (MCSI), pp. 313–318. IEEE (2016)
22. Vermesan, O., et al.: Internet of Things – from research and innovation to market deployment. river publishers series in communication, 141 p. (2014). http://www.internet-of-things-research.eu/pdf/IERC_Cluster_Book_2014_Ch.3_SRIA_WEB.pdf. Accessed 3 Aug 2016
23. Internet of Things and its future. http://www.huawei.com/ilink/en/about-huawei/newsroom/pressrelease/HW_080993?dInID=23407&relatedID=19881&relatedName=HW_076569&dInDocName=HW_076557. Accessed 3 Aug 2016
24. NB-IOT – Enabling new business opportunities. Building a better connection. Huawei Tech. Co., Ltd. http://www.huawei.com/minisite/4-5g/img/NB-IOT.pdf
25. Matat, D.: Internet rechey I tehnotrendi yak oznaki evolyutsIYi suspIlstva. Osvita Ukrayini. http://pedpresa.ua/136666-internet-rechej-i-tehnotrendy-yak-oznaky-evolyutsiyi-suspilstva.html
26. Cisco IoT System Brochure Cisco IoT System Deploy. Accelerate. Innovate, 52 p. (2015). http://www.cisco.com/c/dam/en/us/products/collateral/se/internet-of-things/brochure-c02-734481.pdf
27. Cisco IoT System Security: Mitigate Risk, Simplify Compliance, and Build Trust White Paper, 4 p. (2015). http://www.cisco.com/c/dam/en/us/products/collateral/se/internet-of-things/iot-system-security-wp.pdf
28. No stars for Internet of Things security. http://www.zdnet.com/article/no-stars-for-internet-of-things-security/
29. IoTSF Guest Blog. https://iotsecurityfoundation.org/survey-less-than-10-of-iot-devices-keep-data-secure/
30. PRESS RELEASE. ioactive. http://www.ioactive.com/news-events/iot-products-have-inadequate-security-according-to-practitioner-survey.html Internet of Things security is dreadful. http://www.zdnet.com/article/internet-of-things-security-it-dreadful-heres-what-to-do-to-protect-yourself. Accessed 3 Aug 2016
31. Kaspersky security bulletin 2015, 85 p. (2015). https://securelist.com/files/2015/12/Kaspersky-Security-Bulletin-2015_FINAL_EN.pdf. Accessed 3 Aug 2016
32. Internet of Things. Hewlett Packard Enterprise. http://www.arubanetworks.com/solutions/internet-of-things/. Accessed 3 Aug 2016
33. Al-Fuqaha, M.G., Mohammadi, M., Aledhari, M., Ayyash, M.: Internet of Things: a survey on enabling technologies, protocols, and applications. IEEE Commun. Surv. Tutor. 17(4), 2347–2376 (2015). http://www.comsoc.org/files/Publications/Tech%20Focus/2016/iot/3.pdf
34. Bardis, N., Doukas, N., Markovskyi, O.P.: Effective method to restore data in distributed data storage systems. In: 2015 IEEE Military Communications Conference, MILCOM 2015. IEEE (2015)
35. Blaum, M., Hafner, J.I., Hetzler, S.: Partial MDS codes and their application to RAID type of architectures. IEEE Trans. Inf. Theory 59(7), 4510–4519 (2013)

36. Peterson, W.W., Weldon Jr., E.J.: Error-Correcting Codes. MIT Press, Cambridge (1984)
37. Abdel-Ghaffar, K.A.S., Weber, J.H.: Parity-check matrices separating erasures from errors. IEEE Trans. Inf. Theory. **59**(6), 3332–3346 (2013)
38. Dimakis, A.G., Prabhakaran, V., Ramchandran, K.: Decentralized Erasure Codes for Distributed Networked Storage, p. 176. University of California, Berkeley (2006)
39. Corbett, P., et al.: Row-diagonal parity for double disk failure. In: Proceedings of the Third USENIX Conference on File and Storage Technologies, pp. 1–14 (2004)

Author Index

Printed in the United States
By Bookmasters